Hidden in Plain Sight

The True History Revealed in Shake-speares Sonnets

Peter Rush

Second Edition (Revised),
Second Printing (Revised) 2019

Published by
Real Deal Publications
P.O. Box 4146
Leesburg, VA 20177

ISBN: 978-0-9883959-1-6

Cover design by Forever Press

Images on pages 26, 68, 73, 106, 117, 140, and 228
courtesy of Wikimedia Commons.
Image on page 46 courtesy of
www.hankwhittemore.wordpress.com
Image on page 219 (Tower portrait of Southampton)
by permission of His Grace the Duke of Buccleuch.

The author can be reached via email at
shakespearessonnets@hiddeninplainsight.com,
and he welcomes responses, feedback,
comments, debate and questions
which he will endeavor to respond to.

Also note the author's website and blog,
Hiddeninplainsight.com where blogposts and
articles are posted from time to time,
and where readers may post public comments and questions.

"*Hidden in Plain Sight* is a lucid, penetrating analysis of one of the most difficult-to-understand pieces of literature in the world: *Shakespeares Sonnets*. Peter Rush convincingly amplifies the recent original discoveries of Hank Whittemore, who first lifted the veil of mystery which had obscured interpretation of the *Sonnets* for 400 years....Rush articulately, coherently and believably summarizes the evidence that the *Sonnets* not only identify the true author of Shakespeare's plays and poetry but also reveal hitherto unknown, astonishing details of the decline and fall of the Tudor Era."—Dr. Paul Altrocchi, researcher, scholar of 16th century history, author of *Most Greatly Lived: A Biographical Novel of Edward de Vere.*

"The Rush-Whittemore demonstration is overwhelming in its argument and evidence that the *Sonnets* have a structure and a code that orthodox inquiry has missed completely. Even those of us who have thought they were written by the Earl of Oxford and that the Earl of Southampton was the "Fair Youth" have not seen how precisely the central hundred of them were a detailed commentary on Southampton's time in prison facing a sentence of death, and who this makes the mis-named "Dark Lady" and what the relationship of both was to the writer. This and other revelations make the book both a scholarly delight, a gripping mystery story, a vital addition to Tudor history, and a profound insight into the life and character of the man who was 'Shakespeare.'"—Robin Fox, University Professor, Rutgers University. Member of the National Academy of Sciences and author of many books including, *Shakespeare's Education: Schools, Lawsuits, Theater and the Tudor Miracle.*

"This book is a major achievement. *Hidden in Plain Sight* is important in many ways, especially in reaffirming, building on and extending Hank Whittemore's accomplishment in *The Monument* (2005) in cracking the code of *Shake-speares Sonnets* to reveal their structure and how they tell the story of Southampton's imprisonment. Also very useful is the book's placing Whittemore's work in the context of the wider worlds of Shakespeare criticism, the authorship question and the Oxfordian movement.

"By documenting and expanding our understanding of the historical events revealed in the *Sonnets,* these works [Rush's and Whittemore's] have gone a long way toward filling the hole that has existed at the core of the Oxfordian theory ever since 1920, when J. Thomas Looney in *'Shakespeare' Identified* pointedly refused to speculate about Oxford's motives for hiding his authorship."—James A. Warren, researcher, writer, editor of *An Index to Oxfordian Publications.*

"Peter Rush's *Hidden In Plain Sight* is a significant publishing event in the history of modern Shakespeare studies. It provides the first closely reasoned rebuttal to what mainstream scholars have mistakenly assumed the *Sonnets* were and meant, i.e., a lovelorn diarist infatuated with a boy....The four respected critics of *Shake-speares Sonnets* with whom Rush takes issue, who are universally praised in the periodical press as both profound and insightful, are shown to be no such thing at explaining the poems. The simple reason is that neither they nor modern history has ever known the crucible of historical circumstances from which the poetry painfully emerged....But lacking accurate history, Shakespeare studies is now hopelessly beset with critical generality, an abstraction that evaporates overnight into nothing."—William J. Ray, scholar, researcher, and author.

"This book represents a unique challenge to orthodoxy because it uses four well-known modern scholars on the *Sonnets* as foils to expose the bankruptcy of their readings....It is coherent, varied and persuasive...excellent and brilliant...sober, scientific, at times rightly sardonic. A great job all along."—Ricardo Mena, scholar, editor, author of *Ver, Begin.*

"Critics of Hank Whittemore's Monument Theory of the *Sonnets* have often claimed that it is just another interpretation, no different from any other, and no more 'correct' than any other. Rush's careful, detailed narrative of how the sonnets in fact tell a single, unified story, anchored within a *bona fide* historical context, should once and for all put an end to such claims. It confirms the correctness of Whittemore's original thesis that the 1609 quarto edition of *Shake-speares Sonnets* is both a history of and commentary on the 1590s politics of the succession to Queen Elizabeth I, culminating in the Essex Rebellion in 1601, and it enriches immeasurably our understanding of these magnificent verses."—William Boyle, former editor, *Shakespeare Oxford Newsletter* and *Shakespeare Matters*, founder of Shakespeare Online Authorship Resources (SOAR).

Dedication

This book is dedicated to Edward de Vere, the 17th Earl of Oxford, who was the playwright and poet we know as "Shakespeare," one of the most accomplished, and tragic, figures in human history. He was the greatest dramatist in the English language. He did the most to bring the Italian literary Renaissance to England. He sparked the Elizabethan Renaissance. His influence was beyond measure and his achievements resonate to this day, more than 400 years after his death. Yet, by an improbable turn of events, he was destined to die unrecognized as the flesh-and-blood person behind the "Shakespeare" pseudonym. His authorship of the works of "Shakespeare" was only rediscovered in 1920 and is denied to this day by mainstream academia; his role in sparking the Elizabethan Renaissance has been gradually unearthed in the ensuing decades.

This book presents a compelling reinterpretation of the meaning of Oxford's ("Shakespeare's") sonnets, confirms in the process that Oxford *was* "Shakespeare," and explains *why* Oxford could not reveal himself to the public as Shakespeare. I hope it will help rectify this cruel injustice, and restore Edward de Vere, the seventeenth Earl of Oxford, to his rightful place in history.

Notes on Second Edition Revisions

The original edition was extensively revised in the second edition to enhance the presentation of two core features of the case being made in this book in favor of the Whittemore interpretation of the *Sonnets*. The original first nine chapters were compressed into a single introductory chapter, condensing the arguments presented that are important for establishing the basis for Whittemore's thesis, but which are not unique to it, involving questions such as whether the *Sonnets* was intended for publication, who the "young man" was, or whether the sonnets describe a homosexual relationship. The new introductory chapter also supplies a discussion absent from the first edition of what I term the "Standard Interpretation" of the narrative conventionally presented, involving a hard-to-follow love triangle involving the poet, the young man, and an unidentified lady. The critique of this interpretation was implicit in the development of the Whittemore thesis in the original Parts III and IV, but I felt the ability to appreciate the weakness of the traditional interpretation, and the strength of the alternative thesis presented here, was enhanced by explicitly discussing, and critiquing, the standard interpretation in the introduction.

Also, the original chapters 17-20, were entirely reorganized into current chapters 9-12 to correct some awkwardness in the presentation and to add significant new supporting information, so that Chapter 9 now includes an extended discussion of contemporary literary evidence supporting the core discoveries of the Whittemore thesis, providing the reader a much stronger evidentiary basis for that thesis. In large part, this represented presenting the extensive collection of literary allusions that point to the same conclusions as those presented in this book, which I had not thought to include in the first edition.

In addition to more minor edits to improve clarity or presentation, several additional sonnets have been analyzed in detail, and a new appendix (Appendix III) compiles the proofs from within the sonnets that the author could not have been the traditional "Shakespeare" from Stratford-on-Avon.

Revisions in the Second Printing of the Second Edition are composed of further corrections of minor errata missed in the previous revision, plus improvements of wordings and enhancement of the information or presentation in a number of passages.

Table of Contents

Appendices 303

Acknowledgments

T he central thesis of this book, and of virtually all the scholarship that backs it up, was discovered and/or documented by Hank Whittemore, a remarkable individual in his own right, who has been an actor, an investigative journalist, a producer of television documentaries, and an outstanding Shakespearean scholar and researcher.

Whittemore became convinced of Oxford's authorship of Shakespeare's plays and poems in the late 1980s. Early on he had become convinced that evidence of Oxford's authorship of the Shakespeare works was most likely to be found in his personal sonnets. After spending ten years continually trying to comprehend them, he came to realize (in late 1998) that in writing the sonnets Oxford had used a special language (described in Sonnet 76 as a compression of subject matter, "Why write I still all one, ever the same") that allowed different words to mean the same thing ("So all my best is dressing old words new"), thus creating an illusion of variety. Unlocking this consistent language led to discovering that the sonnets concealed an incredible narrative of the last years of Elizabeth's reign never before recognized by scholars or anyone else. Far from being some species of love poetry, possibly of a homosexual nature, Shakespeare's sonnets turned out to be a highly political document, whose true meaning and purport had lain, "hidden in plain sight," for nearly 400 years until finally discerned by Whittemore.

In mid-1999 I had the good fortune to read a post on a listserve I subscribed to by Whittemore that offered readers a copy of a preliminary draft of a thesis he had developed on the sonnets that claimed to have solved the 400-year-old mystery of what they were really about. I accepted his offer, read his manuscript, and told him that if he could show that his interpretation could be consistently applied over the entire sonnet cycle, I would be convinced. We began a communication that has continued to this day, that has blossomed into a friendship and a collaboration. By 2005, Whittemore was ready to put his discovery out to the world in the form of a 900+ page major tome entitled *The Monument* (article-length expositions of the thesis had already appeared in several Oxfordian newsletters where it had sparked lively debate pro and con). Whittemore also published a popularized, much shorter book, *Shakespeare's Son and His Sonnets* in 2010, hoping to reach a broader audience.

In 2011, I got an idea for an alternate means of presenting Whittemore's breakthrough, one that I felt represented a more effective ordering of the evidence to be found in the sonnets in support of his thesis. I began a manuscript of my own that has now become this book. Over the course of the last five years, Whittemore not only encouraged me in my endeavor, but served as a sounding board and source of expert knowledge as I worked my way through sonnet after sonnet, confirming for myself the validity of Whittemore's readings, and in some instances, enhancing them.

So what I present here is very largely derived from Whittemore's pioneering analysis. My debt to him extends to the many hours he has devoted to helping me noodle through many, many questions I have had. He has checked a number of facts that I wasn't sure of. He has read the manuscript multiple times and provided other very helpful suggestions.

And he has contributed a foreword to this book.

We are all in Hank Whittemore's debt for finally resolving the mystery of *Shake-speares Sonnets* and confirming beyond doubt that Oxford was the human face behind the "Shakespeare" pseudonym. In doing this, he has also unlocked the sonnets themselves, revealing a world of new understandings. Our understanding of each individual sonnet, and of the collection as a unified work, are thereby enriched beyond measure.

I am also indebted to the information and analysis respecting the life of Henry Wriothesley, the Third Earl of Southampton and without doubt the subject (the "younger man") of the sonnets, as presented in Katherine Chiljan's 2011 book *Shakespeare Suppressed.* I have relied on her compilation of the raft of allusions and references to Southampton in the first half of the 1590s that all but cry out that he was special, and likely royal, and on her review of Southampton's career after his release from the Tower by James I on his accession to the crown, which helps unravel both the mystery of why the 1609 publication of the *Sonnets* was a total non-event, certainly suppressed by the authorities, and also why the First Folio of Shakespeare plays was compiled when, and how, it was compiled, including the mystery of why it appears to point to the author as being the man from Stratford without saying it explicitly.

Acknowledgments

Finally, I owe an enormous debt to my editor, Alex McNeil, who edited *The Monument* and to whom I was introduced by Hank Whittemore. Not only has McNeil pruned a good 30% or more of my initial verbiage, sharpening and honing the message in the process, he has also contributed a number of corrections based on his independent knowledge of the material, going far beyond what most editors are able to contribute to their respective authors. And he has stuck with me through five successive passes through the original manuscript, and once more through the significant revisions of the Second Edition. I will be eternally grateful to him for his labors, which, there can be no doubt, have made this book more readable and accessible.

Peter Rush
Leesburg, Virginia
June 2015

Foreword

By Hank Whittemore

The author known to us as Shakespeare used the personal pronoun "I" referring to himself in only two contexts: first, in the dedications of the narrative poems *Venus and Adonis* (1593) and *Lucrece* (1594) to Henry Wriothesley, third Earl of Southampton (1573-1624); and second, in the lines of *Shake-speares Sonnets* (1609), which many commentators believe were also addressed primarily to Southampton. These two instances serve as the opening and closing brackets for all the authorized publishing of "Shakespeare" works from 1593 to 1609, after which came a silence until the printing of *Othello* in 1622 and the First Folio of plays in 1623.

After the two dedications were published in the early 1590s, marking the first appearance of the Shakespeare name in print, never again would the author dedicate a written work to anyone else, thereby uniquely and permanently linking Southampton to "Shakespeare." In the *Lucrece* dedication he declares to the earl, "The love I dedicate to your Lordship is without end"; in the sonnets he makes similar statements, for example, "O know, sweet love, I always write of you, and you and love are still my argument." Clearly, to the greatest writer of the English language there was something particularly important about the Earl of Southampton.

It's in the sonnets where, in the most direct and personal way, we find extraordinary statements that run completely counter to accepted belief: "My name be buried where my body is," the poet writes in Sonnet 72, adding in Sonnet 81 that "I, once gone, to all the world must die." How could the author make such declarations that we perceive as demonstrably untrue of "Shakespeare" as we understand him? The only sensible reading is that "Shakespeare" was not the author's real name, but, rather, a pen name, and that he knew his actual identity was being erased from the record of contemporary history.

So we confront an "authorship question" directly from the pen of the author himself and, crucially, within the context of his statements to Southampton. Logic dictates that the matter of the poet's true identity being expunged from the record is inextricably tied to Southampton. Here is the doorway of a great mystery; we may choose, if we wish, to walk through it into a world that has been forbidden to generations of students.

When I attended the university of Notre Dame, performing in plays and graduating in Communication Arts in 1963, it was never brought to my attention that any mystery about the author of *Hamlet* might exist. Only in 1987 did I learn that a Hamlet-like nobleman of the Elizabethan royal court, Edward de Vere, seventeenth Earl of Oxford (1550-1604), had been identified in 1920 as "Shakespeare" by a British schoolmaster, J. Thomas Looney; only afterward did I realize that a vigorous body of research and writing about Oxford as the author had been continuing ever since. This came as a shock to me and changed my life.

Early on, studying the Elizabethan age and Oxford's life in relation to the Shakespeare works, I became convinced that if there existed any "smoking gun" evidence to confirm his authorship, it was to be found in the *Sonnets*. I went through the 154 consecutively numbered little poems over and over, marking up dozens of editions and filling notebooks with words, lines, hypotheses and ideas, along with insights from scholars over the previous century and a half. I kept searching for some special language and structure that would open up a genuine "story" yielding new, unexpected information; by 1997, after more than a decade, that goal seemed hopeless.

At that point I was offered the chance to "get away" from the *Sonnets* for two years. While working on museum exhibits combining art and science, I completed a book entitled *Your Future Self: A Journey to the Frontiers of the New Molecular Medicine* (Thames & Hudson, 1998); while working on that book it occurred to me that the structure and function of the DNA molecule might suggest a clue to the inner workings of the Shakespeare sonnet sequence. After all, base pairs of DNA can be lined up as pairs of letters, creating a molecular "language" that contains all the genetic information needed to produce the form and functions of an individual human being.

I decided in the fall of 1998 to return to the *Sonnets* for one more round of intense searching for an answer. Despite all the previous work, I was still merely hypothesizing that an answer existed in the first place. My process roughly followed a standard method, setting up a series of hypotheses and following them until they either wound up in dead ends or led to new information and, in turn, further tentative assumptions. And the first such hypothesis— contrary to what many scholars (Oxfordians included) tended to believe—was that the poetical sequence of the *Sonnets* was constructed as a single masterpiece of art, where all its parts worked together to create a unified whole.

Glancing again at the verses, it struck me that I should take the author at his word—that he was building a "monument" for "eyes not yet created." Over and over he speaks of the verses as defying Time by surviving to be read by readers of future generations. "And thou in this shalt find thy monument," he tells Southampton, "When tyrants' crests and tombs of brass are spent." If we take him at his word about writing for readers of the future, I thought, it stands to reason he would give us the means of comprehending it. He would enable us to learn what he wanted us to know by leaving "instructions" about his language and how to use it.

Finding a consistent system of verbal communication would be just the beginning; those communications would have to lead to some new information—a tall order, one which appeared impossible to fill.

As I flew from New York to San Francisco for an Oxfordian conference in November of 1998, however, various connections between sonnets suddenly began to appear to me—as if the brief respite from studying them had allowed my unconscious to work on its own, with the results now floating to the surface. On the plane I began to scribble notes; as the conference began, more thoughts appeared, so that over the next three days I filled several notebooks.

I now saw that the poet had inserted information about "my verse" all over the sonnet sequence, leaving specific descriptions of his language. In Sonnet 76 he speaks of "dressing old words new, spending again what is already spent," and in Sonnet 105 he writes about "varying to other words," adding that "in this change is my invention spent." The methodology of this "invention" gradually became clear to me, leaving no question that the sonnets employ a "special language" to create a "noted weed," or familiar costume, of poetry while simultaneously recording the author's reactions to circumstances and events unfolding in real life in real time.

But would this special use of words lead to any new information? I had no real expectation of such an outcome. As the conference continued, however, I remained in my hotel room with notebooks strewn about, making one attempt after another to follow the poet's double-image language, when—and here I beg the reader's indulgence—the floor below me seemed to move. The realization that came forth was so startling that I became dizzy.

The "how" had been discovered. Now the "what" more or less suddenly sprang into focus: the sonnets had nothing to do with love, beauty, romantic entanglements or anything remotely similar to what virtually every commentator had believed them to be expressing. No, the sonnets were a record of history, a history revolving around the crucial question of dynastic succession in the waning years of Elizabeth's reign, and both Oxford and Southampton were in the middle of this history. The sonnets were telling this story, using the medium of the special language I had begun to understand; and I was, quite literally, "floored."

Specifically, a number of insights flooded my mind, all proving to be accurate as I pursued my analysis over the succeeding weeks. Above all, I had finally found the historical context from which flowed everything else:

- Oxford was recording his thoughts and emotions during the final years of the "succession crisis" that England faced during the 1590s up to the death of Elizabeth I in 1603. The crisis revolved around the Queen's refusal to name a successor. Now that she was turning sixty, a single question daily grew more critical: who would be in position to choose the next monarch when she died? Who would be kingmaker? The power of William Cecil Lord Burghley to control the succession was being challenged by a rising faction of young nobles led by the earls of Essex and Southampton.

- In 1593 Oxford adopted the mask of "Shakespeare" behind which he could lend public support to Southampton. When Burghley died in 1598 and his son Robert Cecil took over, the power struggle quickly escalated, with the "Shakespeare" name suddenly appearing on printed quartos of plays dealing with the politics of succession. In effect Oxford was trying to educate the public about how to judge a potential ruler and ways in which a transfer of crown can be achieved.

- Essex and Southampton were out-maneuvered, leading to their ill-fated Essex rebellion on February 8, 1601—a failed attempt to remove Cecil from his power behind the throne. Both earls were imprisoned as traitors and faced certain death. Now in full control, Cecil orchestrated the course of the trial to its foregone conclusion. Oxford, on the tribunal, voted with the peers in finding both earls guilty of high treason and sentencing them to death. Essex was swiftly executed.

- Amazingly, however, Southampton was spared execution, though he remained in the Tower, a condemned criminal and traitor, for the remainder of Elizabeth's reign. Equally amazing, his unconditional release was ordered within days of King James becoming king, and he went on to have a colorful career in James' court for more than two decades. How and why Southampton's life was spared and his status at court fully restored has been a question which has never really been addressed (or, for that matter, even asked) in any of the histories of this period.

- Another one of my crucial insights was that Oxford had written the majority of the sonnets (which turned out to be exactly one hundred in the middle of the series) about the period described above, focusing on Southampton *after* his February 8, 1601 arrest, and that embedded in them were not only the answers to the historical mysteries that have surrounded the biography of Southampton for four hundred years (e.g., how and why was his life was spared), but many more revelations, both historical and personal to Oxford, that have eluded historians and literary critics alike for the same four hundred years.

With this new historical context now identified, more new insights flooded my mind, and key words began leaping from the page with new meanings. For example, the legal language, rather than being metaphors by which the Poet was expressing his love for the Youth (as all traditional commentary would have it), instead took on direct relationships to specific matters during the Youth's (Southampton's) imprisonment—the crime, the trial, the efforts to save him, the Poet's (Oxford's) sacrifice, and so on. In short, I now saw what I had long suspected, that the key to understanding the sonnets was to see that they were indeed telling a real story about real events.

The Shakespeare sonnets thus offer a puzzle with two halves. One half consists of the words and lines on the printed page; by themselves, they comprise a mystery that has haunted readers for centuries. The other half is the all-important historical-biographical context of time and circumstance. This is Oxford's story of the succession crisis and how the Tudor dynasty finally ended. Now both halves of the puzzle—the poetry on one hand, the contemporary history on the other—fit together perfectly and completely within a single solution.

I leave to this book the exposition of the full thesis that I began developing that long weekend in San Francisco. I did publish several articles presenting it in summary form in Oxfordian newsletters starting in 2000, my book *The Monument,"* in 2005, and a popularized presentation in 2010, *Shakespeare's Son and His Sonnets.*

As Peter stated in his Acknowledgements, he very early on became interested in my thesis, and from the time of publication of *The Monument,* has had no doubt that the riddle of the sonnets had been solved. By that time I had met Peter in person, and we began a friendship that, when he began work in 2011 on what has become this volume, became also a collaboration.

From the beginning, others besides Peter showed an equal interest in my discovery. Two very early adopters of my thesis were Charles and William Boyle; the latter was the editor of both the Shakespeare Oxford Society (SOS) and Shakespeare Fellowship (SF) newsletters during this period, and he immediately, beginning in 1999, gave my thesis wide circulation in those publications, aiming a beam of high intelligence on every aspect of the "Monument theory of the *Sonnets,"* as we came to refer to it. He also made a signal contribution on a topic I did not identify, namely, the significance of the historical meaning of "misprision," thereby solving the historical mystery surrounding the legal basis on which Southampton's life was spared—"misprision of treason" or "misprision of trespass."

Others also came forward offering partial or total support for my thesis, most notably Dr. Paul Altrocchi, the distinguished Oxfordian researcher, and Prof. Daniel Wright of Concordia University in 2005, while other leading Oxfordians dismissed the thesis, unwilling to accept some of the unexpected conclusions that flowed from my analysis.

Peter has been among the most perceptive of those supporting my thesis, especially in identifying where my initial translations and takes on some key sonnet passages was unsatisfying, and he flagged a number of important questions that warranted further thought and research on which we have exchanged views over the last nine years. He also expressed, during our many conversations, his view that more than one pathway could be used to lead others to see the true story recorded by the poet. In particular, he felt that the case for the thesis needed to be presented more as an argument than just a sequential explanation of the true meaning of each sonnet.

I agree. He envisioned a "forensic approach" to presenting the case to a skeptical audience, a pathway to make explicit some of the logical steps underlying my conclusions that I had left merely implicit in *The Monument*. Seeing how the sonnets themselves become evidence for the story unfolded within them, he sought a logical path whereby the truth could be more powerfully presented.

This was exactly the kind of reaction I had hoped for. If what I had accomplished "opened the door" to further exploration, well, such was the function of an initial discovery; any valid new findings should open up other avenues, leading in turn to more discoveries. As Peter embarked on his own path, he saw additional confirmation for readings in *The Monument* as well as more specific ways to understand various passages. He moved on to develop his own readings, which cohere very closely with mine, while also bringing out new details that make the overall argument even stronger.

To my delight and frequently to my surprise, Peter has expanded the original discovery, often clarifying or deepening the meaning of certain lines or even major aspects of whole sonnets, while strengthening their emotional impact. In addition, of no small importance is his demonstration that all traditional commentary on the sonnets is far wide of the mark. He has shown how the failure of scholars, including most Oxfordian scholars, to recognize any of the important passages in the *Sonnets* as demanding explanations that cannot be encompassed within the traditional reading, has doomed all of them to virtual irrelevance as useful interpreters of these poems. And he has shown how their utter failure stands as a strong repudiation of their interpretation and a *de facto* endorsement of our alternate construction.

In sum, Peter Rush in this book offers a new and powerful guide to the important story that I first presented to the world in published form ten years ago. I am in awe of what he has managed to set forth in the following pages, which I hope will receive the widest possible readership and continue to be read over the long haul. Credit should also go to Alex McNeil, who edited *The Monument* a decade ago and has now assiduously edited *Hidden in Plain Sight*, contributing countless observations, insights and suggestions along the way.

By its special language and structure, along with the story it records for all time, the "monument" of the *Sonnets* is—as the title of this book states—"hidden in plain sight." Thanks to Peter Rush for helping us to see it more clearly, vividly and truly.

Nyack, New York, August 2015

Part I: The True Meaning of Shake-speare's Sonnets Revealed

Chapter 1
Introduction and Overview

The Enigma of *Shake-speares Sonnets*

On or around June 19th, 1609, something occurred in London that was truly extraordinary, though subsequent history, while agreeing that it was odd, has all but ignored its importance. On that date, a volume of 154 sonnets (plus one other poem) credited to the incomparable poet and playwright known as William Shakespeare went on sale in London. What made this event extraordinary was that the appearance of this book in two London bookstalls had no reception whatever. Some copies must have been sold—thirteen have survived. There is but one record of anyone purchasing the book (which some scholars believe to be a forgery), and none of anyone commenting on the poems at the time, or in any way acknowledging their existence for more than three decades. How the publication of this book could have received such a total non-response, given that the fame of its author, William Shakespeare, was at an all-time high in 1609, with most of his plays having been performed both in popular theaters and at Court, his name the best-known of any dramatist of his age, and his two long, narrative poems (*Venus and Adonis,* and *Lucrece,* first published in 1593 and 1594 respectively) still in print fifteen years later, is inexplicable to historians. (Imagine, for comparison, a work by Hemingway, or Faulkner, being published while its author was at the height of his popularity, and being similarly ignored and lost to history.)

Another mysterious event, ordinarily not deemed related to this one, was the release six years earlier of Henry Wriostheley, the 3rd Earl of Southampton, from the Tower of London after twenty-six months' confinement for his leading role in the abortive "Essex Rebellion" of February 8, 1601. What made that event extraordinary was first, that Southampton wasn't executed in 1601 along with Essex and all other leaders of the Rebellion, despite having been condemned to death; and second, that his release was one of the very first official acts of the new king James I after he became king at Elizabeth's death in late March of 1603. Documentary evidence is absent as to why and how Southampton was spared execution, an event noted by historians as a mystery but whose significance, again, is universally ignored. No evidence likewise exists to explain why James released him almost immediately, shortly restoring him to full earldom from which position Southampton went on to play a significant role in English history over the next twenty years. (Again, imagine, for comparison, the Rosenbergs being spared execution in 1953 with no reason given [and none publicly asked for], and then released without explanation as one of the first acts of John Kennedy.)

What links these two events is first, that the sonnets were primarily directed to and written about Southampton, and his relationship to Shakespeare. The release of Southampton from the Tower on April 10, 1603, is recorded in Sonnet 107, a fact about which most scholars concur. Second, Southampton and Shakespeare are also forever publicly linked by the fact that *Venus and Adonis* and *Lucrece* were the first works to which the name "Shakespeare" was associated, as the person dedicating these poems to Southampton in language that is effusive bordering on the worshipful. But again, despite the linkage of Shakespeare and Southampton on both counts, neither historians nor Shakespeare scholars have ever sought, to my knowledge, to link these two very odd events, or to try to explain them.

A solution to both mysteries, and what connects them, has only become available in the wake of the extraordinary discovery, first publicly propounded in 2000 by Hank Whittemore, of what the *Sonnets* was all about, a discovery that he fully developed in print in his 2005 magnum opus, *The Monument.* Whittemore's discoveries have completely overturned the traditional reading of the sonnets as a rather weird three-way romantic relationship between Shakespeare, a young man and a sex-craving, manipulative woman, and replaced it with a reading that locates the sonnets in the context of dynastic politics in the waning years of Elizabeth's reign.

(Throughout this book, I will be referring to the sonnets frequently. When the reference is to the volume first published in 1609 under the title "*Shake-speares Sonnets,*" I will usually refer to it using the shortened title "the *Sonnets,*" which, because it refers to a specific publication, will take a singular verb, such as "the *Sonnets* was published in 1609...." In all other situations when I refer to the sonnets that comprise the *Sonnets,* I will refer to them as "the sonnets," such as "the sonnets contain many allusions to Queen Elizabeth.")

Whittemore was certainly far from the first person to try to understand the sonnets. Efforts to do so date back to the late 18th century, necessitated by the surprising number of enigmas posed by them. While most scholars agree that there are three main persons involved—the poet himself, a young man, and the poet's supposed mistress—the general agreement ends there. Questions such as who the young man was, and why the first 126 sonnets appear to be written to him by the poet, as one man to another, are the first of many that have elicited a multitude of proposed solutions by hundreds of scholars and commentators. Other questions revolve around who the woman might have been, and what her relationship was to the poet and the young man. Further questions concern the strange dedication page, whether the sonnets were published with the permission of Shakespeare, and whether they are in a specific order as intended by Shakespeare.

Questions have also swirled for over two hundred years as to the quality of the sonnets. While today, most scholars maintain that they are excellent poems, this view is relatively new, with the bulk of scholarly and general opinion from the late 18th century until the mid-20th century judging them as of indifferent to poor quality, with at best a few excellent poems in the whole lot. That so few of them are generally taught in secondary school or college is an apparent reflection of the inaccessibility of most of them to a general audience.

Examination of the entire set of 154 poems has been left to a handful of scholars who have chosen to serve as editors to collections of the complete series, exercising their editorial function by contributing introductory discussions presenting their best efforts to make sense of some of the difficult questions, and by providing glosses and commentary, line-by-line, for each sonnet.

It has proven to be an arduous task, as sonnet after sonnet has presented thorny problems as to what is actually being said, and as to what narrative, if any, is being related. For starters, what sort of poems are these pesky sonnets? They follow in the wake of many sonnet cycles that stretch two hundred years back to Petrarch's love sonnets to his Laura, which cycles right up to Shakespeare's time followed the same pattern of being love poems to a real or fictive ideal lady. The sonnets of Shakespeare's contemporary Phillip Sidney, published fifteen years before the *Sonnets,* were to a woman named Stella. But *Shake-speares Sonnets* breaks every mold, starting with the fact that over eighty percent of the sonnets are to another man, and the remainder are to a woman who is definitely not being idolized. Many scholars even find passages that they assert must be intentionally mocking the traditional sonnet template, as they are unable to explain the sonnets in any other way.

Yet the sonnets—the only work that Shakespeare wrote in the first and second person—are so deeply personal that the notion that they are satire doesn't ring true. Surely for this reason, plus the fact that they were written by Shakespeare, they have fascinated—and exasperated—scholars and other critics for nearly three centuries, during which time hundreds of anthologies, scores of full-length books, and innumerable articles and essays have discussed, dissected and critiqued these singular poems. A two-volume compilation of the opinions of hundreds of critics was published in 1944 by Hyder Edward Rollins entitled *A Variorum Edition of Shakespeare: The Sonnets.*[1] Rollins meticulously documented the vogue of the *Sonnets* from 1609 to 1944, though he estimated that very few people actually read them during that period.

Rollins also documented many of the mysteries surrounding the sonnets, involving both circumstances of their publication and of their content. He devoted the second volume of his work to cataloguing the varied efforts of dozens of critics to solve these mysteries, allocating an appendix to each issue and summarizing the take of each critic on each issue. The result bespeaks a discipline that has yet to find its way, as every critic has his or her own take on each of the many questions, with no two scholars agreeing on all the same issues.

The outpouring of books and articles on the *Sonnets* has continued apace since that time. As I hope to demonstrate, the best of these scholars in the last several decades have been no more successful than their numerous predecessors in making sense out of these quintessentially enigmatic poems.

One scholar has had the courage to acknowledge the true state of affairs of conventional *Sonnets* analysis. In his introduction to the text of *Shake-speares Sonnets* in the 2002 edition of the *Complete Pelican Shakespeare,* Yale University professor emeritus and Shakespeare scholar John Hollander wrote: "And yet the sonnets as a whole are a great puzzle, and it is equally true that with the key of the sonnet Shakespeare unlocked a chest...full of enigmas of various sorts.... [which] enigmas seem to be nested one inside the other." He explained his reference to the key of a chest by quoting William Wordsworth: "With this [the sonnets], Shakespeare unlocked his heart," to which Hollander rejoined, "if what [Wordsworth] meant is that he [Shakespeare] recorded events in his life and his feelings about them as in a diary—even an enciphered one—then...we would have to conclude that what in fact he unlocked was a cabinet containing a coffer with its own lock whose combination no one has been able to discover." Hollander adds, ruefully, "And thus leaving us, too, with the possibility that it isn't really a combination lock at all, but a dummy set into a door that had been welded shut by circumstance."[2]

But even Hollander does not include the two mysterious events mentioned above as among the deepest—and most consequential— of the enigmas surrounding *Shake-speares Sonnets.* He, like all conventional scholars, persists in seeing the sonnets as reflecting the private, and at times almost sordid, life of the great Shakespeare, a life that to them floats in no particular historical context, not even in a biographical one. For them, the sonnets are *sui generis,* and are believed to tell a story of a three-way romantic triangle and tangle for which not a shred of external evidence, from either history or from Shakespeare's putative biography (or that of Southampton), exists.

Among Whittemore's major conclusions that, to my knowledge, no one before has ever recognized, is his identification of the historical context for Sonnets 27-126, a context which both explains the two historical mysteries cited above, and a great deal else, that permits the sonnets to finally be correctly understood. (It should be noted that Katherine Chiljan, in her 2013 book *Shakespeare Suppressed,* although she does not recognize the context of the sonnets discovered by Whittemore, provides very strong corroboration for Whittemore's answers to the two enigmas that open this book, and amplifies and extends them in her discussion of Southampton's life after his release in 1603.)

In order to appreciate the nature and magnitude of Whittemore's discoveries, which is the purpose of this book, we must first explore and analyze the currently prevailing version of the narrative that is supposedly being related in the sonnets. I will refer throughout to this as the "traditional," "conventional" or "orthodox" view.

The "Standard Interpretation"

Despite the wide divergence among scholars on many of the questions posed by the *Sonnets,* there is, ironically, pretty general agreement that the individual sonnets constitute a narrative of sorts, that tell of a triangular sex/love relationship between the poet, the young man, and a lady presumed to be the mistress of the poet. I refer to this narrative as the "Standard Interpretation" (SI) because some variant of it is common to all commentators save the small minority who believe the sonnets to be purely fictive creations of Shakespeare's imagination.

It is telling that all the best-known sonnets are gender non-specific, such that most who read them do not know that the context is ostensibly love poems to another man. And Sonnets 127-152, directed to a woman, are hardly what one thinks of as love poetry. Unwinding the nature of the intertwined relationships in both sections of sonnets is just the beginning of the challenge that anyone seeking to understand the sonnets must grapple with. The SI is an attempt to extract from each sonnet a coherent piece of the presumed narrative of this triangular relationship. As I shall illustrate throughout this volume, this often leads to incoherence as the inferred presumption of what is happening in one sonnet is unrelated or even in contradiction to what is presumed to be happening in the sonnet or sonnets that precede(s) or follow(s) it/them. The SI as told by each who attempts to supply a narrative for the poems also comes to include extended "backstories" that find no direct support in the text of any sonnet, but which are required to supply a way to understand passages within the sonnets that the commentators can explain in no other way.

A *precis* of the Standard Interpretation's version of this narrative is helpfully included in the edition of *Shakespeare's Sonnets and Poems* published by the Folger Library, contributed by the editors Barbara A. Mowat and Paul Werstine:

> The narrative goes something like this: The poet (i.e. William Shakespeare) begins with a set of 17 sonnets advising a

beautiful young man (seemingly an aristocrat...) to marry and produce a child in the interest of preserving the family name and property but even more in the interest of reproducing the young man's remarkable beauty in his offspring. These poems of advice modulate into a set of sonnets which urge the poet's love for the young man and which claim that the young man's beauty will be preserved in the very poems that we are now reading. This second set of sonnets (Sonnets 18-126), which in the supposed narrative celebrate the poet's love for the young man, includes clusters of poems that seem to tell of such specific events as the young man's mistreatment of the poet, the young man's theft of the poet's mistress, the appearance of "rival poets" who celebrate the young man and gain his favor, the poet's separation from the young man through travel or through the young man's indifference, and the poet's infidelity to the young man. After this set of 109 poems, the *Sonnets* concludes with a set of 28 sonnets to or about a woman who is presented as dark and treacherous and with whom the poet is sexually obsessed. Several of these sonnets seem also to involve the beautiful young man, who is, according to the *Sonnets'* narrative, is also enthralled by the "dark lady."[3]

It is regrettably impossible to list here all of the specific twists and turns in the posited relationships among the poet, young man and woman that constitute the SI. The same edition above helpfully provides a one or two sentence summary of what each sonnet supposedly is about, according to the SI, and to read through these in order is an exercise in madness. For sonnet after sonnet, the sense that is made of each compels statements that imply elaborate "backstories" which come out of nowhere and go nowhere. A few examples will have to suffice to illustrate the point[4]:

Sonnet 30: [The poet] grieves for all that he has lost..." What has he lost, what is he grieving for? Nothing previous suggests he's lost anything or anyone.

Sonnet 31: "The poet sees the many friends now lost to him as contained in his beloved. Thus, the love he once gave to his lost friends is now given wholly to the beloved." What friends? Why are they lost? What does "lost" even mean here? Are *friends* what he has lost in Sonnet 30? How can "lost friends" be "contained" in his beloved?

Sonnet 32: "The poet imagines his poems being read and judged by his beloved after the poet's death, and he asks that the poems, though not as excellent as those written by later writers, be kept..." Why does the poet suddenly veer to discuss his own death? What "later writers" are being referred to?

Sonnet 33: Suddenly, the beloved is "now 'masked' from" the poet. "Masked" how? Why? By whom?

Sonnet 34: "...now the sun/beloved is accused of having betrayed the poet by promising what is not delivered. The poet writes that while the beloved's repentance and shame do not rectify the damage done..." What could possibly be "not delivered" that would constitute betrayal, or that would be so serious that repentance and shame are insufficient to rectify it?

Sonnet 36: "The poet accepts the fact that for the sake of the beloved's honorable name, their lives must be separate and their love unacknowledged." Nothing in the sonnet refers to anyone's "honorable name." If this is really the beginning of a permanent separation, how come another ninety sonnets follow in which the love is clearly acknowledged? And how can it be stated here that their love is "unacknowledged" when ninety more sonnets continue to talk of it?

Sonnet 38: "The poet attributes all that is praiseworthy in his poetry to the beloved, who is his theme and inspiration." So what happened to the total break described two sonnets previous, or the harm done four sonnets ago that couldn't be rectified?

This exercise in incoherent narration where what is allegedly said in sonnet after sonnet is either disconnected from, or in contradiction to, the narrative of the sonnets that precede and follow it, continues throughout the remainder of the Folger rendering of its version of the SI. Just in this set of sonnets, every attempted explanation requires imputing all sorts of "facts not in evidence," betrayals, things, or friends, the poet has "lost," "later poets" who write better than the poet does, something "not delivered" which causes acute shame which is somehow never mentioned again, a "final" separation which lasts for all of one sonnet, etc., etc.

The succeeding episodes in the SI narrative continue an almost impossible-to-follow sequence where: the other man betrays the poet, either with some unmentioned other person or persons, or with the woman the SI claims is the poet's mistress; the woman toys with both of them; the poet betrays the other man (how is never made clear—with the woman or some other man or woman?); and somehow they come back together, separate, disparage each other, and come back again. Reading the narrative in one sitting causes one's head to spin. Finally, Sonnets 127-152 lose all sense of narrative, as they wander all over the map implicating the woman as having snared both men as sex slaves, portraying the poet as begging to get back into her bed (what happened with his attraction to the man?), alternately disparaging and praising her, etc. etc.

The reader is encouraged to obtain a copy of the Folger edition and to peruse the summaries of each sonnet in order to verify for him or herself the incoherent mishmash of a story that they relate. Possibly more accessible is a recent book by the former President of Harvard and Shakespeare scholar Neil L. Rudenstine, entitled *Ideas of Order, A Close Reading of Shakespeare's Sonnets*[5], available online as well as in hard copy, devoted to nothing but a detailed telling of the Standard Interpretation with a few original angles thrown in.

The Crisis of Orthodox Scholarship

It is this quintessential incoherence and mishmash of contradictions and impossible imputed story lines that convicts the SI of being fiction, of being an utterly hopeless rendering of what Shakespeare could possibly have meant to impart in the sonnets. Proponents of the SI (which is to say virtually all conventional scholars) seem to forget that they are talking about Shakespeare, the greatest playwright in history, and an accomplished poet to boot. Would he really have written 154 sonnets to commemorate such a wretched personal life, even if its storyline were more-coherent than the SI understands it to be? Wouldn't it be worthwhile to consider the possibility that some far loftier, more noble story was the substance of the sonnets, something more befitting the greatness not just of Shakespeare as a craftsman of drama, but the nobility of the implicit morals and morality reflected in so many of his plays, both tragedies and comedies?

Right off the bat, the SI confronts a number of obvious questions that make its narrative appear highly improbable:

1. How did Shakespeare manage to carry on these two (or more) affairs? After all, he was married, lived in Stratford-on-Avon, at least three days journey from London, and had to support his wife and three children. What about his wife Anne Hathaway? Was he two-timing her (or three-timing her)? Stratford was a small town, so even if it is supposed that he carried on the affairs only in London, word could easily get back. To my knowledge, no scholar has asked or attempted to answer this obvious question.
2. So Shakespeare had this relationship to this man, but he simultaneously had a mistress, so was he two-timing the man (until the man turned the tables and stole the woman?

Which was before the woman made both men her sex slaves?)? Or was he two-timing the mistress?

3. And so Shakespeare was bisexual? As was the man? And the woman was OK with that? This supposed triangle is remarkably improbable, both in real life and in fiction, in any age, much less the straight-laced era of Elizabethan England.

4. Most adherents to the SI think that the man was a nobleman, generally assumed to be either the Earl of Southampton or the Earl of Pembroke. So how did this commoner go from having one of these gentlemen for a patron to having him as a lover? Class distinctions would make this seem mighty unlikely. It would likely be extremely hard for an earl to hide a liaison with a commoner, and highly risky, given that sodomy was a capital offense, and Elizabethan England was a police state with a very effective internal spy network.

5. Also, if as most scholars believe, the young man was either Southampton or Pembroke, since both of *them* were married, are we to understand that *they* were also two-timing (or three-timing) *their* wives with the poet and the mistress? The mind starts to boggle at the thought.

These are just the beginning of the problems that orthodox scholarship would struggle to answer, hopelessly, in my opinion, if they even tried to discuss them, that none even attempts to address. In addition to the conundrums listed above that concern the sexuality of the poet and the young man, and the class differences among them, are the following further questions that, again, orthodox scholarship is hard pressed to answer:

1. Who was the young man? If, as a majority believe, he was Southampton, how could the commoner Shakespeare and Southampton have maintained the kind of relationship portrayed in the SI completely undetected by contemporaries, over what appears to be a number of years? (This is highly damaging to the credibility of the SI, because so much is known of Southampton's biography that it strains credulity that the poet (who, if he were Shakespeare, would have had a high profile as well) could have been carrying on the type of affair generally portrayed with the flesh and blood Southampton, and do so without so much as a whisper of it getting out to anyone.

Southampton spent most of the 1590s in the association of the 2nd Earl of Essex, and spent considerable time abroad or in other parts of England. Nothing in the SI remotely resembles anything that is known about Southampton. And then, in 1601, Southampton was arrested and convicted of treason for his role in the Essex Rebellion, a terrible disgrace. How could this biography possibly be fit in to the SI account of the relationship triangle of poet, young man (if he were Southampton) and the woman?)

2. How could a commoner have dared, much less gotten away with, addressing a nobleman in the highly disparaging tone of the first seventeen sonnets, or the very familiar and often scolding or critical tone in many of the later sonnets? Such forms of address were simply not done, even between members of the nobility.

3. If the relationship was homosexual, how and why were the sonnets ever published, given that publication would have exposed both men to severe sanctions, even possible execution (sodomy was a capital crime)?

4. If it wasn't homosexual, what was it? A majority of scholars attempt to describe the relationship as close friendship, but the SI that these same scholars adhere to is nothing if not about tangled *romantic* attachments among the two men and the woman, which implies bisexuality or homosexuality on the part of both men.

5. Who the poet, Shakespeare, really was. Several of the questions posed above all but rule out that Shakespeare could have been a commoner, pointing instead to his having to have been a member of the nobility, writing under a pseudonym.

The Sonnets Themselves Speak Out

Whittemore did something not done by traditional scholars: he decided to take the sonnets at their word, to treat what was said in every sonnet as meaning what it appeared to mean. For starters, he noticed that a number of passages referred to the sonnets themselves as an actor in history, to preserve the memory of the poet and Southampton. Amazingly, orthodox scholarship has failed to take these passages seriously as keys to unlock new doors of understanding.

Specifically, in more than a dozen sonnets, the poet explicitly states that his poetry, his "rhymes," will make their subject (Southampton), and/or the sonnets themselves, famous for all future history, even until eternity. The claims made for the power of the sonnets to do this are truly extraordinary. I find it inconceivable that Shakespeare, whoever he was, would have made such claims if the story that would resonate for the rest of history were the tawdry, if not sodomitic, three-way homo- and bi-sexual relationship that is portrayed by the Standard Interpretation.

The following ten passages from eight sonnets illustrate the point:

The author's first reference to his "verse" occurs in Sonnet 17, where he opens the sonnet with

17   1   Who will believe my verse in time to come

and ends it with

17   13   But were some child of yours alive that time,
17   14   You should live twice; in it and in my rhyme.

Why would the poet be concerned in this way with how the sonnets will make the other man live on in them if the SI is what the sonnets are actually about?

Sonnet 18 makes similar references:

18   11   Nor shall Death brag thou wander'st in his shade,
18   12   When in eternal lines to time thou growest:

Here the poet says that the subject of the sonnets will live *eternally* in the sonnets, defying mortal death. To "grow...in eternal lines" implies that people in future generations will read the lines, and so learn of the man. Why would the poet say that the sonnets will help the man cheat death by being memorialized in poems that will be *eternal* if the subject matter is a tawdry love triangle?

Sonnet 19 continues with a similar refrain:

19   13   Yet, do thy worst, old Time: despite thy wrong,
19   14   My love shall in my verse ever live young.

The next such reference is in Sonnet 54, where the poet explicitly says that his verse will show the young man as forever young.

54   13   And so of you, beauteous and lovely youth,
54   14   When that shall fade, my verse distills your truth.

This echoes Sonnet 18, implying that when the subject's youth and beauty pass, the sonnets will capture for all time how beautiful he was. Sonnet 55 continues:

55 1 Not marble, nor the gilded monuments
55 2 Of princes, shall outlive this powerful rhyme;

This couplet is extraordinary, and confounds all by itself any credibility for the SI. How could the standard telling of how the youth has betrayed the poet, and the poet betrayed the youth, and the woman messed around with both, conceivably be something the poet would describe as the subject of "powerful rhyme" that will outlive stone monuments to kings?

Sonnet 60 states again how the sonnets will stand praising the young man:

60 13 And yet to times in hope my verse shall stand,
60 14 Praising thy worth, despite his cruel hand.

Sonnet 81 asserts that the sonnets will be a monument to the man (a monument being a stone tomb generally reserved for important people):

81 8 When you entombed in men's eyes shall lie.
81 9 Your monument shall be my gentle verse,

Sonnet 107 states that the poet will live on in the sonnets after his mortal life is done

107 10 My love looks fresh, and death to me subscribes,
107 11 Since, spite of him, I'll live in this poor rhyme,

and then repeats that the sonnets will be the other man's monument as well, which will last far longer than stone monuments to princes:

107 13 And thou in this shalt find thy monument,
107 14 When tyrants' crests and tombs of brass are spent.

These ten passages are fatal to the SI, by making clear that the poet saw the sonnets as a single body of poetry whose purpose was to memorialize the young man, and preserve knowledge of him until the end of time. That he could desire to do this if the SI were an accurate understanding of the content of the sonnets is all but inconceivable. I am not aware of any orthodox scholar, certainly not the four examined in this book, who attempts to tackle the above challenge to the orthodox view, or who is even aware that such a challenge even exists.

I have presented these passages here because the implications to be drawn from them inform the context in which Whittemore's discoveries became possible. Given the proof that Shakespeare saw both Southampton, and his sonnets, as transcendent, not only does the SI become untenable, but so even the possibility that the traditional candidate is Shakespeare, the commoner from Stratford, appears remote at best. Among other questions that these passages resolve are the following:

1. The relationship of poet to young man was decidedly *not* romantic, *ergo*, not homosexual. Apart from the danger of revealing a homosexual relationship, how can anyone believe that Shakespeare would think that the story of such a relationship would be of interest to and resonate among future generations until the end of time?

2. Nor was the relationship one of close male friendship because, again, why would such a friendship be considered by the poet to be of such transcendent importance.

3. Therefore, whatever the sonnets are chronicling, it *must be* something of importance to England, its current population, and to all future generations.

4. The sonnets were intended for publication. Only if they were published could they possibly have the grandiose effect the author claimed for them. Future generations must read them to learn of the story they tell.

5. The sonnets are in the order the poet intended. This is indicated by the frequent references to the sonnets as a whole, making clear that the poet was constructing an edifice, one he twice calls a "monument," to preserve the story they tell.

6. The author cannot have been the traditionally identified "Shakespeare" from Stratford-upon-Avon, because his known biography rules out that he could conceivably have been the chronicler for information about a top nobleman, the 3rd Earl of Southampton, that was so astounding as to justify the claims made in the passages above, information not known to anyone else that we know of. Only a fellow member of the nobility could possibly have had that kind of access and information.

Other passages in the Sonnets also all but rule out that "Shakespeare" from Stratford was the real author, including:

1. Several lines in Sonnet 81 contrast the fame that the poet claims the young man will have with the absence of fame predicted by the poet for himself. This cannot be explained if the author were the traditional candidate from Stratford who, at the time the sonnets were published in 1609, would have been at the height of his popularity, making it inconceivable that he would characterize himself as destined "to all the world" to die and be buried "in a common grave." Orthodoxy has no explanation for this line.

2. Sonnet 72 echoes a similar theme, saying "My name be buried where my body is," that is, once he is dead, nobody will remember the poet, or even know who he was. Such a story is impossible for the man traditionally identified as Shakespeare, whose plays and published narrative poems were very popular. The name "Shakespeare" could never have been thought to "be buried where my body is," which could only be possible if "Shakespeare" were a pseudonym, that would surely live on, while the true name of the real author would remain unknown forever after his death.

3. Sonnet 66 says that the poet's "art" is "tongue-tied by authority," which means that he is unable to write what he wants on pain of reprisals from the state. This supports the view that the sonnets convey a message threatening to the authorities. No traditional scholar thinks that "Shakespeare" from Stratford had any reason to fear the authorities, so, without a reason to pen this line, he couldn't have been the real Shakespeare.

4. Sonnet 125's opening line, "Wer't ought to me I bore the canopy" is inconsistent with Shakespeare being a commoner, who would never have had the ability or right to bear a canopy, which was carried for official state occasions, typically visits by foreign dignitaries or coronations or funerals of monarchs. Only a member of the nobility would have that right.

Orthodox scholars are not only unable to answer any of the above questions, but possibly for that reason, make no attempt to do so. They do not even recognize that these questions are in need of being answered. Another conundrum faces traditional scholarship —even the best efforts of scholars cannot even fit a great many passages from the sonnets into the Standard Interpretation at all,

15

despite page after page some of them expand in their anthologies trying to explicate these problem passages. Those scholars who edit the complete *Sonnets* in particular find themselves facing the extreme challenge of trying to explain these numerous lines that defy intelligible interpretation under the premise of the SI. When stumped by one or more lines in a sonnet, the scholars typically resort to one of the following subterfuges:

1. They provide often lengthy explanations *qua* exegeses on the possible meaning(s) of key words, without attempting to derive a comprehensible meaning for the entire passage or sonnet.
2. They shoehorn passages into the Standard Interpretation by concocting elaborate "back stories" of invented "facts" that are presumed to be true.
3. Some passages defy their ability to make any connection between them and the SI narrative, so they muse that the poet is discoursing on abstract topics that have no relevance to the narrative, such as the nature of "beauty" in the abstract, the use of cosmetics, or the fashion of wearing wigs.
5. They simply omit to provide any commentary on certain important lines that prove to be devastating to their view of the sonnets, such as the lines quoted above on how the sonnets will make Southampton famous until the end of time. Their avoidance of tough questions merely confirms that they have no actual idea what the sonnets are about, since any such understanding must start by making sense of these most problematic passages.

Understanding the Standard Interpretation, and how inadequate it is to make sense of the sonnets, is important to show why there is need of a sea change in the underlying assumptions on which a correct interpretation must be grounded, and to demonstrate that Whittemore's discoveries offer the *only* interpretation that *does* make sense of the numerous passages that orthodoxy *cannot* make sense of.

One of the purposes of this present volume is to show not only the degree to which Hank Whittemore's discoveries offer a truly coherent and satisfying explanation for the entire sonnet collection, but the degree to which his is the *only* treatment that has any coherence at all. That is, that *versus* the SI, I believe the contest is between a proposed possible solution and a manifest non-solution.

One can accept or reject Whittemore's solution, or accept parts of it and reject other parts, but whichever one does, one *must* reject the SI, even if means concluding, with Hollander, that the *Sonnets* pose a mystery that may never be solved. I go out of my way to demonstrate the inadequacy of the SI both to make the case that there is a *need* for a satisfying solution to the sonnets (that is, that none of the existing proposed solutions is viable), and to highlight the contrast between how Whittemore's interpretation provides a coherent narrative throughout that also explains innumerable problematic passages, with how conventional analysis is helpless to provide such a narrative or to understand the multitude of these problematic passages.

To illustrate this contrast, I have selected four recent editions of the sonnets whose editors are highly respected scholars who have each written extended introductory discussions and extensive glosses and comments on each sonnet. I draw on their comments on the problematic passages frequently throughout this volume to demonstrate their inadequacies and highlight the superiority of the Whittemore interpretation. The four scholars, with the editions they have edited, are: Stephen Booth (*Shakespeare's Sonnets,* Yale University Press),[6] Colin Burrow (*The Complete Sonnets and Poems,* Oxford University Press),[7] Katherine Duncan-Jones (*Shakespeare's Sonnets,* Arden)[8] and John Kerrigan (*The Sonnets and A Lover's Complaint,* Penguin edition).[9]

(One other edition deserves mention, *Shakespeare's Sonnets* (1964) edited by A. L. Rowse. Rowse, uniquely among orthodox scholars, sought to find a few sonnets that might expose the time frame in which the sonnets were written. He found four sonnets (25, 86, 107 and 124) that he believed referred to events between 1592 and 1594, which conclusion allowed him to render the most plausible version of the SI that I have seen. Unfortunately, Rowse made no effort to relate his narrative to hundreds of lines that were incompatible with his version of the narrative, which in the end rendered his solution unviable, but at least he adopted a correct methodology, that presaged Whittemore's by recognizing that establishing an historical context for the sonnets was essential to deciphering their meaning.)

In sum, the sum total of the narrative that comprises what I have termed the "Standard Interpretation" is an impossible solution to the riddle of the sonnets that Hollander so eloquently described. I submit, using the terminology and insights of Thomas Kuhn, whose 1962 book *The Structure of Scientific Revolutions* coined the term "paradigm shift," that only a dramatic such shift from the existing paradigm—that is, the SI—to the new paradigm discovered by Whittemore, can ever unlock the mysteries and solve the enigmas of *Shake-speare's Sonnets*.

A good illustration of the nature of a paradigm shift is provided by one of my favorite Edgar Allan Poe short stories, *The Murders in the Rue Morgue*. The police were baffled by a set of clues that they could not make sense of. Inspector Dupin's solution required examining, then jettisoning, a core assumption that everyone else had, quite understandably, made, since no prior case had ever called it into question. Of course, the assumption was that the murderer was human: the murderer was an orangutan. The Copernican, heliocentric paradigm, replacing the geocentric Ptolemaic one, is another good example of a paradigm shift, as was Einstein's relativity theories supplanting Newtonian mechanics, and Alfred Wegener's theory of continental drift, that, fifty years later, was validated when plate tectonics were discovered.

In the case of *Shake-speares Sonnets,* an equally dramatic paradigm shift is clearly needed. No amount of tweaking or refining the Standard Interpretation holds any promise of answering the enigmas that have so far eluded intelligible interpretation under the conventional paradigm that identifies the three characters as Shakespeare (understood as the man from Stratford), a young man (most likely the 3rd Earl of Southampton, an identification which is in fact correct), and an unidentified woman, involved in a tangled three-way relationship involving homosexuality, bisexuality, and heterosexuality.

I turn now to the most pressing element of that required paradigm shift, without which the sonnets cannot be comprehended—determining who "Shakespeare" really was.

The "Shakespeare Authorship Controversy"

As more and more people are coming to be aware, there is a long-standing controversy as to who the flesh-and-blood man was whose works we know as Shakespeare's. The debate illustrates in an even more important context the importance of being willing to recognize when an existing paradigm is inadequate to account for the known facts of a discipline, in this instance, that of Shakespeare Studies. And it is vitally important to at least tentatively resolve because who the poet/author was bears crucially on what the *Sonnets* is about.

The man currently identified as "Shakespeare" died in 1616. Most people do not know that there is not a single record dated during his lifetime, of anyone in all of England professing to know an actual person of that name as the author of the plays and poems. And on his supposed death in April of 1616, there was not a single eulogy, commentary, obituary, no notice of any kind, that England had lost its greatest playwright—a virtually impossible scenario if the man who died at that time had been the true Shakespeare. For that matter, 13 years before, when Queen Elizabeth had died, while there was an outpouring of writings from virtually every known literary figure of the time, there was, again, nothing from the greatest of them all, Shakespeare. Each of these facts is sufficient to cast extreme doubt that Shakespeare could have been the traditionally identified man from Stratford who died in 1616.

It was not until seven years later, in several short poems in the Preface to the 1623 publication of the *First Folio* of Shakespeare's collected plays that anyone wrote publicly of "Shakespeare" and purported to describe him as a flesh-and-blood person. In Ben Jonson's poem in honor of Shakespeare, he called him "sweet swan of Avon," and Leonard Digges referred in his poem to "thy Stratford Moniment." These two references, taken separately, are both ambiguous, since there are many Avon rivers (and other "Avon" place names), and many Stratfords, both towns and other geographical designations. No subsequent document putting these two references together to identify Stratford-on-Avon as Shakespeare's home town is known until the next century. And at the time of Digges' reference, there *was* a monument to a "William Shakespeare" in Stratford but it shows a man standing with his hands placed on a sack of wool or grain, suggesting a wool or grain merchant, not a writer, which would accord equally well with Shakspere's known business activities, or those of his father.

It took until the early 18th century for people to turn these vague suggestions from the *First Folio* into an unambiguous association of the author of the plays and poems that have become known to us as written by "William Shakespeare" with the flesh-and-blood man William Shakspere (or Shagspere, or Shaxpere, or, as occasionally spelled, Shakespeare) of Stratford-upon-Avon. By that time, nearly a century of Civil War, the Puritan Revolution (and the consequent banning of all theatrical performances for nearly two decades), and the following Restoration, had intervened, such that anyone with first-hand knowledge of "Shakespeare" had long-since died, leaving extant the thinnest of evidence as to who "William Shakespeare" had really been. In the relative vacuum of hard evidence, the *First Folio*'s suggestive references were taken as definitive, and a hunt begun to flesh out the biography of the man from Stratford. Thus began a three hundred year-long quest by proponents of the Stratford "Shakespeare" to find out more about their man, in hopes of solidifying the identification.

The results of the most intense search for biographical information in the history of the arts has turned up just shy of zilch relevant information (none of it conclusive) to buttress the identification of the Stratford "Shakespeare" with Shakespeare the playwright and poet. However, what it *has* turned up is several scores of biographical snippets about the man from Stratford that paint a picture of someone about as unlikely to be capable of being the Shakespeare we know as could be imagined. (In this book, I, like many others, have adopted the convention of referring to the man from Stratford as "Shakspere," in order to make unambiguous when it is he, the flesh-and-blood businessman (every known record of him involves a business or real estate transaction) from Stratford, who is being referred to; the author of the literary corpus, whoever he might have been, will be referred to as "Shakespeare.")

It is unfortunately impossible for me to give proper coverage here to the specifics of the documented life of Shakspere that would demonstrate how utterly improbable, and essentially impossible, it is that he could have authored the works of Shakespeare. I have provided a summary of many of them in Appendix I, and I commend the reader unfamiliar with the debate, or who heretofore has accepted the blanket denials from the academic camp that there is any basis for doubting the Shakspere identification, to read that appendix before continuing.

But I want to add one other observation here, and that is that a minority of Stratfordian scholars (scholars who continue to support the Shakspere identification) are forthright in their concession that the picture painted of the historical Shakspere is diametrically opposite the temperament and background of what common sense would presume the real Shakespeare would have possessed. They, and all other Stratfordians consequently argue that, unlike the case with virtually every other famous literary figure in history, "Shakespeare" put absolutely nothing of his real life, or his real personality, into his writings. This fact alone speaks volumes against Shakspere being Shakespeare.

By the mid-19th century, with the growing sophistication of critical analysis of literary works and the birth of modern historiography, the manifest disconnect between the Shakspere biography and what the content of Shakespeare's works suggested the author should be like lead some people to question the attribution of the works of Shakespeare to the man from Stratford, who seemed to have none of the characteristics that the true author must have possessed. Even in England, two of the most prominent politicians of that century, Lord Palmerston and Benjamin Disraeli, were among the doubters. Thus was born the "Shakespeare authorship controversy," which continues, stronger than ever, to this day.

Among the notables who have doubted Shakspere's authorship are: Mark Twain and a dozen other famous 19th century authors, political figures from Lord Palmerston and Otto von Bismarck to Charles DeGaulle, historians Crane Brinton and David McCullough, Shakespearean actors Sir John Gielgud, Derek Jacobi, Mark Rylance and others, actors Charlie Chaplin and Orson Welles, Sigmund Freud, Helen Keller, and even five members of the U.S. Supreme Court from Oliver Wendell Holmes to John Paul Stevens, and this is far from a complete list. All of them have all been convinced both by the affirmative evidence that Shakspere could not have been Shakespeare, and by the lack of evidence that he was.

If Shakspere wasn't Shakespeare, then who was? The doubt led to a search for who the true author could have been. No satisfactory candidates were proposed until 1920, when one Thomas Looney published *"Shakespeare" Identified,* that pointed to Edward de Vere, 17th Earl of Oxford. In the almost century since, the case for Oxford has grown ever stronger, to the point that almost everyone who doubts it was Shakspere believes that Oxford was definitely or most likely to have been the real Shakespeare. There are many dozens of excellent books, now supplemented by half a dozen periodicals and thousands of articles and websites, that have confirmed and extended Looney's identification of Oxford as the face behind the "Shakespeare" pseudonym. While it would be impossible to do more than scratch the surface of the evidence that supports the Oxford identification in anything short of a book-length treatment, I have included an appendix, Appendix IV, that briefly covers just a fraction of the reasons for believing that Oxford had to be Shakespeare, which the reader unfamiliar with the case for Oxford is commended to read before proceeding.

In the debate between Stratfordians and Oxfordians, the following can be said: neither position can point to any convincing documentary confirmation of their case, meaning evidence such as anything from a manuscript of a Shakespeare play in one or the other's handwriting, or a memoir or letter from a contemporary clearly identifying one or the other as the author, or any other such type of evidence. Both sides rely on literary evidence, both from what's in the plays and poems themselves, and from some allusions in a few other literary works believed to refer to Shakespeare or Shakspere, which they try to match up against the known biographies of Oxford and Shakspere. In a nutshell, the biography of Oxford provides absolutely everything that one might expect to find in the author of the plays, from his education, known domains of knowledge and experience, languages he knew, extended travels in Italy and France, and known attributed or suspected writings, to the psychology one would expect to find (the perspective of a top nobleman) and to innumerable instances in the plays when a strong similarity to incidents in Oxford's life suggests that the incidents are autobiographical. The polar opposite is true for Shakspere, for whom there are zero correlations between what the writings would suggest and anything whatsoever in his known biography.

The curious irony for Stratfordians is that they simultaneously know too little, and too much, about Shakspere. They know too little (effectively nothing) that would confirm him as a writer of any kind, but too much of his actual life, which suggests he was a mean-spirited, ruthless, petty social climber who sued people for as little as two pounds owed him and who hoarded grain in a famine, and who invested in several theaters but yet never received so much as a tuppence from anything he supposedly ever wrote—an incongruity that alone says he couldn't have been the author.

I hope I have provided enough here and in the appendices to lead all readers to recognize that this debate is legitimate, and that there is plenty of reason, at the very least, to raise doubts about the traditional attribution, if not to decide that whether or not Oxford wrote Shakespeare, we can be certain that Shakspere of Stratford could not have. Because of the decades-long campaign by Stratfordian stalwarts to hide the weakness of their case by trying to discourage people from even looking into the controversy, largely through *ad hominem* attacks on Oxfordians, a coalition was formed in 2007 to counter this campaign by soliciting support for a statement asserting that there are legitimate and strong grounds for doubt. The "Shakespeare Authorship Coalition" has now gathered more than 2,700 signatures, many from prominent individuals in many walks of life, to a "Declaration of Reasonable Doubt About the Identity of William Shakespeare." The Declaration itself is a very useful compendium of many of the strongest reasons to doubt, including many points I have not included in my appendix, so I strongly urge the reader to look up this Declaration in addition to reading Appendix I.

I should also mention that I have included an annotated bibliography at the end of the book, to help guide the reader to other sources on all aspects of the controversy.

Orthodoxy's Defense: the Magic of Genius

I have dwelled on the question of authorship because it is essential to a correct reading of the *Sonnets* for the reader to at least be open to considering that the poet was Oxford (and not Shakspere). In a strict sense, it would not be necessary to start with this view, in that in the final analysis the sonnets themselves establish that only if Oxford is the author can they be made sense of. But from the perspective of making the discoveries that Whittemore made in the first place, it would be psychologically almost impossible for someone who was fully convinced that Shakspere was the poet to recognize the evidence pointing to Oxford for what it is. That said, in my presentation, I do not ask the reader to assume at the outset that the poet is Oxford, but rather to suspend judgment until I come to my discussion of Sonnets 30 and 35 several chapters in, where the sonnets themselves show why only Oxford makes sense as the poet.

So how do Stratfordians account for how someone whom they concede had at best (and even this is undocumented) the education that the grammar school in Stratford (which was a small agricultural town) would have provided, growing up in a town where he likely didn't even have access to many books (if he'd even been inclined to want to read books at all since he was the son of illiterate parents whose father's business the young Shakspere would almost certainly have expected to help out with from a young age), manage before age thirty to display intimate knowledge of gardening and botany, birds and animals, astronomy, hunting and falconry, music, classical mythology and literature, medicine, heraldry, history, sailing and seamanship, scripture, and the law, plus fluency in French, Italian, Latin and likely some Greek, plus detailed information that could only have come via first-hand experience of the street layouts of several cities and knowledge of minor artistic figures and other details of Italy, and to wield a vocabulary that dwarfs that of any other figure in English literature including Milton, by a factor of two to three or more to one?

Easy, so claims the defender of the orthodox paradigm. He picked it up by browsing in bookstalls in London, and by conversations in taverns where he talked to people who'd traveled abroad. How anyone can believe this fairy tale is frankly beyond me. An analogy might if Einstein were an elementary school dropout who'd had no mathematics in school, and who browsed in bookstalls to learn physics and math and still came up with the five papers on five different areas of physics, one of which was the theory of special relativity, that Einstein had published in 1905. Einstein was not a professor (he had a job at the Berne patent office), but he'd had extensive academic training in physics. In fact, his mathematics skills were not that high in 1905, such that he had to spend years bringing them up to snuff before he was able to come up with his General Theory of Relativity ten years later. His inborn genius alone couldn't replace the need for knowledge of physics and mathematics—it could only be expressed after he'd put in the time and work to gain the knowledge without which genius cannot be expressed.

Except in the case of Shakespeare, so orthodoxy tells us. The answer typically provided is perfectly captured in in the oft-cited quotation from T. W. Baldwin in his 1944 book *William Shakespeare's Small Latine & Less Greeke*, "At least no miracles are required to account for such knowledge and techniques from the classics as he [Shakespeare] exhibits...[the] Stratford grammar school will furnish all that is required. *The miracle lies elsewhere; it is the world-old miracle of genius...*" [10] (emphasis added). The ascription of "genius" or other comparable words to Shakespeare is the typical answer proffered by orthodoxy to explain (away) every impossible attribute that Shakespeare had that Shakspere demonstrably could not plausibly have had. "Well, he was Shakespeare, and his genius allowed him to intuit in minutes what other mortals require months or years of study to master," go goes the apparent argument.

The "Satan Maneuver"

This appeal to the other-worldly *deus ex machina* of supposed "genius" to negate, with a single affirmative stroke of the pen, the deficit of no training or experience, no conducive home or school environment, no mentors or teachers, and no time to have mastered any of the known fields, is breathtaking. Mark Alexander, in an article on Shakespeare and the law, dubbed this intellectually shoddy tactic the "Satan Maneuver," after seeing an interview with an evangelical minister who, when asked how the world could have been created only 6,000 years ago in light of the existence of vastly older fossils, simply replied "Satan put them [the fossils] there," thereby ending all possibility of further discussion. Alexander continues:

> Unfortunately, the Satan Maneuver appears frequently in Shakespeare studies. When confronted with internal evidence that Shakespeare may have had a high-level education, whether in law or the classics, a scholar will produce a rabbit out of his or her hat by falling back on Shakespeare's genius, which is, like Satan, a phenomenon of no known source or established dimension. For example, A.L. Rowse in his *Shakespeare The Man* explains Shakespeare's comprehensive and wide-ranging experience with classical and contemporary literature and history thus: "He had a marvelous capacity from the outset for making a little go a long way; his real historical reading came later—he was very much a reading man, and he read quickly."
>
> How he has grasped Shakespeare's "marvelous capacity" or knows his reading ability, Rowse does not say. But his meaning is clear; Shakespeare gleaned his incredible wealth of knowledge by having a capacious mind that magically (through the mystery of *genius*) grasped knowledge quickly and easily. British Shakespearean scholar Allardyce Nicoll makes a similar claim in his book *Shakespeare*: "In the wonder of his genius he was able to grasp in lightning speed what could be attained only after dull years of work by ordinary minds." Thus can scholars magically explain away the need for education and leisure that ordinary common sense would argue was required for this writer's immense erudition and the aristocratic nature of his themes and settings. By introducing such statements, scholars cut short arguments in favor of a university education or the kind of experience and leisure that only the nobility had access to in Shakespeare's day. The forum of reason, argument, and evidence dissolves. Genius in the form of a superhuman mind and memory explains all, the magical ability to immediately and photographically apprehend everything, sans education, sans experience, merely from reading a few translations or conversing with travellers.[11]

A comparable tactic is used to defend the standard interpretation of the sonnets. No matter how incoherent, weird or implausible the narrative they derive may be, it's what they go with, with a rationalization that amounts to the Satan Maneuver—"magical thinking" run amok.

Hank Whittemore's Shocking Discovery

Whittemore's recognition that all previous attempts at understanding the sonnets led to an incoherent narrative was a driving force behind his fascination with them. That is, he early on recognized that the conventional interpretation utterly failed to make sense of the sonnets, and that even plugging Oxford in as the author did not of itself resolve the many anomalies in the prevailing view. The other driving force for Whittemore was his belief that, of all places, it would be in the sonnets that the true authorship of Shakespeare's works would most convincingly be revealed because of their intense personal nature and the fact that they were written in the first person, the only works of Shakespeare to be so written.

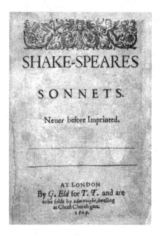

Figure 1 - The enigma of Shake-Speares Sonnets *begins on the cover, with the hyphenated name "Shake-Speare" used at the top, and the two lines beneath bracketing a blank space where normally an author's name would appear.*

What has ensued is a classic instance of a Kuhnian paradigm shift. Whittemore, from outside the field of academic Shakespeare scholarship, was able to recognize that the standard interpretation contained innumerable holes—anomalies—that cried out for explanations that the existing paradigm could not provide. Discovering a new paradigm wasn't easy, and even Whittemore notes that after almost ten years he nearly gave up his quest. Whittemore describes his process of discovery in his Foreword. After the years of fruitless efforts, he took a year away from the project, then returned for one last go at it, and then, more or less suddenly during a conference in late 1998, the outlines of an alternate paradigm that immediately allowed him to make sense of the anomalies and unlocked the sonnets, came to him in a flash.

The picture that emerged represented a shocking discovery—that the sonnets, far from relating a sleazy three-way relationship, with its frequent infidelities and betrayals by all parties of each other, were about reasons of state, were firmly rooted in the history of the last years of Elizabeth's reign, and contained historical information otherwise unknown to history. The new paradigm that he had discovered and the standard interpretation couldn't have been farther removed from each other—easily as far removed as Copernican astronomy was from Ptolemaic.

Whittemore's new understandings saw print in his more than 900-page magnum opus, *The Monument,* published in 2005, providing a parallel "translation" of every sonnet, presenting the hidden meaning that Whittemore had discerned, and including extensive discussions of the meanings and usages of thousands of words and phrases. It also related many of these words to their usage in the plays, to provide further depth to his reading of the *Sonnets.* Aware that the size of the book might deter some readers, in 2010 Whittemore wrote *Shakespeare's Son and His Sonnets,* which presents a summary case in some 200 pages.

When his understanding of the *Sonnets* finally becomes the standard interpretation, as I believe it will, Whittemore's achievement will rank alongside that of Looney in rehabilitating the reputation of the greatest dramatist in any language, while also making public the intensely political, if generally unknown, role that the man we refer to as "William Shakespeare" played in the England of Queen Elizabeth I.

Why this Book

The inspiration for this book came as I read Whittemore's *Monument* and *Shakespeare's Son.* As I worked through them, I realized that I was convinced of the correctness of his interpretations because of what he discovered in certain sonnets that, once understood, led to understanding previously less accessible passages in other sonnets. I felt that his discoveries could more effectively be presented to a wider audience if his thesis was presented by examining sonnets, and sections of sonnets, in the order that I found best built the evidentiary case.

Therefore, in this book, the order of presentation of the sonnets is not numerical (that is, starting with Sonnet 1 and ending with 154), but forensic—starting with whichever sonnet or sonnets provide the clearest evidence for the context of the entire sonnets series, and proceeding from there in order of ease of deciphering each succeeding clue. I believe this is the way any good detective progressively unravels a perplexing criminal case, by seeking to explain items of evidence that initially "don't fit," by beginning with the most readily understandable pieces of evidence and working step by step toward the more and more difficult clues, as previously solved clues help to unravel each in turn.

I have divided my presentation into two parts. Part I presents the basis for the full thesis that Whittemore discovered. As an aid to the reader, I have codified each important conclusion as I develop it in the form of a theorem, modeled on the kind of theorems that Euclid first developed for geometry. I have assembled all the theorems for easy reference in Appendix VII. I have done this to help make transparent the thread of the argument and to highlight the logical progression of my presentation. By the end of Part I, the full thesis that Whittemore discovered is presented, in the course of which presentation twenty-two sonnets are discussed, and nineteen theorems presented.

Part II then applies that thesis to an additional seventy-three sonnets, which all yield intelligible readings based on the new paradigm. Such a degree of success is extraordinary. Space forbids examining all the sonnets (in total, ninety-five out of 154 are discussed in whole or in part), but almost all of those not covered can likewise be unlocked by the key that Whittemore discovered. Part I is therefore the presentation of the discovery of the new paradigm, and Part II presents the empirical testing of that paradigm to confirm that it truly does account for nearly every sonnet.

Although my debt to Whittemore is incalculable, in all cases where I discuss what a sonnet, or part of one, means, I have come up with my own reading. In most cases it is the same, or close to the same, reading as in *The Monument,* but in a significant number of instances, I was unsatisfied with Whittemore's specific take on a sonnet, or some lines from a sonnet. Most often, I determined that Whittemore had applied a too formulaic reading of certain words that Shakespeare uses to stand for concepts other than their ordinary meanings. In all such cases, I insisted on making each sonnet, and within each sonnet each quatrain and the couplet, speak a coherent story. I bounced my new readings off Whittemore, who has been a friend for the last decade and who collaborated intensively in the preparation of this book; in all such cases, he has concurred that my reading are improvements, and was happy to find someone standing on his shoulders refining his initial work.

This book is a challenge to Shakespearean orthodoxy because it comes at the authorship question from a new angle not typically advanced by Oxfordian challengers to the myth of the Stratford man. To my knowledge, no Oxfordian has ever challenged the orthodox reading, including the Standard Interpretation, by taking apart the exegeses of contemporary notable scholars, as this book does, and demonstrating their legion and fatal deficiencies. If orthodox scholars are forced to refute this book, they will find themselves on unfamiliar and uncertain terrain not just in their interpretation of the sonnets, but in their defense of the Stratford man.

This book is also a challenge to another kind of "orthodoxy," this one within the Oxfordian camp, which seeks to deny the truth of Whittemore's discoveries by dismissing them as "impossible" without making the effort to refute the reasoning that led to them. Since Whittemore published his first articles on his thesis in 2000, support within the Oxfordian community has grown to where at the 2015 annual Shakespeare Oxford Fellowship meeting, the attendees split close to 50-50 on whether they supported Whittemore's interpretation of the sonnets. I believe that this book will bolster those who have already concluded that Whittemore is on the right track, and will help many others to better follow the logic that makes Whittemore's case so compelling.

Finally, this book is aimed at a much broader audience than just Stratfordian and Oxfordian devotees, namely, the general public, and especially young people in high school and college, where the spirit of inquiry is typically the strongest, and iconoclasm about handed-down 'truths" is greatest. I am certain that many of this generation will be much more open-minded about the authorship controversy, and not meekly accept their teacher's or professor's attempts to dismiss it as the domain of quacks and crackpots. It is time for the real Shakespeare to take his formal place in history, and I hope that this book will contribute to that end.

Chapter 2
Sonnet 107 — The
Historical Anchor

While most scholars view the *Sonnets* as a narrative of the poet's up and down relationship with the younger man, and while many try to guess when the poems were written, until very recently only A.L. Rowse and Hank Whittemore examined the possibility that the *Sonnets* as a whole was concerned with known historical events.

In fact, the only recognition by most scholars of a possible historical connection is a general belief that Sonnet 107 makes reference to an historical event. Even here, there is not universal agreement as to which particular event is referred to. The sonnet states that "the mortal moon" has "endured" her "eclipse" (line 5); the next four lines herald an unanticipated period of peace. Scholars have proposed several different events that occurred between 1579 and 1603 as the one referenced. Following Whittemore, I concur that this sonnet contains the clearest historical reference of any sonnet and accordingly must be the first sonnet to be analyzed, as holding a central clue that provides a key to unlocking myriad others.

(As we commence analyzing specific sonnets, it should be noted that Shakespeare's sonnets, with a handful of exceptions, are organized as a series of three quatrains of four lines each, followed by a couplet of two lines, with the overall rhyme scheme of *abab cdcd efef gg*. I shall often refer to the first, second or third quatrain, or the couplet. A hallmark of most sonnets is that each quatrain represents a distinct subdomain of meaning which connects to that of the succeeding quatrain. The couplet typically ties the whole sonnet together, providing something akin to a punch line, or in some other way wrapping up the sonnet. Knowing how the poet uses this structure helps unravel the meaning of many of the sonnets. We shall demonstrate in our analysis of Sonnet 107 how the first, second and third quatrains each contain distinct segments of content that build on one another and flow through to the concluding couplet. It is noteworthy that none of the scholars whose analyses we have selected to review provides any discussion or analysis of quatrains and how they relate to each other, and to their couplets. Their glosses are limited to line-by-line commentaries.)

Sonnet 107 reads as follows:

Sonnet 107 and James

107	1	Not mine own fears, nor the prophetic soul
107	2	Of the wide world dreaming on things to come,
107	3	Can yet the lease of my true love control,
107	4	Supposed as forfeit to a confined doom.
107	5	The mortal Moon hath her eclipse endured
107	6	And the sad Augurs mock their own presage;
107	7	Incertainties now crown themselves assured
107	8	And peace proclaims Olives of endless age.
107	9	Now with the drops of this most balmy time
107	10	My love looks fresh, and death to me subscribes,
107	11	Since, spite of him, I'll live in this poor rhyme,
107	12	While he insults o'er dull and speechless tribes:
107	13	And thou in this shalt find thy monument,
107	14	When tyrants' crests and tombs of brass are spent.

The historical anchor is the second quatrain (lines 5-8), within which the words of Line 5 are typically taken as most important, because of the reference to the "mortal moon" enduring "her eclipse." The quatrain so clearly points to the March 1603 death of Elizabeth and accession of James that it amazes me that this conclusion is not universally accepted. Though a good number of scholars do accept this reading, which has much more support than any other, I shall briefly discuss four other events and dates that have been proposed by some number of scholars each as the historical reference here.

The suggested event of earliest date is the defeat of the Spanish Armada in 1588, which deployed in the shape of a crescent (hence, the reference to the eclipsed moon). Although it does make some sense of the hailing of an unexpected peace this date is impossibly early, since it would push all surrounding sonnets a decade or more sooner than anyone believes they were written. The second proposed event is a lunar eclipse in 1595, but this reading doesn't jibe with anything else in the quatrain, and is not in tune with the clear importance attached to this event. The third is that it celebrates Elizabeth's surviving her "climacteric," or 63rd birthday in 1596, thought to be an especially dangerous phase of life, but this reading makes no sense of the rest of the quatrain. The fourth proposes that it refers to Elizabeth's surviving a serious illness in 1599-1600, but since news to that effect proved to be a false rumor, this too seems hardly likely.

Thus, by process of elimination alone, the field narrows to Elizabeth's death and James' accession. Among our four chosen critics, Stephen Booth alone refuses to assign the sonnet to a particular event, writing that "All the theories are inconsequential, but scholars have been producing them for so many years, that the questions about this poem are not now *whether* it alludes to a specific event in Shakespeare's lifetime and *whether* it provides a clue to dating but *which* date the poem gives for its writing[xii]." Colin Burrow, in contrast, reviews the five leading event proposals, concludes that the accession of James "is the most likely," and mentions some of the other resonances between the words in these four lines and England in 1603 at the moment of James' becoming king.

Katherine Duncan-Jones does not disagree that the accession of James is referred to, but suggests a later date for the sonnet. For reasons that surely stem from her advocacy of Pembroke rather than Southampton as the addressee of Sonnets 1-126, she argues that because James' progress through the city of London was delayed nearly a year because of an outbreak of plague, it could be dated to 1604: "Though the coronation took place quietly on July 25th, 1603, it was not until a year after Elizabeth's death that the 'balmy time' of James reign was publicly celebrated. Sonnet 107 may belong to the summer of 1604." A paragraph later, with no additional evidence, she announces that the sonnet "seems to belong to the summer of 1604."

I see no logic in her argument. The palpable relief felt by the populace occurred in 1603, not a year later, after months of political calm had made peace seem the new normal. Her advocacy of Pembroke as the young man in Sonnets 1-126 appears to be driving her need to make this claim, which amounts to circular reasoning— the only reason for seeking a later dating is to validate an improbable identification of the young man. If he wasn't Pembroke, none of Duncan-Jones' arguments on the later dating have any validity. Kerrigan (see below) conclusively shows that this sonnet is about James' accession, not subsequent public coronation, and the remainder of the sonnet only makes sense if the man is Southampton, not Pembroke, so I consider Duncan-Jones' advocacy of Pembroke to be fully disproven.

Alone among our four selected critics, John Kerrigan not only concurs that James' accession is the proper context, but does a masterful job of demonstrating how many words and phrases in lines 5-9 point to specific aspects of that accession. Kerrigan cites multiple references to a popular concern with augurs, and the widespread fear of civil strife or even foreign invasion from Spain. He notes the use of the word "crown." He cites several speeches by James that resonate with the notion of peace, of olives (a reference to peace), of the promise of lasting peace. He points to the word "balm" (used in the coronation ceremony, and a "familiar symbol of regal authority"), giving a double meaning to the phrase "balmy time." His comprehensive presentation[xiii] of this convergence of sonnet with history is too lengthy to reproduce here, but the reader is strongly encouraged to read it.

My summary discussion of this quatrain draws in part on Kerrigan's. The first phrase that stands out is "mortal moon," which almost all scholars agree refers to Elizabeth. Elizabeth was referred to during her lifetime as the Greek or Roman goddess of the moon (Cynthia or Diana, respectively). The word "mortal," in connection with "endur[ing]" an "eclipse," is an apt reference to her death on March 24, 1603. Before her death, astrologers and others had prophesied trouble after her passing, which exactly fits the expression "sad augurs." Those dire warnings proved to be false, such that these augurs later "mock[ed] their own presage." "Incertainties" perfectly describes the widespread fear of rebellion or civil war that might break out on her death, engendered by her failure to have named a successor and the presumed widespread opposition to James. Those fears were belied by the peaceful transition of power, which fits exactly with the assertion that all uncertainties are now certain ("assured"), and that peace portending years more of tranquility ("peace proclaims olives of endless age") is at hand.

Kerrigan points out that the use of "crown" in "crown themselves assured" surely refers to James' being *crowned* king. He also describes multiple initiatives immediately taken by James to bring peace—with Spain, Scotland (because he remained its king), and Ireland—while he laid claim, as a king, in his own words, to "olives of peace." Clearer proof that Line 8 is a direct quotation from James would be hard to find. In sum, every significant phrase in this quatrain fits the context of the fears preceding Elizabeth's death, and the assuaging of those fears upon James' accession.

Many other scholars concur with this reading. While this interpretation is essential for Whittemore's thesis, it is hardly unique to him. What *is* unique to Whittemore is the insight he drew from the remainder of the sonnet in the context of the correct understanding of lines 5-8 as describing the peaceful accession of James.

Theorems 1-4

As I mentioned in the previous chapter, I have employed the device of identifying a series of progressive theorems. Understanding the meaning of lines 5-8 leads to one of them. However, three prior theorems follow from facts established in the previous chapter, which I now list here. The first two derive from the conclusions that can and must be drawn from the passages that proclaim that the sonnets will live forever, as will Southampton in them, which further proves that the sonnets were intended to be published. The third derives from the discussion of the sonnets as a deliberate creation, that is, as a monument.

Theorem 1 confirms that the poet intended the sonnets be published:

Sonnet Theorem 1:

The author of the sonnets intended that they be published, which is the only conclusion that can be drawn from the statements in at least eight sonnets that the author wants the sonnets to be read by the world and last until the end of time.

Theorem 2 rules out the possibility that the relationship is romantic, whether homosexual, bisexual or heterosexual, based on the evidence that the sonnets were intended to be published:

Sonnet Theorem 2:

The relationship of young man to poet in Sonnets 1-126 cannot be homosexual because they were intended for publication (see Theorem 1), and the consequences for both poet and young man would be dire if the poems described such a relationship; nor can it have been some species of "friendship" or "manly love," because that would not justify the claims made that the sonnets, and Southampton's name, would be made famous until the end of time. Therefore, the relationship must be of a different type, such as between blood relatives (e.g., parental, fraternal, etc.)

Theorem 3 states that the sonnets are in authorial order:

Sonnet Theorem 3:

The sonnets are in the order the author intended, demonstrated by the author's description of them as constituting a "monument" and as being an eternal historical record, which bespeaks their being a unitary document in a structured order rather than a mere collection of poems.

Our analysis of lines 5-8 of Sonnet 107 now permits us to posit our fourth theorem:

Sonnet Theorem 4:

Lines 5-8 of Sonnet 107 reference the death of Elizabeth, the accession of James, and the palpable public relief and joy at the peace and calm which marked James' accession.

Sonnet 107 and Southampton

It is essential to recognize that the second quatrain refers to Elizabeth's death and James' accession, but that that reading alone is insufficient to lead to new understandings of other sonnets. Kerrigan, commenting that Line 10's statement "my love looks fresh" jumps out when it is noted that one of the first acts of James on becoming king was to order the release of Southampton, "often thought to be the addressee of Sonnets 1-126," knocks on the door of insight here. Becoming in his words "mildly speculative," Kerrigan says that if Southampton were the addressee of sonnets 1-126, "both he (Southampton) and the poet's affection for him would have been refreshed and renewed by the events of 1603." But having come this close, Kerrigan comes no closer to unraveling the first quatrain, or the remainder of the sonnet.

Duncan-Jones notes that Southampton's release from prison may have been celebrated in this sonnet, but finds reasons to believe it is about Pembroke's being restored to court. Neither Burrow nor Booth even mentions Southampton as possibly referred to here.

Consequently, none of them clearly sees in the first quatrain (combined with Line 10) an unambiguous reference to the release of Southampton from prison on order of James, a reading that not only makes the quatrain transparent, but that also fits with the widespread presumption that Southampton is indeed the addressee in the first 126 sonnets.

But the first quatrain states this clearly. The word "lease" in Line 3 can only be an ellipsis of "release," from the "confined doom" of Line 4, which surely refers to prison, the one venue that would be so characterized from which someone would be released. Combined with the clear dating of the second quatrain to the accession of James as king following the death of Elizabeth, the only person known to have been released from prison in that time frame was Henry Wriothesley, the 3rd Earl of Southampton. As noted in Chapter 1, one of the very first acts of James as king, even before he left Edinburgh, was to order the release of Southampton from the Tower of London. (Southampton had been condemned to death in 1601, and was mysteriously spared, but kept imprisoned, presumably for life, still deemed guilty of treason.)

Lines 3-4 thus clearly establish that this sonnet celebrates the release of Southampton from the Tower of London, which occurred on April 10, 1603. Drawing this conclusion, which should have been obvious, was Whittemore's first step on the road to cracking the central secrets of the sonnets. Whittemore took the next logical step, which was to realize that this sonnet could be dated not just to late March or early April, 1603, but specifically to April 10, the date that Southampton was released. To my knowledge, no commentator has understood this sonnet as having this purpose, nor proposed that date (or any specific date) as its most likely moment of composition. The identification of the exact date of composition opened the door for Whittemore to revolutionize the analysis of the sonnets.

The following theorem codifies this breakthrough recognition:

Sonnet Theorem 5:

Sonnet 107 celebrates the release of Southampton from the Tower on April 10, 1603, by order of James I, and was quite likely written on that date.

It follows that if Sonnet 107 is about Southampton, all previous sonnets must also be about him, which yields our next theorem.

Sonnet Theorem 6:

Because Sonnet 107 describes the release of Southampton from prison, Southampton must be the addressee and subject of all preceding sonnets, as the "friend," "love," "young man," "fair youth," etc. Sonnets 1-106 are therefore to and about Southampton.

By the same logic, the next nineteen sonnets must also be about Southampton:

Sonnet Theorem 7:

Since all sonnets through Sonnet 126 are about the same man, the remainder of the sonnets in this series (Sonnets 108-126) are also to and about Southampton.

Theorems 6 and 7 are not groundbreaking in content, as critics have generally concurred that Southampton was the "young man" of Sonnets 1-126. However, that belief is based entirely on the dedications by Shakespeare to Southampton in Shakespeare's two long narrative poems of 1593 and 1594. The importance of these theorems is that they do not flow from the earlier dedications, which were published some fifteen years before the sonnets were published, and nearly a decade before most of them were written, but from *evidence within the sonnets themselves.* The recognition that Sonnet 107 is a chronicle of Southampton's release from the Tower on April 10, 1603, proves once and for all that Southampton is the "young man" of all the sonnets from Sonnet 1 through Sonnet 126.

Southampton Transcendent

Sonnet 107 not only confirms that Southampton is the "young man" of sonnets 1-126, and celebrates his release from the Tower of London, but also makes clear that his release was an important event, and therefore Southampton himself must be extremely important.

The sonnet opens with the poet's confession that "mine own fears" cannot "control" the "lease" [from prison] of his "true love." In context, "control" must mean "comprehend" or "take in," which is to say that the poet's fears, presumably for the fate of his love in prison, have been utterly relieved by his love's release. But the poet also states that "the prophetic soul of the wide world dreaming on things to come" can likewise not "control" his love's "lease." This line and a half is astonishing, and defies any intelligible reading under conventional assumptions. It can only mean that the release of Southampton is an event of transcendent significance for the public. We must wait until later in our narrative to understand why the poet would make such an assertion, but it confirms that the topic is the release of an important person, who can only be Southampton.

The conclusion of the sonnet reinforces this reading.

The third quatrain states that his "love looks fresh," which, as noted by Kerrigan, supports the notion that Southampton is "fresh" out of prison, and also has a "fresh" start for his life, in the context of the "balmy times" initiated by the accession of James. Then comes the poet's assertion that he has conquered death ("death to me subscribes") because he will live on in his sonnets while death will merely rule over "dull and speechless tribes." Switching suddenly to address "his love" in the second person, he tells Southampton that he too will live on in the sonnets, which shall be his "monument" that will outlive the brass tombs of kings. The full significance of these final lines of this most remarkable sonnet will become clear later.

Whittemore's Crucial Insight

Theorem 5 brings us to the threshold of the signal breakthrough that propelled Whittemore on his successful journey of discovery of what the sonnets were really about.

As close as Kerrigan came to seeing not only James' accession in lines 5-8, but also Southampton's release in lines 1-4 (and the first four words of Line 10), no critic to my knowledge made what should have been the obvious inference that the precise *date* of Southampton's release was also being celebrated in the sonnet. Whittemore, uniquely as far as I know, drew this conclusion. Only by seeing this sonnet as commemorating such a specific date did Whittemore ask the crucial next question, pursuing which unlocked the secret to understanding one hundred sonnets at the center of the *Sonnets*. Namely, if Sonnet 107 describes Southampton's release from twenty-six months in the Tower of London, then might not the immediately preceding sonnets reference the period when Southampton was still *in* the Tower? If so, must there not also be a sonnet that refers to the *first* day that Southampton was incarcerated there, the date of his arrest, February 8, 1601? Whittemore's pursuit of answers to these two questions led him to his first critical breakthrough, from which flowed a cornucopia of further insights into the core of what the sonnets are about. This breakthrough discovery is the subject of the next chapter.

Chapter 3
Prison Sonnets?

T he failure to understand that Sonnet 107 is all about Southampton and his release from the Tower on April 10, 1603, ensures that all commentators will fail to ask the obvious questions posed by our new understanding of it: if the first 126 sonnets are about Southampton, and if Sonnet 107 marks the *end* of his imprisonment, is there a sonnet that marks its *beginning*? If so, might all the sonnets between that "arrest" sonnet and 107 have been written during that twenty-six-month period? Conventional critics' failure to make such inquiries is consistent with their refusal to examine Southampton's biography in any meaningful way. That Southampton was imprisoned from February 1601 to April 1603 is universally ignored, even though most critics recognize Southampton as the addressee of the first 126 sonnets.

The failure to see any connection is even more surprising when so many of the sonnets from 27 to 106 reflect anguish and despair, refer to some major crime or trespass that Southampton has committed, and use words suggesting blackness and death. These are clues to the real reason that these sonnets were written—that they are the poet's reaction to his "friend" Southampton's imprisonment, condemnation to death, and prolonged stay in the Tower—that have lain "hidden in plain sight" for over 300 years.

Whittemore's next critical discovery was finding the sonnet that recorded the day that Southampton was arrested and *began* his incarceration. Finding it was easy—the only challenge was in assuming it existed. Once Whittemore posited that it did exist, he recognized that Sonnet 27 had to relate to the events of February 8, 1601, just as clearly as Sonnet 107 referred to the events of April 10, 1603. Beginning with Sonnet 27, the tone of the sonnets changes dramatically. Throughout the first twenty-six sonnets the tone is generally upbeat. The poet is down on himself here and there, but there is no hint of death, despair, clouds, graves, night, blackness, moans, and other words that appear frequently beginning with Sonnet 27.

The following lines from five sonnets between Sonnets 27 and

35 illustrate this dramatic change in tone:

27	1	Weary with toil, I haste me to my bed,
27	8	Looking on darkness which the blind do see
27	10	Presents thy shadow to my sightless view,
27	11	Which, like a jewel hung in ghastly night,
27	14	For thee and for myself no quiet find
28	1	How can I then return in happy plight,
28	2	That am debarr'd the benefit of rest?
28	3	When day's oppression is not eased by night,
28	4	But day by night, and night by day, oppress'd?
28	13	But day doth daily draw my sorrows longer
28	14	And night doth nightly make grief's strength seem stronger.
30	6	For precious friends hid in death's dateless night,
30	10	And heavily from woe to woe tell o'er
31	9	Thou art the grave where buried love doth live,
35	1	No more be grieved at that which thou hast done:

Clearly, something has gone terribly wrong, starting at Sonnet 27. This strongly suggests that Sonnet 27 begins the story of Southampton's arrest and imprisonment, which justifies stating the following two hypotheses:

Sonnet Hypothesis 1:

Sonnet 27 was written on February 8, 1601, the night Southampton was arrested, along with Essex and several dozen other conspirators, for his role in the Essex Rebellion.

Sonnet Hypothesis 2:

Sonnets 27-106, a series of eighty sonnets, were all written between February 8, 1601, and April 9, 1603.

With a clue that some catastrophe has occurred, let us start by examining the sonnet where this is first recorded.

Sonnet 27

The first two quatrains are as follows:

27 1 Weary with toil, I haste me to my bed,
27 2 The dear repose for limbs with travail tired;
27 3 But then begins a journey in my head,
27 4 To work my mind, when body's work's expired:
27 5 For then my thoughts, from far where I abide,
27 6 Intend a zealous pilgrimage to thee,
27 7 And keep my drooping eyelids open wide,
27 8 Looking on darkness which the blind do see

While the word "travail" in Line 2 can mean either "labor" or "travel," most commentators assign the latter meaning. This is surely wrong. In context, "travail" is clearly a synonym for the "toil" of Line 1: "weary with toil" means "with travail tired." The poet hastes himself to "*my* bed," which surely refers to the bed one sleeps in when one is home, not traveling, supported by Line 5's statement that the loved one is far "from where I *abide,* which is to say, one's home, not some lodging while traveling. The poet is clearly weary from "toil," not from "travel." Lines 3 and 4 further support this reading, where "journey in my head" refers to "work" his mind must do when the body's "work" is done.

By glossing "travel" for "travail," conventional scholars avoid confronting the *caesura* that this sonnet represents. They permit themselves to misread what follows as simply the emotional pain of temporary separation from a loved one, rather than the apprehension of what may be a permanent separation, and likely the death by execution of the loved one.

The second quatrain does suggest distance from the beloved, mainly because of the word "pilgrimage." But "pilgrimage" would hardly be the word of choice if the poet had just left on a trip and was already missing his beloved. The reference to "looking on darkness" belies any connotation that the issue here is mere separation. The conventional reading of these eight lines shows the bias of traditional scholars, who see the sonnets only as a species of love poetry. They fail to realize that if this were really describing the reaction of someone in love to having to be apart from the loved one for a few days, it is so overwrought as to be a caricature of true love.

The final quatrain and couplet continue in the same vein:

27 9 Save that my soul's imaginary sight
27 10 Presents thy shadow to my sightless view,
27 11 Which, like a jewel (hung in ghastly night),
27 12 Makes black night beauteous and her old face new.
27 13 Lo! thus, by day my limbs, by night my mind,
27 14 For thee and for myself no quiet find.

The language continues to darken, with the beloved appearing only as a "shadow" to the poet's "sightless" view, and, most starkly, in one of the most dramatic images in the entire sonnet sequence, as a "jewel (hung in ghastly night)." What stronger image could have been conjured to capture the awfulness of his beloved Southampton arrested and in the Tower, facing the capital charge of treason? While conventional analysis might suggest that the image of the "jewel" making the night beauteous and "her old face new" belies the notion that something bad has happened, the couplet dispels any interpretation other than that, relative to the preceding sonnets, something has gone drastically wrong. Southampton, the "jewel," is of course the bright spot, but the statement that "for thee" and "for myself," the poet can find "no quiet" makes the reality clear. It says that by day, his limbs find no quiet (proving that the poet's activity during the day is not traveling away from the beloved, but engaging in "travail" on the beloved's part), while at night, his mind is likewise obsessed with what has happened and suffers a like inability to find quiet. Line 14 confirms that this is not about the poet's lovesick reaction to a separation, but a situation that equally denies "quiet" to poet and beloved alike.

Read conventionally, these lines are incongruous, even absurd; what aspect of a merely temporary separation from a loved one—a separation that had begun less than twenty-four hours earlier, no less—would warrant such hyperbole, no matter how strong the love?

Additional confirmation of the existence of a break between Sonnets 26 and 27 is provided by the structure, discussed above in Chapter 2, where conventional critics concur that Sonnet 26 is an envoy sonnet to those that precede it, and that Sonnet 27 begins a new series. Even though the significance of the change in tone is overlooked, the fact that Sonnet 27 begins a series of exactly 100 sonnets cements the conclusion that it represents a dramatic break with the first twenty-six. In view of the general recognition that Sonnets 26 and 126 are "envoy" sonnets, and the sudden change in tone with Sonnet 27, it is puzzling that conventional commentators don't recognize Sonnet 27 as the initiating sonnet of the next 100. None of them appears to have "done the math." Had any of them done so, the existence of a 100-sonnet middle series would have jumped out at them, and they might have looked for something that unified the set. But they did not.

Sonnet 28 picks up where Sonnet 27 leaves off, this time in an extended statement of how neither day nor night can bring the poet relief or solace but rather both conspire to deepen his misery.

Sonnet 28

28	1	How can I then return in happy plight,
28	2	That am debarr'd the benefit of rest?
28	3	When day's oppression is not eased by night,
28	4	But day by night, and night by day, oppress'd?
28	5	And each (though enemies to either's reign)
28	6	Do in consent shake hands to torture me;
28	7	The one by toil, the other to complain
28	8	How far I toil, still farther off from thee.
28	9	I tell the Day, to please him thou art bright
28	10	And dost him grace when clouds do blot the heaven:
28	11	So flatter I the swart-complexion'd night,
28	12	When sparkling stars twire not thou gild'st the even.
28	13	But day doth daily draw my sorrows longer
28	14	And night doth nightly make grief's length seem stronger.

The first two lines state that the poet cannot find happiness in anything, nor even get any rest. Lines 3 and 4 attest that both day and night "oppress" him, the two cooperating ("consent [to] shake hands") to "torture me" (line 6), despite their normal posture of being "enemies to either's reign." Lines 7-8 elaborate that day tortures "by toil" (a further refutation of the reading of "travel" for "travail" in Sonnet 27), night by thoughts of how far away the beloved is (not in linear distance, but in accessibility).

The third quatrain is extraordinary, and subtle, and confirms the reading of Sonnets 27 and 28 to this point. In it, the poet becomes a supplicant to both day and night, entreating them to release Southampton from his plight, on the ground that Southampton can enhance both. He tells day that on a cloudy day, Southampton will be bright in the sky, and night that on a starless night, Southampton will "gild'st (light up) the even [evening]."

The couplet acknowledges that his supplication has failed—day is lengthening his list of sorrows and night is amplifying the depth of his grief. What stronger evidence is needed to show that the poet is suffering because something dire has happened to his beloved, something that is *external* to their personal relationship? The poet says that he is suffering deep sorrows that are only worsening, and grief that is growing stronger. Such words totally cohere with the cause, assuming that Southampton has been arrested for capital treason, as we maintain. What in the Standard Interpretation could possibly justify these emotions?

Nevertheless, conventional scholars ascribe the anguish expressed in Sonnets 27-28 to the poet's reaction to being temporarily separated from his beloved. Kerrigan goes so far as to read the phrase "oppressed by night" to refer to "oppressive weather" that "makes travel exhausting and sleep hard to come by." He cites the interplay between day and night as expressing monotony. Duncan-Jones describes Sonnets 27 and 28 as the first two of five sonnets "in which the solitary poet meditates on his friend: 27-8 are on night and sleeplessness."

Remarkably, not one of them even mentions "sorrow" or "grief" from lines 13-14 of Sonnet 28. This appears to be another instance where an inability to make sense of something leads them to forgo commentary on it because they can't explain it. Yet these two words, among the most powerful in either sonnet, prove that something dreadful has befallen Southampton, and demolish any possibility that the Standard Interpretation can be correct.

Sonnet 29—one of the most famous of all the sonnets, beginning "When in disgrace with Fortune and mens eyes,"—will be discussed later (see chapter 17) as its interpretation requires discoveries not yet presented.

What is noteworthy at this point is the incoherence of our commentators' attempts to make sense of this sonnet in the context of the two that precede it. If Sonnets 27-28 were about the poet's anguish at being separated from his beloved, and plagued by exhaustion from travel and heat, why would Sonnet 29 suddenly shift to something bearing no relationship to either theme? Duncan-Jones opines, "Lonely and outcast, the speaker envies the prosperity and talent of others, until he remembers his friend, whose love compensates him for everything." This contradicts what she believes the preceding two sonnets are about, where thoughts of the beloved are *causing* mental anguish, not compensating for it. And why, in the context she posits, would the poet be lonely or outcast? Burrow sees the poet as "isolated and apparently deprived of all means of comfort until thoughts of the friend dispel the gloom," again, contradicting the reading of the preceding sonnets. Booth sees a discourse on Christian theology (even more irrelevant), and Kerrigan passes on making any comment.

Sonnet 30

Sonnet 30 continues the theme from Sonnets 27 and 28 that something is drastically wrong, and also contains further confirmations that this group of sonnets deals with the arrest and forthcoming trial of Southampton.

30	1	When to the sessions of sweet silent thought
30	2	I summon up remembrance of things past,
30	3	I sigh the lack of many a thing I sought,
30	4	And with old woes new wail my dear time's waste:
30	5	Then can I drown an eye (unused to flow)
30	6	For precious friends hid in death's dateless night,
30	7	And weep afresh love's long since cancell'd woe,
30	8	And moan the expense of many a vanish'd sight:
30	9	Then can I grieve at grievances foregone,
30	10	And heavily from woe to woe tell o'er
30	11	The sad account of fore-bemoaned moan,
30	12	Which I new pay as if not paid before.
30	13	But if the while I think on thee (dear friend)
30	14	All losses are restored and sorrows end.

The poet says that he has old woes and a sudden set of new ones, described as "my dear time's waste." In lines 5-6, he describes himself weeping copiously for "precious friends hid in death's dateless night," as clear a reference to imprisonment in the Tower as one could ask for, strongly recalling Sonnet 27's "ghastly night," and referring either to Southampton only (using a plural for a singular), or to Essex and the other conspirators as well. In lines 7-8, the poet is again weeping, bemoaning something that has vanished. Lines 9-12 talk of old woes which have now returned with a vengeance. The apparent meaning of the final couplet is belied by the rest of the sonnet; it suggests that the thought of his beloved brings only temporary relief from multiple griefs.

The first two lines remind us that justice moved swiftly in those days. Indictments were produced on February 17, just nine days after the offense, and two days later the trial took place. Treason trials of noblemen necessitated convening a jury composed of the preeminent peers of the land; and first among those, by hereditary right, was the Earl of Oxford—the real Shakespeare—who would now need to sit in judgment of Southampton, and perforce agree with the inevitable guilty verdict that would send him to the executioner.

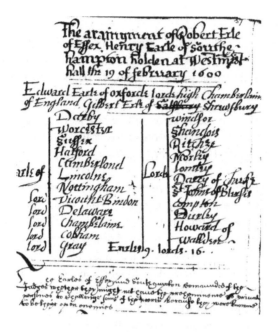

Figure 2 - The announcement for the arraignment of the earls of Essex and Southampton, which includes Edward, Earl of Oxford, at the head of the list of jurors "summoned."

If Oxford wrote Sonnet 27 on the night of the arrest, February 8, and began writing a sonnet a day, Sonnet 30 would have been written on February 11, six days before the trial started. Almost certainly, notice had been sent by that time to the nobles whose attendance would be required at the trial (some would need time to travel to London); in legal parlance, they had been officially "summoned" to a "session." In that context, the appearance of the words "summon" and "sessions" on consecutive lines is striking. "The sessions of sweet silent thought" is a strange phrase—who would normally describe himself absorbed in a reverie as having a "session" of thought, much less multiple "sessions"? When we later confirm that the poet is Oxford, this opening couplet provides convincing collateral evidence for that conclusion, and for the precise dating of this sonnet.

Sonnet 34 will also be discussed later. However, the third quatrain of sonnet 34 is reproduced here, because it again strongly suggests Southampton has committed an offense that has caused him great shame, one for which repentance is insufficient for expiation.

34   9 Nor can thy shame give physic to my grief;
34 10 Though thou repent, yet I have still the loss:
34 11 The offender's sorrow lends but weak relief
34 12 To him that bears the strong offence's loss.

Sonnet 35 continues this thought, and is even more explicit, for the first time assigning blame to the loved one:

35   1 No more be grieved at that which thou hast done:

"That which thou hast done." The beloved has done something. What? In the context of the preceding eight sonnets, it is obvious that something extremely serious has happened, not merely a personal affront to the poet or a snag in their relationship.

Even in the face of repeated statements that something serious has happened to the poet's beloved, traditional scholars assure us that the event is merely a personal transgression against the poet by the young man. Where Southampton's biography shows his arrest for the crime of high treason, the description of which fits exactly the lines we read in these sonnets, conventional critics refuse to make any such connection, instead concocting imagined transgressions by the "friend" against the poet for which the text provides no support. Such is the power of belief in an established paradigm that new evidence can all but slap one in the face, and one still does not see it!

Duncan-Jones states: "the speaker [is] betrayed by his young friend, addressed as the sun" (Sonnet 34) and "the young man has wronged his friend" (referring to Sonnet 35). Kerrigan in Sonnet 34 glosses "disgrace" in Line 8 as "dishonor (suffered by the poet when rejected by the youth)." Burrow speculates: "the disgrace concerned could be the ignominy suffered by the poet or the ungracious conduct of the friend." Booth, discussing Sonnet 35, fantasizes: "Quatrain 1 seems to be a loving effort to relieve the beloved's sense of guilt, but the easiness of its not-quite-appropriate platitudes gives it a lack of conviction that advertises the speaker's earnest benevolence rather than the justice of the defense he offers…. The [second] quatrain develops a competition of guilt between the speaker and the beloved...[the speaker] goes on to belittle the beloved...and to assert the beloved's wrongdoing."

These interpretations exemplify the gulf that separates Whittemore's approach from the non-analytical, improvised approach of traditional scholarship, which grasps at surface meanings while avoiding the singularities that could lead to enlightenment. Each critic is compelled to invent what I call a "plausible backstory" for what *might* be going on: "backstory" because each critic infers other aspects of the relationship for which no evidence is adduced (nor does it exist) that would supply the context needed for it to be true; "plausible" because the backstories are all pure speculation. For example, Burrow's reading of "disgrace" requires him to fabricate a backstory that the poet was treated "ungraciously" by the friend, and Kerrigan's reading of "dishonour" leads him to invent a backstory that the youth rejected the poet. Evidence for neither of these stories can be found in the sonnets; they are simply concocted.

Furthermore, each backstory applies only to the sonnet being discussed, as the critic attempts to explain its specific text. Because none of the backstories is true, nor are the readings; as the critics move from sonnet to sonnet the *ad hoc* stories they need to create frequently become unconnected to each other, leading to a narrative that cannot be comprehended. The failure of conventional critics to find a coherent, consistent backstory that carries through all the sonnets provides a further demonstration that the problem is not their lack of critical ability, but their marriage to an erroneous paradigm.

To recap, according to conventional analysis the poet (a) has taken a trip somewhere and is physically separated from his beloved for a couple of sonnets; (b) he feels alone and outcast; (c) the young man is described as greatly loved by the poet; and (d) suddenly the young man has betrayed the poet, for which the poet proves remarkably forgiving. The incoherence of such a narrative should be obvious.

In the real context discovered by Whittemore, Southampton, the subject of the sonnets, has in fact committed a horrendous transgression—the crime of high treason. It is therefore to be *expected* that the tone of the sonnets would change dramatically. The continuation of this new tone confirms that each of the next seventy-nine sonnets following Sonnet 27 was also written while Southampton was imprisoned. The contrast between the plausibility and likelihood of this construction and the irrationality and randomness of the conventional commentators could not be more dramatic. As we will see, the perfect fit between our reading and so many of the sonnets confirms the validity of this reading by explaining the sonnets in a coherent way.

Sonnets 27-106 must therefore be recognized as the "Prison Sonnets," an understanding that will properly orient all further analysis. Our analysis of these sonnets will reveal a lot about Oxford's thoughts during Southampton's imprisonment, about the reality of who Southampton really was, and even some important historical facts not documented anywhere else. Recognizing that Sonnets 27-106 are "Prison Sonnets" is the next key to unlocking the rest of the story, a key truly "hidden in plain sight" for over three hundred years.

We can now restate our two initial hypotheses as theorems:

Sonnet Theorem 8:

Sonnet 27 was written on, and chronicles the night of, the failed Essex Rebellion, February 8, 1601, when Southampton and others were arrested for high treason and put in the Tower of London.

Sonnet Theorem 9:

The series of eighty sonnets from Sonnet 27 to 106 chronicles Southampton's period of confinement in the Tower of London from the day of his arrest on February 8, 1601, until the day of his release on April 10, 1603, and should therefore be identified as the "Prison Sonnets."

Chapter 4
Sonnet 87 — Reprieve
By Misprision

With the context of Sonnets 27-106 now established, we move ahead to another singular passage, in Sonnet 87, to further confirm our thesis and to resolve a deep historical mystery in the process.

An obvious feature of the sonnets is the frequent use of words which have two or more meanings. Much of the conventional critical analysis of specific sonnets is concerned with determining possible meanings of such words, and deciding which are the most likely. Most editions provide extensive glosses of meanings that existed in Shakespeare's day but are now archaic or rare. Critics typically attempt to extract a narrative from their readings.

What Whittemore discovered is that Shakespeare wrote the *entire sonnet series* on two distinct levels. On the "surface" level, the words have an apparent meaning. That is the level at which conventional scholarship starts and ends. Whittemore discovered the deeper, "real" level that tells another story altogether.

One of the keys that permitted Whittemore to unlock this deeper level of meaning is the presence of various words and phrases that appear *not* to fit well with the surface meaning. The large bulk of what I have termed anomalies are of this nature. These words actually function as a Rosetta Stone, a key to unlocking this deeper, true level of meaning.

In this and the next several chapters, we shall focus on words that have legal connotations, bearing in mind that with Sonnet Theorem 9, we have established that Sonnets 27-106 were written sequentially during the period of Southampton's imprisonment, which began on February 8, 1601.

The Mystery of Southampton's Redemption

The most dramatic example of use of a word that makes sense only under the new paradigm is found in Sonnet 87; to understand it, some historical background is necessary. Southampton's physical survival, after his conviction for high treason and sentence of execution, is one of the great mysteries of English history. Following his release from confinement, Southampton experienced a colorful career in the court of James I, and played a leading role in the founding of settlements in Virginia (Hampton Roads is named for him). But no surviving record explains why he wasn't executed shortly after Essex, who was beheaded on February 25, 1601. Crowds went every day to the execution grounds in the Tower until March 18, when the last two executions were carried out, expecting to see Southampton go to his final resting place.

England was a bureaucratic society, where everything done was documented and laws were followed (even monarchs had to appear to follow the rule of law). If someone was convicted of high treason, they *were* executed unless their sentence was commuted or they were pardoned, an act which *would be documented*. Except in the case of Southampton.

In his excellent 2009 article on the *Sonnets,*[xiv] Bill Boyle examined this issue. His findings highlight the extraordinariness of Southampton's eventual fate. Boyle cites evidence that literally all the conspirators arrested (whether tried or not) were assessed enormous fines, which they eventually paid at least some of. Among this number was the diplomat Sir Henry Neville, who was only marginally involved in the rebellion, yet wound up held in the Tower for almost two years, charged with "misprision of treason,"[xv] and ended up paying almost £3,000 of a £10,000 fine. He and Southampton were the only conspirators imprisoned for so long. He was released (under a royal warrant from James) on April 10, 1603, the same day as Southampton.

All those sentenced to die were executed (in February or March 1601) with two exceptions. One exception was the conspirator John Davis, who cooperated fully with the State in condemning himself and four others at a trial held *after* Essex had been executed, leading to their all being convicted and sentenced to death in March 1601. Yet, while four of them were then executed within weeks of their sentences, Davis was released and pardoned within a year. This certainly must have been a *quid pro quo*, much as prosecutors today offer plea bargains to guilty parties who agree to inform on others.

The second exception was Southampton. Citing Charlotte Stopes' biography of Southampton, Boyle notes that the Privy Council "turned itself to mercy, in order to ingratiate themselves with the people," but that mercy was almost always "mercantile mercy, measured in proportion, not to the degree of the offender's guilt, but of his capacity to pay." More importantly, the Council did so only after the ringleaders had been executed, and Southampton was surely a ringleader. There is no evidence that Southampton paid a fine, nor is there evidence of a *quid pro quo* of any kind in the official record.

Why was his life spared? Why were his titles and estates restored? Why was he made a Knight of the Garter, all within a few months of James' accession? The answers to these questions, discovered by Whittemore, lie in the sonnets, once again "hidden in plain sight," where all could have seen them, but none has.

Here, we focus on the fact that one sonnet reveals what no extant historical document has—the legal maneuver that had to have been used to spare Southampton's life. It was a legal device used when a monarch wanted to commute a treason conviction from death to something less. It was called "misprision of treason."

In a 1567 legal lexicon by Rastell,[xvi] "misprision of trespasse" is defined thusly: "that in every treason or felonie is included *misprision*, and where any hath committed treason or felonie the [Queen] may cause the same to be indited and [arraigned] but of *misprision* only if she will."[xvii] This makes clear, as well, that "trespass" was clearly understood at the time to mean "treason" or some other high crime ("felony").

The Oxford English Dictionary renders a similar meaning for "misprision," defining it as "an offence or misdemeanor akin to treason or felony, but involving a lesser degree of guilt, and not liable to the capital penalty," which accords perfectly with the 1567 description. The term came to be understood as meaning concealing one's knowledge of treasonable actions. It was always understood as a legal term.

Mysteriously, no official documentation exists of Southampton's sentence reduction (surely there must have been documents), but to escape execution Southampton's conviction must have been converted by royal order to misprision of treason. No other legal means existed short of outright pardon.

A number of letters from Southampton to the Privy Council, written from the Tower in February and March of 1601 pleading for his life, are extant. They reflect his knowledge of the distinction between treason and misprision of treason, as Southampton lays out the case that he really had no idea where the action led by Essex, of which he was the second in command, was going. He begs mercy for his "fault" in not informing the authorities of what was going on—exactly fitting the definition of misprision. That this defense was a patent lie mattered less than that it provided a pretext, should the authorities be so inclined, to spare his life.

It is in this context that we encounter, in Sonnet 87, the word "misprision."

87 11 So thy great gift, upon misprision growing,
87 12 Comes home again, on better judgment making.

The use of "misprision," with its special legal significance, in a sonnet that we have provisionally dated to the period of Southampton's imprisonment, can hardly be coincidence. Further, it is used in a poetic sentence suggesting that something *good* has happened to Southampton *because* of the misprision. This contradicts any interpretation of misprision as something bad. The sonnets thereby contain the only documentation, the only historical record, that explains how Southampton was spared execution.

A further implication flows from this reading of "misprision" in the sonnets. How did the poet know that Southampton's conviction had been commuted to misprision? Knowledge of it has been lost to history. It surely was not widely known at the time either. It is safe to surmise that only a few of the Queen's closest advisors and perhaps a few top nobles would have been privy to this information. Shakspere could not possibly have known. But Oxford, as the first earl of the realm, could readily have been in the tiny circle of those who knew. This fact alone argues conclusively that Oxford had to have been Shakespeare.

Reading "misprision" as Whittemore does lets us see if other lines from the sonnet support this interpretation. We are not yet at a point where we can make sense of every Line in this sonnet, but we will note several lines that strongly support this reading.

87 3 The charter of thy worth gives thee releasing;

If "upon misprision" means "on being deemed guilty of misprision of treason instead of high treason," then Southampton has been "released" from a death sentence. The "charter of thy worth" might well refer to the actual order reducing the sentence, a "charter" or document that must have existed.

If "thy great gift" in Line 11 is read, logically in this context, as Southampton's life, now given renewed expectation of continuing, then "upon misprision" it (his life) could certainly be described as "growing" (line 11), and also as "coming home again" (line 12). Syntactically, while "on better judgment making," appears to have

53

"thy great gift" as its subject, if "making" is read as "having been made," the lines support the interpretation that they refer to the authorities having made a "better judgment" about Southampton's fate than execution. ("Judgment" is also a legal term; an order reducing a conviction is a legal judgment, which further supports this reading.) Within the sonnets, syntax often has to be sacrificed on the altar of condensation.

The contrast between the new reading of this sonnet, and those of our commentators, couldn't be starker. It should come as no surprise that the conventional commentators choose banal alternate meanings that make little sense even on the surface level. Their inability to provide satisfying glosses of "misprision" reinforces the conclusion that the word can only refer to Southampton's reduced sentence.

Our four commentators all converge on some variant of "error" as the meaning of "misprision": to Duncan-Jones, it means "false estimate"; to Booth, "error, misprizing, mistaking of one thing for another"; to Kerrigan, "one word for 'error' covers both the not knowing of Line 9 and the mistaking of 10"; and to Burrow, "error or oversight."

The importance of this unusual word in confirming our thesis and establishing that Sonnets 27-106 are indeed "Prison Sonnets" justifies examining the conventional commentators in greater depth. Burrow writes of Line 11 (which contains "misprision") that something, presumably, is "occurring as a result of error or oversight," and on Line 12, that "[it] reverts back to you on the making of a properly informed judgment." But he provides no hint of what the line may refer to. What has actually "occur[red] as a result of error or oversight"? What is the "gift"? Interpreting "misprision" as "error or oversight" requires these two lines to mean "so thy great gift, occurring as a result of error or oversight, reverts back to you on making of a properly informed judgment." This reading defies intelligible rendering.

Booth does no better, glossing Line 12 as "having changed your mind," leading to an absurdity similar to Burrow's, that the great gift, "being grounded on an error," comes home again "having changed your mind."

Duncan-Jones offers no reading of Line 12, and translates "upon misprision growing" as "coming into existence as the result of a false estimate." Her description of the entire sonnet is telling: "Using legal and financial imagery, the speaker relinquishes his claim to the young man, which was based on misjudgment or misprision, the youth having underestimated his own value and overestimated that of the speaker." If this is a valid reading, why isn't it the final sonnet? Why would the poet devote another thirty-eight sonnets to the youth, in light of the thorough emotional thrashing that such a reading would imply?

Kerrigan offers a novel, but no more helpful, meaning for Line 11, "the young man's *gift* was grounded in and arose from misprision. Perhaps Shakespeare means to suggest that the gift grew, became more precious, while it lodged mistakenly with the poet." As with the passage above from Burrow, this defies intelligibility.

The new reading—that Sonnet 87 chronicles the explanation of how Southampton was spared execution—gains strength not only from its power, simplicity and logic, but also from the inability of all alternate attempts to make sense of the word "misprision." More importantly, the new reading confirms that an entirely different paradigm is required to understand the word, and the sonnet. The coherence of the new reading in turn confirms the truth of the new paradigm.

This is the evidence that permits us to assert Theorem 10:

Sonnet Theorem 10:

Sonnet 87 chronicles the legal device that must have been used in Southampton's case, namely, that his conviction was reduced from the capital offense of high treason to the non-capital offense of misprision of treason.

Chapter 5
Sonnet 35 – Trial and Trespass

S onnet 35 defies coherent interpretation by our critics, but bristles with new revelations when correctly located in the context of Southampton's arrest and impending trial for capital treason. It is another strong example of the productivity of seeing the post-Sonnet 26 poems as about Southampton after his arrest and Oxford's reaction to his predicament, contrasted with the impotence of the standard view. The sonnet announces for the first time that Southampton's troubles are due to something that he "hast done," and includes a stunning revelation about the role that Oxford is playing on Southampton's behalf.

Sonnet 35

35	1	No more be grieved at that which thou hast done:
35	2	Roses have thorns, and silver fountains mud;
35	3	Clouds and eclipses stain both Moon and Sunne,
35	4	And loathsome canker lives in sweetest bud.
35	5	All men make faults, and even I in this,
35	6	Authorizing thy trespass with compare,
35	7	Myself corrupting, salving thy amiss,
35	8	Excusing thy sins more than thy sins are;
35	9	For to thy sensual fault I bring in sense--
35	10	Thy adverse party is thy Advocate--
35	11	And 'gainst myself a lawful plea commence:
35	12	Such civil war is in my love and hate
35	13	That I an accessary needs must be
35	14	To that sweet thief which sourly robs from me.

This sonnet contains the first direct statement that Southampton has done something seriously wrong ("that which thou hast done")—heretofore we have been told only that something serious has happened to him. In Line 6 the wrong is described as "thy trespass." The conventional reading—that the young man has somehow offended or transgressed against the poet—is rendered untenable because of the legal meaning of "trespass" at that time. In a 1979 book, *The Tudor Law of Treason,* Prof. John Bellamy (cited by Whittemore in an article in 2004[xviii]) establishes that by the 16th century, "trespass" had come to mean transgression against the state, that is, treason. Bellamy cites a 1517 riot in London against foreigners, where thirteen participants were drawn and quartered as traitors, accused of the crime of "trespass." And, as noted, in 1567 Rastell in his legal dictionary referred to "misprision of trespasse" as encompassing treason, clearly associating the words.

And sure enough, Shakespeare uses trespass as a synonym for treason in several instances, most notably in *1 Henry VI* (II.iv.92-94), as cited by Whittemore, where he writes "And by his treason stand'st not thou attainted, corrupted, and exempt from gentry? His trespass yet lives guilty in thy blood." He also has Hamlet accuse his mother Gertrude of "trespass" when he charges her in the bedroom scene with killing his father the king, an act of treason.

In Sonnet 35 the context is the phrase "authorizing thy trespass with compare" (line 6). Some background is required to understand this reference. The day before the Essex Rebellion, Essex (or possibly Southampton) specially contracted for a public performance of Shakespeare's play *Richard II*, the theme of which is the overthrow of the monarch; the performance was intended to rally supporters to their cause. The play includes a scene showing the actual deposition, where Bolingbroke receives the crown from Richard II, who is compelled to accept the situation. The play as originally published did not contain this scene, which first appeared in a 1608 edition. Some scholars believe that the scene was added by Shakespeare (whoever he was) at the express request of Essex and/or Southampton for that performance, precisely because it depicted their own intent—to ask Elizabeth to step down and make Essex King. Queen Elizabeth is known to have afterward remarked about this performance that "I am Richard II, know ye not that?" If indeed this scene was added by Shakespeare at that time, it means that Shakespeare was directly aiding the conspirators, and thus bore significant responsibility for helping them get in trouble, even if he was never directly charged.

All four of our conventional critics see this sonnet as the poet trying to make light of the friend's guilt (for doing *what* is never asked). When they come to Line 6, they concur that it means "I justify your fault by comparing it to" the "comparisons" in the first quatrain—i.e., you are no more at fault than the rose for having thorns, or the sun and moon for having eclipses, or the bud for having a canker. This is an impossible reading of "authorizing," which is not a synonym for "justifying," but rather implies prior permission, making the authorizer complicit in the action he authorized. If "authorized" is read correctly, it cannot mean excusing or rationalizing the trespass after the fact, but rather giving prior approval and support for it.

Nevertheless, Duncan-Jones understands Line 7 as saying that "by letting you off the hook this way, I am compromising ('corrupting') myself." The other critics do not even attempt to explain "corrupting." Again we see inability to cogently explain the words used. What sense does it make for the poet to tell his friend that his trespass is justified, only to say in the next breath that by letting the friend off the hook this way, the poet is corrupting himself?

The true meaning of "authorizing thy trespass with compare" is now transparent. As this is the ninth sonnet since Sonnet 27 (written the night of Southampton's arrest), it is likely that it was written just before the trial, which began some eleven days after the arrest. Since the rebellion was treason, "trespass" clearly refers to Southampton's commission of treason by participating in the rebellion.

In Line 6 the poet is saying that he authorized the trespass "with compare." If the trespass was Southampton's role in the rebellion, then how could Shakespeare have authorized it? Only by agreeing to the performance of *Richard II* on the eve of the rebellion, and writing a new scene depicting the actual deposition of a monarch. Shakespeare "authorized" Southampton's crime by "compar[ing]" it to the actions of Bolingbroke in deposing Richard II, thereby legitimizing it.

Lines 7 and 8 can now be seen to refer to the effort that Shakespeare is making to try to mitigate Southampton's crime—he is trying to heal (salve) his "amiss"—by trying to find excuses for it. "Myself corrupting" could now mean that the poet properly shares his guilt, even though he's not in any legal jeopardy for it— "I corrupted myself by sanctioning your crime, even abetting it."

Turning to Line 10, we find the biggest anomaly in the sonnet: the poet's description of himself as both Southampton's "Advocate" *and* his "adverse party" ("Advocate" is capitalized in the original text). Again, these are legal terms, as the conventional critics recognize. Line 10 is explicit—whatever trouble Southampton is in, Shakespeare is acting both as his defense lawyer (advocate) and as prosecutor, judge and/or juror (adverse party). To deny this reading is to argue that these legal terms are being used figuratively. But any such attempt runs aground on the inability to explain why the poet would say he was the subject's "adverse party"—the preceding lines, by the conventional reading, labor to show the poet as the friend's justifier, trying to minimize and excuse away his fault. Only our thesis can make full sense of Line 10. The following line hammers home what is at stake: "And 'gainst myself a lawful plea commence." The word "lawful" puts to rest any argument that Shakespeare is not using "advocate" and "adverse party" in their strictly legal senses.

None of the conventional critics makes sense of Line 10. Booth does not attempt an explanation. Duncan-Jones ("your (legal) opponent is also your (legal) defender") and Kerrigan ("the client of the prosecution speaks for the defence") get the literal sense right, but make no attempt to integrate that meaning into the rest of the sonnet. What legal proceeding is the friend involved in? According to their readings, this sonnet is about the poet justifying the friend's unnamed transgression, which is against the poet, not a legal case involving the commission of a crime. Burrow's interpretation is "your opponent, who should be pleading against you, is in fact pleading for you," which follows his comments on the preceding lines yet is devoid of any connection to them. That Burrow's take on this line is a *non sequitur* highlights how bankrupt is his, and all conventional, readings of this crucial line. Burrows gets it wrong even in a literal sense: If the "adverse party" is *not* pleading against him, then he is no longer an adverse party—the only possible reading is that he is simultaneously pleading both for and against him, a sense that eludes Burrows. Burrows seems to have overlooked that it is the author who is both adverse party and advocate, calling him "your opponent," who the author clearly was not.

These critics choke on applying both words ("advocate" and "adverse party") to their theory of the case, which involves only *two* parties, the friend and the poet; in this context the existence of a *third* party is required. An "advocate" is one who pleads another's case to a third party, generally a court. But the critics have the poet "advocating" for the friend against himself. And in what capacity is the author acting as the "adverse party" against the friend—the same friend that he is also arguing for?

The clear meaning is that Shakespeare is referring to himself as both "thy adverse party" and "thy advocate" in a case that is before a *court*. Line 11 makes clear that the poet is at war with himself, conducting a plea against himself, and in Line 12 actually labels this internal conflict a "civil war."

This indicates that Shakespeare was simultaneously acting as Southampton's lawyer ("Advocate") and his accuser, i.e., an opposing lawyer or a juror ("adverse party"). Under the conventional paradigm, such a possibility poses insuperable difficulties. As conventional scholarship cannot satisfactorily account for the use of these two terms in any other sense, their appearance here is a powerful indication, from the "smoking gun" of the sonnets, that Shakspere is not our man, and that Oxford is. If Oxford is Shakespeare, these terms can be easily explained, and the entire sonnet can be read in a consistent and intelligible manner.

Edward de Vere, 17th Earl of Oxford, was the first earl of the realm, the first among the twenty-five peers summoned on short notice to sit as the jury for the treason trial of the Essex Rebellion conspirators in mid-February of 1601. If he were Shakespeare, he would be the author of these sonnets, which would mean that he had a very close relationship to Southampton. But at the treason trial, despite that relationship, as a member of the jury he would have had no choice but to find him guilty of high treason, a capital crime. This unavoidable duty would have made Oxford Southampton's "adverse party."

At the same time, as someone with possible direct access to the Queen, and with assured access to her top lieutenant, Robert Cecil (Oxford literally grew up with Robert as a *de facto* stepbrother in Burghley's household), Oxford also would have had the opportunity to work behind the scenes to spare Southampton's life.

We lack external documentary proof that Oxford did any such thing. Is such a possibility mere speculation? Not if we choose to believe the sonnets. Oxford was not Southampton's legal advocate in the sense of being his lawyer at the trial itself—Southampton assuredly had none. So, what possible meaning is there other than that Shakespeare/Oxford is saying that he is working *behind the scenes* to save Southampton from execution?

If this is the meaning, Line 9 adds support: "For to thy sensual fault I bring in sense," would then mean "Against your crime and guilt, I bring in contrary argument" to try to spare you.

As noted, Southampton wrote letters to the Privy Council after his conviction, pleading for mercy. They are so well written from a legal standpoint that they appear to be from someone who has the assistance of counsel, "telling him exactly what to say and how to say it," as Boyle puts it.[xix] Given Oxford's previous legal training at Gray's Inn, and the myriad legal references throughout the plays and poems demonstrating that he had a firm grasp of the law, it is likely that Oxford was Southampton's *de facto* defense counsel (his "Advocate") after the trial. If so, this would lend even further weight to our interpretation of this sonnet.

Finally, the quatrain all but confirms that Oxford had to have been the author, and that the context for being Southampton's "adverse party" was that he had to sit in judgment on Southampton: "That I an accessory needs must be/ to that sweet thief which sourly robs from me." Oxford must be an accessory to "that sweet thief" (the forthcoming trial, or perhaps to Robert Cecil who was orchestrating it) by convicting Southampton, which will rob Oxford of Southampton. Oxford is compelled to be an opponent in a court of law ("adverse party"), in a proceeding that will remove the subject ("thou") from Oxford altogether. I am unable to come up with any way to make sense of the quatrain under the conventional interpretation.

The above explanation is the only coherent one that anyone has advanced. It constitutes strong proof not only that these sonnets are about Southampton's trial and imprisonment, but also that Oxford was the author of the sonnets, and was "Shakespeare." This is the first item of evidence from within the sonnets that convincingly establishes that Oxford must be the author.

Sonnet Theorem 11:

The early prison sonnets, especially Sonnet 35, establish that Southampton has committed a serious crime or "trespass," i.e., treason, arising from his role in the Essex Rebellion.

Sonnet Theorem 12:

Sonnet 30 chronicles how Edward de Vere, the Earl of Oxford, was "summoned" to the "sessions" of the House of Lords to be part of a jury to condemn the Essex Rebellion conspirators.

Sonnet Theorem 13:

Sonnet 35's reference to the poet being simultaneously the "Advocate" and the "adverse party" of Southampton bears only one possible interpretation: that Oxford, as a member of the jury that must condemn Southampton to death is his "adverse party," but that he is simultaneously doing what he can behind the scenes to save his life, as his "advocate."

Sonnet Theorem 14:

Based on Theorems 12 and 13, it is now conclusively established that the poet is Edward de Vere, 17th Earl of Oxford, who sat in the sessions that condemned Southampton and others to death. As the commoner Shakspere could not have had anything to do with the trial, he could have been neither Southampton's advocate nor adverse party, and hence could not have been "Shakespeare."

Another item of evidence that the sonnets are about Southampton and Oxford's efforts to spare his life after his conviction for treason is provided by the recent discovery of a poem written by Southampton to Queen Elizabeth, most likely in March of 1601. As analyzed by Whittemore in a recent article,[xx] there are strong resonances between the poem and the sonnets that, by Whittemore's hypothesis, would have been written between February 8 and mid-March of 1601, strongly suggesting that Southampton had those sonnets in his possession when he composed the poem, and that he used them to help formulate the language to be used in it. Major excerpts from Whittemore's article appear in Appendix V.

Prison Sonnets: Essence of the *Sonnets*

We have now established that a series of eighty sonnets, from Sonnet 27 to Sonnet 106, more than half of the total, span the period that Southampton was in the Tower, from his arrest on February 8, 1601, to his release on April 10, 1603. Far from being about a "fair youth," as conventionally understood, they are about a ringleader of a quixotic attempted rebellion against Queen Elizabeth, who was arrested, tried, condemned to death, mysteriously spared execution, and just as mysteriously released with no lingering adverse consequences. I contend that this series forms the core of the *Sonnets,* and that Southampton's arrest and incarceration led to the creation of what we today know as *Shake-speare's Sonnets.* The first twenty-six sonnets, and perhaps a few more, might have been all Shakespeare ever wrote, absent Southampton's arrest.

I shall return to a detailed examination of several dozen of the prison sonnets in Part II, which will provide further understanding of what these sonnets are about. That discussion will leave little doubt about the validity of the reading of them as being to and about Southampton while in the Tower, and as recording Oxford's emotional state as he deals with this situation.

The notion that a majority of the sonnets pertain to Southampton's twenty-six months in the Tower is one of Whittemore's major, and unique, contributions. This discovery expands the historical "hooks" or "anchors" from Sonnet 107 to encompass the eighty-one sonnets from 27-107, all but the last of which written while Southampton was in prison. It also permits us to find a number of other historical hooks and anchors, as we have seen, from the night that Southampton was arrested (Sonnet 27) to Oxford's role in his trial (Sonnet 35) to the reason he was spared execution (Sonnet 87).

The case for this reading is extremely strong, and several chapters in Part II will further bolster this reading. If this was all that Whittemore had discovered, it would be a monumental achievement (no pun intended), completely overturning the Standard Interpretation and the paradigm it rests on, and replacing it with a new and exciting one.

However, this turns out to merely provide the historical *context* for the *real* story, which was mightily important, but which wou have lain buried forever but for it   s being preserved in the sonnets. To understand *this* story now that we've established the basis for a new paradigm, we must begin at the beginning, with Sonnets 1-17, and uncover the amazing truth buried there, "hidden in plain sight."

.

Chapter 6
The "Procreate Sonnets"

It is safe to say that when Oxford began to write the first sonnet he had no idea that Southampton would end up in the Tower. Why he began writing them at all is another of the enigmas that plague traditional analysis, hamstrung, as always, by having the wrong poet. It turns out that the first seventeen sonnets share a common theme, one which is so obvious that no one disputes the rationale for grouping them together. In recognition of the ostensible common theme, these sonnets are almost universally dubbed the "Marriage Sonnets," an inaccurate and highly unfortunate designation. There is not a single reference in any of them to marriage, nor is there any mention of a marriage partner. The putative basis for this label derives from the fact that almost every one of these sonnets strongly urges the young man to produce an offspring, which would have implied having to be married (especially in that era).

By shifting the focus of attention away from procreation, those who identify these sonnets with marriage overlook a crucial question: Why is Shakespeare so obsessed with urging this young man to create a child while showing no concern for marriage, or a marriage partner? This is just the first of a series of questions, the true answers to which rock the foundation of the orthodox view. These sonnets use the word "love" over a dozen times, yet they are clearly *not* about love as most of us would understand it. And they talk about the importance of Southampton's passing on his "beauty" in ways that confound any ordinary rendering of that word.

I call the first seventeen sonnets the "Procreate Sonnets" because of their insistence that the "young man" (Southampton) do exactly that. It is something specific to procreation that will prove to be a key to unlocking the true meaning and purpose of this set of sonnets.

Marriage Without a Bride?

Dating the sonnets has long been recognized to be as important as it is difficult. Other than the historical marker of April 1603, for

Sonnet 107, traditional scholars have had no firm date for any sonnet. Whittemore's discovery that Sonnet 27 marks the arrest of Southampton on February 8, 1601, provides a final date by which the preceding twenty-six sonnets had to have been written. Coincidentally, or more likely not, Southampton would have been twenty-six years old until a few months before his arrest. Presuming that Oxford had not yet composed his planned sonnet to correspond with Southampton being twenty-seven at the time of his arrest, then the first twenty-six sonnets match one-to-one with Southampton's age.

This accords with a belief shared by many conventional scholars that Sonnets 1-17 were composed as a group after Southampton had turned seventeen in 1590, their number intentionally matching his age. Seventeen was the age at which men were considered to have come of age, and was therefore also the year when Southampton was introduced to the Court. It was also the year when Lord Burghley, Elizabeth's chief counselor, and possibly Elizabeth herself, began importuning Southampton to marry Elizabeth Vere, who was, not coincidentally, Oxford's daughter, a fact which appears to support the view these sonnets were indeed intended to urge Southampton to agree to the marriage.

However, if these were truly "Marriage Sonnets," intended to convince Southampton to marry a particular young woman, why is there no reference to a single characteristic of the woman—to her beauty, character, lineage or other desirable traits—nor even to the importance of having a wife, or to the benefits of married life? If the purpose of these sonnets had been to encourage Southampton to marry Elizabeth Vere, they must be judged inept in the extreme, bereft of so much as a single line that would hit Southampton's "hot button." Rather, they are primarily an extended scold that would almost certainly annoy, not convince. If any emotion was intended to be induced in Southampton, it would appear to be shame, as we shall see. On what basis could shame be effective if marriage *per se* were the goal?

It should be obvious that marriage *per se* is not the focus or purpose of these sonnets. Which woman the young man uses to produce an offspring is of no consequence to the poet—any woman will do, and nothing needs to be said about her. This oddity is never noted by conventional critics.

These sonnets contain another oddity, namely, if the desired result is merely that the young man produce a child before he's too old to do so, why is it so urgent that he do so now, when he's still in his teens? This anomaly is likewise never addressed in conventional discussions.

The reason given for advocating procreation is also odd: the sole reason given is to perpetuate Southampton's *own* "beauty." These sonnets do not show the least concern for the usual reasons that men of means would have for desiring a male heir, namely, to be able to pass on an estate, a hereditary title, or wealth and possessions. *Southampton's* "beauty" is praised as exceptional; twelve of the first fourteen sonnets refer to it. As we shall see, the use of this special word is a touchstone for a correct analysis, in which its real meaning leads to a new understanding. I dare to speculate that no other poems, much less sonnets in a cycle, before or since, ever asserted the importance of a *male* passing on *his* "beauty," a truly singular theme.

Love, Actually?

These sonnets conceal yet another anomaly: If they were addressed to either a homosexual lover, or to a "friend" toward whom the poet feels "manly love," where's the love?

Under the homosexual conjecture, if the poet were sexually interested in the young man, what sense would it make for him to be exhorting him to have children, which would necessitate marriage to, and sexual intercourse with, a woman?

The tone and content of these sonnets likewise makes no sense if intended to express some sort of abstract, "manly," or other type of "friendship" love as well. In short, despite the frequency of the word "love," these sonnets have nothing to do with any kind of affection of the poet toward Southampton. Something else is going on. Stephen Booth remarks to this effect in his commentary on Line 13 of Sonnet 10:

10   13   Make thee another self, for love of me,

Booth writes "that this is the first point in the 1609 sequence where the speaker implies close personal friendship between himself and the young man he is addressing." Booth notes that there is only one other instance of the use of the word "love" in a context suggesting affection within the first seventeen sonnets, in the first line of Sonnet 13:

13   1   O, that you were yourself! but, love, you are

Booth notes, "[T]he grounds for referring to the young man of sonnets 1-17 as 'the beloved' are derived from previous readings of the rest of the collection."[xxi]

These sonnets begin the entire series of 154 poems. If the first 126 are written to a young man with whom the author has a strong friendship, invoking the supposedly "manly" or "Renaissance" concept of love as basically platonic, why is such love barely mentioned in the very first group? The series lacks an introductory sonnet. That we think of these "marriage" sonnets as reflecting the love of the poet for the young man is, as Booth observes, based on importing that view from later sonnets.

The standard interpretation is that Shakespeare started writing these sonnets and only afterward did he either reveal his existing affection for the young man, or begin to love him. Neither explanation makes sense, because neither accounts for why Shakespeare began writing them in the first place, why he was so interested in urging the young man to procreate, or why as early as Sonnets 17-18, he is already talking about how the sonnets will preserve Southampton's essence for eternity. This suggests that the relationship between poet and Southampton never varied, and remained constant through the transition from the first seventeen sonnets to all the succeeding ones. The notion that the poet's affection for the young man evolved into a full-blown romantic attachment after Sonnet 17 is not supportable.

The Patron Perplex

The traditional view is compelled to posit that the relationship of Shakespeare to Southampton was client to patron—no other possibility can be imagined that would account for how "Shakespeare" (presumed to be the man from Stratford) could even have known Southampton, much less have written sonnets to and for him. Not a shred of supporting documentary evidence suggests that Southampton was ever Shakespeare's patron, or even knew him in any capacity. The conjecture is based entirely on the fact, already noted, that Shakespeare had dedicated his two narrative poems that were published in 1593 and 1594 to Southampton, in very effusive and subservient tones. That Shakespeare secured Southampton as a patron is a bedrock component of the Stratfordian paradigm, accepted by all traditional scholars, despite this utter lack of independent or plausible evidence to support this conjecture.

As far as I have been able to determine, not a single orthodox scholar has noticed that the conjecture that Southampton became Shakespeare's patron around 1594 fatally conflicts with the possibility that Shakespeare could have written Sonnets 1-17 to him three years earlier when Southampton was seventeen years old—in 1590. If Southampton only became Shakespeare's patron in 1593 at the earliest, what possible relationship could he have had in 1590 that permitted him to lecture the young nobleman with such scolding and critical words? By Stratfordian chronology (an exercise in fiction from start to finish), Shakspere first arrived in London as an actor (not yet a playwright) no earlier than 1589 or 1590. How could he immediately have been commissioned to write this first set of sonnets?

Figure 3 – 3ʳᵈ Earl of Southampton as painted by Nicholas Hilliard in 1594.

Simply put, how could Shakspere, a recent arrival from the provincial small town of Stratford (speaking a very distinctive "hick" accent) with no literary accomplishments, no contacts and no academic credentials, have written a series of sonnets in 1590 to and for Southampton, much less ones urging him to procreate? Why would he? He couldn't have secured Southampton, a high nobleman and royal ward of the Queen living in Burghley's household, as a patron yet. By what means would he have gotten them to Southampton in the first place, and what would have prevented Southampton from having him locked up for the impertinence of addressing a top nobleman as these sonnets do?

Therefore, the necessity of the "marriage sonnets" to have been written no later than 1590 is by itself conclusive proof that they couldn't have been written by Shakspere. (We haven't even factored in how it would have been possible for Shakspere at the very beginning of his career to have authored such incredibly accomplished poems as his first literary output of any kind.) Such a possibility also conflicts with the necessity (under the Stratford paradigm) of Southampton's becoming Shakspere's patron no earlier than the publication date of *Venus and Adonis* in 1593, three years later than Sonnets 1-17 must have been composed.

The Little Matter of Class

Another prominent feature of the "Procreate Sonnets" also vitiates the premise that they were written by Shakspere to Southampton. The tone of many lines is impossible coming from a lowly commoner to a prominent young earl—how could he possibly have penned them. Only someone who was at least the social equal of an earl could have done so. Compare the language, for instance, with which Oxford addressed Lord Burghley on many occasions, numerous examples of which are preserved in the records; the tone is, to our modern ear, highly deferential and respectful, almost craven at times. If this is how the scion of the leading house of England addressed another lord (a lowlier one, in fact), how much more deferentially must noble patrons have typically been addressed by their commoner clients?

The highly familiar and often superior-sounding tone of every sonnet in this series, and frequent descriptions of Southampton as conceited, selfish, and not willing to share of himself by passing on his fine qualities (above all, his beauty) to the next generation, are simply inconceivable coming from commoner Shakspere to the 3rd Earl of Southampton. No commoner (and arguably almost no noblemen either) could have penned the following lines, among others, and not paid the price, at the very least, of incarceration:

| 1 | 5 | But thou, contracted to thine own bright eyes, |
| 1 | 6 | Feed'st thy light'st flame with self-substantial fuel, |

| 4 | 1 | Unthrifty loveliness, why dost thou spend |
| 4 | 2 | Upon thyself thy beauty's legacy? |

| 4 | 5 | Then, beauteous niggard, why dost thou abuse |
| 4 | 6 | The bounteous largess given thee to give? |

4	7	Profitless usurer, why dost thou use
4	8	So great a sum of sums, yet canst not live?
4	9	For having traffic with thyself alone,
4	10	Thou of thyself thy sweet self dost deceive.

| 9 | 13 | No love toward others in that bosom sits |
| 9 | 14 | That on himself such murderous shame commits. |

| 10 | 1 | For shame! deny that thou bear'st love to any, |
| 10 | 2 | Who for thyself art so unprovident. |

10	5	For thou art so possess'd with murderous hate
10	6	That 'gainst thyself thou stick'st not to conspire.
10	7	Seeking that beauteous roof to ruinate
10	8	Which to repair should be thy chief desire.

We can therefore for the several reasons presented above conclusively rule out Shakspere as the author of the *Sonnets,* which is to say that the content of these first seventeen sonnets alone constitutes sufficient proof that Shakspere was not Shakespeare.

Sonnet Theorem 15:

Shakspere was not Shakespeare, because, as the subject of the sonnets is Southampton (Theorems 6 and 7), it is impossible that twenty-six-year-old Shakspere could have written these sonnets in 1590, when Southampton was sixteen; Shakspere had yet to produce anything that would commend him as competent to write poetry, or plays, nor is it credible that a commoner could write poetry that so scolds and patronizes one of the highest noblemen in the land.

Oxford Fills the Bill

We have already identified conclusive evidence from some of the early prison sonnets that the author of the sonnets could have been no one other than the Earl of Oxford. Let us see how well this hypothesis fits the "Procreate Sonnets."

Oxford surely knew Southampton from an early age, likely as young as eight, when he joined the Burghley household as a royal ward in 1581, following the death of the 2nd Earl of Southampton. That year Oxford had reconciled with his wife Anne, Burghley's daughter, and would have resumed close contact with Burghley House. We infer that Oxford joined with Burghley (and Queen Elizabeth) in 1590 to urge Southampton to marry Oxford's daughter

Elizabeth Vere. As an older earl (Oxford was forty in 1590, some twenty-three years older than Southampton), and as one who had known Southampton growing up, he would be in a position to adopt the tone of this series of sonnets. No one else in England would have been in a better position to do so.

Southampton's young age is no impediment to the Oxford thesis—in fact, it supports it. There is no paradox of the patron issue surrounding the dedications to Southampton of the 1593 and 1594 poems as there is for Shakspere, as Oxford was not seeking a patron; the dedications can be seen as an attempt to promote Southampton to the London literary world (we will shortly see the real reason). The scolding tone in some of these early sonnets also makes sense if seen as coming from an old ward of Burghley's to the young ward.

Thus, with Oxford posited as Shakespeare, the anomalies that cannot be explained under the Stratfordian paradigm are no longer impossible to countenance. However, this still leaves unexplained why Oxford would have written these sonnets, and what Oxford's relationship to Southampton was. Specifically, why would anyone not related by blood to Southampton care whether he procreated? Who would be more concerned about the young man having children than about whom he might marry for that purpose? A friend? A lover? We turn now to an examination of the meaning of "beauty" in these first seventeen sonnets for answers to these questions.

Chapter 7
"Beauty" Reinterpreted

A very important key to unpacking the true meaning hidden in Sonnets 1-17 lies in recognizing the actual intended meaning of the word "beauty." Obsessed with the notion that the sonnets are love poetry of some kind, holders of the orthodox view see "beauty" as ordinary *physical* beauty, describing the physiognomic characteristics of the young man, presumably Southampton. That Southampton was known to have had somewhat feminine features undoubtedly reassures holders of this view that it is correct. My analysis will show this view to be untenable, as nothing in the discussion of beauty in these sonnets relates to a single feature associated with physical beauty. Rather, "beauty" is clearly used to refer to something which is inheritable (which physical beauty manifestly is not). And the importance of this "beauty" is made clear by the fact that the word occurs nineteen times in twelve of the seventeen sonnets.

Oxford is clearly repurposing the word to refer to something else, something readily revealed upon close analysis of the text of these sonnets. That orthodox scholars have for over a century failed to see what is plainly meant here is a testament to the power of a false paradigm to cloud one's reason and limit one's imagination to that which is "possible" under the prevailing paradigm. (Among other things, this reading disposes of the myth that *Shake-speares Sonnets* can be located in the tradition of previous sonnet cycles, where physical beauty—of the [female]) beloved—is all-important.)

A note on my methodology is in order. While I include the complete texts of five of these seventeen sonnets, and discuss parts of several others, in this chapter my purpose is limited to showing that "beauty" must mean something other than physical beauty, which will prove to be a very important clue to what the sonnets are all about. This approach means that in this chapter, I will not be able to discuss the full meaning of these five sonnets, the basis for which discussion has not yet been laid. I shall return to reveal the full meaning of them in a subsequent chapter, at which point the reader will be encouraged to return to the texts of these sonnets in order to follow the analysis.

The key word "beauty" makes its debut early, in line two of the very first sonnet, to which we now turn our attention:

Sonnet 1

The first two lines state:

1 1 From fairest creatures we desire increase,
1 2 That thereby beauty's *Rose* might never die,

The first line appears to be a general statement about nature, or at least about all beautiful creatures in nature. But this reading becomes strained by Line 2's reference to "beauty's *Rose*" (capitalized and italicized in the 1609 printing). Our commentators divide on this emphasis given to "*Rose*," with Burrow and Booth ascribing the apparent emphasis to a typographer's whim, and Kerrigan and Duncan-Jones attempting to find some general

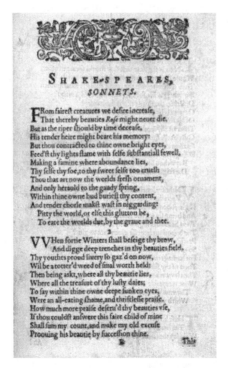

*Figure 2 – The first page in
the 1609 quarto edition of*
Shake-Speares Sonnets.

73

reference to beauty that would explain it.

It should be noted that "beauty's *Rose"* is singular, which compels reading "fairest creatures" in the previous line as a plural form disguising a singular subject. Since the remainder of the sonnet, and the succeeding sixteen, are all about one young man who is being urged to procreate, "fairest creatures" can only refer to him. The second line is stated as a consequence of the first line. "That thereby beauty's Rose may never die" is the reason that "fairest creatures"—our male subject of these sonnets—need to reproduce. And as we've established, that male subject, the so-called "young man" or "fair youth," is Southampton.

What exactly is meant by "beauty's rose"? In the seventeen procreate sonnets, "beauty" is the most frequently used noun in the series, but this first instance does not refer to "beauty" itself, but to "beauty's rose." Duncan-Jones notes unhelpfully that the rose was "often associated with female beauty and, more specifically, with female genitalia." But we know that this sonnet, and all succeeding ones, are about what a *man* passes on, so "beauty's rose" can hardly refer to female beauty or to female genitalia that might be passed on. Booth proposes several meanings—"the bloom of youth," "the most perfect example of beauty" and "the beauty of the rose," none of which is elucidating. (We will return to discuss the full meaning of this allusion later, when we have established the context to do so.)

The rest of the sonnet follows:

1	3	But as the riper should by time decease,
1	4	His tender heir might bear his memory:
1	5	But thou, contracted to thine own bright eyes,
1	6	Feed'st thy light'st flame with self-substantial fuel,
1	7	Making a famine where abundance lies,
1	8	Thyself thy foe, to thy sweet self too cruel.
1	9	Thou that art now the world's fresh ornament
1	10	And only herald to the gaudy spring,
1	11	Within thine own bud buriest thy content
1	12	And, tender churl, makest waste in niggarding.
1	13	Pity the world, or else this glutton be,
1	14	To eat the world's due, by the grave and thee.

Lines 3 and 4 appear to refer to any parent-child situation, as the "riper" of the two, the parent, approaches death, the child, the "heir," carries forward the memory of the parent. The poet finally arrives at "thou" in Line 5, and immediately derides his subject for being self-obsessed (lines 5-6), for making a famine in place of abundance (line 7), and for being his own worst enemy, acting cruelly to his own self (line 8). These lines reinforce the reading of "fairest creatures" as the same person referred to by "His" (line 4), "thou" (line 5), "thy" (line 6), and "thyself" (line 8).

Lines 9-10 present an important anomaly. Our four traditionalist critics fail to make sense of them. They gloss the words "herald" and "gaudy," but not the meaning of the entire line. None tries to explain why the poet would call the young man "the world's fresh ornament." What could the poet mean by "world's"? Why would the "thou"—Southampton at age seventeen—be of interest or concern to the "world," however defined? What could be intended by calling him "fresh ornament"? The silence of our four selected critics is another self-condemnation of their approach—if you can't make sense of it, pretend it doesn't exist, and hope nobody notices.

Line 10 finds the annotators glossing several words, struggling to make sense of the line. To Burrow, the friend, "like an early rose …is presented as one who precedes the arrival of spring in its full panoply." This parsing raises more questions than it answers. It ignores why the young man would be the "only" such herald. What does this have to do with what immediately precedes it, about how selfish he is by not reproducing himself? To Duncan-Jones, Line 10 suggests that the young man may show "great promise as a courtier," which is subject to the same criticism. (The insistence of our commentators in calling Southampton the "young man," even when some of them elsewhere acknowledge that he is Southampton, creates a difficulty of reference for my presentation. In general, I will use "Southampton" when referring to the younger man the poet is addressing, keeping in mind that none of the commentators use his name in their sonnet-by-sonnet glosses and exegeses.)

Lines 11-12 pose no difficulties, merely saying that Southampton is being niggardly with his "content," which will be buried with him if he fails to procreate. But the couplet (lines 13 and 14) returns to the subject of Line 9, again mentioning "the world," which is to be pitied because of Southampton's decision to "bur[y] thy content" in "thine own bud," a clear reference to his refusal to contemplate creating an offspring. Why the "world" should care is the obvious question posed, but is neither noticed *as* a question, nor answered, by conventional critics. Why would Southampton's offspring be considered to be "the world's due" that he is "eat[ing]" in Line 14? What could be so important as to warrant such lofty language?

That "something" can only be something genetic. This series of sonnets is about Southampton's male heir(s) *inheriting* something from him that *can be inherited* (unlike physical beauty). *What that something is* is the paramount question to be answered here, but I know of no critic who has considered it, much less answered it.

Sonnet 2

Sonnet 2 brings us to the doorstep of a set of understandings that will unlock the secret world that Oxford created:

2	1	When forty Winters shall besiege thy brow,
2	2	And dig deep trenches in thy beauty's field,
2	3	Thy youth's proud livery, so gazed on now,
2	4	Will be a totter'd weed, of small worth held:
2	5	Then being ask'd where all thy beauty lies,
2	6	Where all the treasure of thy lusty days,
2	7	To say, within thine own deep-sunken eyes,
2	8	Were an all-eating shame and thriftless praise.
2	9	How much more praise deserved thy beauty's use,
2	10	If thou couldst answer 'This fair child of mine
2	11	Shall sum my count and make my old excuse,'
2	12	Proving his beauty by succession thine!
2	13	This were to be new made when thou art old,
2	14	And see thy blood warm when thou feel'st it cold.

The surface meaning is clear. When "thou" are age forty, your present beauty will be a tattered weed, and it will be locked in your sunken eyes (lines 1-8). If you instead had had a child, if you had "used" your "beauty," you could have passed it on (lines 9-12). In the final couplet, your beauty would be made new, and you would see "thy" blood in your child as you approached death.

The occurrence of "beauty" three times confronts us immediately. Why is Oxford so concerned about Southampton passing on his "beauty" "to this fair child of [his]"? That question is posed each time the word "beauty" appears in the succeeding fifteen sonnets. The question that confronts the conventional critics is whether "beauty," conventionally taken to mean *physical* beauty, is the likely meaning here?

It cannot be. First, if physical beauty were the intended meaning, it would require that Shakespeare believe that it can reliably be passed on from parent to child—even in Shakespeare's age, people knew better than that. More interestingly, even if it were certain that an offspring would inherit physical beauty, the real question is why the poet is so concerned that the young man *pass on* his "beauty"? If the young man is the object of the poet's love, manly or otherwise, it is *his* physical beauty, and the fact that it will fade as he gets older, that would be of concern, so why would a paramour or admirer care whether it were passed on? A contention that the poet is concerned about beauty for its own sake is not supported by the text.

Surely the object of the poet's love must also have some inner qualities to commend him. But in these first seventeen sonnets the focus is exclusively on his "beauty."

These questions cry out for an interpretation that uncovers another meaning for "beauty." We begin by analyzing Line 12 of Sonnet 2:

2 12 Proving his beauty by succession thine!

Shakespeare often plays games with syntax to conform to the strictures of the meter and rhyme scheme, and also to facilitate the condensation that he needs in order to pile content into a short poem. It helps us to unwind the syntax, which in this case is straightforward: "Proving his beauty by succession thine" means that "his (your son's) beauty is proved to be your beauty by the fact of his succession from you." In other words, the fact that your son has inherited your beauty is proved by the fact that he succeeds you.

The glosses by three of our commentators on this line are as curious as they are futile. Burrow interprets Line 12 as "proving your son to be yours in perpetuity, rather than by gift or conquest." Kerrigan glosses "succession" as "right of inheritance." Booth misses the simple syntax of the line, expending twenty-five lines explaining (erroneously) something that doesn't need explaining. He tells us that "proving" and "by succession" refer to a son's "right to his deceased father's possessions," despite the absence of a reference to "possessions," and despite the fact that the father may be old, but is not dead.

Duncan-Jones reads "proving" as "demonstrating, or discovering, or both," and "by succession" as "beauty inherited legally by inherited right." Though she gets the sense right, she fails to realize its necessary implication, that "beauty" as used here cannot be physical beauty, which is incapable of being legally inherited. One has to wonder what *she* meant by "beauty inherited legally."

Line 12 makes clear that whatever "beauty" is, it isn't physical beauty, which would hardly be "proved" by the mere fact of a son being his father's lawful offspring. "Beauty" must be something internal that is *passed hereditarily*, and is relevant to the notion of legal succession.

A clue is provided in the final couplet whose meaning our commentators, uncharacteristically, come close to correctly grasping. Duncan-Jones comments that "the (no longer) young man will perceive the renewal of his blood-line and beauty when his own body has undergone the wintry process of aging." Kerrigan correctly notes that this reflects the belief that the son carried the same blood as the father (also noting the belief that the blood of a young man would be hotter than that of an older one). Burrow has a succinct and basically accurate read: "to see your own blood vigorously alive in your son."

Duncan-Jones and Burrow correctly perceive that the issue is inheritance—passing on of the young man's bloodline. But, lacking a context to recognize the implications of this reading, and working within an incorrect paradigm, they made no use of an insight that might have led them to anticipate Whittemore's breakthrough understanding of these sonnets.

To turn to the couplet, Line 13 says that "This [beauty] were to be new made, when thou art old," followed by Line 14, "and see thy blood warm when thou feel'st it cold." That is, "beauty" is "new-made" in the son, when the young man (his father) will no longer be young.

Thus, "beauty" *must mean blood*—specifically, "blood" as in "bloodline," which could refer to the "blood" that is being inherited, descent from a common ancestor, parental lineage, kinship or, especially relevant here, "descent from noble or royal lineage" (from the FreeDictionary.com). Rereading Sonnet 2 in this light, we now understand the first two lines to say that when you are forty years old and have deep wrinkles on your noble brow, your great opportunity (lines 3 and 4) to pass on your bloodline will be gone. At that point (lines 5-6), if you are asked where that bloodline is and if it is nowhere except in yourself, that would warrant no praise (lines 7-8). However (lines 9-12), if you had produced a child, you could answer that he will inherit your accounts and justify your life, demonstrating that, in succeeding you, he inherited your blood. Your blood would be thus made new when you are old, and you will see it in your son as you approach death.

Sonnet 4

Sonnet 4 provides a proving ground for our re-interpretation of "beauty." It is also a marvelous example of how Shakespeare crafts individual sonnets around certain *motifs*, here the notion of lending money or valuables:

4	1	Unthrifty loveliness, why dost thou spend
4	2	Upon thyself thy beauty's legacy?
4	3	Nature's bequest gives nothing but doth lend,
4	4	And being frank she lends to those are free.
4	5	Then, beauteous niggard, why dost thou abuse
4	6	The bounteous largess given thee to give?
4	7	Profitless usurer, why dost thou use
4	8	So great a sum of sums, yet canst not live?
4	9	For having traffic with thyself alone,
4	10	Thou of thyself thy sweet self dost deceive.
4	11	Then how, when nature calls thee to be gone,
4	12	What acceptable *Audit* canst thou leave?
4	13	Thy unused beauty must be tomb'd with thee,
4	14	Which, used, lives th' executor to be.

"Beauty" first occurs in Line 2, where the meaning of the first two lines becomes (reading "loveliness" as Southampton), "unthrifty person, why do you spend the legacy of your bloodline on yourself (rather than pass it on)?" The use of the word "legacy" makes it unambiguous that we are speaking of something that is inherited (the best applicable definition of legacy is "something transmitted by or received from an ancestor or predecessor"). No one would normally consider physical beauty to be a legacy.

Then follows an extended section on how his beauty has been lent, not given, to him, but so far he has in turn re-lent it only to himself, without profit, so that his audit will show he squandered the loan by not increasing it (by creating offspring). Again, if "beauty" meant physical beauty, what sense would it make to say that it was merely borrowed? Would anyone think, for example, that a beautiful woman had "borrowed" her beauty from her *mother*?

Lines 13-14 conclude, "Your unused bloodline must go with you to the grave, which, had you 'used' it (passed it on), it (in the form of your son) would be your executor."

Duncan-Jones seems to have forgotten her correct reading of "beauty" as "bloodline" in the previous sonnet, and reverts to the standard reading of "beauty's legacy" as referring to physical beauty. "His beauty is unique, and, if not reproduced, will die with him."

In this sonnet Shakespeare makes the same point he has made in the three preceding ones, here using the metaphor of lending money. To anticipate a much later line, he is continually "dressing old words new" (76.11) with the same theme. But what richness he creates in these "newly dressed" words!

Sonnets 5-6

Sonnet 5 reinforces our interpretation of beauty:

5	1	Those hours, that with gentle work did frame
5	2	The lovely gaze where every eye doth dwell,
5	3	Will play the tyrants to the very same
5	4	And that unfair which fairly doth excel:
5	5	For never-resting time leads summer on
5	6	To hideous winter and confounds him there;
5	7	Sap check'd with frost and lusty leaves quite gone,
5	8	Beauty o'ersnow'd and bareness every where:
5	9	Then, were not summer's distillation left,
5	10	A liquid prisoner pent in walls of glass,
5	11	Beauty's effect with beauty were bereft,
5	12	Nor it nor no remembrance what it was:
5	13	But flowers distill'd though they with winter meet,
5	14	Leese but their show; their substance still lives sweet.

This sonnet is an extended metaphor about how Time allows a person his "summer," when he had better reproduce himself, on pain of reaching the winter of his life (death) with nothing by which his bloodline ("substance") can continue. Though the sonnet appears to lack an explicit subject, a "thou," Line 2 evokes the same notion presented in Sonnet 1, that the subject is the focus of the "gaze" of "every eye," which can only be Southampton. We will see later that several other words confirm that Southampton is indeed the subject.

"Those hours" in Line 1 is "time" (mentioned explicitly in Line 5), which allows the subject a period of life (line 2), but just as surely will destroy that life ("will play the tyrants to the very same") before too long. The second quatrain adds the metaphor of seasons—Time will replace the "Summer" of Line 5 with "hideous winter" (death).

The third quatrain introduces another metaphor that all four conventional commentators have missed by taking it literally. The quatrain warns that "summer's distillation" must be preserved in a metaphorical vial (the "liquid prisoner pent in walls of glass," a reading confirmed in the next sonnet). That the "distillation" must be an offspring is confirmed in Line 11, which says that if this is *not* done, both beauty and "beauty's effect" will be bereft—that is, "bereft of existence." "Beauty's effect" surely means the child that won't exist. Line 12 reinforces this with "neither beauty (your bloodline) nor even the remembrance of beauty [of] what it was [will exist after you're gone]."

Line 13 then says that "flowers distilled" (the subject), though they will die ("with winter meet"), they will lose ("leese") only their outward appearance (their show), while their "substance" (their fragrance) will continue ("still lives sweet"). The metaphor is continued into the first quatrain of Sonnet 6 (see discussion of lines 1-4 of Sonnet 6 on page 82). Substituting the real subject, Southampton, for the metaphorical flowers, Southampton with an heir ("flowers distilled"), though he die ("winter meet"), will lose only his mortal self (his "show"), while his heir, his bloodline (his "substance") will live on ("live(s) sweet").

Taking literally the apparent discussion of distilling flowers, Booth reads "summer's distillation" as "the essence of summer as perfumes made from flowers." Burrow and Kerrigan concur. Duncan-Jones comes up with "rose water," which she explains as referring back to "beauty's Rose" in Sonnet 1, which is correct, but with a different meaning for both "beauty" and "rose." All fail to see that what is distilled is the same thing that has been the subject of all five sonnets so far, "beauty" or noble bloodline.

"Beauty o'ersnowed" (line 8) is commented on only by Duncan-Jones: "[this] suggests both a verdant landscape now covered with snow, and white hair on a human head," which makes no sense in context, as "beauty" is glossed here not as physical beauty of the young man, but as the general beauty of nature.

Burrow reads "substance" in Line 14 as "possessions, goods, estate," as if the sonnet were about ordinary inheritance. Kerrigan notes usefully that "leese" was probably an intended pun, reflecting both "lease" and "lose," and notes that the expression "more show than substance" was in use then.

Only Duncan-Jones attempts a general summary of the poem, which I quote in full to demonstrate its shortcomings: "the process which has brought the young man to his present physical perfection will in the same manner bring him to decay. However...the speaker tells him that he can preserve the essence of his beauty, even as Elizabethan housewives preserve roses by distilling rose water."

What sense is there in saying that the "process" that brought the young man to his present physical perfection (her reading of "beauty" here) will also bring him to decay? There is nothing in the sonnet of a "process" that brought him to his present state. Nor will he decay through the "same process," but rather by time, which is a recurring theme throughout the sonnets. Nor does the sonnet say that he can preserve the essence of his (physical) beauty.

To compare the preserving of the "essence" of his "physical perfection" to Elizabethan housewives preserving roses by distilling rose water is ludicrous. How could a person's *physical* perfection be distilled into, and thereby preserved, anything analogous to rose water? Has Duncan-Jones never heard of metaphor?

I have quoted the critics here at length to well illustrate the difficulty they have making sense of a sonnet that, once understood from the new perspective, becomes transparent.

The first quatrain of Sonnet 6 continues the distilled flowers metaphor, this time so graphically that it is surprising that it has eluded conventional scholars:

6 1 Then let not winter's ragged hand deface
6 2 In thee thy summer, ere thou be distill'd:
6 3 Make sweet some vial; treasure thou some place
6 4 With beauty's treasure, ere it be self-kill'd.

Here, the direction is to "make sweet some vial" by "treasur[ing] thou some place with beauty's treasure." Of our four commentators, only two perceive that this is about procreating, that "vial" is a woman's womb, to be impregnated with his "treasure," his seed. But Line 4, which is explicit that the treasure belongs to beauty ("beauty's treasure)," eludes them, as they fail to recognize that beauty can only be something that is transmitted by the seed, namely, the bloodline.

The remainder of the sonnet confirms that procreation is the subject of both sonnets, not the distillation of flowers.

6 5 That use is not forbidden usury,
6 6 Which happies those that pay the willing loan;
6 7 That's for thyself to breed another thee,
6 8 Or ten times happier, be it ten for one;
6 9 Ten times thyself were happier than thou art,
6 10 If ten of thine ten times refigured thee:
6 11 Then what could death do, if thou shouldst depart,

82

6	12	Leaving thee living in posterity?
6	13	Be not self-will'd, for thou art much too fair
6	14	To be death's conquest and make worms thine heir.

Line 5 says that "that use" (referring to lines 3-4) is permitted (is "not forbidden usury"), and is "for thy self to breed another thee" (line 7). With such an offspring (and even better with ten such), death would be defeated, even after "thy" death, since "thou" would be left "living in (thy) posterity."

Sonnets 9-14

In Sonnet 9 we find another reference to beauty:

9	11	But beauty's waste hath in the world an end,
9	12	And kept unused, the user so destroys it.
9	13	No love toward others in that bosom sits
9	14	That on himself such murderous shame commits.

Again, the sense defies reading "beauty" as "physical beauty." Duncan-Jones displays the traditionalist dilemma with this sonnet, translating part of Line 11 as "the waste, or consumption, of physical beauty," and Line 12 as "Beauty which is so preserved (kept unused) is destroyed in the process." She has concocted an oxymoron: If "beauty's waste" is the consumption of physical beauty, then such consumption would be the opposite of keeping it unused. She fails to address what "unused" physical beauty could mean. How does one "not use" physical beauty? One *has* it, one does not "use" it. Since Line 12 says that *unuse* is the destroyer or waste of beauty, it is only intelligible if "beauty" is inherited bloodline—its "use" is its being passed through procreation. The "waste" is in not "using" it, i.e., not passing it to the next generation, thereby destroying it.

Sonnet 10's use of beauty is equally transparent under our interpretation:

10	13	Make thee another self, for love of me,
10	14	That beauty still may live in thine or thee.

Read as bloodline, "beauty" here can be passed to offspring, as the couplet says. Once again, none of the commentators ask how physical beauty can be passed with certainty to one's offspring. Line 13 also foreshadows the relationship between the author ("me") and the subject ("thee"), since "for love of me" suggests a blood relationship between the author and the subject, and that the author's bloodline is also in jeopardy if the young man does not procreate.

Sonnets 12, 13 and 14 each contain similar uses for "beauty." Sonnet 12 again refers to the danger that if not passed on, his beauty will be wasted. In Sonnets 13 and 14, the incompatibility of "beauty" with any notion of physical beauty is even more clearly manifested than in the preceding sonnets.

The incoherent and illogical way that our four traditionalist critics are compelled to understand "beauty" in these sonnets can be seen as another powerful reason to jettison the old paradigm. "Beauty" clearly refers to the bloodline that Southampton is being asked to ensure gets passed on to an offspring.

We can now formulate our new understanding of the meaning of the word "beauty" into a theorem. This is an interim theorem, as the meaning and use of "beauty" will be further refined in subsequent chapters:

Sonnet Theorem 16:

"Beauty" as used in the "Procreate Sonnets" refers not to physical beauty, but to the bloodline that the poet desires Southampton to pass on.

Oxford as Southampton's Father

One further conclusion from the above discussion is compelling: only if Oxford were Southampton's father would he show such concern that Southampton pass on his bloodline to the next generation. What unrelated person would be so obsessed, as the author of Sonnets 1-17 clearly is, with repeatedly reiterating this concern? Why would Oxford (or anyone not related to Southampton) care whether Southampton continued the Southampton lineage or not?

That Oxford *was,* indeed, Southampton's father will be amply confirmed in the analysis to follow, including, among many other markers, the number of times where Southampton is referred to as the "sun," clearly punning on the word "son." Also, who else but a parent (or other close relative) would hazard advocating for a condemned traitor, presumably at significant personal risk, as Oxford indicated he was doing in Sonnet 35, or maintain contact and concern over a period of years for someone condemned, possibly for life, in the Tower of London? Certainly not a status-conscious social climber like Shakspere seeking patronage from members of the nobility.

The strongest reason to conclude that Oxford had to be Southampton's father is that such a relationship provides the *only* explanation for what type of "love" actually existed between them, after ruling out any type of romantic (homosexual or bisexual) love or some species of "friendship." The word "love" is just as legitimately used in parent-child relationships as in romantic ones. Most of the usages in the sonnets are as a term of reference to the man himself ("my love" as a term of address) rather than describing the *emotion* of love.

In complete contradiction to the narrative of the Standard Interpretation, in fact there is no sonnet in which the poet is anything but supportive of and loyal to Southampton, through thick and thin, again bespeaking the type of loyalty that a father would have for a son (*not* for a fickle, on-again-off-again romantic partner), and likely for no other man not closely related to him. This permits us to formulate our next theorem:

Sonnet Theorem 17:

Southampton had to have been Oxford's son. Having ruled out that the relationship between Shakespeare and Southampton could be either homosexual or some species of "manly friendship," we must conclude that it had to have been one based on blood (parental or close relative). The relative ages of Oxford and Southampton, and the concern expressed in Sonnets 1-17 that Southampton pass on his bloodline (his "beauty") practically rule out that the relationship was anything but father and son.

Chapter 8
Southampton Transcendent

T hat "beauty" refers to Southampton's noble bloodline, even if that bloodline is actually inherited from Oxford, still would not suffice to warrant the extraordinary praise that the sonnets say is owing to Southampton and that will resonate through all of history to come. We have already looked summarily at several passages that make these seemingly over-the-top statements. We will now take a closer look at the sonnets that contain them to determine what is it about Southampton that warrants such grandiose description and the need to preserve it for future generations.

Preserving Southampton in the Sonnets

We have already seen several passages within the sonnets that refer to the sonnets themselves, essentially as "actors" in the narrative the sonnets are telling. Many more such references to the sonnets as an actor occur in other sonnets we have yet to consider. This usage is highly singular, and I don't believe anything like it occurs anywhere else in the corpus of English poetry. This fact should further confirm that any conventional reading of the sonnets is off the mark.

Between Sonnets 15 and 17, the poet first makes the first such reference to the sonnets ("my barren rhyme" in sonnet 16, prefigured in Line 14 of Sonnet 15) and second, for the last time urges Southampton to pass on his "beauty" (which we now understand to be his bloodline). After Sonnet 17, no further reference is made to the importance of doing this; instead future sonnets say that the sonnets themselves will be the instruments to pass something on to posterity. (We will see later the signal importance of this alteration of the message.)

Next we must ask what these self-referential passages are saying is being preserved in the sonnets. It cannot possibly be the bloodline itself since the sonnets, as poetry, can only convey information. Therefore, it can only be the *knowledge* of what that

86

bloodline is that the sonnets preserve. And for the knowledge of Southampton's bloodline to be so overarchingly important, the bloodline itself must be something extraordinary—something more important even than Oxford's own bloodline. We shall now explore what this "something" must be.

As noted, the first sonnets to reference the sonnets as a whole are Sonnets 15 and 16, with Sonnet 15 flowing seamlessly into Sonnet 16 as if they were a single poem.

Sonnet 15

15	1	When I consider every thing that grows
15	2	Holds in perfection but a little moment,
15	3	That this huge stage presenteth nought but shows
15	4	Whereon the Stars in secret influence comment;
15	5	When I perceive that men as plants increase,
15	6	Cheered and check'd even by the self-same sky,
15	7	Vaunt in their youthful sap, at height decrease,
15	8	And wear their brave state out of memory;
15	9	Then the conceit of this inconstant stay
15	10	Sets you most rich in youth before my sight,
15	11	Where wasteful time debateth with Decay,
15	12	To change your day of youth to sullied night;
15	13	And all in war with Time for love of you,
15	14	As he takes from you, I engraft you new.

This delightful sonnet is extraordinary for its succinct commentary on the ephemeralness of life, especially that portion of one's life when one is at the youthful height of one's powers—a topic of interest to the poet because of its application to Southampton. Line 2 notes that "every thing that grows" "holds in (stays in a state of) perfection but (for only) a little (short) moment" where the "huge stage of life" merely presents these moments as short-lived appearances ("shows") that entertain the heavens. The second quatrain likens men to plants that grow to their maximum heights in their youth, only to immediately start shrinking until they die (are "out of memory"). The third quatrain brings in Southampton, calling the height of youthful vigor "the conceit of this inconstant stay" in that state, where he appears "most rich in youth before my sight," while time and decay are meanwhile conspiring to start him on the road to death ("to change your day of youth to sullied night").

The couplet completes the thought, summing up the situation to say that Oxford is in a war with Time, in which as Time draws Southampton inexorably toward death ("takes [life] from you), Oxford rescues him from that fate by ensuring his immortality in the sonnets ("I ingraft you new"). The mechanism by which Oxford will "ingraft" Southampton is not explicitly mentioned in this sonnet, a defect remedied in the first quatrain of Sonnet 16 with a reference to "my barren rhyme." "Ingraft" refers to the practice of grafting the body of one plant onto another to give it new life—a perfect metaphor for how Oxford intends to graft the essence of Southampton to the corpus of sonnets that will long outlive his corporeal body.

Sonnet 16 begins by contrasting the power of such an "ingrafting" to the efficacy of actually procreating and creating an offspring whose existence would represent a much more powerful way to preserve himself and his essence. The poem makes clear that the latter is far more effective, and hence far preferable. The mention of "means more blessed" surely is intended to evoke a "blessed event," that is, the birth of a child.

16	1	But wherefore do not you a mightier way
16	2	Make war upon this bloody tyrant, time?
16	3	And fortify yourself in your decay
16	4	With means more blessed than my barren rhyme?

None of our commentators understands this meaning, nor sees the seamless flow of meaning from Sonnet 15 to Sonnet 16. Most of them consider Line 4 of Sonnet 16 to be a self-deprecatory statement that the poet thinks his poetic efforts aren't good, that they're "barren." Duncan-Jones comes the closest to understanding it, observing that the verse is "barren" because "it can generate only verbal images of the youth, not living children," but then strays by interpreting "barren" as inability to conceive. (It is actually barren because it preserves the mere *memory* of Southampton and his bloodline; how much better to have the bloodline actually continue via flesh-and-blood offspring.) Her discussion of the word "blessed" confirms that she has not grasped the true purport, commenting that "marriage [a word not mentioned anywhere] is a more blessed form of renewal than writing…because it offers 'bliss' or happiness, in addition to the blessing of children" not seeing that the issue is not children, *per se*, much less marital bliss, but *children as carriers of Southampton's blood.* Burrow thinks that the line "shockingly denies the vitality implicitly granted to verse" in Sonnet 15. Kerrigan sees this as an elegant apology for writing bad poetry (sic), both men failing to see the meaning of "barren" as even Duncan-Jones does, as characterizing the contrast of mere poetry to a living child. Booth says nothing about this line.

The remainder of Sonnet 16 reprises yet again how Southampton must conduct this warfare against Time:

16	5	Now stand you on the top of happy hours,
16	6	And many maiden gardens yet unset
16	7	With virtuous wish would bear your living flowers,
16	8	Much liker than your painted counterfeit:
16	9	So should the lines of life that life repair,
16	10	Which this (Time's pencil, or my pupil pen)
16	11	Neither in inward worth nor outward fair,
16	12	Can make you live yourself in eyes of men.
16	13	To give away yourself keeps yourself still,
16	14	And you must live, drawn by your own sweet skill.

Continuing the theme of Sonnet 15, Lines 5-8 say that Southampton "now stand(s) on the top of happy hours" (is at his youthful peak), and states more clearly than ever that there are any number of young women who would gladly bear his children ("many maiden gardens [young women] yet unset [virgin]" who would happily "bear your living flowers [offspring]." Such "flowers" will much more closely resemble him than will his portrait in the sonnets ("your painted counterfeit").

The third quatrain says that only Southampton himself can so preserve his life: Line 9 declares that the "lines of life" (Southampton) should "repair" that life ("repair" surely means fix the flaw of mortality, "fix" life so that it doesn't die at his mortal death), that is, avail himself of the possibility of procreation while he is young enough to do so. The next three lines assert that neither Time nor the poet can make Southampton do this, incidentally playing with the metaphors of a pencil and pen that Time and the poet use to write "lines"—"lines of life" for Time, lines of poetry for the poet. Line 13 picks up grammatically from Line 9, saying that "to give away yourself" (find a suitable woman and have her bear your children) preserves himself ("keeps your self still"), and that "you must live" (forever), based on your own effort ("drawn by your own sweet skill").

Presumably, only fifteen other sonnets had been composed by the time of Sonnet 16, the penultimate one of the first series. After Sonnet 17, the poet abandons the theme of procreation. In Sonnets 15 and 16, the poet says to Southampton that if he doesn't procreate and pass on his bloodline ("make war" on "Time" by passing himself on, thus defeating death), these sonnets will be only a "barren" *record* of his bloodline, in place of the perpetuation of the *actual* bloodline.

Sonnet 17

Sonnet 17 is one of several truly extraordinary sonnets within the complete collection. Here, the sonnets ("my verse") become the subject of the entire sonnet, identified as the vehicle that will tell the world about Southampton:

17	1	Who will believe my verse in time to come,
17	2	If it were fill'd with your most high deserts?
17	3	Though yet, heaven knows, it is but as a tomb
17	4	Which hides your life and shows not half your parts.
17	5	If I could write the beauty of your eyes
17	6	And in fresh numbers number all your graces,
17	7	The age to come would say 'This Poet lies:
17	8	Such heavenly touches ne'er touch'd earthly faces.'
17	9	So should my papers (yellow'd with their age)
17	10	Be scorn'd like old men of less truth than tongue,
17	11	And your true rights be term'd a Poet's rage
17	12	And stretched metre of an Antique song:
17	13	But were some child of yours alive that time,
17	14	You should live twice; in it and in my rhyme.

This sonnet rises to new levels in describing Southampton, saying that the true description of his qualities ("your most high deserts"), if captured in the sonnets, will scarcely be believed in ages to come. Lines 3-4 say that even this description will not come close to capturing his true qualities, being "as a tomb" hiding "your life" and not showing the half of the reality.

Line 5 refers to the "beauty of your eyes," certainly the same "beauty" (that is, bloodline) that we have already discussed. Lines 6-8 say that if additional sonnets listed all of Southampton's graces, future ages would say they were lies, that such heavenly perfection could never exist in a mortal. The third quatrain adds that the sonnets ("my papers") will likely be "scorned" and Southampton's "true rights" will be deemed a literary fiction ("a Poet's rage", the exaggerated rhythm of an "Antique song"). The couplet then reprises for the last time the refrain that Southampton can live on in reality, not just in the sonnets, if only "some child of yours [were] alive that time."

Sonnet 17 completes the "procreate sonnets" series, reaching a crescendo of seemingly exaggerated claims for Southampton's personal qualities (of which his "beauty" is the only one to be enumerated), while repeating the plea to him to have a child in order to pass on these qualities. Yet not one of our commentators finds this excessive praise to be at all noteworthy, strange, or in need of explanation. The question why Oxford praises Southampton with such superlatives cries out to be addressed and answered, or, for Stratfordians, why the commoner Shakspere would write such hyperbolic comments about Southampton, and why his account of them in the sonnets may come to be "scorned" in future.

Line 11 holds the first clue as to what this deeper meaning might be, a clue whose true meaning is again overlooked by our commentators: the reference to Southampton's "true rights." All four commentators agree that "rights" refers to what is "due" the youth: "praise" (Kerrigan and Burrow), "estimation" (Booth) and "what is truly your due" (Duncan-Jones). None tries to explain why the youth deserves such praise, nor from whom it would be due. All four also see a likely or certain pun on "rights" (Line 11), reading it as actually meaning "rites," described as "appropriate ceremonies" (Duncan-Jones), "rituals of worship which you deserve" (Burrow) and "ritual of praise appropriate to you" (Kerrigan). What might constitute a "rite" or "ritual" of praise to an ordinary person, much less to this particular youth, is not specified, and is hard to picture. Why "rights" should even be understood as "praise" is justified by none, nor is the even more improbable pun on "rites," which forces them to concoct alleged "facts not in evidence" about "ceremonies" and "rituals" which nothing in the sonnet remotely suggests.

The word "rights" is above all a legal term, and more so in Shakespeare's time than today. The numerous legal references throughout the sonnets should attune any scholar to the strong likelihood that "true rights" here are *legal* rights. And by calling them "*true*" rights, and specifying that they may not be believed (by being written off as a poet's invention ["rage"]), it is further indicated that they are *rights that are not being recognized.*

Knowing that "beauty" represents bloodline, we can anticipate that the "rights" in question involve Southampton's bloodline. We shall soon comprehend the full nature of these "true rights."

Sonnets 18-19

Sonnet 18 continues the theme of preservation of Southampton in the sonnets, but abruptly abandons the theme that the preferred course is to preserve himself by means of procreation. This sonnet states that Southampton will live on in Oxford's rhyme alone. The last six lines make an astounding assertion in this regard:

18	9	But thy eternal Summer shall not fade
18	10	Nor lose possession of that fair thou owest;
18	11	Nor shall Death brag thou wander'st in his shade,
18	12	When in eternal lines to time thou growest:
18	13	So long as men can breathe or eyes can see,
18	14	So long lives this and this gives life to thee.

In stark contrast to Sonnet 16, Southampton will now become immortal—his summer will never end, his qualities ("that fair") will not fade, Death shall not claim him. The message is stunning: my sonnets will live as long as mankind lives, and will give eternal life to Southampton.

The two themes—the eternal importance of the sonnets, and that Southampton will remain alive in them—compel a conclusion that there is something extremely important about Southampton that has not been stated explicitly. Southampton, and the sonnets themselves, reinforce each other's importance—Southampton is important in ways the world does not know about, except as they learn of them from the sonnets, which in turn makes the sonnets important as the sole imparters of these important truths.

The clear meaning of Sonnet 18 is missed by every one of our commentators. Not one understands it to say that the sonnets will immortalize their subject for eternity; they thereby relieve themselves of the inconvenient necessity of explaining *why* the poet would think his subject is worthy of being so remembered by generations to come.

Instead, we get from Duncan-Jones a recognition of the contrast in message from that in Sonnets 16 and 17, to Sonnet 18's statement that the sonnets "will endure until the end of time," and that their message is "an affirmation of the youth's beauty and virtue." Booth contributes a long exegesis on the possible meanings of "lines" from Line 12, but says nothing about lines 13-14. Kerrigan says of Line 12 that "in time thou grow'st" means that "the young man will flourish as long as *time* stands, waxing *towards* its unknown limit, since his growth through *eternal limits* is also grafted *in* (bound by eternal lines) *to* the root stock of *time*" (emphasis in original). Burrow reads the same phrase as "you become a living part of time....The addressee is like a shoot grafted into time's substance, and continues to live through either the poet's lines or his own bloodlines." These latter two exegeses defy intelligible readings.

The couplet of Sonnet 19 returns to the assertion that the role of the sonnets is to preserve the memory of Southampton, the last such reference until Sonnet 32, under very changed circumstances:

19 13   Yet, do thy worst, old Time: despite thy wrong,
19 14   My love shall in my verse ever live young.

Sonnet 54

Reference is made to the sonnets themselves in Sonnets 32, 38, and 54. Of interest here is Sonnet 54 which, while not returning to Sonnet 18's assertion of the timelessness of the sonnets, does imply that it is now too late for Southampton to procreate, and that the only medium for Southampton to be known to posterity is through the sonnets.

54 1   O, how much more doth beauty beauteous seem
54 2   By that sweet ornament which truth doth give!
54 3   The Rose looks fair, but fairer we it deem
54 4   For that sweet odour which doth in it live.
54 5   The Canker-blooms have full as deep a dye
54 6   As the perfumed tincture of the Roses,
54 7   Hang on such thorns and play as wantonly
54 8   When summer's breath their masked buds discloses:
54 9   But, for their virtue only is their show,
54 10   They live unwoo'd and unrespected fade,
54 11   Die to themselves. Sweet Roses do not so;
54 12   Of their sweet deaths are sweetest odors made:
54 13   And so of you, beauteous and lovely youth,
54 14   When that shall vade, my verse distills your truth.

The commentators understand this poem on one level, and aren't quite so far off base here. The overall metaphor is a comparison between the rose and the canker-bloom. The former has not only bright colors, but also a pleasing odor that can be preserved by distilling it into perfume ("tincture"). The latter ("Canker-blooms" refer either to wild roses [sometimes called "dog roses"], which have very little odor, or poppies, which have no odor but mimic the color of roses) have only the virtue of show, which inevitably fades; when they die, they are gone forever. Roses therefore are more beautiful because of their odor, which can be preserved. The couplet then compares the youth to the rose who, when he fades (or "vades," meaning to pass away), will be "distilled" into the sonnets ("my verse distills your truth") and so preserved. "Rose" also carries as always the connotation of the Tudor rose, emphasized here by being capitalized all three times.

The commentators all interpret Sonnet 54 as saying that the sonnets themselves replace the offspring desired in the first seventeen sonnets, and are as the odor to the rose; but they continue to understand "beauty" only as physical beauty. Burrow has "when your beauty shall pass away my verse will preserve the essence of your truthfulness." Duncan-Jones has "by means of verse your truth is preserved and transmitted to future generations." She continues, saying that in contrast to Sonnets 1 and 5, where procreation can preserve "beauty's rose," here poetry can do so. Both understand that the metaphor of the preserved scent refers to the "poetic distillation" (Duncan-Jones) of the man's "beauty," and also of his "truth" (or "truthfulness" for Burrow). Duncan-Jones adds that the process of preserving the scent of the rose into rose water "is analogous to the poet's artistic preservation of the young man's quintessential substance."

It is curious that when the poet suddenly mentions preserving not the man's "beauty," but his "truth" (a formulation that appears nowhere else), the commentators merely report the fact. Burrow's alternation to "truthfulness" changes the sense entirely, and I think erroneously. Booth glosses a possible meaning for "truth" as used in Line 14: "reality, nature, essence."

Consistent with our reading of sonnets 16-18, the "truth" of Line 14 is clearly the same thing that the "procreate sonnets" seek to preserve in poetry, what we have provisionally identified as knowledge of Southampton's bloodline. Again, the "truth" being transmitted is something more than just the bloodline. It is the truth of who Southampton is.

"Truth" also appears in Line 2, here as the agency that produces "that sweet ornament", the sonnets. "Sweet ornament" refers to the rose's scent, which is then identified as a metaphor for the "verse," the sonnets. So, the use of "truth" in Line 2 is a reference to the poet himself, as the one who "doth give" (produce) the ornament (the sonnets). That "truth" is also part of Oxford's personal motto (see Chapter 18) is surely an intentional self-reference. And just as the scent of roses is made more beautiful by being preserved as "perfumed tincture," so Southampton's essence is made more beautiful by being preserved in the sonnets.

Sonnet 54 picks up where Sonnet 18 leaves off, with neither one referencing procreating as an option. In Sonnet 18, the context is that the option to procreate is off the table, at least for the moment. By Sonnet 54, with Southampton in the Tower facing execution, it is too late to reproduce. All that can be salvaged from this dire situation is to capture Southampton's essence in poetry, in his father's sonnets.

Sonnet 55

Sonnet 55 is another of the sonnets that carries an extraordinary message. In it, Oxford makes an astounding claim for the sonnets and for the coming fame of Southampton—that generations to come will praise Southampton even to the Judgment Day, via the medium of the sonnets—an assertion that traditional analysis fatally chokes on:

55	1	Not marble, nor the gilded monuments
55	2	Of Princes, shall outlive this powerful rhyme;
55	3	But you shall shine more bright in these contents
55	4	Than unswept stone besmear'd with sluttish time.
55	5	When wasteful war shall *Statues* overturn,
55	6	And broils root out the work of masonry,
55	7	Nor Mars his sword nor war's quick fire shall burn
55	8	The living record of your memory.
55	9	'Gainst death and all-oblivious enmity
55	10	Shall you pace forth; your praise shall still find room
55	11	Even in the eyes of all posterity
55	12	That wear this world out to the ending doom.
55	13	So, till the judgment that yourself arise,
55	14	You live in this, and dwell in lover's eyes.

"Hyperbole" barely suffices to describe the claims made for both the sonnets and for Southampton in this sonnet. Though it repeats what has been stated earlier, it goes on to assert that these sonnets will outlive the "gilded monuments of princes" and "statues" destroyed in wars yet to come; the poems will not be destroyed by the sword of war ("Mars") nor by war's "fire." As "the living record of your memory" they will allow the young man to "pace forth" against death; his praise will be celebrated by "all posterity" until the end of time ("out to the ending doom" (Doomsday).

Our commentators agree with the reading that Shakespeare is saying that his sonnets, and the memory and praises of his subject, will endure until the Last Judgment. But not one of them asks *why* he would make such an astounding assertion. It is another testament to the power of a false paradigm that, perhaps imperceptibly, it constrains its adherents not to ask themselves questions that cannot be answered within that paradigm. In fact, this sonnet confirms that there is something extremely important about Southampton and his story, which leads to another theorem:

Sonnet Theorem 18:

There is something transcendent about Southampton and his bloodline (his "beauty" as presented in the "procreate sonnets"), the subject of the sonnet series, which leads Oxford to state that the truth about him will be of interest and import to future ages, as evidenced by his increasingly grandiose claims for the importance of the sonnets and what they reveal about the subject, as most strongly demonstrated in Sonnets 54 and 55.

Chapter 9
Prince Southampton

S onnet 55 is arguably the most anomalous sonnet of all from the perspective of the traditional paradigm. Why would Shakespeare think that the whole world would forever praise Southampton based on what he'd written about him in the sonnets? Lines 10 and 11 can be read as even comparing Southampton to Jesus. Numerous other sonnets echo comparable assertions of the importance of Southampton not only for his time, but for all future generations. What reality could conceivably generate such seemingly outlandish claims for someone who was a member of the upper nobility, but from a recently minted and already tarnished lineage, and who had few accomplishments to his name?

Nothing short of Southampton having royal blood could have warranted Oxford's seemingly inflated claims for the importance of Southampton for all future history. That is, *Southampton had to have been Elizabeth's biological son.* Since we've just established Oxford as Southampton's father, it follows that Southampton must have been Oxford's and Elizabeth's bastard son. Southampton's "beauty" as it appears in the sonnets is his *royal nature,* his *royal Tudor bloodline, Elizabeth's blood* running through his veins. *Such a cause, and such a cause alone, would justify the language employed in Sonnet 55.* And it would readily explain Oxford's abiding concern for Southampton throughout the *Sonnets* (and much else besides).

His royal status was obviously unknown to the general public because Elizabeth refused to publicly acknowledge him as her son, but it had to have been a rather open secret among the upper nobility and related *cognoscenti,* and, as we shall see, documentary literary and related evidence abounds to show exactly that, as putatively unwarranted acclaim and praise greeted Southampton from the moment he was introduced at court, and for several years thereafter.

The only alternative to this interpretation is that Shakespeare was talking through his hat, that his incredible claims for Southampton and the sonnets were just so much fatuous hot air, the bloviated, narcissistic rantings of someone proposing that the shady (if not also illegal) elements of his private romantic life were world-important. One can't have it both ways. Either Shakespeare's claims were grounded in reality, or were flights of extreme fantasy. The latter view makes nonsense of the sonnets and must be rejected. Shakespeare (aka Oxford) had good reasons for his elevated opinion of the importance of Southampton and of his story as told in the sonnets.

The recognition that Southampton had to be Elizabeth's royal bastard son by Oxford confirms that the *Sonnets* are about the forbidden topic of the succession, and concern the highest matters of state. First among the concerns of any top members of the nobility as the 1590s unfolded was the continuation of the Tudor Dynasty, an increasingly urgent matter as Elizabeth had passed beyond child-bearing age without an apparent heir, and refused to address the issue of who would succeed her and whether, and how, her dynasty might persist.

Oxford, as one of the leading lords of the nation, was very deeply invested in the Tudor dynasty—his great-great-grandfather, John de Vere, the 13th Earl of Oxford, had been a crucial supporter of Henry Tudor when he set out to become king a century before, and had led forces that turned the tide of battle against Richard III at the Battle of Bosworth in 1475 as a result of which Henry Tudor was installed as Henry VII. Henry immediately restored the 13th earl to all of his lands and the 13th Earl became one of the leading men at Henry's court. The continuation of the Tudor dynasty would therefore have been of paramount importance to Edward de Vere, the 17th Earl of Oxford. And if Southampton were of royal blood and therefore a potential heir and future king, it is certain that Oxford would make the claims such as those in Sonnet 55—all the more so if Southampton were his own son.

If a true prince existed who could inherit the crown from Elizabeth and carry on the Tudor legacy, but was being denied his royal right because Elizabeth refused to acknowledge him, and if it was a capital crime to discuss the succession, where but disguised in a piece of literature, of poetry (the chosen medium of the time for allegory and allusion where meanings could be apparent to those in the know but deniable if challenged by the authorities), could someone like Oxford stash the truth in a format that he hoped would be transparent to the politically savvy. Oxford was a "Tudor patriot," more loyal to the Tudor brand than the actual Tudor ruler Elizabeth, and it is no stretch to imagine that he felt that if Southampton could never be acknowledged as the rightful king he was by blood, that it mattered to at least preserve knowledge of who he really was for future generations to understand.

Other than Southampton's being royal, I can't come up with any hypothesis that would justify the language of Sonnet 55, that states that knowledge of Southampton will outlive stone monuments and last until Eternity.

A. Conan Doyle's "Sherlock Holmes" character is noted for saying that "when you have eliminated the impossible, whatever remains, no matter how improbable, must be the truth," and for putting it in slightly different words: "Eliminate all other factors, and the one which remains must be the truth." Both versions of the dictum apply to our contention that Southampton had to have been Elizabeth's royal, but unacknowledged, son by Oxford. It is impossible that the poet would have said what he did in Sonnet 55 if the Standard Interpretation were correct. It is impossible that Shakspere could have been Shakespeare. And it is impossible that Shakespeare would have written Sonnet 55, and several others with a similar message, unless they conveyed something extremely important about Southampton and of consequence for England. That Southampton must have been royal is what remains after the above impossibles have been eliminated.

With this discovery, the vista glimpsed with the revelation that Sonnets 27-106 are "prison sonnets" now expands to reveal a new panorama laden with possibilities to finally unravel the meaning of all the sonnets. If Oxford is not only telling us in Sonnet 27 that Southampton is in the Tower, but is also telling us throughout the sonnets that he is Elizabeth's royal bastard son, "Prince Southampton" in fact, even if unacknowledged, almost every enigma we have encountered can suddenly be solved. Once we adopt the new paradigm, our eyes and minds are instantly opened to recognizing in a great many passages an array of additional references throughout the sonnets that confirm that Southampton is of royal blood, passages that could not have been so recognized before.

Royal References in the Sonnets

The moment we see that the "young man" of the sonnets, Southampton, is or might be royal, we can recognize that the sonnets are replete with royal terminology and references, many of which I shall now list. While a modern audience might assume that every one of these can be taken metaphorically, a contemporary audience would hear them differently. As we'll discuss below, Elizabethan England was the "Age of Allusion," where writers used allusions of all kinds to a far greater degree than in later centuries. Terms that suggested royalty would suggest actual royalty to an educated Elizabethan Englishman or woman, and would not be read merely as a metaphor.

The following list is copied without context, merely to demonstrate the frequency with which words that denote or relate to royalty are used in the sonnets. Some of these examples will be discussed in my analysis of specific sonnets. Some of the references are to Southampton himself, while others confirm that the subject matter is the domain of the royal court, and concerns and issues of state and/or monarchs, which is the context for Whittemore's paradigm:

1. "King", "Kingly":

63	6	And all those beauties whereof now he's king
64	6	Advantage on the kingdom of the shore,
70	14	Then thou alone kingdoms of hearts shouldst owe.
87	14	In sleep a king, but waking no such matter.
114	10	And my great mind most kingly drinks it up:
115	6	Creep in 'twixt vows and change decrees of kings,
114	10	And my great mind most kingly drinks it up:

2. "Crown"

37	7	Entitled in thy parts do crowned sit,
60	6	Crawls to maturity, wherewith being crown'd,
69	5	Thy outward thus with outward praise is crown'd;
107	7	Incertainties now crown themselves assured
114	1	Or whether doth my mind, being crown'd with you,
115	12	Crowning the present, doubting of the rest?

3. "Sun"

25	6	But as the marigold at the sun's eye,
33	9	Even so my sun one early morn did shine
33	14	Suns of the world may stain when heaven's sun staineth.
35	3	Clouds and eclipses stain both moon and sun,
76	13	For as the sun is daily new and old,
148	12	The sun itself sees not till heaven clears.

4. "Grace," "Gracious"

7	1	Lo! in the orient when the gracious light
10	11	Be, as thy presence is, gracious and kind,
17	6	And in fresh numbers number all your graces,
28	10	And dost him grace when clouds do blot the heaven:
40	13	Lascivious grace, in whom all ill well shows,
53	13	In all external grace you have some part,
67	2	And with his presence grace impiety,
78	8	And given grace a double majesty.
78	12	And arts with thy sweet graces graced be;
79	2	My verse alone had all thy gentle grace,
94	5	They rightly do inherit heaven's graces
96	2	Some say thy grace is youth and gentle sport;
96	3	Both grace and faults are loved of more and less;
96	4	Thou makest faults graces that to thee resort.
103	12	Than of your graces and your gifts to tell;
132	11	To mourn for me, since mourning doth thee grace,
150	4	And swear that brightness doth not grace the day?
26	10	Points on me graciously with fair aspect
62	5	Methinks no face so gracious is as mine,
79	3	But now my gracious numbers are decay'd

5. "Succession," "Successive," "Succeeding"

2	12	Proving his beauty by succession thine!
19	12	For beauty's pattern to succeeding men.
127	3	But now is black beauty's successive heir,

6. "Monarch"

114	2	Drink up the monarch's plague, this flattery?

7. "Homage"

7	3	Doth homage to his new-appearing sight,

8. "Sovereign"

33	2	Flatter the mountain-tops with sovereign eye,
57	6	Whilst I, my sovereign, watch the clock for you,
126	5	If Nature, sovereign mistress over wrack,
153	8	Against strange maladies a sovereign cure.

9. "Majesty"

| 7 | 4 | Serving with looks his sacred majesty; |
| 78 | 8 | And given grace a double majesty. |

The Age of Allusion

A modern reader would be astounded by the degree to which the relatively tiny community of writers—of poetry, plays, novels and essays—in Elizabethan England employed allusions of all sorts in their writings. Allusions took various forms, but one of the most common was quoting expressions or short passages from other writers, either verbatim or with slight changes, or by using the same or similar words in the same context. Some allusions were to other members of the literary community, or to prominent public or political figures, emphatically including the monarch. Allusions were employed for many reasons, including both praise and satire. Freedom of speech was a concept no one could accuse Elizabeth's England of honoring, so writers who wanted to express ideas that might land them in trouble had to employ allusions to provide deniability of their true meaning. Writers frequently alluded to each others' works, such that an implicit dialogue often took place. Modern scholars who fail to recognize the degree to which literature was used for such extra-literary purposes underestimate or miss altogether the true meaning of much of the literary output of the period.

Poetry, in particular, held a prominent place in public discourse. It was through poems that information was imparted that in later centuries would more commonly be expressed in prose form, such as in essays. Thus it is that all of the introductory material to the First Folio of Shakespeare's plays was in the form of poems (including the two that contain the first allusions that suggested that Shakespeare might have been from Stratford-upon-Avon). Poetry permitted a wide field for the use of metaphor, indirection, and allusion. Often the only source for certain historical information is the nominally "literary" evidence to be extracted from poems, novels and plays.

The Shakespearean scholar implicitly acknowledges the validity of using allusions when it advances (or appears to advance) his or her argument for Shakspere. In the absence of any documentary evidence during his lifetime that pertains to

Shakspere's alleged acting or playwriting career, scholars have latched on to a few allusions in writings of the time, two of which from 1592 are vital to the Stratfordian case. Unfortunately, orthodox scholars ignore a much greater cache of allusions in scores of poems and other works that do not fit into their paradigm.

Deciphering allusions involves literary interpretation, as allusions obviously don't explicitly reference their objects. The two allusions on which the case for Shakspere relies to place him in London as early as 1592, and as an actor (though not as a playwright), are found in an odd three-page screed by the dying writer Robert Greene, appended to the end of a novel called *Greene's Groats-worth of Wit,* registered in September of 1592, seventeen days after Greene had died. The standard interpretation of these two allusions is essential for the Stratfordian proposition; a convincing challenge to it makes the Stratfordian position all but untenable.

The two allusions are a repurposed line from Shakespeare's *Henry VI, Part 3* (a play performed in the early 1590s but not printed until 1623), and an allusion to a "Shake-scene" whom Greene claimed was a danger to three alluded-to but unnamed fellow writers. While the possibility that William Shakespeare might be "Shake-scene" is plausible at first glance, "Shake-scene" is far more likely a reference to the well-known actor and theater manager Edward Alleyn, who fits the description perfectly, including being a "shake-scene" on stage, known for belting out bombastic lines and adding his own words to the parts he played. Since allusion only works when it is recognizable to an audience, Shakspere would already have to have been a well-known actor for this allusion to have been understood to be to him. Even then, it is improbable that Greene would have used a name ("Shake-scene") so transparently suggestive of "Shake-speare" had someone with a name so closely similar to "Shake-scene" been the target. Shakspere (or Shakespeare) was unknown in the London acting scene in any capacity in 1592, hence he couldn't have been "Shake-Scene."

And the play from which the line from *Henry* VI is taken was anonymous at that time, so its use by Greene could not have been an allusion to Shakespeare as its author. The adaptation of this line by Greene is a perfect example of the kind of "borrowing" lines from other's works that was frequently employed at that time.

So, neither allusion can credibly be read as referring to Shakspere (or Shakespeare), which throws out the window the sole items of putative evidence that the Stratford Shakspere was in

London and receiving notice, if not notoriety, as early as 1592.

By contrast with this unfortunate orthodox attempt to use allusion, the sonnets are riddled with allusions that would have been recognizable to a contemporary audience, that all but shout out that the Whittemore interpretation is the correct one. The words listed above that allude to royalty are only one type of such allusions. We will return below to other allusions within the sonnets.

But allusions in *other* works of the time provide powerful confirmation of the Oxfordian thesis, including those suggesting that "Shakespeare" was a pseudonym, that the true author was a nobleman (possibly Oxford), and supporting Whittemore's contention that Southampton was Elizabeth's royal son. I am indebted to Katherine Chiljan (*Shakespeare Suppressed*) who has assembled scores of such allusions and from whose book many of my examples in this section and elsewhere are taken.

On "Shake-speare" as a pseudonym, Chiljan has found more than a dozen allusions to Shakespeare, many of which involve references to "speares" or comparable military instruments, confirming that "Shake-speare" is itself a military allusion and therefore clearly a pseudonym. A number of these also allude to the author as being Oxford, or at least to his being a nobleman who had to disguise his authorship on that account.

Allusions to Southampton being royal, that is, the son of Elizabeth, also abound, primarily in the time period from 1590 to 1593, corresponding to the first years that Southampton was at court. During these years, he received undeserved praise and special honors, which could be explained only were he actually a prince (and that fact were an open secret). We will cover these allusions when we discuss Southampton's early biography in a later chapter.

Within the sonnets themselves, references to Southampton as royal, or kingly, or sovereign, occur in numerous locations, as listed above. The following five references are representative of how Oxford used these royal allusions to state the truth about Southampton.

In Elizabeth's day the word "sovereign" referred to the monarch. This meaning is unmistakable in Sonnet 33:

33 2 Flatter the mountain-tops with sovereign eye,

The image developed in the sonnet is of the sun as Southampton, whose eye that is that of the sovereign.

Sonnet 57 has a more explicit reference:

104

57   6   Whilst I (my sovereign) watch the clock for you,

Oxford here all but swears fealty to Southampton, addressing him as his "sovereign," after opening the sonnet with "Being your slave." Why would the first among equals of all noblemen in England, the Earl of Oxford, address a lesser member of the nobility in this way under any other reading of the sonnets?

At least two of the more than half dozen references to "king" or "kingdom" clearly reference Southampton as "king." Sonnet 63 says that Southampton is "king" of "all those beauties," that is, he is king of his royal (Tudor) blood, and by extension, he is a Tudor king:

63   6   And all those beauties whereof now he's King

The couplet of Sonnet 70 (written after Oxford learned of the reprieve of Southampton's death sentence) is revealing:

70   13   If some suspect of ill mask'd not thy show,
70   14   Then thou alone kingdoms of hearts shouldst owe.

The meaning is that if Southampton hadn't been "suspect" (guilty) of "ill" (the wrongdoing that landed him in the Tower), his "show" (that he would have been visible to all as the royal heir) would not have been masked, in which case the populace would owe him "kingdoms of hearts." That Oxford is saying that Southampton was by rights a future king could hardly be more clear.

Sonnet 87 ends with perhaps the most explicit reference to Southampton's royal blood:

87   13   Thus have I had thee, as a dream doth flatter,
87   14   In sleep a King, but waking no such matter.

The poet deems Southampton a "king" at night, in his dreams, but not upon awakening. It is another way of saying that rSouthampton's royal blood is a secret of which few are aware, but knowledge of which haunts Oxford. He knows that Southampton should be a king, but his knowledge of that fact is like a dream since nobody else knows it.

The critics' failure to make sense of Line 14 is a stunning confirmation of their inability to understand the meanings of key words and phrases. Kerrigan and Burrow don't even recognize that "King" is a reference to the young man. Kerrigan translates the last line as "a dream of wealth and power which, on waking, proves insubstantial, nothing of the kind, a fraud," which is a *non sequitur* from what comes before, and refers to the poet, not the young man. Burrow has "while I was asleep I dreamed I was a king who owned all (sic)" but woke to find it not true, and has Line 13 as "So I have possessed you as in a self-deceptive dream." Booth punts, writing "(1) I am a king; (2) you are a king" and says no more on the use of "King." He gives "possessed" as the meaning of "had" in Line 13, with a suggestion of "possessed sexually." Only Duncan-Jones suggests that the addressee *might* be the young man, "elevated to kingly status...only in the speaker's imagination." She neglects to suggest why the poet would imagine him as a king, here or anywhere in the sonnets. The simple meaning of these two lines as "I had thee as a king in my dream, but not on waking" eludes the others, and the significance of calling him a "King," capitalized for emphasis, eludes all.

Finally, there are a number of allusions, both in Shakespeare's other sonnets, and several other works, that all but proclaim that Elizabeth and Oxford were lovers, and that Southampton was their offspring, which we review at the end of this chapter. The totality of evidence from these allusions vastly overshadows both the quantity and quality of the allusions assembled on behalf of the case for Shakspere, and constitutes further evidence for the hypothesis that Southampton was a royal son of Elizabeth and Oxford.

Motto as Signature

One of the richest sources for allegory was the practice of royalty and the nobility of having personal mottos that were typically written on their coats of arms, and for important members of the nobility these mottos were well known. We will review the mottos of Elizabeth, Oxford and Southampton; allusions to each of

their mottos in a number of sonnets lends further weight to the identification of these individuals as the sole *dramatis personae* of the *Sonnets.*

One of Queen Elizabeth's mottos was in Latin, *Semper Eadem*, translated as "Always the same" or "Ever the same." Her coat of arms bears this motto (as seen above in Figure 5).

Southampton's motto was in French, *Ung par tout, tout par ung*, rendered as "One for all, all for one."

Oxford's motto was in Latin, *Vero Nihil Verius*, translated as "Nothing truer than truth." The family name was de Vere, stemming from the Ver region of Normandy. The motto may have been chosen because of the pun on the family name; Oxford certainly considered "Ver" as standing for "true" or "truth," based on the occurrence of those three letters twice in a three-word motto. "Ver" is the root of the French word for truth, "verité," the Latin "veritas," and the English "veritable." Oxford used "Truth" to refer to himself in Sonnets 14 and 101.

Oxford also appropriated the word "ever" as a sort of signature, making a pun on his name "E. Ver" (E[dward de] Ver[e]). Similarly, he appropriated "never" as "ever's" rhyme and paired opposite.

A dramatic example of the "ever/never" self-reference appears in the epistle added to the second printing of *Troilus and Cressida* in 1609, which, along with *Pericles* appearing in the same year, were the last new Shakespeare plays to appear before *Othello* was printed in 1622 and the First Folio in 1623. The epistle is titled: "A Never Writer to an Ever Reader: News:" When improbable formulations occur, especially in a context such as this, there must be a reason. Reading it as "[From] an E. Ver Writer to an E. Ver Reader" is irresistible once Oxford is understood as the author. The reference to Oxford as the "never writer" could be because he was dead by 1609, and/or because as Oxford, he was not recognized as the writer known as Shakespeare.

In 1598, when the Shakespeare name first appeared in print as the author of a number of the plays, and Oxford was named in print as one of the best writers of comedies—and when Oxford was still very much alive—writer Thomas Marston hailed a great, but unacknowledged, writer, with these lines:

Far fly thy fame
Most, most of me beloved! Whose silent name
One letter bounds. Thy true judicial style
I ever honor; and, if my love beguile
Not much my hopes, then thy unvalued worth

Shall mount fair place, when apes are turned forth

These six lines cry out: "Edward de Vere." The letter "e" "bounds" his [silent] name ("*E*"[dward de Ver]"*e*")—silent, because it is masked by the Shakespeare pseudonym. No other candidate's name fits this description, no other candidate's name could be said to be "silent," much less "beloved" of the author or whose name was so bounded. "Far fly thy fame" characterizes this unnamed author just as Shakespeare's fame was "flying far" that year, with the first publication of six of his plays bearing his name, and the first reference to him in print as a leading playwright. "Thy unvalued worth" has to refer to someone who is accomplished but is not being recognized, to which Marston adds the hint that this situation is caused by people in power, and can only be changed when these "apes are turned forth"—fall from power. Finally, the use in Line 4 of "ever," Oxford's favorite term of self-reference, cannot be coincidental.

This passage illustrates the use of allusion, with allusions to the real Shakespeare, to Edward de Vere, to the fact that his true name was unknown, to the fact that he was unvalued (under his own name) and to the authorities, the "apes" keeping him unknown to the public.

Queen Elizabeth is clearly referenced by allusion to her motto in Line 5 of Sonnet 76:

76   5   Why write I still all one, ever the same,

"Ever the same" is literally her motto, well known to all, and is therefore a virtual signature here. This evidence alone confirms that the sonnets are in significant part about Elizabeth—if Elizabeth is referenced here, in a line that says that the poet is writing the same thing over and over again, then she is present, explicitly or implicitly, in all previous (and likely all succeeding) sonnets.

Southampton's motto "All for One" is also alluded to here in the otherwise awkward locution "why write I still *all one*," (emphasis added), which appears to be an ellipsis for "all one way." A modern reader might downplay the significance of these two phrases, but in the Elizabethan context, where mottos were important and well known, such usages were never accidental.

Line 4 of Sonnet 105 also strongly suggests the mottos of Southampton and Elizabeth:

105   4   To one, of one, still such, and ever so.

"To one, of one," with the repetition of "one," recalls Southampton's motto, while "Ever so" is an adequate translation of *Semper Eadem*, "ever the same," Elizabeth's motto again. This sense is borne out later in this sonnet, with "ever" doing double duty as recalling Oxford.

"Truth," an allusion Oxford used for himself based on his motto, occurs in multiple locations where they are clear allusions to Oxford himself, which will be noted later.

Summing up, clear allusions in a number of sonnets to the mottos of Southampton, Elizabeth and Oxford provide further confirmation that the sonnets are about *these* three personages, not Shakspere, Southampton and an unidentified lady. Above all, if Elizabeth is the woman referenced in a few of the first 126 sonnets, and is the subject of 127-152, the sonnets cannot be remotely related to the Standard Interpretation, as neither Shakspere nor even Oxford could have had Queen Elizabeth as his mistress as the SI's narrative requires, much less that she would have carried on a three-way relationship with Southampton and ended up snaring both of them sexually.

Truth and Beauty

I now come to the most conclusive of all allusions to the relationship between Oxford and Elizabeth, that occur in a pair of sonnets and in a separate collection of poems published in 1601 that includes a short poem by "Shakespeare"—"truth" and "beauty." These two allusions are first paired in Sonnet 14, written as we have determined in 1590. Oxford says (line 11) that if Southampton would only "convert" himself "to store," meaning produce an offspring, then "truth and beauty shall together thrive," whereas if he fails to do so, "Thy end (Southampton's death) is Truth's and Beauty's doom and date" (line 14). These allusions to "Truth" and "Beauty" all but cry out as referring to Oxford and Elizabeth.

"Truth," as we have established, was one of Oxford's self-allusions, derived from his name, his ancestral home in France, and his motto (and probably also from his self-conception as a truth teller in a society awash in lies and secrets). And we have shown that "beauty" refers to the Tudor bloodline, that is, Elizabeth's blood. It is no stretch to recognize that Beauty can mean Queen Elizabeth herself, depending on context. In fact, "Beauty" was one of a raft of superlatives used for Elizabeth, about whom panegyrics were universal. Writers of the time outdid themselves in finding exaggerated praise for every quality that Elizabeth might be said to possess. Good examples of such usage occur in the extended poem *Love's Martyr* by Robert Chester, published in 1601, which included, among others, the following: "beauty that exceeded all beauty on earth," her "princely eyes," her "majestical" appearance, her chastity, her "deep counsels," her eloquence, the "sweet accents of her tongue," and her being a Phoenix, "Earth's beauteous Phoenix."

The message imparted in Sonnet 14 therefore becomes transparent: If Southampton carries on the Tudor lineage by procreating (which means that he is a prince), "Truth" (Oxford) and "Beauty" (Elizabeth) will live on through the extension of the Tudor dynasty ("together thrive"), whereas if he fails to do so, when he dies, so will the Tudor lineage. The import is clear: Southampton is the only person through whom the Tudor Dynasty can continue. (The next chapter explores the rest of the sonnet, and exposes the emptiness of the traditional attempt to understand these two words as meaning "truth" and "beauty" in the ordinary sense, as qualities, not as persons.)

Confirmation that Beauty was understood to refer to Elizabeth comes from a 1599 book of poems about Elizabeth by John Davies one of which, entitled "To the Rose," is a six-line poem where the first letters of each line spell "REGINA," a title referring to Elizabeth. Line 4 refers to her as "Beauty's Rose." Verses addressed to her during a 1602 visit to a nobleman's house also included a reference to her as "Beauty's Rose." (Both references are cited by Chiljan[xxii].) These examples confirm that the second line of Sonnet 1, from 1590, "that thereby beauty's *Rose* might never die" was unambiguously referring to Elizabeth, the Tudor Dynasty, and the issue of the succession, since "Beauty's Rose" was in danger of dying without an heir to carry it on. "Rose" was an unmistakable allusion to the Tudor Dynasty, which had the rose as its symbol. "Beauty's Rose" clearly meant "Elizabeth's Tudor blood."

Thus, from the very outset, the *Sonnets* proclaim that Southampton is a royal prince, Elizabeth his mother, and that the survival of the dynasty depends on his being recognized as the rightful heir when Elizabeth dies. This conclusion cannot be disputed without refusing to accept the allusion to Elizabeth in "Beauty's *Rose*."

Astoundingly, not one of the eight modern scholars cited in this book, who, of all people, should have the greatest ability to grasp how words would be understood in Shakespeare's day, has recognized this allusion. Only Duncan-Jones made any mention that this might have brought to mind the widespread desire that

Elizabeth marry and have a child. She, and all the rest, ascribe nothing but commonplace meanings to "rose" and "beauty." Their refusal to recognize that the phrase "beauty's rose" would instantly bring to mind Queen Elizabeth, and not be understood by a contemporary reader as a metaphor of how a rose is a symbol of beauty in general, is one more testimony to the power of an erroneous paradigm to paralyze analytic thinking.

"Truth" and "beauty" are paired again in Sonnet 101 (discussed in more detail in Chapter 20), and the *cognoscenti,* certainly those at Court, would likely recognize this allusion as well.

In this sonnet (line 3), truth and beauty depend on "my love," who is clearly Southampton. By Whittemore's chronology, this sonnet would have been written in late 1602, well into Southampton's second year in the Tower and at a time when Elizabeth's death was anticipated in the near future. With no chance that Southampton will become king, the poem states that the only hope is to make knowledge of who Southampton was available to future ages via the sonnets, so in that sense the perpetuation of the knowledge of truth (Oxford) and beauty (Elizabeth as Southampton's mother) depend on the knowledge about Southampton surviving the mortal death of Oxford and Elizabeth.

The Phoenix and Turtle

Chester's book, *Love's Martyr,* which contains a short poem by Shakespeare, is extraordinary for several reasons, and reveals vital information of relevance to our story. The full title (as it appeared on the title page) was *Love's Martyr or, Rosalins Complaint. Allegorically shadowing the truth of Love, In the constant Fate of the Phoenix and Turtle,* and its publication in the second half of 1601, just months after the Essex Rebellion, was almost certainly seditious. The book consisted of a long poem by Chester, followed by a section that featured fourteen poems, some by well-known poets, including Shakespeare and Ben Jonson, all on the same theme as Chester's lead poem—the Phoenix and her lover, a Turtledove ("Turtle"). As published, Shakespeare's poem bore no title, and the one given to it in 1807, *The Phoenix and Turtle,* is therefore often used. (Much of what follows is a summary of Chiljan's lengthy presentation and analysis of the content of this poem in *Shakespeare Suppressed.*[xxiii])

The Phoenix was an undisguised allusion to Queen Elizabeth. The phoenix was her personal symbol; a medallion struck in 1574 featured her on one side and a phoenix on the other; and many other items associated her with the phoenix. What Chester's poem says about the Phoenix-Queen is truly astounding.

The title of the book says that the poem "allegorically shadow[s]" the "truth of Love," which will be the love between the phoenix and the turtle dove, making clear that both the phoenix and turtle dove were real people, i.e., it is about Elizabeth and a lover alluded to as the "Turtle Dove." Another title for the book appeared on the first page: "Rosalin's Complaint, metaphorically applied to Dame Nature at a Parliament held (in the high Star-chamber) by the Gods, for the preservation and increase of *Earth's beauteous Phoenix.*" Elizabeth's Court at Westminster Palace is unmistakable as the location where "Parliament" met and where the courtroom named "Star-Chamber" was located. Early in the poem, "Dame Nature" (Rosalin) proceeds to describe the Phoenix as a woman, while the Turtle Dove describes the Phoenix in several places as "rose," "queen," and "sovereignty," ratifying the association of the Phoenix with Elizabeth.

The final line of the second title foreshadows the central theme of the poem, mentioning the "preservation and increase of Earth's beauteous Phoenix." With the Phoenix being Elizabeth, the mention of her "preservation and increase" can only refer to the succession, highly relevant in 1601 in light of her physical decline. But any reference to the succession would have risked running afoul of the authorities, as Elizabeth, backed by Parliament, had years earlier forbade it to be discussed. Since the only way she could be "preserved," much less "increased" after her death was if she had already produced an eligible offspring, this all but shouts that she did, in fact, have a child (now grown). Indeed, the poem concludes by proclaiming that a "new, Princely Phoenix" had arisen to succeed her after her death. The poem therefore proclaims that a "Prince Tudor" existed, ready to succeed her.

The poem has a narrator, "Dame Nature," who fears that the Phoenix will die childless, thus ending the Phoenix's dynasty—reflecting the widespread fear that Elizabeth would die without an heir. Dame Nature, who is also apparently the "Rosalin" of the title (Rosalin is a reference to the Tudor Rose and may also allude to all of Elizabeth's Tudor ancestors, who want the dynasty to continue), is instructed by Jove to take the Phoenix to the island of Paphos to meet her mate, the Turtle Dove. There, they pair up and commit to "sacrifice" their bodies "to revive one name," presumably the Tudor name. The poem thus proclaims that Elizabeth had a consort.

As many who have commented on this poem note, to all but

openly state that the Queen not only had a lover, but a love-child by him, and to discuss the succession and propose that this offspring was a "New Princely Phoenix" who would succeed her on her death, was bold to the point of recklessness. But the poem plunged on to virtually identify the child as Southampton.

The Phoenix then says: "Of my bones must the Princely Phoenix arise," a "Creature" that "shall possess both our authority," again, a description of what an heir would possess. In the final passage, the poem states that at the end, "Another princely Phoenix upright stood...Sprung from the bosom of the Turtle-Dove. Long may the new uprising bird increase...." "Uprising" can only be understood as an allusion to the Essex Rebellion, which nails the "Princely Phoenix" as Southampton, who was a leader of that "uprising." Earlier, the poem had referred to the Essex Rebellion, when the Phoenix complained that "Lady Fortune "did conspire/My downfall" by sending "Envy," the initial "E" most likely referring to Essex. This book was published just months after the Essex Rebellion. To wish Southampton, then languishing in the Tower for his role in it, a long and fecund life was outright treasonable.

The story told, of a phoenix being brought to mate with a turtle dove, is another remarkable feature of both Chester's poem and all the shorter poems contributed by others, because it overturns the traditional story of the phoenix. The bird is normally male; here it is female. A turtle dove is normally female in literature; here, it is male. No previous work of poetry or literature associates a phoenix with a turtle dove. The phoenix is supposed to self-immolate every 500 years and be reborn. Here, it perishes in the fire and is replaced by a new, "princely" phoenix. Such deliberate violation of a well-known trope emphasizes the importance and singularity of what is being said about the actual people who are the subjects of the allusions.

Who is the Turtle Dove? If the allusion was clear to a contemporary audience, that clarity exists no longer. Scholars have sought in vain to discover his identity, some even proposing Essex, though that makes no sense just months after he was beheaded for treason. Some modern scholars, including Colin Burrow, think the Turtle Dove is the people of England, and the new prince James of Scotland, but this makes nonsense out of the notion that both birds self-immolate in order to produce a *new* phoenix. In fact, the field of possible candidates is extremely narrow, limited to anyone who might have had a sexual alliance with Elizabeth and produced an offspring. While Chester's poems do not point a more precise finger, Shakespeare's poem does.

Shakespeare's untitled poem is all about the Phoenix and Turtle Dove's tragic love, which ends in their mutual immolation. Like Chester's, it violates the normal story, which doesn't include a turtle dove, and from which the phoenix emerges anew from the ashes. The main body of the short poem describes a relationship between the phoenix and turtle dove that darts back and forth in tantalizing but obscure ways, playing on words that connote "two" ("twain," "division," "separate") and "one," such as "two distincts, division none," "neither two nor one was called," "Reason...saw division grow together," and "How true a twain /Seemeth this concordant one." One line also makes explicit that the Phoenix is Elizabeth: "and no space was seen/'Twixt this *Turtle* and his Queen." There are also hints that a third party may be involved.

From the standpoint of allusion, the most important feature of the poem is a final section labeled "Threnos," sometimes misconstrued as a separate poem. The word "threnos" is defined as "a lyrical lament over a victim of the catastrophe in a tragedy," which aptly describes the five stanzas that follow, proving that the "threnos" was an integral part of the preceding poem, the label being purely descriptive. The first line of the preceding stanza states that "Reason...made this threne," that is, the "threnos," further confirming that the "Threnos" was part of the single poem. This matters because the linkage between the final stanza preceding it and the content of the "Threnos" reveals the identity of the turtle dove.

The final preceding stanza says that the threne is made "to the phoenix and the dove...as chorus to their tragic scene." The Threnos then commences: "Beauty, truth and rarity,/Grace in all simplicity,/Here enclosed, in cinders lie." The association of the phoenix with beauty and the turtle dove with truth is inescapable. The fourth stanza repeats how truth and beauty are dead, saying "Truth and beauty buried be." This representation of truth and beauty is the same as that in Sonnets 14 and 101, described above. All three poems are by the same author, "Shakespeare," and all three discuss "truth and beauty" as dying or in danger of dying. In the case of the two sonnets, we have already shown truth to be Oxford (and beauty as Elizabeth), so "truth" in the Threnos—the turtle dove—must also be Oxford. Oxford must therefore be the turtle dove in *Love's Martyr* and the other poems in the collection.

The Threnos has not just truth and beauty perishing in cinders, but also "Rarity." Rarity can only be their royal offspring, whom we know to be Southampton. This then becomes a perfect metaphor for the mess that Elizabeth has made of the Tudor lineage, by having a son who can become an heir, but, by not acknowledging him, condemning the Tudor line to go extinct with her death, equivalent to the death of all three of them. The third stanza describes the phoenix and turtle as "leaving no posterity," since "Rarity" was destroyed along with them in the immolation.

Shakespeare's poem conflicts with Chester's (and with several of the others in the collection) by saying there was no surviving posterity, no "new Princely Phoenix" to carry on the lineage. Very little is known about this unique work, so the motivations of Chester and the other poets can only be inferred from their poems. Chester clearly was advocating that Elizabeth ensure that she designate a natural heir, and was claiming that such an heir existed, the "new Princely Phoenix"; he strongly alludes to him as Southampton, the "uprising bird." Shakespeare (Oxford) was clearly despairing, believing that all hope for Southampton to be named was now lost.

This view was reflected in Sonnet 73, which contains an unmistakable allusion to his poem in *Love's Martyr.* Line 4 refers to "Bare ruined choirs where late the sweet birds sang." The allusion compels identifying the "sweet birds" with the phoenix and turtle of his poem. Sonnet 73 would have been written in late March of 1601, right about the time Shakespeare would have been composing the *Phoenix and Turtle* poem, for publication a few months later. "Ruined choirs" in Sonnet 73 echoes the "cinders" of the poem, and "late" indicates the birds are now dead.

What happened to Chester's book, and even exactly when it was put on sale, are not known, but its reception was similar to that for the *Sonnets* eight years later. Given its seditious nature, it would be logical to assume that it was suppressed. Oddly, there is no record of it in the Stationers' Registry. However, no one suffered any consequences from contributing poems to it. The book could not have been a private enterprise by the otherwise obscure Robert Chester. Chester's identity is not even clear, but he was likely a servant in the household of the prominent Welsh nobleman Salusbury, who helped put down the Essex Rebellion and to whom the work is dedicated. Perhaps publishing it under cover of Salusbury was an attempt to protect the work, and its authors, from taint of association with the Essex Rebellion. In any event, it must have had some powerful protectors; given that the story was about Elizabeth and Southampton, and probably Oxford, there is a strong probability that Oxford was behind the entire publication—his role obscured by being merely one among many secondary contributors.

In any event, *"The Phoenix and Turtle* is the final poem by "Shakespeare" published during Oxford's lifetime.

The allusions in Chester's poem, which are echoed in the fourteen accompanying short poems, clearly related to the desire by some persons to see Elizabeth have a Tudor successor. The work asserted that she had a lover by whom she had a child, and that on her death, this successor should emerge as the new sovereign, the "new Princely Phoenix." It can be assumed that these allusions would only have been published were they understandable and credible to an intended audience. That the book exists and was put on sale sometime in the latter half of 1601 proves that there was a widespread belief that the "Virgin Queen" had a living heir who could be named to succeed her, and almost certainly that it was Southampton. The numerous references in the early 1590s to Southampton as a prince (see Chapter 11) may have died out in the intervening years, but certainly people in 1601 remembered who he was, to which recollections *Love's Martyr* alluded.

The Narrative Poems Weigh In

In 1593, *Venus and Adonis* was published, with a dedication to Southampton by "William Shakespeare," establishing him as the author. It was a highly accomplished narrative poem and was an instant hit, and became perhaps the most popular poem in all of England for the next half century, going through at least sixteen reprintings. There can be little doubt that Venus was an allusion to Elizabeth, who was often compared to the classical goddesses Cynthia, Diana and Venus (even though modern critics do not make this association). That this was the contemporary understanding, however, is shown by the comment on *Venus and Adonis* by a purchaser of the poem in 1593, William Reynolds, who wrote that he believed Venus to be an almost transparent allegory about Elizabeth.[xxiv] Venus is portrayed as pursuing Adonis, who kills himself by letting a boar impale him, after which issues forth from his blood a purple flower, representing a child, which at the end of the poem Venus refuses to acknowledge publicly.

That Adonis is Oxford and the child Southampton is thus strongly suggested. If so, the poem might be recounting the period from 1571 to 1573 when Elizabeth was showering favor on Oxford, newly arrived at Court, and quite likely pursuing him. This poem would be the first such to portray Oxford's relationship with Elizabeth. Despite its highly erotic content, the license for it was issued by

Archbishop John Whitgift in his own hand, which Whittemore believes indicates that Elizabeth "ordered special treatment for the book in keeping it free from government censorship."[xxv]

Remarkably, six stanzas scattered in three locations in the poem, in the voice of Venus entreating Adonis to accept her advances, carry the same message as that in Sonnets 1-17, repeating the theme that one's duty is to reproduce, on pain of wasting one's essence ("seeds spring from seeds, and beauty breedeth beauty," "By law of nature thou are bound to breed," "Be prodigal," "posterity,/Which by rights of time thou needs must have," etc.). Although here addressed to Adonis, the message was surely intended for Southampton, echoing that in the early sonnets. If Adonis was not Oxford, these lines make little sense.

Today, this poem is almost exclusively remembered for the one-paragraph dedication in which "Shakespeare" presented the poem to Southampton in highly deferential and self-deprecating terms. Three elements of this dedication are rarely, if ever, commented on. First, it is signed "Your Honors in all duty, William Shakespeare." This is notable in two respects. First, this is the first appearance in print of the name "William Shakespeare." Were he actually Shakspere, or any other previously unknown person using this as a pseudonym, neither the dedication nor the way in which it

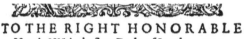

TO THE RIGHT HONORABLE
Henrie VVriothefley, Earle of Southampton,
and Baron of Titchfield.

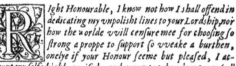

Ight Honourable, I know not how I shall offend in dedicating my vnpolisht lines to your Lordship, nor how the world will cenfure mee for choofing fo ftrong a proppe to fupport fo weake a burthen, onelye if your Honour feeme but pleafed, I account my felfe highly praifed, and vowe to take aduantage of all idle houres, till I haue honoured you with fome grauer labour. But if the firft heire of my inuention proue deformed, I fhall be forie it had fo noble a god-father : and neuer after eare fo barren a land, for feare it yeeld me ftill fo bad a harueft, I leaue it to your Honourable furuey, and your Honor to your hearts content, which I wifh may alwaies anfwere your owne wifh, and the worlds hopefull expectation.

Your Honors in all dutie,

William Shakefpeare.

Figure 6–The 1593 dedication of Venus and Adonis *to Southampton signed by the first appearance of the name "William Shakespeare"*

was published (by the well-known printer Richard Field), nor the personal approval by the Archbishop (implying the approval of the Queen), would make any sense. These factors require that the true author be a well-known personage, almost certainly from the nobility. The second feature is the phrase "Your Honors in all duty." A nobleman did not owe "duty" to another nobleman, but only liege duty to his sovereign, the monarch. If "Shakespeare" were a nobleman, this address is how he would address one of royal blood.

Finally (universally missed by every commentator I have read), is the last line of the dedication, where he asks that Southampton's "heart's content...may always answer your own wish, and the world's hopeful expectation." This clearly echoes the phrase in Line 9 of the first sonnet, telling Southampton he is the "world's fresh ornament." And of itself, what could it mean? If Southampton is royal, the meaning is transparent—he is the hope of "the world" (England) to continue the glorious Tudor Dynasty, something which Oxford hopes will happen in the near future. No conventional critics venture to explain why Shakspere would call the twenty-year-old Southampton "the world's hopeful expectation." That Shakespeare meant this phrase to refer to a monarch-in-waiting, a prince, is confirmed by its appearance in *Henry IV, part 1,* where Henry refers to Prince Hal as "the hope and expectation of thy time," and again in *Part 2,* where Hal describes himself as "the expectation of the world," both instances applying these words to a prince in waiting.

Lucrece, published in 1594, reverses the relationship between the woman and the man, with Tarquin pursuing Lucrece and raping her, producing a child. Whittemore argues that Lucrece is likewise Elizabeth and Tarquin Oxford. If so, it would mean that all three poems ever published by "Shakespeare" during Oxford's lifetime were about the relationship with Elizabeth that produced Southampton. Oxford included another dedication to Southampton in this poem, dedicating himself to "your Lordship...without end," basically saying he was at Southampton's service.

That both narrative poems were effusively dedicated to Southampton further suggests that this was Oxford promoting his son, Prince Southampton, and using the poems to tell those in the know about his royal origin.

(Appendix V includes a discussion by Whittemore of these two poems as allegories of the relationship between Elizabeth and Oxford, as he contends are also *The Phoenix and Turtle,* and finally *Lover's Complaint,* published in 1609 together with the *Sonnets.*)

Prince Southampton

Apart from his sonnet-by-sonnet, line-by-line translation of every sonnet, Whittemore has identified two broad facts that constitute the heart of his new paradigm. The first is the recognition that Sonnets 27-106 represent Southampton's term in the Tower. The second is his demonstration that the sonnets in their entirety are about Oxford, Elizabeth and their bastard son Southampton. These twin discoveries permit reading entirely different meanings into every sonnet, completely overturning conventional understandings of them. Because the second of these contentions is so controversial, in this chapter I have assembled many of the numerous examples from the sonnets and other literary works of the time that indicate that many people at the time knew the truth about Southampton, and wrote about it—allegorically or via allusion, to be sure—confirming the truth of Whittemore's otherwise astounding discovery.

To summarize, evidence from within the sonnets, backed up by allusions in contemporary writings, make highly credible Whittemore's contention that Southampton was Elizabeth's son by Oxford. Chapter 11 will present further evidence that contemporaries recognized Southampton as a prince in writings published between 1590 and 1593.

The notion that Elizabeth had at least one, and possibly several, children, including one by her long-time consort the Earl of Leicester (who turned up in Spain in 1587 claiming to be her son) was widely believed at the time. If Southampton were indeed her son, how the pregnancy could have been disguised, and the switch to have him raised by the 2nd Earl of Southampton carried out, can be readily surmised, as discussed in detail in Chapter 11.

The modern view that Southampton was Oxford's and Elizabeth's son is not original with Whittemore. Beginning in the 1930s, a few Oxfordians came to this conclusion. The history and specific arguments of what has come to be known as the "Prince Tudor" (Southampton would be a Tudor prince were he the son of Elizabeth) theory are beyond the scope of this book (see the bibliography for several books by "PT" Oxfordians). It is enough to say that the "PT" theorists correctly identified the relationship between Elizabeth, Oxford and Southampton, based on a small subset of the evidence in the *Sonnets* (and from the other poems) that Whittemore ultimately amassed in support of his much broader theory of what the *Sonnets* is all about.

However, they never put together the narrative story that ties all the sonnets together, they failed to uncover the historical context of the sonnets, they deciphered only a small portion of the special language Oxford employed to disguise the true meaning of the *Sonnets*, and they did not solve any of the other issues and mysteries surrounding the sonnets. Until the appearance of Whittemore's thesis, holders of this view remained a small minority within the Oxfordian community. (Since Whittemore made his case not only in his books but also in presentations to the Shakespeare Oxford Fellowship, and individually to many members of that premier Oxfordian organization in the United States, roughly 50% of members in several polls have come to accept some or all of Whittemore's reinterpretation of what the sonnets are about, and most importantly that Queen Elizabeth figures as the "dark lady.")

A special note is required on Katherine Chiljan's view. Chiljan has assembled a detailed compilation of relevant literary evidence on many aspects of the authorship issue in her book *Shakespeare Suppressed,* on which I have relied for many of my examples in this chapter. She has also pieced together the likely story of how Shakspere came to be credited with being Shakespeare, and of how the publication of the *Sonnets* in 1609 triggered the decision to propagate this fraud. Part of the story she presents draws heavily on a number of passages from the sonnets and from *The Phoenix and Turtle* to show that Southampton was Elizabeth's royal son. She then demonstrates that Shakespeare, whoever he was, was Southampton's father. Since she acknowledges in her introduction that she has no doubt that Shakespeare was Oxford's pseudonym, even though she does *not* discuss Oxford as being Shakespeare in the body of her book, she clearly places herself in the "Prince Tudor" camp. Interestingly, her book has gotten strong favorable reviews from many Oxfordians, but for the most part, they have remained silent on this part of her thesis, with which they apparently disagree.

However, Chiljan does not directly address Whittemore's thesis. This is a shame, because I believe that Whittemore's thesis only strengthens the powerful case that Chiljan makes. Instead, she presents a view of the sonnets that is flawed, first, in that she appears to think the sonnets are assembled in random order, since she jumps around and assigns assumed dates to some of the sonnets that scramble the chronological ordering. Second, she discerns Elizabeth to be referenced in the first 126 sonnets, and even in Sonnet 127, only to adopt the standard view that the remainder of the "dark lady" sonnets (128-152) are about someone else in Elizabeth's court, a switch that makes no sense.

Chapter 10
Sonnets 1-17 Revisited

W e are finally able to understand the true meaning and purpose of the "Procreate Sonnets," Sonnets 1-17. They urge Southampton to have a child *to ensure the survival and succession of the Tudor dynasty*. Since any overt discussion of the succession to Elizabeth had been declared a capital crime, Oxford could hardly proclaim Southampton to be in the line of succession. He therefore chose the subterfuge of entreating him to ensure that his bloodline would continue beyond himself, while embedding multiple references in these sonnets that the *cognoscenti* would recognize as identifying Southampton as of royal blood. We have seen how the *Sonnets* can now be seen to contain numerous allusions to royalty, and how allusions in external writings including "beauty" as an allusion to Elizabeth, support our interpretation. The true burden of proof is on those who dispute Whittemore's interpretation to show why all of these allusions are invalid.

We shall now review many of the sonnets from 1-17 that we have already discussed (see chapter 6), and several we have not, from our new perspective of seeing Southampton as a royal, if unacknowledged, prince, the son of Elizabeth and Oxford. And we will examine two of the three that immediately followed these first seventeen.

Sonnet 1

We have discussed how the first two lines, which state that "from fairest creatures we desire increase" in order that "beauties *Rose* might never die," refer to Southampton ("fairest creatures"), who must procreate in order that Elizabeth's Tudor Dynasty (aka her blood) will not die out with her death. Line 9's representation of Southampton as a "fresh ornament" can now be understood to refer to him as the newly available royal heir (just arrived at Court), and the "only herald to the gaudy spring" as saying he is the only one with royal blood, who can usher in a new spring for the Tudor lineage. The full expression "the world's fresh ornament" confirms this reading, as the only possible reason for Southampton to be the "*world's*" "fresh ornament" would be if he possessed royal blood and was a potential future monarch, "the world" referring to the people of England, his future subjects. The couplet can now be understood as saying that if Southampton is a glutton by "eating" what is due the world (the continuation of his royal Tudor lineage), and if he does not continue the Tudor line, the world (i.e., England) should be pitied.

Line 12 first introduces a metaphor we have seen in other sonnets, that of "wasting" his lineage by being stingy with it, by storing it within himself. I should note two words that are repeated frequently and often refer to Southampton's royal status: "fair" and "sweet." "From fairest creatures" can now be read as "from the most royal of personages..." (you, Southampton). Line 8's reference to his being "to thy sweet self too cruel" can now be read as "to thy royal self [you are] too cruel."

Sonnet 2

In Sonnet 2, Line 2 becomes "[when time has] dug deep wrinkles in your royal brow," reading "royal" for "beauty's" and "brow" for Line 5 becomes "If you are asked where your royal blood exists," and lines 9-10 "how much more would you be praised if you had passed your royal blood (which is also Elizabeth's) on to a child." Line 12 would now read "Demonstrating your son's blood to be royal since he has succeeded from you."

The word "succession" would now mean the succession from one monarch to another—the meaning that would occur first to any contemporary reader.

If Sonnet 2 was written in 1590, Oxford was then forty years old, and the opening line, "When forty winters..." would be autobiographical. It is hard to explain the use of this phrase by twenty-seven-year-old Shakspere.

Sonnet 4

In Sonnet 4, the couplet's "unused beauty" means the royalty Southampton failed to pass on, that died with him, and the couplet would now mean "Your royal blood, not passed on to anyone, will die with you, ending your (Tudor) dynasty," whereas if "you" had used it (to leave a successor), that successor will manage the royal "estate" you leave behind.

Note here the return of the metaphor of stinginess with his royalty in "beauteous niggard," translated as "royal miser," not "lending" "nature's bequest" (Queen Elizabeth's loan of royalty) that was but lent to him to perpetuate the line, not to use it up on himself. "Profitless usurer" is a marvelous metaphor signifying that he is "lending" to himself, consuming himself (wasting, as indicated in Sonnet 1) by failing to ensure that his royalty passes to the next generation.

Sonnet 5

In Sonnet 5, the metaphor of the distillation of flowers (also used in Sonnet 54 for the sonnets themselves) now refers to the preservation of the royal bloodline. When the flowers (Southampton) lose their external appearance in winter, their "substance," his child, will still be alive and royal ("live sweet"). If this is not done, the Tudor bloodline will be "bereft" and will fade from memory.

Sonnet 6

Sonnet 6 continues the extended metaphor about money, usury and lending. "Treasure thou some place with beauty's treasure ere it be self-killed" now means "Find a woman with whom to produce a royal heir before you kill the royal blood [by dying childless]." "That use is not forbidden usury" means that using your royal blood by passing it on is permitted use, not forbidden —harking back to Sonnet 4's "profitless usurer," who "lends" to himself only, yielding no profit (interest) or royal offspring.

Sonnet 7

Sonnet 7 likens Southampton to the sun, and plays on the pun between "sun" and "son."

7	1	Lo! in the Orient when the gracious light
7	2	Lifts up his burning head, each under eye
7	3	Doth homage to his new-appearing sight,
7	4	Serving with looks his sacred majesty;
7	5	And having climb'd the steep-up heavenly hill,
7	6	Resembling strong youth in his middle age,
7	7	Yet mortal looks adore his beauty still,
7	8	Attending on his golden pilgrimage;
7	9	But when from highmost pitch, with weary car,
7	10	Like feeble age, he reeleth from the day,
7	11	The eyes ('fore duteous) now converted are
7	12	From his low tract and look another way:

7   13   So thou, thyself out-going in thy noon,
7   14   Unlook'd on diest, unless thou get a sonne.

The double metaphor is that of the sun, rising in the east (first quatrain), being overhead at midday (second quatrain), and leaving the sky at nightfall (third quatrain), and of the people, adoring the sun until abandoning it when it finally sets. The final couplet begins with "So thou," indicating that the sun is a metaphor for Southampton, reinforced by "thy self out-going in thy noon" and by a final statement that he will die "unlooked-on" unless he gets "a sonne," an obvious pun on "sun."

Likening Southampton to the sun, we can read "each eye" doing "homage" as referring to the universal loyalty of the population to Southampton as the heir, "serving with looks his sacred majesty." "Sacred majesty" is not a suitable appellation for the sun. It is a virtually undisguised reference to Southampton as his "majesty," the king. "Gracious" is also a term used in reference to royalty, and the statement that every eye ("each under eye") "doth homage" defies any interpretation other than the obvious one—that homage is being rendered to the king, the sovereign.

In the second quatrain, "mortal looks" (the king's subjects) adore his royalty ("beauty"). In the third quatrain, "the eyes" previously "duteous" now no longer look at him, but look for a different successor; that leads to the couplet, where Southampton will be "unlooked-on" unless he has produced a son to replace himself.

The productivity of the royalty hypothesis is amply shown here, and contrasts with the profitless analysis of our commentators. Duncan-Jones' "Even as the sun is gazed on and admired as it rises to its height, but neglected in its setting, so the young man will lose the admiration he now enjoys unless he begets a child," well exemplifies the bankruptcy of their analysis—what admiration does the young man now enjoy, and why he would lose it if he doesn't beget a child, are nowhere addressed.

Sonnet 9

We see that in Sonnet 9, the last four lines return to the notion of the "waste" of "beauty," the failure to pass on the royal bloodline: "your royalty, if you waste it by not using it, can come to an end, and if you keep it unused, you will thereby destroy it." The couplet levels the charge that Southampton will be displaying a high disregard ("no love") for his subjects ("others"), that is, the people of England, if Southampton "commits…such murderous shame…on himself" by not procreating and continuing the royal lineage. Lines 4 and 5 reinforce that it is all England ("the world") that Southampton will betray if he continues pursuing his current course:

9	4	The world will wail thee, like a makeless wife;
9	5	The world will be thy widow and still weep

The people of England deserve their rightful monarch, and will collectively wail should Southampton die childless, leaving the nation and all its inhabitants figuratively "widows."

As with the statements of the importance of the story of Southampton as related in the sonnets in Sonnet 55 and others, so the traditional critics have no explanation for why "the world" would care about the subject of the sonnets, whether he was Southampton or someone else. Why would the world "wail thee," why would it be "thy widow," and why would it "still weep"? Why, returning to Sonnet 1, would "the world" need to be pitied (line 13), and why would Southampton "eat the world's due" if he fails to procreate? Southampton understood as a royal prince makes self-evident why "the world," that is, the people of England, and England as a country, would care about whether he were to maintain the Tudor Dynasty.

Sonnet 10

Sonnet 10 now yields a treasure trove of meaning:

10	1	For shame! deny that thou bear'st love to any,
10	2	Who for thyself art so unprovident.
10	3	Grant, if thou wilt, thou art beloved of many,
10	4	But that thou none lovest is most evident;
10	5	For thou art so possess'd with murderous hate
10	6	That 'gainst thyself thou stick'st not to conspire.
10	7	Seeking that beauteous roof to ruinate
10	8	Which to repair should be thy chief desire.
10	9	O, change thy thought, that I may change my mind!
10	10	Shall hate be fairer lodged than gentle love?
10	11	Be, as thy presence is, gracious and kind,
10	12	Or to thyself at least kind-hearted prove:
10	13	Make thee another self, for love of me,
10	14	That beauty still may live in thine or thee.

The first quatrain is a compact restatement of the argument

being made, that Southampton is selfishly thinking only of himself, and not of the people of whom he is "beloved" ("thou art beloved of many"). This presumably reflected the fact that even at the very young age of seventeen, Southampton was not only being introduced at Court, but was already a Court favorite. The "many" whom Southampton does not love in return at this point, is another reference to the people of England ("the world"). Not one of our commentators glosses "beloved of many."

Such a way of describing Southampton makes no sense if viewed as written by a young, unknown Shakspere praising Southampton just as he starts his career at Court. But under our interpretation, it perfectly sets up the second quatrain, where it is Southampton's royalty that is at issue. Line 7 cries out Southampton's royalty. Even Stratfordians understand that the "roof" that he seeks to "ruinate" refers to his family's "house," so by their reading, it is the "house" of Southampton that is in jeopardy. Understanding that "beauteous" means "royal," the "house" here is actually the House of Tudor. "Which to repair" further confirms this reading, as there would have been no reason to "repair" the Southampton lineage, since with Southampton in the prime of late youth, it was in no present jeopardy, unlike the House of Tudor.

The third quatrain contains further proof, and represents an explicit entreaty from Oxford to Southampton to change his mind: "O, change thy thought…." "Gentle love" is the "gentle" love of a sovereign for his subjects, harking back to the many whom he is "beloved" of, but to whom he hasn't been returning his love. "Thy presence" is his royalness, which he is asked to embrace, by being "gracious" and "kind," both appellations often applied to royalty.

The couplet's "for love of me" only makes sense if Oxford is his father; otherwise, why would a man say that another man's child should be conceived for love of him? The final line reiterates that only by having a child can Southampton's royalty be acknowledged in him or his offspring.

It is hard to imagine that when this was written, anyone, at least in Oxford's circle, could have failed to understand its true meaning. Furthermore, it must be that these early sonnets were those referred to in 1598 in Francis Meres' *Palladis Tamia* as Shakespeare's "sugar'd sonnets" being circulated among the author's "private friends."

Sonnet 13

Sonnet 13 reveals its full meaning:

13	1	O, that you were yourself! but, love, you are
13	2	No longer yours than you yourself here live:
13	3	Against this coming end you should prepare,
13	4	And your sweet semblance to some other give.
13	5	So should that beauty which you hold in lease
13	6	Find no determination: then you were
13	7	Yourself again after yourself's decease,
13	8	When your sweet issue your sweet form should bear.
13	9	Who lets so fair a house fall to decay,
13	10	Which husbandry in honour might uphold
13	11	Against the stormy gusts of winter's day
13	12	And barren rage of death's eternal cold?
13	13	O, none but unthrifts! Dear my love, you know
13	14	You had a Father: let your Son say so.

The use of "love" in the first line, the first such use in direct address to Southampton, means more than "son," or "my son." It means "my royal son." The remainder of the sonnet follows the now familiar pattern: Lines 3-4 urge him to prepare against "this coming end" (death) by creating a "semblance" of himself. The second quatrain says that he has merely a "lease" on beauty, which, so long as it isn't allowed to expire ("find(s) no determination"), would continue to exist after his own death, living vicariously through his "issue."

The third quatrain asks what kind of person would permit "so fair a house" to collapse for want of "husbandry" (procreation). "House" again evokes the House of Tudor, with "fair" meaning "royal." The "house" of Southampton was only two generations old at that point, and had recently been in disgrace under Southampton's father, so it could not possibly warrant the phrase "so fair."

Finally, the couplet answers the preceding quatrain with "only the unthrifty would do so," and again directly addresses the subject, "dear my love, you know *you* had a Father; let your *Son* say so" too. Again, in context, "my love" is "my royal son."

This sonnet also introduces the word "sweet," in conjunction with "love," that has a cognate meaning. Line 4 has "your sweet semblance," which he should give to another. Line 8 uses the word twice, "your sweet issue" and "your sweet form." What characteristic do his "semblance" and his "issue" have in common—they both are royal. "Your sweet form" is "your royal form."

There are no more references to Southampton as "my love" in the remainder of the "Procreate Sonnets," the word appearing next in Sonnet 19, Line 14: "My love shall in my verse ever live young." "Love" again should be read as "my royal son."

One of the most consistent allusional practices is Oxford's use of personification. Certain nouns and adjectives are used to refer to persons. This usage confounds the conventional scholar, who flounders around, seeing discourses on abstract topics, such as fashion in wigs, when the words in question really refer to Southampton, Elizabeth, Oxford or concepts such as the Tudor lineage. This is true for words such as "nature," "time," "fair," "kind," and "true," among others.

Oxford employs these words flexibly, the exact meaning determined by context. In analyzing Sonnet 14, for example, we will see "beauty" used to refer to Queen Elizabeth herself, whereas previously it referred to her royal Tudor lineage

We have already discussed the meaning of "Truth and Beauty" in the lines 11 and 14 of Sonnet 14. We now turn to the remainder of the sonnet.

Sonnet 14

14	1	Not from the stars do I my judgment pluck;
14	2	And yet methinks I have astronomy,
14	3	But not to tell of good or evil luck,
14	4	Of plagues, of dearths, or seasons' quality;
14	5	Nor can I fortune to brief minutes tell,
14	6	Pointing to each his thunder, rain and wind,
14	7	Or say with Princes if it shall go well,
14	8	By oft predict that I in heaven find:
14	9	But from thine eyes my knowledge I derive,
14	10	And, constant stars, in them I read such art
14	11	As truth and beauty shall together thrive,
14	12	If from thyself to store thou wouldst convert;
14	13	Or else of thee this I prognosticate:
14	14	Thy end is Truth's and Beauty's doom and date.

The first eight lines are a foil for the third quatrain and the couplet, saying that the poet's knowledge does not enable him to predict the future. Rather (lines 9-14), his knowledge comes "from thine eyes," from which he perceives, as we've already noted, that "truth and beauty" shall thrive together if Southampton will only "convert himself to store" (procreate), and that should he not do so, when he dies that failure will be "Truth's and Beauty's doom and date." We have established that "Truth" is Oxford and "Beauty" Elizabeth (see Chapter 9).

Lacking this understanding, our conventional critics make no effort to make sense of the repeated reference to "truth and beauty." In short, they fail to recognize that there is anything in need of explanation, and by so doing, leave standing a *de facto* interpretation in which the author is saying that truth and beauty, as abstract qualities, will die, meet their "doom and death," if the young man doesn't have a child—an absurd proposition. Booth doesn't recognize that breeding is the import of Line 12, and his gloss merely defines "doom" and "date." Burrow does recognize that Line 12 is about "turn[ing] away from your preoccupation with yourself to breed," but likewise just provides definitions for "truth" and "beauty" in his analysis of Line 14. Kerrigan reads Line 12 as saying "if you would turn from yourself (eschewing narcissism) and breed children," and at least wrestles with what might be meant by Line 14, saying it suggests the young man "purpose[s] the destruction of *truth* and *beauty*," whatever that could really mean. He adds that these last six lines are saying that if the young man does not breed, "those eyes decree destruction to themselves and to the *truth* and *beauty* which in one sense they are."

Duncan-Jones' reading goes the farthest in stating overtly the absurdity that the conventional view is compelled to adopt. While it's not clear whether she sees Line 12 as referring to the young man breeding, her gloss on Line 14 begins: "When you are dead, truth and beauty will also come to an end," echoing Kerrigan's interpretation. She attempts to explain this by asserting that Shakespeare "used the conceit of all beauty being encompassed in the love object frequently," citing two couplets from *Venus and Adonis* and three lines from *The Phoenix and Turtle*. She appears to be saying that Shakespeare is conveying that all beauty is encompassed in the loved one, such that when that person dies, beauty dies with it. In a paragraph introducing the sonnet, Duncan-Jones makes even clearer how she understands these lines:

> The poet claims that he has knowledge of the stars, but not of superstitious astrology, being directed by his friend's eyes, which tell him that in him alone lies responsibility for the future survival of truth and beauty.

None of these interpretations makes sense. This sonnet is clearly saying that "truth" and "beauty" will continue if the young man breeds, so Duncan-Jones' assertion that this is about how the love object "encompasses" "all beauty" is off the mark. Her statement does not even refer to the conditional nature of the prognostication, that only "if" the young man fails to breed will truth and beauty meet their doom. Her introductory note is explicit: the young man ascribes to himself "responsibility for the future survival of truth and beauty," with "truth" and "beauty" clearly understood as abstract qualities.

How could such a reading possibly be the correct one? Why would Shakespeare, or any poet, make such a fatuous and silly assertion?

Even more damning to all conventional interpretations is their failure to tackle a reason for the inclusion here of "truth" where previously only the young man's "beauty" has been mentioned. Not one commentator provides a gloss on what "truth" might mean in this context, nor why it was here added to "beauty," which appears sixteen times through Sonnet 13. Even if the notion were that the young man's "beauty" (however that is understood) will die with him if he fails to procreate, what could the death of "truth" possibly mean? The critics are silent.

Tellingly, not one of the four critics' books maintain the capitalization of "truth" and "beauty" in Line 14, not even Booth, whose edition prints the facsimile of the original opposite his modernized version.

The meaning is clear once the context provided by the new thesis is recognized. This sonnet is an extended discourse on the ability to predict the future, where the first eight lines dismiss conventional methods used to foretell the future, in order to set up the basis for the certitude of the prognostications of lines 11 (that "truth and beauty shall together thrive") under one scenario, or will meet their "doom and date" under the other. The source of this certitude is the "knowledge" the author "derive[s]" from "thine eyes." Knowing what we do, this "knowledge" in which he can "read such art" is surely the knowledge of Southampton's royal blood.

I have dwelled at some length on the conventional reading of this sonnet to highlight the inability of any orthodox scholar to correctly understand allusion, and to recognize that seeing "truth" and "beauty" as *qualities* leads to absurd interpretations, whereas when correctly recognized as personifications—as allusions to specific people—all mystery vanishes. If "Beauty" stands for Elizabeth, and "Truth" for Oxford, these six lines become clear: Oxford's and Elizabeth's royal bloodline will live on ("thrive") in a continued Tudor lineage, if Southampton procreates, but if he doesn't they will die for all history when he dies. It is significant that the poet says it is from Southampton's "eyes" that he derives this knowledge, the eyes clearly being a metaphor for his essence, his royal blood. (This reading is confirmed in Sonnet 17 where he writes "If I could write the beauty of your eyes," which means "If I could write openly about your royal blood.")

Sonnet 17

We can now conclude our analysis of Sonnet 17. Its seemingly exaggerated praise of Southampton—that future ages will think the poet is lying because no one could be so heavenly—now informs us that Southampton is, or should be, king, a position as close to heaven as mortals can achieve. The reference in Line 11 to "true rights" means the "right of inheritance" or "royal succession." The sonnets ("my verse") are like a "tomb which hides your life and shows not half your parts" because they must be written in veiled language, unable to openly state who Southampton really is. The "beauty of your eyes" is his royal blood, his "graces" all the qualities characteristic of a monarch, as well as a reference to how royalty is addressed ("your grace"). His "heavenly touches" would be his royal demeanor, contrasted with non-royal ("earthly") subjects.

Our analysis of Sonnets 1-17 thus confirms the reading we first affirmed in the previous chapter, that Southampton was Elizabeth's and Oxford's royal son. This allows us to state our final theorem:

Sonnet Theorem 19:

Southampton was the royal son of Queen Elizabeth and Oxford, and his royal blood is the subject of Sonnets 1-126. The word "beauty" in Sonnets 1-18 is a coded reference to this royal blood, which must be passed on so that the Tudor dynasty will not die out. The fact of his having royal Tudor blood in direct succession from Elizabeth, making him perhaps the only living person other than Elizabeth to have such blood, and hence that he carried within himself possibly the only means to continue the House of Tudor, explains the poet's far-reaching statement of the importance of Southampton that will make him live on, in the sonnets at least, for ages to come.

Sonnet 19

Though it is not one of the procreate sonnets, Sonnet 19 contains an unambiguous reference to the fact that Southampton is royal, and needs to pass his royalty on to future generations of rulers. The poet tells Time, in reference to Southampton:

19	11	Him in thy course untainted do allow
19	12	For beauty's pattern to succeeding men.

That is, Time, leave Southampton alone long enough to permit him to pass on his royalty ("beauty's pattern") to future monarchs of the Tudor lineage ("succeeding men"). Reflecting their inability to make sense of this couplet, three of our four commentators are mum on what these lines might mean. Only Burrow even tries, and he floats "leave him unsullied as an ideal example of beauty for later ages" as an explanation, which fails on several counts. This misreads the role that "time," a common personification in poetry of the age, plays, which is to bring on death, not to sully someone. It misreads "succeeding," which refers to the royal succession, and correspondingly "men," who are not "later ages," but later Tudor kings. Under our reading, these two lines all but transparently yield a meaning that coheres with the rest of the sonnet, and with all preceding ones.

Aesopian Language

We have seen how central the uses of allegory and allusion were to literature in late 16th century England. We have identified many allusions in the sonnets so far that confirm that they are about Southampton as the royal son of Elizabeth and Oxford. However, Whittemore discovered that the sonnets constituted something distinct from any other poems or literary works, and that merely pointing out allusions was insufficient to their full understanding.

One of Whittemore's crucial breakthroughs was discovering that the *Sonnets* employed a "special language" throughout where words that might normally be understood to mean one thing were actually used to mean something quite different. We have already seen many instances of this, such as, in the early sonnets, the true meaning of "beauty," which we now see refers either to Elizabeth, or to her royal Tudor blood, or "sweet" and "fair," meaning royal. In contrast to the meanings identified by the conventional scholar, the true meanings are part of a consistent story that spans the entire sonnet series.

We now understand why the author had to do this: He had no other means to speak about the subject matter that was his only interest—his royal son Southampton by his union with Queen Elizabeth. Using words with hidden meanings enabled Oxford to speak of his father-son relationship with Southampton, of Elizabeth as Southampton's mother, and Southampton as a royal prince, while appearing to speak of an ordinary love relationship. In addition to "beauty" as Elizabeth, or her royal blood, other common words, such as "time," "love," "true," "kind," "fair," "fresh," and "sweet," also carry hidden meanings in the sonnets that permitted Oxford to safely discuss the situation that he and Southampton faced, and even in some sonnets to rail against the Queen.

The apparent surface meaning of the sonnets and of these key words created ample room for deniability should anyone suspect something and ask questions. The author needed to make sure that their true meanings were not transparent (a task he ultimately succeeded in all too well). Even Oxford would not have been immune from disaster had he directly revealed Southampton's lineage from Elizabeth—something eminently deniable on her part—or publicly promoted him as Elizabeth's successor.

In touting his rhyme as the vehicle that would reveal the truth to future ages, Oxford was relying on there being enough *cognoscenti* who would know the true meaning, and who would ensure that it became public knowledge at some point in the future. Oxford must have expected that the sonnets would be sufficiently transparent for later ages to understand their true meaning. We will see shortly how this fact most likely explains the momentous aftermath of the 1609 publication of the *Sonnets*.

While the mode of writing employed by Oxford is akin to allegory, it is properly called Aesopian. An allegory is a story that is a metaphor for another story that is similar, but about different people. *Pilgrim's Progress* is an allegory, in which the progress of a pilgrim on earth is also the progress of someone saving his soul. The supposed children's stories of C.S. Lewis are extended Christian allegories, where the lion is revealed to be Christ. Chester's *Love's Martyr* is another example of an allegory.

While Aesopian writing uses allegorical techniques in places, the principal method of communicating the intended message is to use words and phrases with alternate, or dual, meanings. This type of writing is called "Aesopian" because the fables attributed to Aesop convey hidden political meanings beneath the apparently harmless moral tales about animals. Aesopian language is often the only means for people in repressive or authoritarian societies to communicate with each other publicly, especially in print, where censors monitor everything that gets published. Russian Marxists in the 19th century employed this technique widely to produce writings that passed muster with Czarist censors, but were actually used to recruit those who would later become the backbone of the Bolshevik Party.

Here is a composite definition of "Aesopian" taken from several dictionaries:

> Employing or having an ambiguous or allegorical meaning, conveying meaning by hint, euphemism, innuendo, or the like, especially a political meaning, usually to elude political censorship, and often intended to convey meaning only to those in a secret movement.

This definition describes everything we have already seen: words, such as "beauty," having an ambiguous, or allegorical meaning; words conveying meaning by hints, such as "misprision" or "adverse party;" and a hidden story which is intensely political. Once the sonnets are understood as written in Aesopian language, the reader can focus on ascertaining what hidden meaning is being imparted in all passages. The shift of focus to this task in turn reveals that the surface story is seriously flawed and lacking in consistency and continuity from sonnet to sonnet—as we have seen when examining the readings of our chosen commentators. Discarding the presumption that the surface story is all there is frees one's mind to bypass the suspension of disbelief that typically occurs among traditional analysts when confronted by these anomalies.

In contrast, the conventional view permits, and perhaps even encourages, its adherents to see each sonnet as more or less *ad hoc*. While groups of two or three sonnets (and in one instance nine), are understood to be linked thematically, the bulk of the sonnets are analyzed one by one and interpreted as if each were best understood as a stand-alone work. This compels the conventional critic to come up with an individualized meaning for every sonnet or small group of sonnets. This critic is not ignorant of the multiple possible meanings of a great many words and phrases, and in the effort to make sense of these poems, great erudition is sometimes shown in researching possible meanings. However, this approach fails to make sense of the sonnet series as a whole. This also explains why the Standard Interpretation is so incoherent: the real narrative has nothing to do with it, so it must be shoehorned into poems where it will never fit properly.

The *Sonnets* are unlike any other literary work I know of. The sonnets were not composed for the purpose of creating great literature. While they are, in fact, superb examples of poetry, the verse was merely the disguise under which Oxford cloaked the real story, that of Southampton and the hope that he might be realized as the next king of England, and of Oxford's travail as he endured the torment of seeing Southampton locked up in the Tower for treason, be condemned to death, and later face a presumed life in confinement. Oxford poured out his personal anguish as he struggled to save Southampton, his feelings of having betrayed both himself and Southampton by the deals he was forced to make, and his ambivalent feelings of liege loyalty toward but also rage at Elizabeth for refusing to acknowledge Southampton as her heir.

From the Oxfordian perspective, it needs to be noted that there is not a single Oxfordian attempt to discuss or explain every sonnet, other than Whittemore's. This is perhaps to be explained by the fact that prior to Whittemore, Oxfordians were little more successful than Stratfordians in understanding the sonnets. The "PT" wing of the Oxfordian party at least got right that Southampton was Elizabeth's and Oxford's son, but that was a far cry from unraveling the meaning of every sonnet. Mainstream Oxfordians are almost as clueless as Stratfordians when it comes to the sonnets, being ahead only by correctly identifying the poet.

Whittemore's discovery of the secret language opened up the ability to read the entire true story, hidden under its Aesopian disguise.

Sonnet 20

Sonnet 20 marvelously illustrates Oxford's use of his secret language to write on two levels at once. It is perhaps the one most often cited in defense of the view that the poet was sexually interested in the young man, and is therefore a linchpin in the case that the relationship was homosexual. I discuss why I believe it does not support that view in Appendix II. Here I wish to show how applying the correct understanding shows this sonnet to be saying very important things about Southampton, while making several apparently sexual innuendos:

| 20 | 1 | A Woman's face with Nature's own hand painted |
| 20 | 2 | Hast thou, the Master Mistress of my passion; |

20	3	A woman's gentle heart, but not acquainted
20	4	With shifting change, as is false women's fashion;
20	5	An eye more bright than theirs, less false in rolling,
20	6	Gilding the object whereupon it gazeth;
20	7	A man in hew, all *Hews* in his controlling,
20	8	Much steals men's eyes and women's souls amazeth.
20	9	And for a woman wert thou first created;
20	10	Till nature, as she wrought thee, fell a-doting,
20	11	And by addition me of thee defeated,
20	12	By adding one thing to my purpose nothing.
20	13	But since she prickt thee out for women's pleasure,
20	14	Mine be thy love and thy love's use their treasure.

All of our four critics confess that making sense of this sonnet is unusually difficult, and all of them provide extensive notes on it.

The most important aid in understanding Sonnet 20 is to dispense with any notion that romantic love or physical attraction is involved, since we now know it isn't. This sonnet, as Sonnets 76 and 105 (to be discussed) point out, is about how the poet says the same thing in every sonnet, merely "dressing old words new," "telling what is told," etc. In that context, we are able to recognize the allusions to Elizabeth which provide the keys to comprehend it.

"A Woman's face" (Line 1), is not a reference to Southampton appearing effeminate, as is generally read, but to Elizabeth, whose "face" (royalty) Southampton inherited as her son. "Nature" is also Elizabeth, who "painted," that is, created, Southampton. "Master Mistress of my passion" has engendered endless discussions on what the phrase could mean. We know that "Master Mistress" refers to Southampton, and, as noted by Booth, "passion" had a possible meaning of "poem" (Booth notes that "poems and speeches that expressed strong feelings often were called passions," and the poems in the *Hekatompathia* are called "passions.") That Southampton was the constant subject of the sonnets strongly supports that this is the meaning here, not romantic love passion, as most critics read it. If so, this states that Southampton is the controller, the sovereign, of the sonnets.

"A woman's gentle heart" would be Elizabeth's royal blood ("gentle" would refer to noble breeding, not "gentleness"), without her fickleness ("shifting change"), presumably describing her continuing refusal to acknowledge Southampton. His eye "gilding the object" it gazes at suggests the action of the sun, another reference to the sovereign. The repetition of 'hew/Hews" is almost certainly a put on an abbreviation of Southampton's name, "He"[nry] "W"[riothesley], and "his controlling" would be his royal power ("controlling" has this connotation in several of the plays). As this sonnet was likely written in 1594, the year of Southampton's twenty-first birthday, Oxford could well be referring to Southampton's reaching an age at which, given his royal pedigree, he will start to command men's attention, and amaze Elizabeth.

"For a woman wert thou first created" can hardly mean that he was created a woman, until nature decided to add a penis and make him a man, as these lines are typically interpreted by those who believe the sonnets are about a homosexual relationship, because he was created "for," not "as," a woman. He was created "for" Elizabeth, to carry on her dynasty, which would imply Oxford being acknowledged as his father, until Elizabeth ("nature") "defeated" (cheated, deprived) him of such acknowledgement, "adding…to my purpose nothing," that is, not acknowledging Southampton, whose "purpose" was to be the royal heir. The surface reading that the third quatrain refers to adding a penis is likely intentional, but has nothing to do with the real meaning. And fatal to the homosexual reading is the fact that if Southampton *were* created a female, to whom a penis was added at the last moment turning her into a man, why would this be "to my purpose nothing" for a homosexual—why wouldn't it be "to my purpose everything," since in this case the poet would now be able to enjoy this beautiful creature *as* a man.

The final line states that, Oxford, will retain his love for Southampton, but that the "use" of "thy love," meaning Southampton's royal blood, will be Elizabeth's ("their") treasure, to be used to perpetuate the Tudor dynasty. While "prickt" can have the obvious sexual meaning, it also meant to select, as Booth notes ("to 'prick' someone is to mark his name with a puncture or a dot"). Line 13 would now mean "since Elizabeth created you for her purposes," a meaning entirely coherent with the rest of the sonnet, and with the thesis of the entire first 126 sonnets.

Chapter 11
Southampton: From Royal Heir to Monument

If Southampton was Queen Elizabeth's son by Oxford, it remains to explore how it could have happened.

This chapter will offer a plausible explanation, and will examine Southampton's biography from his life as a ward of Lord Burghley up through his release from the Tower on April 10, 1603. The following chapter will pick up the story with his release, and trace his rather odd, if not mysterious, twenty-year post-prison career in the court of James I, including its ups and downs that included both high honors and periods of imprisonment. This chapter will draw on new research and hypotheses on the role that the 1609 publication of the *Sonnets* had on his career, and on the fabrication of the myth that Shakspere was Shakespeare, first propagated in print in the 1623 First Folio of Shakespeare's plays. It will end with his mysterious death which most likely was caused by murder, for reasons that point directly to the Whittemore thesis of Southampton's royal blood.

Neither historians nor Shakespeare scholars have recognized the importance of Southampton for the history of England in the last decade of Elizabeth's reign and almost the entirety of James'. That so many circumstances of Southampton's life, from oddities about his birth, as we've reported, to the exaggerated praise received during his early years at Court, to why he would have participated with Essex in an attempted putsch, to why he was spared execution, to why he was released as one of James first acts as king, to why he was periodically re-arrested by James, to the suspicious circumstances of his death, are each and all shrouded in mystery, should have alerted scholars to the likelihood that something about Southampton made him important beyond anything reported in the documentary record. Whittemore's solution to the manifold riddles of the *Sonnets,* combined with hypotheses from Katherine Chiljan on Southampton's post-prison career, provide highly plausible and satisfying solutions that resolve every element of the mystery, and firmly establish why Southampton was so central to English history from 1590 to 1624. No other theory exists that provides solutions to these mysteries. If what is presented here does not provide the solutions, then what better theory can

The "Virgin Queen" a Mother?

The easiest part of the story to imagine is how it came to pass that Oxford was chosen by Elizabeth for a sexual relationship. To imagine that Elizabeth remained celibate for her entire life merely because she never married is an utterly improbable scenario—a woman with the power that she possessed surely desired sexual satisfaction, and had the means to secure it without it becoming public knowledge. Rumors abounded before and after that time that the Queen was no virgin. A number of men were said to have been her lovers, first among them her long-time male confidant Robert Dudley, the Earl of Leicester. For years, Leicester had rooms immediately adjacent to those of the Queen in one of her palaces; for what other possible purpose would that proximity have been established? There were rumors that she had had a son by him, and someone claiming to be that son turned up in the Spanish Court in Madrid in 1587.

Oxford was Elizabeth's favorite at court in 1573, when Southampton would have been conceived, and it requires no stretch of imagination to believe that she did have sexual relations with him, whether or not that led to conception. Oxford had come to Court in 1571, at age twenty-one, when Elizabeth was thirty-seven. As described by Whittemore in *The Monument,* "he quickly rose at Court in the highest personal favor of the Queen, to the point it became Palace gossip that they were as lovers."[xxvi] He remained at Court through the first half of 1574, traveling with the Queen's entourage whenever she went on progress. In 1573, Elizabeth was thirty-nine and, within a few years, she would be toying with the French, leading them to believe she was interested in marrying the Duke d'Alençon, nineteen years her junior, when in reality she had no such intention. That she might have wanted to produce an heir while she still could, so as to keep the Tudor dynasty from dying out with her, is indeed plausible. And as Oxford was her acknowledged favorite at that time, if she had any such intention, it would have been carried out with him.

A curious item of documentary evidence supports the likelihood of this union. As recounted in the Prologue to *The*

Monument,[xxvii] "One young observer of the Court, Gilbert Talbot, writes to his father the Earl of Shrewsbury, 'My Lord of Oxford is lately grown into great credit, for the Queen's Majesty delighteth more in his personage and his dancing and his valiantness than any other.'" Talbot goes on to say that the Lady Burghley, Lord Burghley's wife and mother of Anne, Oxford's wife (but with whom it is likely Oxford had not yet consummated his marriage), "hath declared herself, as it were, jealous," to which the Queen became "offended." Tellingly, he concludes, "At all these love matters my Lord Treasurer (Burghley) winketh, and will not meddle in any way." Burghley's motives for favoring a union of Oxford and Elizabeth at this time are easy to surmise—with the window closing on Elizabeth choosing a royal husband from France, foreclosing the possibility of having a legitimate heir, reasons of state would dictate creating an illegitimate one who could yet be acknowledged in the future to ensure a smooth succession and maintain the Tudor Dynasty.

Figure 7 – One of several portraits of Queen Elizabeth holding a "sieve," symbolic of chastity and virginity (painting by Quentin Metsys the Younger, 1583).

It should also be noted that the cult of Elizabeth's virginity postdated by nearly a decade the time that she and Oxford would have mated. It did not get into full swing until the 1580s, after her childbearing days were behind her. Once established (and Elizabeth herself did not directly promote the cult), this reputation might have deterred her from later acknowledging Southampton, but it would not have been a factor in any decision about having a child in 1573.

Therefore, if the evidence buried in the *Sonnets* points to the necessity that Southampton was Elizabeth's and Oxford's illegitimate son, the absence of historical confirmation that she and Oxford were lovers and indeed had a son is not dispositive against this conclusion. That even one report of rumors suggesting that the Queen and Oxford might have been lovers has found its way through the intervening years to us today is a pretty strong indication that at the time such a liaison would likely have been an open secret.

Hiding a Royal Pregnancy

If Elizabeth became pregnant by Oxford in the late summer of 1573, as our hypothesis calls for, how could such a pregnancy be hidden? Whittemore, Chiljan and others before them have spelled out likely answers to these questions.

The Prologue to *The Monument* provides an excellent summary of Elizabeth's recorded whereabouts and activities in 1573 and 1574, above all during the latter period of what our hypothesis estimates would have been her pregnancy—April-June, 1574. Its timeline of Elizabeth's whereabouts establishes that she was largely absent from sight during the critical months of what would have begun her third trimester.[xxviii] According to Whittemore, Elizabeth attended a public sermon in March of 1574, but remained "in virtual seclusion during [the rest of] March and April, and all of May and June. In terms of any documentary record of her activities, she will not be visible until the beginning of her royal progress in July." Elizabeth did entertain private audiences with a few people during this time, but she was always seated well apart from her audience. In early June, when the French ambassador Fenelon sought an audience on the occasion of the death of King Charles IX of France, she refused to see him—exactly at the moment when our theory suggests she was about to give birth, or possibly had just done so. No one records actually seeing Elizabeth until the first week of July, according to Whittemore.

That she would have been so secluded is hard to explain otherwise, given the momentous developments occurring at that time, including the turmoil in France following the Saint Bartholomew's Day Massacre in 1572, the growing danger of a Spanish invasion, and the negotiations with France over a visit of

Alençon to be followed by a possible marriage to him.

Another unexplained incident occurred in early July of 1574—the sudden departure of Oxford not just from Court, but from England, an unauthorized act that normally would be severely punished. Fears that Oxford was supporting Catholic nobles plotting against Elizabeth proved unfounded; Elizabeth sent someone to fetch him home, and he returned before the end of July. Far from being severely punished, or even reprimanded, he was welcomed back with open arms. If he left out of pique that Elizabeth, having delivered their son, was refusing to publicly recognize him as such, the entire incident is readily explained. Elizabeth, knowing why he left, clearly had no fear that he had treason in his heart, and had no reason to chastise him on his return.

Placing a Changeling Son

Placing a child born in 1574 in the Southampton household likewise would have been easier than it might appear. By a single scrap of documentary evidence, a letter dated October 6, 1573, from the 2nd Earl of Southampton, we are informed that his wife had given birth to "a goodly boy." There is no further record of the child, not even of his name, for more than nine months. There is no record of his baptism, and no record of his having had godparents, a strange occurrence for a noble-born child. Did that child die shortly after his birth? What else could explain the absence of any record of his existence until late July of 1574? On July 26, 1574, the boy's grandmother bequeathed various items to "my Son's son, Harry, Lord Wriothesley" in her will. This date is a month to six weeks after the likely birth of Elizabeth's and Oxford's child, by our theory, and so could very well have been referring to the changeling, not to the baby born on October 6 of the previous year.

Many other circumstances surrounding his birth, and the fortunes of the 2nd Earl of Southampton, are equally mysterious in terms of the known historical record, but would be explained by our theory. The 2nd Earl was in perennial trouble, on suspicion of being a secret Catholic, and was arrested at the end of October 1571 and put into the Tower of London, where he spent the next eighteen months. His son would likely have had to have been conceived in January, some four months before the 2nd Earl's release; he could only be the father if his wife had had a conjugal visit with him in January of 1573, a very unlikely event—Whittemore reports that the Privy Council never allowed such visits. Absent such a visit, the child could not have been his. In this event, anticipating the birth of her child by this time, Elizabeth would have had the perfect solution to her problem of what to do with her baby. Whether the baby born on October 6 died of natural causes or was removed on orders from Elizabeth to be raised by someone else, Elizabeth had ample power to compel the 2nd Earl and his wife to raise her baby in its place. At any time, she could have had the 2nd Earl rearrested, or even executed, for treason.

Were the child Elizabeth's, it wouldn't do for him to be raised into manhood by the Southamptons. Therefore, it appears too convenient that at just about the age that he would start to be groomed for a future as a possible king, his apparent father, the 2nd Earl, was rearrested in 1581, when the boy would have been seven. The 2nd Earl's health declined rapidly after his arrest, despite his having been in excellent health when he went in, so his death in October of that year, strongly suggests foul play, perhaps via torture or poison. The boy was immediately declared a "child of state," that is, a royal ward of Elizabeth's, to be raised in the Burghley household, just as young Oxford had been at age twelve almost twenty years before. Elizabeth was now his legal mother.

Little of this reconstruction can be proved from contemporary documentary evidence, but neither can various elements of that evidence be explained under the accepted narrative. The case that Southampton was Elizabeth's and Oxford's son derives its strength from its ability to unlock a consistent meaning and narrative for the entire corpus of sonnets, and is bolstered by the fact that it also better explains the historical anomalies cited above. The laws of probability defy the likelihood that a conclusion so productive in making sense of sonnet after sonnet that conventional analysis chokes on is false, not to mention that the same conclusion would unravel multiple historical mysteries. And it is confirmed by allusions in the contemporary literary record proving that Southampton's royal parentage was an open secret among at least the literati, and presumably also the nobility, in late Elizabethan England.

End of the "Procreate Sonnets"

With Sonnet 18, the urging to Southampton to procreate that pervades the first seventeen sonnets abruptly vanishes, never to recur. Clearly, something changed dramatically between Sonnets 17 and 18. While Sonnet 18, as well as Sonnet 19, retain and even expand the theme that Southampton will live eternally in the sonnets, the core content, and the tenor, are starkly different from those of the previous seventeen.

Nothing within the sonnets provides a definitive resolution to the mystery. We are left to hypothesize without the ability to be certain of the truth. The first, most likely scenario, is that Oxford had some reason to believe that the Queen would recognize Southampton as her royal son on his turning seventeen and being introduced at Court, and that Sonnets 1-17 were written in anticipation of that occurring. When it did not, Oxford believed (perhaps temporarily) that Southampton might never be acknowledged, which would account for the references in Sonnets 18 and 19 to Southampton living eternally, but only in the sonnets. By Whittemore's hypothesis, Sonnet 18 would have been written when Southampton was eighteen, and Sonnet 19 when he was nineteen.

Another possibility is the conjecture that Sonnets 1-17 were written as part of a campaign by Lord Burghley to get Southampton's acquiescence to marrying Oxford's own daughter, Elizabeth, then fifteen. That Burghley very strongly supported this is well known, though the reasons he so fiercely desired it have never been revealed. Since Burghley surely knew that Southampton was Elizabeth's royal son, the only plausible explanation for Burghley's years-long campaign to pressure Southampton to marry Elizabeth Vere, his granddaughter, was that, when such a marriage would be consummated and a child born, that child, Burghley's great-grandchild, would be a potential future king or queen, making Burghley a progenitor of a future monarch.

Following this scenario, if Burghley desired the match for this reason, with his enormous influence with Elizabeth, he would be able to convince her to acknowledge Southampton as her son. Oxford wrote the first seventeen sonnets in support of the campaign to convince Southampton to marry his daughter Elizabeth. But because he could not publicly advocate such a course, he had to resort to the subterfuge of urging Southampton to be sure to procreate, which would of course imply taking a wife first—that wife being Elizabeth Vere. And since Southampton clearly opposed the match, presumably because he wanted to choose a wife for love rather than succumb to an arranged marriage (as Oxford had done), Oxford eschewed trying to convince Southampton of Elizabeth's excellent qualities, and focused on what was, for him, of paramount importance—getting Southampton recognized as heir apparent, hence the argument, really the only argument, in Sonnets 1-17, that being able to pass on his royal lineage, and save England (and the Tudor dynasty) in the process, was his duty and obligation, to himself, to Queen Elizabeth, to Oxford, and to present and all future generations.

Hence we find Oxford chiding Southampton in Sonnets 1-17, accusing him of selfishly consuming his "beauty," and acting selfishly toward both his own legacy, and the world. Interestingly, a poem, *Narcissus*, written in 1591 by Burghley's secretary, John Clapham and dedicated to Southampton, may have been commissioned by Burghley as part of his effort to get Southampton to marry Elizabeth Vere by suggesting he was being narcissistic in rejecting the union—mirroring the theme reflected in a majority of this group of sonnets.

The significance of turning seventeen is that that was the first age at which Southampton could legally reject the marriage that Burghley had tried to arrange for him. By this reconstruction, Oxford ceased to promote the marriage after Southampton's rejection of it. Burghley continued to push for it for four more years before finally throwing in the towel at Southampton's twenty-first birthday on October 6, 1594, when Southampton ceased to be Burghley's ward, at which point Burghley was reported to have fined Southampton the enormous sum of £5,000.

Had this been the plan, it would appear to have constituted incest, as both Southampton and Elizabeth Vere were Oxford's offspring. While this would have been a difficulty, there are multiple avenues that could have been pursued to get around it. In laying them out, we are admittedly in the realm of speculation, and will doubtless never know for sure how Burghley, or Oxford, were planning to circumvent this roadblock.

One possibility would have been not to identify Oxford as Southampton's father, but to claim that the identity of the father had to remain a state secret. Another would have been to revert to the story that Oxford told for six years, that Elizabeth Vere was not his child. That would require explaining who her father was, with the imputation that Burghley's daughter Anne (by this time deceased) has committed adultery. However, it could also have been claimed that Anne had been raped—bringing up the child of the rapist (whose identity could be claimed was unknown) would not have been considered scandalous. This story would have the added advantage of explaining that Oxford's liaison with Queen Elizabeth was not adulterous because he had not yet consummated his marriage with Anne.

Lord Burghley was immensely influential, and the Elizabethan regime was a virtual dictatorship. Many things are possible in dictatorships when there is a will to make them happen. Perhaps Burghley had some other means to avoid the imputation of incest if Southampton and Elizabeth Vere had married. What is clear is that Sonnets 1-17 all but explicitly identify Southampton as of royal blood, and urge him not to squander it, but to ensure that Tudor Rose blood is passed on to future generations. And a wealth of other literary evidence, as we've seen, points to the same conclusion. Why this theme abruptly ended with Sonnet 17 is a matter for speculation; what Sonnets 1-17 import is not.

Southampton's Meteoric Rise at Court

The marriage fiasco had no discernable immediate impact on what can only be described as a fairy tale from the time Southampton was introduced at Court until at least 1593. The mysteries that surrounded the birth and infancy of Southampton—that the boy born on October 6, 1573, almost certainly couldn't have been his putative father's, that nothing more is heard of or about him for more than nine months, and that no record exists of his baptism or of his having godparents—are only the first of many mysteries about Southampton's life and death. The convenient death of his father in 1581, when he was seven, permitting him to be raised and educated as befitting an heir to the throne in the household of Lord Burghley and as the legal child of the Queen, is another.

The extraordinary favor shown him from day one at Court is yet another mystery. Oxford, scion of the first noble family of England, was introduced to Court at the age of twenty-one; but Southampton, from a far less distinguished family, was introduced there to much fanfare and acclaim at the age of seventeen. He was an immediate Court favorite and remained so for several years. The favor showered on him during these years is all the more surprising, given his problematic parentage—the 2nd Earl had been in and out of favor, suspected at times of being a secret Catholic, or an outright traitor. It was almost certainly this background that gave Burghley the leverage to order him to raise Southampton as his son, in place of the boy born to the Countess, his wife. To the world, then, the 3rd Earl would normally have been seen as handicapped by the fact of who his father was. In any event, the lineage of Southampton was very new, putting it low in the courtly pecking order. Yet, Southampton sailed to prominence as if he had been the 18th Earl of Oxford or of some other prominent house.

Very shortly after his arrival at Court in 1790, he was the subject of a dedication of the poem, already mentioned, entitled *Narcissus* by John Clapham, secretary to Lord Burghley, who described Southampton as "most famous" and "most distinguished"—odd appellations for one so young, so recently arrived at Court and so without accomplishment, but understandable if Burghley sought to help bring a potential future prince of England to public prominence.

A year later, on the occasion of a visit by Queen Elizabeth to Magdalen College, Oxford University, the college chaplain John Sanford composed a Latin poem describing the banquet for the Queen in which he referred to Southampton as *dynasta,* which translates as "prince," followed by the description, "illustrious lineage, whom as a great hero the rich House of Southampton lawfully lays claim to as one of its own." To call him a prince in front of the Queen, were he not one, would be scandalous; to call him a "hero" without having done anything to deserve it is odd; and to describe the house of Southampton as of "illustrious lineage" was absurd, unless Southampton were, in fact, the prince so described. The very word "lawfully" suggests that law, rather than bloodline, made him a Southampton. In fact, the entire locution could be read as saying that Southampton was of an illustrious lineage, namely, the Tudor lineage, that the House of Southampton merely "laid claim to" ("as one of its own"), possibly suggesting that Southampton wasn't originally from that lineage. All of this suggests that his royal birth was known (at least to some) at the time.

Further honors followed, such as his nomination, at the age of nineteen, for Knight of the Garter in 1593. Having done nothing to deserve the honor, he didn't receive it that year, but the nomination itself was, at the least, surprising. Writing verses about the winner of the honor that year, Henry Percy, the well-known author George Peele inserted five lines about Southampton, literally saying he wished Southampton "all fortune" in the eyes of "Cynthia" (the Greek goddess Cynthia was a well-known allusion to Elizabeth), and concluding, "With all the stares (stars) in her (Cynthia-Elizabeth's) fair firmament,/ Bright may he (Southampton) rise and shine immortally," surely hyperbolic appellations unless Southampton were in fact royal.

Confirming how unusual this nomination was, historian Sidney

Lee noted that the nomination "was, at his age, unprecedented outside the circle of the sovereign's kinsmen." (This and many of the following citations are from *The Monument*[xxix].) Southampton biographer Charlotte Stopes concurred, writing, "the fact of his name having been proposed was in itself an honor so great at his early age that it had never before been paid to anyone not of Royal Blood." That Southampton *was* of royal blood evidently never occurred to any scholars.

Other high praise for the young Southampton came in May of 1593, when Barnabe Barnes published a collection of poems including a sonnet to Southampton, referring to his "sacred hands which sacred Muses make their instrument," again, extraordinary words for such a young lord. Also in 1593, George Peele, in his work *the Honour of the Garter,* according to G.P.V. Akrigg, "made a non-existent Earl of Southampton an original member of the Order [of the Garter, referencing Southampton's nomination that year] and then worked in a smooth compliment to 'Gentle Wriothesley, South-Hamptons starre."

Oxford entered the field of praise for Southampton the same year with his dedication of "Shakespeare's" *Venus and Adonis.* Given the immediate popularity of this poem, its dedication to Southampton would have gotten very wide public exposure, the outcome surely hoped for by Oxford. While the poem itself was certainly about Elizabeth as Venus, and almost as certainly about Oxford as Adonis, with Southampton springing as a purple flower from Adonis' blood, as we've seen, it was the dedication that was most important in promoting Southampton to the public. Calling him "the world's hopeful expectation" certainly indicated that there was something special about Southampton that would hardly have been appropriate for anyone not of royal blood, carrying the same signification as Sonnet 1's appellation of "the world's fresh ornament."

The tone and language of the dedication is replicated in a dedication by poet Thomas Nashe of his *The Unfortunate Traveller, or the Life of Jacke Wilton* to Southampton in June of 1593. Foreshadowing "Shakespeare's" second dedication to Southampton a year later, Nashe used the following phrases, among others, to present a picture of worshipfulness of Southampton, the attitude due a monarch: "My reverent *dutiful* thoughts (even from their infancy) have been retainers to your glory," "Incomprehensible is the height of your spirit...", "Of your gracious favor..." and "Your Lordship is the large spreading branch of renown." Such seemingly exaggerated degree of praise and fealty would only be appropriate toward one of royal blood.

Also in 1593, Nashe dedicated a poem to "Lord S.a.," presumably Southampton (two lines in his poem associated "Lord S.a." with the "fair youth" of the sonnets, which also confirms that the first seventeen were in private circulation by 1593), two lines of which strongly alluded to his royal birth: "Pardon, sweet flower of matchless poetry,/And fairest bud the red rose ever bore." "Sweet," "flower," and "bud" were all terms used in the sonnets for Southampton, so "matchless poetry" must refer to the first set of sonnets already circulating privately. "Red rose" was an unmistakable allusion to Queen Elizabeth, which is to say that this line says that she "bore" Southampton.

Oxford returned to literature again in 1594 with his *Lucrece,* with another dedication to Southampton from "Shakespeare," this one more worshipful and subservient than the previous one. Oxford (aka "Shakespeare") states, "The love I dedicate to your Lordship is without end…. What I have done is yours, what I have to do is yours, being part in all I have, devoted yours." From the Earl of Oxford to the Earl of Southampton, such slavish devotion could only be understandable if Southampton were Oxford's sovereign, the royal heir to the throne, which would elevate him to a station above that of Oxford. And it is saying that Oxford is dedicated one hundred percent to helping Southampton—"to help him become king" is the unspoken purpose of the devotion.

There can be little doubt that Oxford's purpose in writing both poems, and dedicating them as he did, was to galvanize interest in Southampton, and to remind those in the know that he was by right a royal heir who deserved to be recognized as such. Such high praise for an untested young lord who was just turning twenty-one is otherwise inexplicable.

As with so much else concerning Southampton, little is known from documentary sources about possible answers to our questions, such as exactly when he began to lose favor, and why. However, it appears that from the literary evidence that 1593 was the high-water mark of his presence at Elizabeth's Court—his star may have already started to wane by 1594. Other than Oxford's dedication of *Lucrece* to him, no other works were dedicated to him after 1594. The record of his presence at Court basically falls silent.

Akrigg identified late 1595 as the date of Southampton's fall from grace: "The year 1595 saw the handsome young Earl of Southampton emerging at the court of Queen Elizabeth as a budding favorite who might well replace Essex."xxx It is unclear on what evidence Akrigg based his evaluation, but, as he documents, Southampton had suddenly fallen out of favor by October of that year. It was reported in September that Southampton was courting Elizabeth Vernon, one of Elizabeth's maids of honor, something that always raised Elizabeth's ire. Elizabeth perennially opposed anyone at Court getting involved with her maids of honor. The same observer reported the next month that "My Lord of Southampton offering to help the Queen to her horse, was refused; he is gone from the Court and not yet returned." I believe that Southampton did not again appear at Court until the day of the Rebellion more than five years later.

If, as seems more likely, his fall from favor began in 1593, it would correspond to the date of his final refusal to marry Elizabeth Vere, the strongly pursued choice of Lord Burghley, as we've seen, and, it can be inferred, of Elizabeth. Given Burghley's persistence over four years in this matter, and his closeness to Elizabeth, it would be a reasonable conjecture that Elizabeth would have recognized Southampton as part of the deal, had Southampton acceded.

The precise role that the early sonnets played in contributing to the elevation of Southampton is not known. The first published mention of any of "Shakespeare's" sonnets appeared in 1598 in *Palladis Tamia,* with the famous reference to the circulation of his "sugar'd sonnets among his private friends." Nashe's apparent familiarity with the language of these early sonnets indicates that they were in circulation by 1593, if not earlier. Since their picture of Southampton is not flattering, whether they would have contributed to helping elevate his public profile cannot be known, unless the fact of his royal birth were so transparent in them that they served to propagate this open secret.

If the first seventeen sonnets corresponded to Southampton's first seventeen years, it appears **that each** of the nine succeeding sonnets was written to correspond with one year of his life. By this reckoning, Sonnet 26 would have corresponded to his being age twenty-six for most of the year 1600 (he would turn twenty-seven on September 6), so Sonnet 27 would normally have been written sometime before his twenty-eighth birthday, until circumstances intervened to disrupt this pattern. This conjecture explains the otherwise odd choice of twenty-six sonnets that precede the climactic change of tone and content that begins with Sonnet 27.

Captain (Cec)Ill vs. Essex-Southampton

The backdrop to Southampton's years at Court was the "elephant in the tent" of Elizabethan politics in the waning years of Elizabeth's reign: the issue of the succession. If Southampton were known to be Elizabeth's son, even if illegitimate, he was *ipso facto* a crucial player in the drama that was being played out. With the collapse of the Spanish Armada in 1589 and the consequent removal of the imminent threat of war with Spain, politics in the last decade of the sixteenth century turned inward, and got ugly. Having failed to produce a lawful heir, Elizabeth also failed to designate a successor, who, had she done so, would almost certainly have had little trouble in taking the reins of power after her death.

Her failure to resolve this issue left different factions free to form around those vying to gain control over the choice of a successor, hence the rivalry between the Cecils and Essex. James VI of Scotland had the strongest claim to the throne by means of consanguinity, but was a Catholic and a foreigner. Plenty of Englishmen would have preferred an Englishman, and a Protestant. There was also the ever-present danger of a Catholic uprising with its prospect of civil war.

So, behind the scenes, starting just about the time that Southampton arrived at Court, a fierce political fight was joined between two factions. One, headed by Burghley and his son Robert Cecil, had the inside track. Robert Cecil had taken control of Elizabeth's secret service after the death of Francis Walsingham in 1589. The elder Cecil, Lord Burghley, continued to have Elizabeth's trust and ear as her very long-serving personal secretary and Lord Treasurer.

Opposed to the Cecils was a loose group that looked to Robert Devereaux, 2nd Earl of Essex, who emerged by at 1590 as highly popular and as a military leader, and who had aspirations to supplant the Cecils. From 1590 to 1596, Elizabeth showered favor on Essex, without diminishing her support for Burghley, in effect playing off both men and their respective supporters against each other. Essex's high-water mark was his successful raid on the Spanish naval city of Cadiz in mid-1596, where he destroyed forty ships and likely averted the sailing of a second armada.

Since Elizabeth had forbidden any discussion about the succession, the fight was driven into the shadows, and the battle was over popularity, and access to and influence over the Queen. Throughout the decade, it appears that Essex won the popularity contest, but the Cecils won control of Elizabeth, which would prove decisive.

For reasons we can only guess at, Southampton had decided early in the decade to throw in his lot with Essex, rejecting not only Lord Burghley's entreaties to marry Oxford's daughter, but an alliance with the powerful Cecil father and son team. His choice was momentous, and ultimately fatal to his prospects.

Southampton sought to (and when given permission by the Queen, did) fight side by side with Essex in military campaigns, and became his right-hand man and a close friend. Since Essex was still in high favor with Elizabeth as of 1596, Southampton's joining him doesn't appear a likely reason for his falling out of favor with her several years earlier, but he clearly had, either because of the Elizabeth Vernon courtship (they eventually got married), or because of his earlier refusal to marry into Burghley's (and Oxford's) family and perhaps thereby be acknowledged as her son.

By the late 1590s Essex and Southampton seem to have concluded that they had no other way to exert influence than to bypass the Cecils and get direct access to Elizabeth; but those efforts were thwarted at every step. Their first setback, likely the decisive one in light of subsequent events, was Elizabeth's appointment of Robert Cecil as her Personal Secretary in mid-1596, succeeding his father in that post, even as Essex was on his victorious mission to Cadiz. It appears that Essex lacked the ability to operate an effective faction at Court. Instead, while he sought further military victories, he found military disaster when deployed against first the Welsh and then the Irish, disobeyed orders from Elizabeth (orders that couldn't have been followed), and made other blunders. Denied permission to have an audience with the Queen, a frustrated Essex barged in on Elizabeth while she was still dressing one time, after which he was not allowed to see her again.

Robert Cecil was undoubtedly the evil genius behind Essex's fall from grace. It is highly likely that Cecil orchestrated the assignment of Essex to the Welsh and Irish campaigns, knowing that the likelihood of success was slim to none, and counting on the almost assured failure of both missions to lower Essex in the eyes of the Queen.

Robert Cecil walked with a limp and was hunchbacked. It appears that he was highly unpopular, but stayed in power first through his father, and later through having gotten Queen Elizabeth's confidence. He knew how to use power. In Sonnet 66, Oxford referred to him as "Captain Ill," making a pun on his name, whose second syllable sounds as "ill." Other allusions to him appear, using the word "crooked," or references to walking with "limping sway.". As modern research has found no basis for thinking that King Richard III was a hunchback, as so famously portrayed in Shakespeare's play, there is good reason to believe that Richard was intended to represent Robert Cecil and that Oxford simply made the character a hunchback to drive home the allusion.

It is impossible to know today what sort of support existed for Essex, either at Court or in the country. There are good reasons to think that he was quite popular, certainly more so than Cecil. Essex thought he was popular enough that when he made his move on Elizabeth's quarters on February 8, 1601, enough of London would rise up behind him to make him unstoppable. His problem was in not understanding that people don't risk everything on a momentary call to rise up.

After the failed rebellion and the execution of Essex, Cecil threw in his lot with James and worked to ensure his accession. His scheming worked. Upon Elizabeth's death on March 24, 1603, James took over peacefully, and Cecil was appointed as his chief counselor, remaining the most powerful man in James' court during the first decade of his reign.

Disaster

There is little mystery surrounding the actual events of February 8, 1601, where Essex and Southampton were out maneuvered by Cecil in their attempts to gain access to the Queen (an excellent article by Dr. Paul Hammer in *Shakespeare Quarterly* in 2008[xxxi] reviews the events of the Rebellion and what the earls' goals may have been, and how Robert Cecil clearly outfoxed them). That they had grossly miscalculated the strength that they would rally is beyond doubt. It is likely that they played right into Cecil's hands. Cecil certainly knew of their plans and made sure that they attempted to carry them out, ensuring their arrest and likely execution, thereby removing the threat from Essex to Cecil's power. Cecil had previously driven Essex to such a point of desperation by preventing him access to the Queen.

So, what did Essex and Southampton intend to demand of Elizabeth had they secured the audience with her that they so desperately sought? The simple fact is that no one knows for sure. Did they simply want to have Cecil removed from power (replaced perhaps by Essex), thus taking control of the succession issue? Did they intend to demand her abdication, and if so, would Essex have become king, or Southampton? Or did they want to force her to acknowledge Southampton as her heir when she died? If Southampton was really her son by Oxford/Shakespeare, the enterprise would appear far less crazy than it otherwise has appeared to history. Unless Essex himself had a similar claim (some believe he might have been an earlier son of Elizabeth by Robert Dudley, the Earl of Leicester), it seems that Southampton must have, since Essex and Southampton could hardly have expected to seize and maintain the monarchy without a strong claim to it by virtue of inherited royal blood.

What, if anything, Oxford did behind the scenes between 1594 and 1601 to continue his campaign to have Elizabeth recognize Southampton as her heir, is also not known. Oxford retired from Court in 1591, the year that Southampton entered it; finding himself in greatly reduced financial circumstances, he had to curtail his previous patronage of numerous writers and playwrights, and largely dropped from public sight. We can infer that he worked hard on polishing, even rewriting, many of his plays, which by the late 1590s were frequently being performed both at Court, where they were favorites of the Queen, and in public theaters. He did continue to receive a £1,000 annual subsidy from Elizabeth until the end of her life, indicating that he stayed in her good graces (James renewed the grant when he became King).

Whether Oxford had advance notice of the intended insurrection is another unknown, but it is known, as mentioned earlier, that the Essex conspirators commissioned a performance the night before the failed action of Shakespeare's *Richard II*, which ends in Richard's abdication to Bolingbroke, the future King Henry IV, a plot line clearly intended to inspire them to feel justified in deposing Elizabeth. Essex's men are reported to have cheered the scene which depicted the deposition. This circumstance is the only clue that suggests that deposing the Queen was their intent.

It is generally believed that this performance included a new scene (4.1.154-318), not included in the then-published 1597 quarto version, that graphically depicted the deposition (the scene did not appear in print until the fourth quarto in 1608). If Oxford had indeed written that scene for this occasion, then he would have been a direct accessory to the rebellion itself. As noted, a suggestion of his complicity appears in Sonnet 35, lines 5-6: "All men make faults, and even I, in this/Authorizing thy trespass with compare...," which says "I authorized your treasonous action by comparing it," presumably to the deposition of Richard II.

As the events transpired, the populace of London did not rise in support of Essex and Southampton. The conspirators, their initial 200 members dwindling by the minute, engaged in a brief skirmish with armed men sent by Cecil to detain them before fleeing by boat back to Essex's house, where, around 10:00 that night, after a second skirmish, they were overpowered, and Essex, Southampton and several dozen others were taken to the Tower.

For Oxford, all hope for the Queen to acknowledge Southampton and proclaim him her heir was now lost. This night, as explained, is memorialized in Sonnet 27, with Oxford in the depths of despair.

The nobles of the land were "summoned" to a "session" at which Essex, Southampton and a number of their top co-conspirators were tried over a two-day period, with conviction a foregone conclusion. Essex claimed that Cecil had been conspiring with the Spanish to give Spain the succession, a charge that has never been verified. Essex was beheaded on February 25, and all expected Southampton to follow shortly thereafter. As we know, he never did.

Southampton's Poem

We have already shown how the sonnets that commence with Sonnet 27 reflect Oxford's day-by-day chronicle of his wrestling with the aftermath of the failed insurrection and his anguish at the trial and inevitable conviction of Southampton for capital treason. They are also clearly missives to Southampton in sonnet form. That they were about, addressed to, and delivered to Southampton is all but proved by the remarkable discovery in 2011 of a 74-line poem written by Southampton to Elizabeth while in the Tower and before his sentence had been reduced to misprision. It is the only known poem by Southampton, and while not of the quality of Shakespeare's sonnets, it shows considerable polish and competence.

More importantly, when compared to the contents of the forty sonnets written between his arrest and March 20, 1601, when he was evidently spared execution, this brief poem is shown to use at least forty significant words that also appear in this set of sonnets in similar contexts. The usage of a few of them in both poems (the sonnets being considered collectively) might be considered coincidence; the occurrence of so many important words in common cannot be. Southampton almost certainly had these sonnets by Oxford/"Shakespeare" in his possession when he composed the poem. The poem is also in iambic pentameter, the same meter used in the sonnets. It is even possible that Oxford might have had a hand in helping him compose the poem, which is a moving plea for Elizabeth to spare his life.

This poem is documentary evidence that the author of the sonnets was in touch with Southampton and was providing him copies of new sonnets as they were written. It is inconceivable that had Shakespeare been Shakspere, he could have had this access, nor is it the least bit likely that he would have wanted such access to a former patron now in such disgrace. The evidence of and in Southampton's poem strongly corroborates that the first forty sonnets were written in the same time frame as his letter—late February to March 20, 1601—and that they were written by Oxford.

A detailed discussion of this poem and the ways it appears connected to the sonnets, written by Hank Whittemore, is provided in Appendix V.

The Monument Is Born

It appears that Oxford made the decision to construct the sonnets as an ordered collection during this time frame: Two sonnets in the post-Sonnet 27 sequence alternately compare the sonnets themselves to the monuments of princes (Sonnet 55) or identify them *as* a "monument" to Southampton (Sonnet 81). We now revisit several sonnets already introduced:

Sonnet 54

Returning to Sonnet 54, written, as Whittemore believes, in early March of 1601, when all still expect Southampton to be executed, we can assume that Oxford/Shakespeare also fears the worst for Southampton, even as he works feverishly behind the scenes to save him.

At this point, realizing that Southampton's royalty will never be acknowledged by Elizabeth (the only one with the power to do so), Oxford is telling Southampton that, when he dies, still "beauteous" (royal) and "lovely" (also royal) but publicly unknown to be so, he would, like the canker-bloom, be lost to the memory of mankind but for the sonnets, through which his "truth," knowledge of his royal blood, will be preserved and made known.

Sonnet 55

By Sonnet 55, which Whittemore surmises was written just one day later, Oxford's tone changes. Perhaps this is when Oxford conceived of his grand project to turn his sonnets into a monument for Southampton. A "monument" was a large tomb built for monarchs or other important people. Sonnet 55 can now be understood as Oxford rationalizing that if he couldn't save Southampton's life, he could memorialize him in a collection of sonnets, which he hoped would be understood correctly, despite having to cloak their true meaning. Here, Oxford states that Southampton will "shine more bright in these contents" (the sonnets) than will the stone monuments of princes; "this powerful rhyme" will outlive such monuments.

The last line ("You live in this [the sonnets], and dwell in lover's eyes") is Oxford's swan song for Southampton if he is put to death: "[After you are executed] you will live in these sonnets, and through them in the eyes of the world."

Sonnet 81

In Sonnet 81, Oxford anticipates his reference to a "monument" in Sonnet 107, stating that "Your monument shall be my gentle verse" which people not even born yet will come to read in ages hence, when all those currently alive are dead.

Doubtless by this time, Oxford, having decided to use the sonnets to permanently preserve the story of Southampton's royalty, conceived of the project not just as a collection of sonnets, but as a symmetrical, highly structured series, just as a stone monument would have a symmetrical structure. This was to be a true monument, albeit in ink on paper rather than in stone. This notion appears to have gestated until Sonnet 67 at the earliest, when Oxford reports Southampton will live. Only after learning this news would the context for shaping the sonnets into a symmetrical monument have existed. If it wasn't a conscious plan before Sonnet 81, crafting the sonnets into the form of a monument was surely intentional thereafter.

Sonnet 107

The full significance of the final two lines of Sonnet 107 can now be fully appreciated: "And thou in this ["this poor rhyme"] shalt find they monument,/when tyrants' crests and tombs of brass are spent." Again, Oxford here openly states that the sonnets will be Southampton's monument that will outlast all the monuments to those who actually became monarchs.

Chapter 12
Southampton Under James I

It is beyond doubt that Henry Wriothesley, the 3rd Earl of Southampton, is the central figure of the sonnets, the *raison d'être* for their creation. But his role bears no relationship to that conventionally assigned to him, of younger lover of the poet who blows hot and cold, and steals the poet's mistress. The flesh and blood Southampton is Oxford/Shakespeare's royal son by Queen Elizabeth, conceived as a "Plan B" which Elizabeth ultimately chose not to adopt. The sonnets alone provide proof of this contention, but it is backed up, as we've shown, by considerable literary evidence that Southampton was understood to be royal. We cannot know how many people at the time knew his real identity, but we can be certain that when he was introduced to Elizabeth's court at age seventeen, he became a factor in Court politics with an importance that exceeds what history has ascribed to him.

Southampton's life, as we've already presented, is filled with unanswered questions and unexplained events. The mysteries started with those listed above about his birth, why he got moved to the Burghley household, why he was a Court sensation at age seventeen, and why he was hailed as a "hero" and a "prince" before he'd done anything to merit such praise. Why the Queen took such a personal interest in him during the early 1590s cries out for an explanation, as does what his intentions were for the Rebellion. We have seen how he was spared execution, released from the Tower by order of James (as one of his very first acts as king), restored to his former title and properties, and even elevated. And as we lay out below, mysteries continued to surround his life from his release in 1603 until his death twenty-one years later.

All of these mysteries are explained by our hypothesis that he was the illegitimate royal son of Oxford and Elizabeth. That is, Whittemore's solution to the riddle of the *Sonnets* is not only the unique key to making sense of all of the sonnets, but it also explains every anomaly in Southampton's real life.

Southampton came of age in the twilight of Elizabeth's reign, when Court politics increasingly revolved around who her successor would be. A son, even if illegitimate, would have a very strong claim. But such a son could not just announce himself as the heir apparent, nor could others announce his existence—only the Queen could have done that. This decision would have been fraught with complications, including how to explain to the world that the "virgin queen" had had a child, whether to identify the father, or even whether to misrepresent who the father was.

While Southampton's stock with Elizabeth was clearly already in decline by 1600, the Essex Rebellion sealed his fate. Most of the sonnets written after the date of this disaster rue what has been lost, and no longer suggest that Southampton has any chance to pass on his royal blood—the theme of the early sonnets. But by our construction, the sonnets to and about Southampton end with the funeral of Elizabeth on April 28, 1603. An illustrious career still awaited Southampton, but of this, even about his first year after captivity which Oxford lived to witness, nothing is chronicled in the *Sonnets*. Its purpose was not to relate Southampton's life *per se*, but to preserve the story, impossible to tell openly, of his royal parentage and claim to be king, a claim that Oxford surely assumed had died for all time with the end of Elizabeth's reign, demarcated by her funeral. (By Whittemore's hypothesis, Sonnets 127-152, in which focus is shifted from Southampton to Elizabeth, relate to the same time period that the prison sonnets do—they do not continue in time past Elizabeth's interment on April 28, 1603.)

James and Southampton

However, after Oxford's death Southampton went on to have an illustrious career in King James I's court. Still, true to form, his life continued to be replete with mysteries. The knowledge that the *Sonnets* uniquely reveal—about Southampton's royal nature, that his father was Oxford, and that Oxford was "Shakespeare,"—continued to be a threat, if not be outright seditious, during James' reign. This fact, unknown to historians and Shakespeare scholars, explains not only the up-and-down nature of Southampton's relationship to James, but also the circumstances of the publication of the First Folio in 1623. Katherine Chiljan has masterfully documented the solution to the mysteries surrounding the 1623 publication of the *First Folio* of Shakespeare's plays, and the origin of the myth that the semi-literate money-grubber from Stratford-upon-Avon, Shakspere, was Shakespeare.[xxxii]

First among these is the very fact of James' release of

Southampton, the quick restoration of his title and property within months of his release, and his appointments to the Order of the Garter and to the captaincy of the Isle of Wight within the year. Before the Rebellion, Essex, with Southampton as his second in command, was the biggest roadblock to James' claim to the throne of England, and with Essex's swift removal from the scene the way was cleared for James. Why would James honor someone who had been a leader of his primary opponent's attempted rebellion slightly more than two years previously? (While it has often been claimed that Essex supported James' claim to the English throne, Chiljan shows conclusively that this was almost certainly not the case.[xxxiii])

Some speculate that Southampton's release was mandated by sealed orders from Queen Elizabeth, which James chose to honor. This theory does not lessen the mystery, since James did much more than just release him. As with so many other episodes during this momentous period of history, historians seem unwilling to ask why would James treat the released Southampton so generously? As we shall see, the relationship was more complicated than such a simple summary would imply. Although Southampton was restored to the nobility, he was given only minor posts for many years. He was also arrested on three occasions, two within a year or so of his release from the Tower, for reasons that history cannot explain. His relationship with James was clearly "complicated," blowing hotter and colder at different times.

Southampton's first arrest occurred barely three months after his release, based on an argument in front of Queen Anne with Lord Grey concerning the Essex Rebellion. The second arrest occurred on June 24, 1604, when he and four others, including two former Essex supporters, were put in the Tower. Southampton was questioned, and his papers were seized. Mysteriously, the incident was not recorded in state papers (or at least not preserved). We only know of it from the reports of two ambassadors, one of whom reported: "James had gone into a complete panic and could not sleep that night even though he had a guard of his Scots posted around his quarters. Presumably to protect his heir, he sent orders to Prince Henry that he must not stir out of his chamber."[xxxiv]

That James felt threatened that night by Southampton and other former Essex supporters cannot be doubted. Chiljan reports that "Historians still do not know the cause," and she offers none either. However, it can hardly be coincidence that June 24, 1604, was the date of Oxford's death. The fact that Southampton and other Essex supporters were arrested on that very night, while James feared a possible attempt on his and his son's life, proves that there remained a very strong connection between Oxford and Southampton.

Perhaps James feared that the death of Oxford, Southampton's mentor and protector, was the signal for Southampton to revive his claim to the throne. It would appear that James' fears were unjustified, as he had Southampton and the others released the next day, something he would hardly have done if he had had evidence to back up his fears.

As documented by Chiljan, the years after 1604 saw Southampton passed over for many posts for which he was qualified, even while he ostensibly remained in high favor in James' Court. The explanation for such a seemingly ambivalent relationship between them is apparent under our theory. We must assume, as we've noted, that support for Essex in 1601 was much stronger than conventionally believed, suggesting that Essex played his hand badly, and might have succeeded had he been able to find a way to harness that support. If so, James would have faced a danger of an attempt by Essex's supporters to remove him and install Southampton as rightful king while announcing Southampton's royal blood.

Under this interpretation, James clearly feared executing Southampton, or locking him up again, because there was no clear evidence to justify such actions, and because that might inflame Southampton's supporters and bring about the very uprising he sought to avoid. But he also feared giving Southampton too much power at Court, hence his relegating Southampton to minor posts until late in the 1610s when Southampton finally joined the Privy Council. James was apparently carrying out the time-honored maxim "Keep your friends close, and your enemies closer."

The Grand *Sonnets* Mystery

Chiljan covers at length the mysteries surrounding the 1609 publication of *Shake-speares Sonnets*.[xxxv] The deafening silence with which the book was received is truly puzzling. Chiljan shows that a significant number of people *did* get hold of it, read the sonnets, and cherished them—but only privately. As with so much else surrounding this book, the non-event of its publication is a huge embarrassment for conventional critics, who cannot explain why, at the putative height of his popularity, "Shakespeare" would publish a new collection of poems that would receive no public notice.

The best explanation is that the book was suppressed by the

authorities as soon as it appeared, an action inexplicable under the Shakspere theory. Multiple items of evidence point to Southampton as the person who had it published, including references in the dedication, and also Southampton's association with the publisher, Thomas Thorpe, both before and after its publication.

Why Southampton chose May of 1609 to publish something that presumably could have been published at any point in the previous five years may never be known. Foreign ambassadors reported that James' popularity, especially among the nobility, had been dropping ever since his coronation, so Southampton might have sensed that James was vulnerable. He had recently been slighted by James, so maybe this was his way of threatening to reveal his royal claim in order to force James to honor him more. He could have counted on the publication to reaffirm his royal status to those who already knew, or he could even have hoped that its publication would serve to revive the Essex movement behind his candidacy for the throne.

Had Southampton had any of these aims, what actually happened could not have been more adverse to his ability to attain them. Chiljan cites evidence that strongly suggests that James and his allies retaliated against all publishers of Shakespeare works, starting with Thorpe, and in subtle ways against Southampton himself. During his August 1609 visit to Southampton's country home, James commanded the city of Southampton to provide him with an armed guard of twenty-four men, considered at the time a strange request—all but signaling that he felt unsafe there. Also, from June 1609 until 1613, no new works were dedicated to Southampton, suggesting that authors stopped seeking his patronage, presumably out of fear.

It hardly seems a coincidence that four months after the *Sonnets* appeared James called for a new parliamentary session, which convened on February 9, 1610, and at which all peers were required to take a new Oath of Allegiance to James recognizing the king's sovereignty, something that would appear superfluous unless he feared that someone (Southampton?) might challenge his legitimacy.

As to the works of Shakespeare, no new editions of either of the still popular poems *Venus and Adonis* and *Lucrece* appeared between 1609 and 1615, which meant that their laudatory dedications to Southampton also did not get republished during this time either. More noteworthy, the publication of new Shakespeare plays ceased in 1609 with the publication of *Troilus and Cressida* and *Pericles,* not to resume for thirteen years. The publication of the former play contains another mystery. The first printing occurred a few months before *Sonnets* was printed; it was followed by a second printing shortly after the *Sonnets* appeared, to which an unsigned letter was appended, titled, strangely, "A Never Writer, to an Ever Reader. News." The "news" was a warning of a coming shortage of new Shakespeare plays caused by the "wills" of "the grand possessors," a warning that proved accurate.

The very locution "grand possessors" strongly suggested that "Shakespeare" (or whoever had used that pseudonym) was no longer alive, and that a group of high noblemen controlled the texts of his plays. Had Shakspere been Shakespeare, it is hard to imagine how he could have lost control of his plays to such a cabal, nor why such a cabal would exist in the first place that would have sought such control. In any case, had Shakspere been Shakespeare, it is hard to imagine that he wouldn't have been publishing his plays himself for profit. The evidence clearly indicates that Shakspere was not involved in publishing any of his plays, roughly half of which had appeared in quarto form by 1609. This fact constitutes another strong item of proof that Shakspere wasn't Shakespeare.

Pembroke and the First Folio

Who were the "grand possessors"? The only reference to their existence was this 1609 epistle. However, it appears that the Herbert brothers, William, the 3rd Earl of Pembroke, and Philip, the Earl of Montgomery, were two of them—perhaps they were the only two. Chiljan presents much evidence of their role, starting with the fact that the two brothers were the driving force behind the preparation of the First Folio of Shakespeare plays that appeared in November of 1623. It contained eighteen plays never printed before, most likely from a trove of plays controlled by the "grand possessors," who ordered all printings of new plays stopped from 1609 until 1623 (*Othello* was printed in 1622, the first new play since 1609).

Pembroke looms large in the remainder of the "Great Shakespeare Mystery." Pembroke was a top favorite with James from his accession, occupying important posts and finally becoming the Lord Chamberlain in December 1615; in that position he controlled the office of the Master of the Revels, which oversaw the publication and performance of plays. On his taking this post, *all reprintings* of Shakespeare plays ceased for over four years, with a single exception (which was clearly done in defiance of an order from Pembroke). It appears he wanted to centralize the Shakespeare legacy in the First Folio, plans for which had likely been made as early as 1615, if not before.

Thus, it is highly likely that, ironically, the very publication of the *Sonnets* in 1609 catalyzed the effort to create an alter-identity for the author of the Shakespeare works, that of "William Shakespeare" of Stratford-on-Avon, which would not only continue to obscure any public knowledge that Oxford was Shakespeare, but bury the ability of anyone to ever uncover the truth of the matter. The same master stroke would prevent any association of Southampton with Oxford or Shakespeare, and hide the true story of Southampton's royalty told in the *Sonnets,* should the publication ever resurface.

The obvious intent of such an effort would have been additional protection against the continuing threat that Southampton represented so long as he lived and so long as there were persons who knew the truth.

How else can the weird features of the *First Folio* be explained? It is clear that Ben Jonson, a rival of "Shakespeare" during the latter's lifetime, was under Pembroke's control by at least by 1615, when Jonson assembled his collected works in a folio edition which almost certainly was the inspiration to do the same with the far more extensive collection of Shakespeare's plays. The Shakespeare Folio contains an odd collection of front matter, including a number of poems that appear to say that the author might have hailed from Stratford-on-Avon without ever saying so explicitly. Jonson had begun in 1615 to create the impression that someone named "Shakespeare" was a flesh-and-blood person who had been an actor in some of his (Jonson's) plays over a decade before that (in 1601).

But perhaps the oddest feature of Shakespeare's First Folio is that it contains none of his poems; Jonson's Folio contained both plays and poetry. This omission confirms an intention to further sever the connection between the real-life Shakespeare and Southampton. Chiljan's meticulous research on this topic provides a convincing reconstruction of how Stratford's petty businessman Shakspere came to be seen as Shakespeare. It makes sense of information that otherwise defies logical explanation. All of it harks back to the fact of Southampton's continued potential threat to the rule of James and his heirs.

Thus, the same explanation that unlocks the mystery of the *Sonnets* also unlocks the multiple mysteries surrounding both the entire life of Southampton, and that of the First Folio and the false ascription of the works of Shakespeare to the semiliterate grain merchant and sometime playhouse investor Shakspere. If Chiljan is correct, the publication of the *Sonnets* in 1609 was the event that set in motion the move to create the myth of the Stratford Shakespeare and bury, it was hoped for all time, the possibility of the true authorship or of Southampton's royal heritage ever coming out.

This reconstruction is Chiljan's alone, so far as I know, and I regard it as a brilliant, highly probably scenario. It explains both the oddities of the First Folio front matter, the reason it was published at all, and the reason and means for pointing to Shakspere of Stratford as Shakespeare

The hoax that Shakspere wrote Shakespeare succeeded for 300 years in obscuring Oxford's authorship, and for almost 400 years in hiding the true meaning of the *Sonnets*. It is high time to recognize that the traditional view of Shakespeare of Stratford-on-Avon is just as much a hoax as the Piltdown man—a deliberate fraud perpetrated, in the case of Shakespeare, for political reasons.

Southampton's Suspicious Death

Southampton finally became a member of the Privy Council in 1619, only to be held under house arrest, not allowed to communicate with anyone, for ten weeks starting on June 15, 1621. Apparently he was suspected of raising discontent in Parliament. According to Chiljan, the Venetian ambassador described Southampton as "a leading nobleman, very popular throughout the country, and is considered here to be almost the only person capable of commanding an army." If so, it is no wonder that James and his top lieutenant, the Duke of Buckingham, were fearful of him. If this report is correct, it would suggest that the remnants of the Essex faction of two decades earlier had maintained themselves throughout James' reign, with Southampton as their unofficial leader, and possibly were growing more numerous, perhaps in response to discontent with the Stuart regime.

In this light, it is highly suspicious that in mid-1624, Southampton was finally granted an army to command in the Netherlands, fighting the Spanish, a position he had sought for many years. His son James accompanied him, only to fall ill and die on November 5. Southampton accompanied his body to the port of Bergen to sail home when he, too, fell ill and died on November 10. His death is highly suspicious, as a servant reported that Southampton was quite well on November 7, and only fell extremely ill immediately upon his physician administering him an enema. Since an enema was a known method of administering poison, the suspicion of foul play is well founded. King James' own physician, George Eglisham, wrote in a pamphlet in 1626 that Buckingham had poisoned King James himself the year before, along with Southampton and three other top nobles, and that others were on his hit list. Eglisham published his pamphlet abroad, but offered to come to England to prove his charges if he were granted safe conduct. In response, the newly throned King Charles suddenly dissolved Parliament, ending any possibility of an inquiry.

Whether or not they can ever be corroborated, Eglisham's charges are credible. Buckingham was a ruthless and unscrupulous operative loyal to Charles, James' son, who yearned to become king sooner rather than later. Charles was such an unpopular ruler that he lost his crown, and his head, to the Puritan Revolution twenty years later. Buckingham was so hated that he was assassinated in 1628. It is plausible that Charles feared that on James' death, Southampton might make his move to be king, and might well succeed given the unpopularity of Charles. With Southampton removed from the scene, one can readily surmise that hastening James' death came naturally.

Conclusion

The intertwined stories of Southampton and Oxford/ Shakespeare comprise a historical reality which historians and English professors have alike gotten wrong, a reality that calls for rewriting the history of England from 1590 to 1626. The publication of the *Sonnets* appears to have triggered the creation of the Stratford man myth that made unraveling the true meaning of the sonnets almost impossible, not to mention its role in helping to bury forever Oxford's true identity. Yet, had the *Sonnets* not been published, we might never have known the true nature of the relationship between Oxford/Shakespeare and Southampton, and Southampton's royal parentage, and even more unfortunately, the First Folio might never have been compiled and published, depriving us of the texts of half of Shakespeare's plays, and of having much less corrupted versions of the others previously published in quarto versions. If so, the irony that the failure of the *Sonnets* to lead to the hoped-for outcome, that of making public the true nature of Southampton and his royal blood, was likely responsible for preserving the full set of Shakespeare plays, is extreme.

Part II: The Prison Sonnets and Beyond

In Part I, we established the context required to understand the *Sonnets:* That the sonnets are all about Southampton, the royal son of Elizabeth, the Queen, and Oxford/Shakespeare, the poet, and center on the tragedy that prevented Southampton from ever becoming king—his role in the Essex Rebellion—and that forced Oxford to renounce any plan to reveal himself as the flesh and blood "Shakespeare." We adopted the method of a forensic investigation, working progressively from the clearest references in various sonnets to ever more obscure ones, with each discovery illuminating the next. A series of nineteen theorems was laid out, intended to document the steps. The complete list of theorems is included as Appendix VI.

In Part II, we apply the new understanding to see how productive it is in helping elucidate the true meaning of the sonnets. We unfold Oxford's mental state, his reactions to what has happened, the fact of his deal with Cecil, his guilt over having to make it, his despair, and his conflicted relationship to Elizabeth. Our purpose in this part is to elucidate the meanings of over half of the sonnets (discussing every sonnet would make the book too long), based on the context we have established. We start with Sonnets 76 and 105, which are strikingly similar and extremely revealing. We will then analyze several sets of eight to ten sonnets from the "Prison Sonnet" series (Sonnets 27-106). Next, we examine the remaining sonnets in three groups: Sonnets 107-126 (a block of twenty sonnets, which Whittemore correlates with the nineteen days from Southampton's release from the Tower on April 10 to the funeral for Queen Elizabeth on April 28, 1603, capped by an "envoy" sonnet). We then discuss Sonnets 127-152, the series of twenty-six so-called "Dark Lady" sonnets (matching the number of sonnets that preceded Southampton's arrest), all focused on Queen Elizabeth; and Sonnets 153-154, the final two, which all commentators agree are tacked on and are distinct in many ways from the rest (with which Whittemore agrees, but with a startling twist that wraps up his book).

167

Chapter 13
"Ever the Same," "Three Themes In One"

We come now to Sonnets 76 and 105, two of the most significant in the entire collection. From our new perspective they open up to an intelligible interpretation that is impossible under the conventional paradigm. In twenty-eight lines, the poet tells us what he is doing, describes his method, confirms his identity as Oxford, and further confirms that the sonnets are all about Oxford, Elizabeth and Southampton.

As we have noted several times, Oxford often makes reference to the sonnets themselves as a single work, not a collection of separate poems. In Sonnets 76 and 105, he goes farther in characterizing all of the sonnets as to substance, and all but explicitly states their nature and purpose.

As we read these two sonnets, the "message in a bottle" that Oxford threw into the ocean of history when he wrote them becomes an open book—a book made intelligible by having the correct context, the right characters and the correct relationship among them for our paradigm.

Sonnet 76: "Ever the Same...Still Telling What Is Told"

76	1	Why is my verse so barren of new pride,
76	2	So far from variation or quick change?
76	3	Why with the time do I not glance aside
76	4	To new-found methods and to compounds strange?
76	5	Why write I still all one, ever the same,
76	6	And keep invention in a noted weed,
76	7	That every word doth almost tell my name,
76	8	Showing their birth and where they did proceed?
76	9	O, know, sweet love, I always write of you,
76	10	And you and love are still my argument;
76	11	So all my best is dressing old words new,
76	12	Spending again what is already spent:

| 76 | 13 | For as the Sun is daily new and old, |
| 76 | 14 | So is my love still telling what is told. |

I am struck by the depth of content this sonnet conveys.

For the majority of the sonnet—nine lines—the poet tells us in multiple ways that *all* of his sonnets are saying the same thing. From the Stratfordian perspective what sense can be made of such repeated assertions? To the contrary, according to their telling, there is tremendous variation in those sonnets, with ups and downs in the supposed relationships and numerous subgroupings of poems that relate to distinct phases of those supposed vagaries. This discrepancy is a glaring anomaly that the Stratfordian camp is unable to resolve, and is one more strong item of evidence against that perspective and in favor of the new paradigm.

Under our interpretation Sonnet 76 is transparent. It says that every sonnet is really about Southampton as the carrier of Tudor blood, and the impending tragedy that he will not be acknowledged by Elizabeth. While the *content* of the sonnets shifts upon Southampton's arrest, shifts again upon his reprieve from execution, and yet again upon his eventual release, and while the *focus* turns from celebrating him as a potential heir to the throne to preserving the memory of his royal birth and rights, the underlying theme stays the same.

The latter point is made clear at the beginning of the third quatrain. Answering the question posed in the first quatrain and restated in Line 5 ("why write I still all one, ever the same"), Line 9 replies that it is because "I always write of you," followed in Line 10 by "you and love are still my argument." Line 10 is the key to understanding this sonnet. (Note also the clear reference to Southampton's and Elizabeth's mottos, "all one" (Southampton's, and "ever the same" (Elizabeth's) respectively.)

To understand it, we first examine the word "argument," which, as early as the 14th century, according to the Online Etymology Dictionary, had a meaning of "statements and reasoning in support of a proposition." This meaning would make no sense under a conventional reading—what would be the "proposition" that would have "statements and reasoning" to support it? But if the proposition were that Southampton had royal blood, then the sonnets would be the "statements" and "reasoning" that support and document this secret truth. This understanding helps us see Line 10 as intending "you and love" to stand for "you and your royal blood," where "love" here means the same thing that "beauty" means in other sonnets. This line would now become "You and your royal blood are [still] the only thing I write about" ("my argument").

Only in this sense could all of the sonnets meaningfully be said to be "barren of new pride," to not vary, to be constantly "dressing old words new." The poet is not talking about superficial differences within the sonnets; he is saying that every one is about Southampton and his royal blood.

This meaning for "argument" is strongly reinforced by the first usage of this word in the sonnets, in Sonnet 38, where the poet says his "Muse" "pour'st into my verse, Thine own sweet argument" (lines 2-3), immediately described as "too excellent for every vulgar paper to rehearse." We have established that "sweet" is another coded word meaning "royal," and "sweet argument" can therefore only mean "the story of your royal blood, of your royal nature." The concluding words of Sonnet 38 ("but thine shall be the praise") refer to what Southampton will receive in ages to come because of what his "Muse" has written in these sonnets—recognition of his having had royal blood.

By the conventional reading, no intelligible meaning for "argument" is adducible in Sonnet 38 or 76.

"Argument" also appears in Sonnet 79 (to be discussed later), where the poet says "thy lovely argument" deserves a "worthier pen," which also supports its meaning as "the reality of your royalty," and in Sonnets 100 and 103, where "subject matter" (that is, his royalty) captures the same sense. Read conventionally, where the "worthier pen" would only be writing of the young man's beauty or other fine qualities, "argument" would have to mean such beauty or other qualities—no such contemporary meaning of "argument" existed.

Paired with "argument" is "invention." The two words appear together in Sonnets 38, 76, 103 and 105. In Sonnet 76, the poet asks in Line 6 why he always writes the same thing "and keep[s] invention in a noted weed." Following the previous five lines that loudly declaim that the sonnets are devoid of variation or change, and that they are "ever the same," "invention" can only refer to this feature of the sonnets—the "invention" is the convention Oxford has adopted of writing about the same thing in every sonnet.

Sonnet 38 supports this reading, saying that it is Southampton who "dost give invention light," meaning that the poet through his "invention" is writing exclusively of "thine own sweet argument," which refers to Southampton's royalty. In Sonnet 103, when the poet appears to be disparaging himself and the quality of the sonnets, he says that Southampton himself "over-goes my blunt invention quite," that is, Southampton's actual royalty greatly surpasses the poet's description of it. In Sonnet 105, "invention" is explicitly explained as the methodology of saying the same thing over and over, merely "varying to other words." Oxford first used the word "invention" in print in the preface to *Venus and Adonis* back in 1593, where he described that long poem as "the first heir of my invention." Some Oxfordians take the word to refer to the first appearance of the Shakespeare pseudonym, but I disagree. "Invention" was used commonly in Shakespeare's day to describe a poet's imagination, his gift for writing. I believe it means his method of focusing on a single matter—Southampton's royalty—and doing so in more than one work, as we have seen.

In the *Venus and Adonis* dedication, the poet said that if this first use of his "invention" should "prove deformed," he would abandon it. Whittemore's analysis of *Venus and Adonis* posits that Venus is Queen Elizabeth, and Adonis is Oxford, so that the *Sonnets* represents an extension of *Venus and Adonis* to include Southampton as a component of the "invention."

Sonnet 76 also provides the clearest statement of Oxford's underlying method, what we have termed his Aesopian language and message, written on two levels, using common words to disguise a second meaning. Having stated that the sonnets are all the same in lines 1-5, he then explains why they may not seem so, when he says in Line 11 that he is "dressing old words new." I read this as revealing that he is taking ordinary ("old") words, words like "beauty," "love," and the other Aesopian words we have discussed, and giving them "new" meanings, in the labor of "spending again what is already spent," that is, retelling the story. Many of these newly dressed "old words" are employed to describe the same concept, such as "beauty," "love," and "sweet" to connote royalty, that is, they become synonyms in Oxford's Aesopian system of "special language."

The words "noted weed" in Line 6 have attracted much attention. "Weed" has been glossed by the traditional commentators as "clothing," "garb," "livery," and "noted" has been glossed as "familiar." I read the phrase, drawing on Whittemore, to mean that his "invention"—his "argument"—is hidden within a familiar garment (the sonnet form), lending the connotation of "disguise," one so thin that his authorship was "almost" revealed with "every word." "Noted weed" then translates as "familiar disguise."

Lines 7-8 extend the revelation, stating "that every word [in every sonnet] doth almost tell my name." Conventional analysis gags on these lines because it would be fatuous for a poet whose name was clearly identified as that of the author to make such an assertion. But it makes sense if the author is *not* identified by the name publicly associated with him—that is, if he is writing under a pseudonym. The poet is saying that his words almost give away his true identity, which would surely be the case if people correctly understood them—the "argument" in every sonnet that identifies him as Southampton's father by Elizabeth. These words clearly show their "birth" (begat by Oxford), and whence "they did proceed" (again, Oxford, or his pen).

These two lines are incompatible with the Stratford conjecture and by themselves render it untenable. They refute the possibility that Shakspere could have been the author of the *Sonnets*, as the notion that the author's name was otherwise *not* told makes no sense if Shakspere was Shakespeare.

This remarkable sonnet, written shortly after Oxford learned that Southampton would not be executed, foreshadows an even more remarkable one written just before Southampton's release from the Tower in 1603.

Sonnet 105: "To Constancy Confined...Three Themes In One"

Sonnet 105 contains a confirmation that the sonnets are about Elizabeth, Oxford and Southampton as a royal family, using allusions to all three that should have been transparent. Needless to say, the conventional view fails to see these key words *as* allusions, and thereby misreads the entire sonnet.

The sonnet reprises at least six themes from Sonnet 76, while making even more explicit what all the sonnets are about, and recording a stunning claim in its concluding couplet. Coming only two sonnets before Sonnet 107, the "historical anchor" that many traditional commentators *correctly* understand (at least in part), Sonnet 105 is universally *mis*understood. There is a deep gulf between what the commentators choose to note about it and its true meaning that becomes transparent under the new paradigm. I would argue that it is precisely *because* Sonnet 105 makes such dramatic revelations that it is so badly understood.

Most commentators do not even recognize the striking similarities between Sonnets 105 and 76.

172

105	1	Let not my love be call'd Idolatry,
105	2	Nor my beloved as an idol show,
105	3	Since all alike my songs and praises be
105	4	To one, of one, still such, and ever so.
105	5	Kind is my love to-day, to-morrow kind,
105	6	Still constant in a wondrous excellence;
105	7	Therefore my verse to constancy confined,
105	8	One thing expressing, leaves out difference.
105	9	Fair, kind and true is all my argument,
105	10	Fair, kind, and true varying to other words;
105	11	And in this change is my invention spent,
105	12	Three themes in one, which wondrous scope affords.
105	13	Fair, kind, and true, have often lived alone,
105	14	Which three till now never kept seat in one.

In Line 4, "to one, of one, still such, and ever so" recalls Sonnet 76's "all one, ever the same," where "to one, of one" references Southampton's motto, and "ever so" (an alternate translation of "ever the same") evokes Elizabeth's motto.

Lines 7-8 recall the statements in Sonnet 76 that all the sonnets are about the same thing, expressing the idea here with the words "my verse" is "confined" to "constancy" and "leave(s) out difference" "one thing expressing."

"Varying to other words" (line 10) harks back to Sonnet 76's "dressing old words new." Line 10 reiterates the assertion from Sonnet 76 that Oxford is substituting other words to convey his (unitary) message, i.e., that he is writing in Aesopian language. Line 11 states that finding ever different ways to talk about "fair, kind and true" defines the scope of his "invention" (the subject), even while doing so nonetheless provides him a "wondrous scope" for his poetic faculties (line 12).

Sonnet 105 also employs "invention" and "argument" in ways similar to their use in Sonnet 76. In Sonnet 105 the poet says that "my invention" is "spent" in simply putting the same argument into "other words," just as Sonnet 76 used "invention" to refer to the description of his method of "dressing old words new." Strikingly, both sonnets use "spend" or "spent" to say that the entirety of Oxford's labor in these sonnets is constrained to a single theme. "Argument" is also used identically, in Sonnet 76 to say that Southampton and his royalty "are still my argument," and in Sonnet 105, that "Fair, kind and true" is "all my argument."

The expansion in Sonnet 105 of Sonnet 76's description of the poet's "argument" provides the clearest revelation of who and what the sonnets are about, all but explicitly naming the *dramatis personae*. Where Sonnet 76 says "you [Southampton] and love [your royal blood] are still my argument," in Sonnet 105, "fair, kind and true" are now identified as "all my argument." Two themes have become three. His verse is now defined as confined to the "constancy" of these "three themes in one." (This locution, surely not accidentally, evokes the Holy Trinity, "three persons in one God," an evocation that would have been obvious to any contemporary reader.)

Identifying what the poet intends by "fair, kind and true," we cement a cornerstone of the new thesis. These three words are used in a singular fashion, since grammatically, they are adjectives. Here, they are the subject of three successive verbs, functioning syntactically as nouns. In Line 9, they are treated as a collective noun ("is all my argument"), in Line 10 they are described as "varying to other words," and most clearly, in Line 13 they are identified as three distinct persons who "have often lived alone" and "never kept seat in one." That is, they are not ordinary adjectives, but allusions to actual individuals,.

No traditional critic can afford to recognize "fair," "kind," and "true" to be persons because that would require specifying which of the three is the poet, which the young man, and which the woman. It's not that they can't accept that the sonnets are about three people; it is that under their paradigm, the adjectives "fair," "kind" and "true" make no sense if they are taken to characterize the traditional threesome. They must see the three words as adjectives all describing the young man, and deny their unmistakable use as nouns, which compels them to untenable readings of this sonnet.

If "fair, kind and true" are persons, the difficulty evaporates. The correct identifications are readily made. "True" evokes "truer" from Oxford's motto. "Fair" means royal, and no doubt refers to Elizabeth. "Kind" associates with "kindred" and "kin," rendering "kind" as child, Oxford's and Elizabeth's offspring. Lines 9-10 thus proclaim that the sonnets are about Elizabeth, Southampton, and Oxford. If his words did not "almost tell my name," as hinted in Sonnet 76, the words of Sonnet 105 rectified that deficiency.

So understood, the "constancy" that "my verse" is "confined" to is the same as that in Sonnet 76: the story of Southampton's parentage and royalty, and all that they imply, both before and after the events of February 8, 1601. This is the "one thing [that his verse is] expressing," "leav[ing] out difference"—never straying from this subject. (It is also, therefore, a story of impending dynastic ruin, as "time" ticks away the remaining years of Elizabeth's reign, and buries the story of the three of them.)

The third quatrain's "fair, kind and true" is thus the first explicit reference to Oxford's "holy family," or rather, "royal family," which he states are "all [his] argument." That Southampton is the *primary* subject of every sonnet (as indicated also in Sonnet 76) is made clear in lines 3-6, where all of the poet's "songs and praises" are "to one, of one," words which reference Southampton's motto. "Kind is my love today, tomorrow kind" says that "Southampton is my son today, and always." Line 6's "wondrous excellence" is Southampton's royalty, which is "still constant (cannot be gainsaid or erased)." The third quatrain brings in Elizabeth to complete Oxford's "trinity," "three themes in one."

The couplet makes a stunning assertion: "fair, kind and true" "have often lived alone," and "have never kept seat in one." The words of the couplet contradict the reading that every one of our critics derives from the rest of the sonnet. Understood within the new paradigm, however, it is such a clear statement that one wonders if Oxford feared he was being too obvious: that he, Elizabeth and Southampton have lived separately for most of their lives ("have often lived alone"), never together as a family should have ("never kept seat in one"). "Seat" would have evoked the royal seat, the seat of power, which is what all three would have occupied together had Elizabeth acknowledged Southampton.

Appearing in a sonnet that was most likely written when Oxford knew Elizabeth was dying or already dead, the description of his "trinity"—himself, Elizabeth and Southampton—represents Oxford's abandonment of all hope that all three would ever be acknowledged as the family that they were. Surely, the opening two lines are intended to anticipate criticism that he was seeking to conflate *his* trinity with the Holy Trinity, while still evoking that comparison.

The Conventional View Strikes Out

I am hard pressed to find another sonnet for which the conventional readings are as far afield from what I believe is the true meaning of Sonnet 105.

The respective readings of Sonnet 105 of our four commentators are incoherent and make no attempt to provide a clear explanation of the sonnet. Duncan-Jones, briefest of the four, sees the opening quatrain as expressing the poet's idolizing the friend, celebrating him "in threefold terms which recall the Trinity," of course attributing all three qualities to "his friend." She fails to ask why the "speaker" would do this, nor does she regard this as a reference to a trinity of three persons. She glosses Line 7 ("constancy confined") as "restricted to (the celebration of) undeviating kindness," presumably referring to "my verse," thereby contradicting much of what she says elsewhere, as she cites numerous instances of the "friend" *not* being "kind." She has no comment on the first appearance of "fair, kind and true" in Line 9, instead merely defining "argument" as "subject matter." She says that the repetition of "fair, kind and true" in Line 10 "exemplified the constancy of his verse," but adds "yet immediately undercuts it in 'varying to other words.'" She makes no comment on the substance of lines 13-14. She has effectively ignored this sonnet.

Burrow makes explicit that he sees the poet worshiping the friend as the epitome of "fair, kind and true." He, like Duncan-Jones, is silent on lines 13-14, which, read in the traditional context, would clearly refute their reading of "fair, kind and true," since these lines contradict the possibility that the friend embodies all three qualities; the couplet says that they do *not* reside together. Not one of Burrow's glosses illuminates any of the important sections of these lines.

Kerrigan and Booth devote much more space to Sonnet 105 than do Burrow and Duncan-Jones. Discussing Line 7, Kerrigan takes a stab at making sense of what is written, noting that "to constancy confined" means "restricted in subject-matter to the theme of sameness-and-fidelity." But he surely can't think that all the sonnets are devoted to this theme, as would be required if his reading of the line were correct. His discussion of Line 9's "fair, kind and true," like Burrow's, expands on the meaning of these three qualities without connecting them to what they mean in the context of the sonnet. He does note that Line 13 means "lodged separately (in different people)." He never explicitly states that he thinks that "fair, kind and true" pertain to the friend—he never states *what* he thinks they pertain to.

Booth devotes three and a half pages to this sonnet, with no more useful result. He fills out his commentary with multiple extended but irrelevant *ad hoc* exegeses. As with the others, most of his commentaries on specific words merely offer possible meanings of those words, without attempting to explain what they mean in context. His note on Line 7 is limited to discussing "constancy": "(1) sameness, being always the same; (2) the theme of faithfulness in love (and the beloved's faithfulness in particular)." Having ascribed constancy to the friend, not to the poetry, he gags on Line 8, trying to make sense of what "leav[ing] out difference" might mean in reference to the friend. As to the final couplet he says virtually nothing. In fact, all commentators are tacit on Line 14 except for glossing the word "seat," all observing that it refers to "residence" or "residing," all missing the obvious connotation of "seat of power." (Ironically, Duncan-Jones glosses "sit" in Line 13 of Sonnet 103 as "be enthroned," which would lead to a rendering that "Your own glass shows you [to be] much, much more than can be enthroned in my verse," an unnecessary substitution, while she misses the clear inference that "kept seat" in Sonnet 105 carries the connotation of "enthroned.")

Sonnet 105 aptly illustrates the principle known as Occam's razor. As it pertains here, it could be paraphrased as "start with the simplest explanation, and avoid needless addition of disparate explanations." That is, simplicity and coherence characterize the reading of this sonnet under the new paradigm; confusion, rambling and incoherence characterize all readings under the traditional paradigm.

Chapter 14
Southampton's Expected Execution, Oxford's Depression

We turn now to Sonnets 60-66. I agree with Whittemore that Oxford began this series of eight sonnets in March 1601, about five weeks after Southampton's arrest, when it seemed certain that Southampton would be executed. One of Whittemore's conclusions is that Oxford assigned one sonnet to each of the sixty days from February 8 to April 8, 1601, which appear as numbers 27-86. While there is no way of knowing whether Oxford actually wrote one sonnet per day, or merely assigned these sixty sonnets to each day when arranging them later, the content of Sonnets 60-66 strongly implies that this group of sonnets was composed in the days just before the 40th day after Southampton's arrest.

By this chronology, Sonnet 60 corresponds to March 13, 1601, and Sonnet 66 to March 19, the 34th and 40th days since Southampton's arrest, respectively. Several convicted conspirators were still to be executed as of March 13, and it was expected that Southampton would be among them. The evidence within these sonnets all but confirms that Oxford did not know that Southampton would be spared—indeed, that decision may not have yet been made—so the despair displayed in this series surely reflects Oxford's true state of mind. The last executions took place on March 18, so Sonnet 66 would have likely been written one day after, presumably the day before Southampton would finally meet his fate.

Sonnets 60 and 63 are remarkably similar, on the surface describing the process of time taking away youth, and life. With the knowledge that Oxford is writing on two levels, we can see that "time" and several other words are doing double duty as they tell a dual story. Here, "time" can be read as ordinary time, and as Elizabeth about to take away Southampton's life (and with it his royal blood). Both sonnets end on the same theme, of how the sonnets will give him life even after he is no more. Sonnets 61 and

62 are about the poet's intense love for his beloved. Sonnets 64-65 both feature "rage" that trumps monuments of stone, a metaphor for Elizabeth destroying the legacy of her forebears. Sonnet 66, written possibly just hours before Oxford expected to hear of Southampton's execution, is a unique lament, reflecting Oxford's belief that all is now lost. Taken as a group, these sonnets stand as testimony written in real time that Oxford, along with all England, believed that Southampton was living his last days on earth.

In contrast, our traditionalist critics have no idea what these sonnets mean, see no coherence in the series of seven, have no explanation for the despairing tone of Sonnet 66, and can't even relate them to the "love triangle" theme by which they purport to understand most other sonnets.

On the surface, Sonnet 60 laments the normal course of life, but buried in it are words that reveal the deeper meanings: that Southampton's expected execution is imminent, and that the Tudor dynasty will come to an end when Elizabeth dies:

60	1	Like as the waves make towards the pebbled shore,
60	2	So do our minutes hasten to their end;
60	3	Each changing place with that which goes before,
60	4	In sequent toil all forwards do contend.
60	5	Nativity, once in the main of light,
60	6	Crawls to maturity, wherewith being crown'd,
60	7	Crooked eclipses 'gainst his glory fight,
60	8	And time that gave doth now his gift confound.
60	9	Time doth transfix the flourish set on youth
60	10	And delves the parallels in beauty's brow,
60	11	Feeds on the rarities of nature's truth,
60	12	And nothing stands but for his scythe to mow:
60	13	And yet to times in hope, my verse shall stand
60	14	Praising thy worth, despite his cruel hand.

The first quatrain refers simultaneously to the expiring time of Queen Elizabeth's reign, to Southampton's expected demise, and likely to Oxford's anticipation of his own death. The simile of the sea coming ashore in waves evokes the notion of a sovereign, and most likely the anticipated arrival of James of Scotland on Elizabeth's death. Line 2 confirms this reading, as the "end" would be the end of Elizabeth's life, with "our" signifying the royal "we." Lines 3-4 expand on the image. The second quatrain shifts to refer to Southampton. The first word, "Nativity," is a reference to Southampton as their child, who could have been in line for the succession ("once in the main of light"), reaching his maturity with the hope of being crowned ("wherewith being crowned"—the use of "crown" demands a meaning of royalty), only to find his way blocked by Robert Cecil. "Crooked" is a clear reference to Cecil, a hunchback with a "crooked" walk, who "eclipses (blocks Southampton's way by executing him) 'gainst his glory fight" while Elizabeth ("time") "that gave (him life and royal blood) doth now his gift confound" (takes away his royal future).

That the second quatrain is about Southampton also demands a reading that the "minutes hasten(ing) to their end" in Line 2 also refers to Southampton's imminent demise.

The third quatrain confirms the metaphor of "time" (Elizabeth, with the double meaning of "death" and death's "scythe," and the further meaning of Elizabeth *as* death) being about to come down on Southampton, concluding that "nothing stands but for his scythe to mow," which "feeds on the rarities of nature's truth" ("nature" is Elizabeth, "truth" is Oxford, and the "rarity" is Southampton and his royal blood—recall "Beauty, Truth and Rarity" from *The Phoenix and Turtle*).

The sonnet sounds the only positive note, that despite the failure of Southampton to become king (or even, perhaps, to avoid execution) the sonnets will survive and tell his story.

Duncan-Jones' reading is typical of the conventional view:

> Developing the temporal meditations of the preceding sonnet, the speaker considers the inevitable process of maturity and decay in the natural world, only to be counteracted by his own verse in praise of the young man.

Duncan-Jones fails to realize that this sonnet, like all the rest, is about Southampton, instead seeing it as a general discourse on the life and death in the natural world, which makes it a *non sequitur*.

Sonnet 61 expresses how Oxford is consumed by his concern for Southampton, which keeps him awake nights, "defeat(ing)" his "rest" as he "play(s) the watchman" for Southampton—suggesting he is working behind the scenes to try to spare his life. The final couplet is suggestive:

61 13 For thee watch I whilst thou dost wake elsewhere,
61 14 From me far off, with others all too near.

Southampton is "elsewhere"—namely, in the Tower—surrounded by those who would execute him ("with others all too near") while Oxford watches and works on his behalf.

Sonnet 62 makes a related point. The first twelve lines apparently describe how the poet is consumed with self-love. Since this theme resonates with nothing else in the entire collection, and would be a *non sequitur* if meant as a sudden lament for a personal quality of the poet that contradicts the sense of the entire sonnet series to this point, it cannot be the poet confessing to be a narcissist. The solution is provided in the couplet:

62　13　'Tis thee (myself) that for myself I praise,
62　14　Painting my age with beauty of thy days.

The only intelligible reading is that what appears to be self-love is really love for "thee," and that the poet lives in the reflection of the royal blood ("beauty") of Southampton.

Sonnet 63

Sonnet 63 harks back to Sonnet 60, on the surface describing the normal progress of life toward death, while embedding indications that it is really about the impending execution of Southampton. Again, the couplet has the only redeeming news, namely, that Southampton's royal blood ("His beauty") shall live, and Southampton will still be alive "in these black lines."

63　1　Against my love shall be, as I am now,
63　2　With time's injurious hand crush'd and o'er-worn;
63　3　When hours have drain'd his blood and fill'd his brow
63　4　With lines and wrinkles; when his youthful morn
63　5　Hath travell'd on to Age's steepy night,
63　6　And all those beauties whereof now he's King
63　7　Are vanishing, or vanish'd out of sight,
63　8　Stealing away the treasure of his Spring;
63　9　For such a time do I now fortify
63　10　Against confounding Age's cruel knife,
63　11　That he shall never cut from memory
63　12　My sweet love's beauty, though my lover's life:
63　13　His beauty shall in these black lines be seen,
63　14　And they shall live, and he in them still green.

As in Sonnet 60, the second quatrain reveals the deeper meaning. "Beauties," as we have established, refers to Southampton's royal blood, which here is tied to a reference to his being "King" (capitalization in the original), if only in Oxford's mind. The word "king" was not, and would not be, lightly used, and surely connotes an actual or potential king. This line also foreshadows the use of this word in Sonnet 87, "In sleep a King, but waking no such matter."

The "beauties" that are "vanishing, or vanished out of sight" is a clear reference to Southampton's imminent execution.

The image in the third quatrain of "Age," whose "steepy night" is mentioned in the second quatrain, as wielding a "cruel knife," suggests execution by beheading. The reference to the poet (Oxford) now fortifying himself against the loss of Southampton's life, confirms this reading; in the normal course of aging (were this about Southampton's being old many years in the future), Oxford would be dead long before that time. The strong suggestion is that the fortifying must be done now, by the medium of the sonnets, and that what must be preserved is "my sweet love's beauty," "sweet" being an Aesopian word for "royal," and "beauty" for "royal blood." The couplet reiterates that whatever happens to Southampton, his "beauty" will "be seen" in the sonnets, which will survive him, and Southampton will be "green" (alive) in them.

Again, our commentators do not recognize that it would be fatuous of Shakespeare to be moaning now about a distant future loss of physical beauty of his beloved, and to claim that the beloved will live forever through that beauty preserved in the sonnets— which is their reading of this sonnet. Why would any future generations care about someone long dead merely described in a poem as having been beautiful?

Sonnet 64

With Sonnets 64-66, we come to Oxford's lowest moments, when he evidently considers it certain that Southampton will be executed, and ruminates on the ruin of the Tudor dynasty. Sonnet 64 is also a supreme test of Whittemore's thesis and method. For this sonnet, more than for most, the conventional interpretations are useless, with readings that have no connection even to the surface story of the poet's tortured love for the young man, whereas our Aesopian reading turns it into an open book.

Under Whittemore's chronology, Sonnet 64 was written to refer to the events of March 17, 1601. On the following morning Charles Danvers and Christopher Blount were publicly beheaded on Tower Hill. Of those who had been condemned to death, only Southampton remained. This reinforces the presumption that Oxford still expected him to die:

64	1	When I have seen by time's fell hand defaced
64	2	The rich proud cost of outworn buried age;
64	3	When sometime lofty towers I see down-razed
64	4	And brass eternal slave to mortal rage;
64	5	When I have seen the hungry Ocean gain
64	6	Advantage on the Kingdom of the shore,
64	7	And the firm soil win of the watery main,
64	8	Increasing store with loss and loss with store;
64	9	When I have seen such interchange of state,
64	10	Or state itself confounded to decay;
64	11	Ruin hath taught me thus to ruminate,
64	12	That time will come and take my love away.
64	13	This thought is as a death, which cannot choose
64	14	But weep to have that which it fears to lose.

Conventional commentators posit that lines 5-8 are literally about how the sea erodes land, but sediment creates new land out of sea; they then impute that is what is meant in lines 9 and 10 by "interchange of state." Why the poet would suddenly digress to such an irrelevant topic none even attempts to explain.

Based on our knowledge that Oxford (and all of London) expects Southampton's imminent execution, we can see an entirely different narrative. Oxford is brooding over Southampton's impending death, choosing here not even to mention the role of the sonnets in preserving his memory, an exception to his normal pattern. The third quatrain posits that "Ruin" (the word that sums up the message of the first ten lines) has taught the poet to recognize that "time," read as both Elizabeth and Death, will indeed take Southampton's life ("time will come and take my love away"). Oxford is sure that Elizabeth will never acknowledge Southampton, and therefore has no reason to prevent his execution.

Oxford's efforts to save Southampton's life seem to have been in vain. The thought of his death causes Oxford to weep over the life of the person that he is about to lose, the thought itself being "as a death," perhaps foreshadowing thoughts of his own desire for death expressed in the next few sonnets.

Awareness of the rigorous rules of sonnet construction helps to avoid incoherent or contradictory readings.

The first quatrain appears to say that durable physical substances such as brass or stone can be made subject to, or be controlled by, something mortal ("mortal rage"). Duncan-Jones, alone of all the commentators, has a helpful read of what might be meant in Line 2, noting that "rich proud cost" "suggests the expensive splendor of elaborate funeral monuments, such as those to be seen in Westminster Abbey or St. Paul's," and that "outworn buried age" would refer to "men who have grown old and exhausted, or who lived long ago, and are now interred." By this reading, "rich proud cost" refers to expensive funeral monuments, but of whom? To answer this, we must ask what the entire sonnet series is about so far. The answer is that it is about the Tudor dynasty, and the fact that it requires a blood heir to continue. If "rich proud cost," "sometime lofty towers" and "brass eternal" are understood to mean the tombs of Elizabeth's Tudor predecessors, this quatrain is revealed to say that "mortal rage" is destroying the legacy of the Tudor lineage.

"Mortal rage" then refers to Elizabeth herself, who has refused to do what was necessary to continue the Tudor legacy. She failed to marry and create an heir by the normal route; she never acknowledged Southampton as her natural issue during the years before the Essex Rebellion when she could have done so; now she is about to execute him. Her "rage," which characterizes her arbitrariness, is defacing the monuments to her Tudor predecessors, "raz(ing)" the lofty towers that celebrate them, and making their brass tombs "slave" to her decision to dishonor them by letting their lineage expire. This reading also fits perfectly with the last four lines, imparting to "ruin" the meaning "ruin of the Tudor dynasty."

The second quatrain must be read in conjunction with the first two lines of the third one. The capitalized "Ocean" of Line 5 must be read as a monarch or monarchy, since it is contrasted as something equal to the "Kingdom" of Line 6. Again, except for Duncan-Jones, our commentators are able only to see the poet talking about the ebb and flow between land and sea.

Support for the traditional view does come from two lines in Golding's translation of Ovid's *Metamorphoses*, where such a tug of war between land and sea is described; I have no doubt that Oxford intended this to be the surface reading. But why would the poet interject that meaning here? By any traditional reading of the remainder of the sonnet, what does it have to do with the "ruin" or "time" about to take his love away? What does it have to do with the first quatrain? The true meaning must be one that fits with the structure and coherence of each line, quatrain and couplet. By that test, the traditional reading fails.

By 1601, it was generally understood that James VI of Scotland, who had a comparatively strong claim to the throne, would succeed

Elizabeth. Robert Cecil, Burghley's son and the most powerful man in England, worked hard to arrange that outcome starting immediately after the Essex Rebellion, intending (successfully, as it turned out) to become his top advisor as well. But there remained concerns that James might not be accepted by the people of England, which would invite other claimants to compete for the crown, creating the danger of rebellion or even civil war.

In that light, the second quatrain refers to the likely change of dynasty, all but explicitly referred to in Line 9: "an interchange of state." (Duncan-Jones alone sees the obvious connection, noting that "state" can be taken in the "political sense, anticipated in the image of dry land's kingdom in Line 6. For readers in 1609 an allusion to the end of Elizabeth's long reign and the beginning of James in 1603 must have been irresistible.")

That meaning is confirmed by Line 10, "or state itself confounded to decay," read as referring to the possibility of rebellion or civil war if the transition of power does not go smoothly. Then, Line 5's "hungry Ocean" would be James, coming from afar to take over ("gain advantage on") England by becoming its king. "Ocean" or "sea" was often used to mean "king" by Shakespeare and other contemporary writers, according to scholar Leslie Hotson (*Mr. W.H.*) and Shakespeare employs this usage explicitly in *King John* 5.4.57: "Even to our Ocean, our great King John." Line 7 would then be read to say "and the firm soil (of England) win [won] [by] the watery main (James)."

Line 8 refers to the first two quatrains, summing them up by saying that James' "store" (the establishment of the Stuart dynasty) has increased, at the expense of the "loss" (end, ruin) of the Tudor dynasty, and that the loss is heightened by the transition to Stuart rule.

The conventional reading of this sonnet is incoherent. It makes no connection between its understanding of the second quatrain and the first quatrain's discussion of Time and "mortal rage" defacing monuments of stone and brass; it fails to explain what "state confounded to decay" could mean if "state" is the interchange of sand between land and ocean; and it cannot explain why any of this would lead the poet to "ruminate" about Time taking his love away.

Sonnet 65

Sonnet 65 picks up where Sonnet 64 ends, again stating Oxford's conviction that Southampton will be executed:

65	1	Since brass, nor stone, nor earth, nor boundless sea,
65	2	But sad mortality o'er-sways their power,
65	3	How with this rage shall beauty hold a plea,
65	4	Whose action is no stronger than a flower?
65	5	O, how shall summer's honey breath hold out
65	6	Against the wreckful siege of battering days,
65	7	When rocks impregnable are not so stout,
65	8	Nor gates of steel so strong, but Time decays?
65	9	O fearful meditation! where, alack,
65	10	Shall Time's best jewel from Time's chest lie hid?
65	11	Or what strong hand can hold his swift foot back?
65	12	Or who his spoil of beauty can forbid?
65	13	O, none, unless this miracle have might,
65	14	That in black ink my love may still shine bright.

The sonnet reprises "brass" and "stone" from Sonnet 64, followed by "sad mortality" in Line 2, and "this rage" in Line 3, recalling "mortal rage" from Sonnet 64. The addition of "nor earth, nor boundless sea" might also be a reprise of the Ocean and the Kingdom of Sonnet 64, indicating that "sad mortality," Queen Elizabeth, is determining all of these.

Against the power of this "rage" (Elizabeth's assumed decision to execute Southampton) Oxford refers explicitly to the plea for Southampton's life—"how with this rage shall beauty hold a plea" ("beauty" again being Southampton's royal blood, which Elizabeth should have sought to perpetuate). Among the traditionalist commentators, Burrow correctly identifies "hold a plea" as a legal term, meaning "successfully present a legal suit." Duncan-Jones concurs that it means "legal process, legal action," as does Kerrigan, with "uphold a suit, prevail in (legal) argument." "Beauty's" action is portrayed as "no stronger than a flower," with "flower" surely a reference to the Tudor Rose; Southampton's only argument, the strength of his "action" (another legal term), is that he is a living embodiment of the Tudor "flower," the Tudor bloodline.

The second quatrain restates the point, asking how Southampton, "summer's honey breath," can possibly hold out against the "siege"—Elizabeth and the circumstances of his coming execution—if neither rocks nor "gates of steel" can prevail against her ("time"); that is, she makes them decay (equivalent to "ruin" of Line 11 of Sonnet 64). Line 9's "fearful meditation" recalls the "thought" expressed in Line 13 of Sonnet 64, whether anything can now save Southampton. "Where...shall time's best Jewel"

186

identifies "time" as Elizabeth, whose "best Jewel" can only be Southampton, with the sense that "Is there any place that Southampton can be hidden to escape his fate ('time's chest')." Line 11 asks if any power ("strong hand") can hold back Elizabeth's ("his," time's) swift movement toward the execution ("foot" read as marching toward the event). Line 12 asks if any can stop ("forbid") her spoiling him (executing "beauty").

The couplet restates that nothing can stop it; all that can now be done is to preserve, in the "black ink" of the sonnets, the memory of Southampton and his royal blood.

Sonnet 65 is remarkable for the degree to which, under the correct paradigm, its true meaning becomes apparent. The use in Line 3 of "plea," a legal term (Shakespeare is acknowledged to have been a master at using legal language correctly and precisely), is so obvious that even the traditionalists read it that way, but they cannot explain why it would appear here. The phrase "action is no stronger than a flower" seems odd unless and until the Tudor Rose is understood as the meaning of "flower." Among our four commentators Booth is honest enough to confess that "to hold a plea" is a legal phrase that does not make sense in this context because its precise meaning is "to try a case."

None of this is understood by our commentators, who continue to flounder in *non sequiturs*. Kerrigan opines that "sad mortality is a monarch stronger than brass, stone and the rest; he o'ersways because he curbs their power by oscillation, mutability, what 64.9 calls interchange of state." What (male) monarch, and what it means to say he "curbs their [whose?] power by oscillation, mutability" are left unspecified. Duncan-Jones opines, "Recapitulating his survey of time's power to transform the world, the speaker searches desperately for a means to preserve human beauty," nothing of which makes sense. Why would "time's power to transform the world," whatever that might mean, threaten the existence of human beauty? And if it would, how could the sonnets forestall this eventuality? Burrow fares no better, glossing Line 10: "The friend is the treasured possession of Time, which cannot be prevented from returning to his coffers....Time, though, simply wants to have his possession, the friend, locked away securely, as the poet had done in [Sonnet] 52."

Sonnet 66

Sonnet 66 is singular, not least because of its structure.

Although the rhyme scheme conforms to the sonnet format, the first twelve lines do not form three quatrains. The poem begins with a line about how Oxford is tired of life and ready to leave it, followed by eleven lines of lamentation, each beginning with "And." It concludes with a couplet that proclaims that "I" would happily depart this world, but for the fact that it would leave "my love" alone. Resigned to the inevitable, exhausted with his apparently unsuccessful efforts to secure Southampton's survival, Oxford catalogs the present sorry state of affairs:

66	1	Tired with all these, for restful death I cry,
66	2	As, to behold desert a beggar born,
66	3	And needy Nothing trimm'd in jollity,
66	4	And purest faith unhappily forsworn,
66	5	And guilded honour shamefully misplaced,
66	6	And maiden virtue rudely strumpeted,
66	7	And right perfection wrongfully disgraced,
66	8	And strength by limping sway disabled,
66	9	And art made tongue-tied by authority,
66	10	And Folly (Doctor-like) controlling skill,
66	11	And simple-Truth miscalled Simplicity,
66	12	And captive good attending Captain ill:
66	13	Tired with all these, from these would I be gone,
66	14	Save that, to die, I leave my love alone.

The first four words of Line 1 are repeated in the couplet, bracketing the list of eleven ills that are the causes of his wish for death. That list is interpreted one way by conventional analysis, and entirely differently under an Aesopian one. Understood as the conventional commentators see it, it is a random list of complaints. It is not clear why these complaints would lead the poet to welcome death, or why he would be choosing this moment in the sonnet cycle to enumerate them.

Correctly understood, the list describes the present circumstance and fate of Southampton, and Oxford's relation to them. In Line 2, according to the orthodox critics, "desert" means "deserving merit" (Burrow), "merit" or "a deserving individual" (Kerrigan), "synecdoche for 'those who are deserving'" (Duncan-Jones), or "worthiness" (Booth). The sonnets are about Southampton. If he is Elizabeth's unacknowledged son, the line is about him—he was "a beggar born" out of wedlock, a bastard, but fully deserving ("desert").

In Line 3, "jollity" is universally understood as "finery." All of the commentators read the line as "worthless people dressed up in extravagant clothes" (Duncan-Jones), or close variants.

Whittemore reads Line 3 as "And see him (Southampton) become a nobody given an earldom," which he explains by saying that Southampton has now become a "nobody" in prison, stripped of his title and estates, but who once had "jollity," which he reads as "dressed up as an earl in great splendor, as Southampton was before this tragedy." I concur that the reference to "nobody" surely pertains to Southampton's current state, but think it more likely that the "jollity" signifies that Southampton in prison was permitted to dress in clothes that befitted his former station. This forces "jollity" to be used ironically, if not sardonically.

The remainder of the lines have been well parsed by Whittemore. I paraphrase him.

Line 4 reflects the poet's faith in Elizabeth that has been betrayed ("forsworn"). I read "faith" in many senses—the "faith" that the English people put in her to perpetuate a stable dynasty, Oxford's "faith" that she would acknowledge their son, and Southampton's "faith" that she would protect and eventually acknowledge him. Line 5 refers to the high honor that Southampton should have had as the heir apparent, which has now been ("misplaced") in another. The "maiden virtue" of Line 6 would refer to Southampton's "beauty" (his carrying of Tudor blood), "strumpeted" meaning it was taken from him. Line 7 is Southampton's disgrace, despite his inner perfection as the prince who should become king.

Lines 8 and 9 contain the clearest topical references. To readers of the time, "Limping sway" would refer to the hunchbacked Robert Cecil. What other meaning could identify "strength" (Southampton) as disabled by it? Line 10 is Oxford's lament that he cannot write what he wants, because of censorship, his "art" being "tongue-tied" by the authorities.

Finally, "Folly (Doctor-like)" may refer to a specific person or persons (suggested by the capital letters), but in a general sense must refer to the "folly" of executing Southampton, which is trumping his "skill" (his royal blood, and the qualities that would have made him a good king). Line 11's "simple-Truth" is a reference to Oxford himself, who uses "truth" throughout the sonnets and elsewhere in the Shakespeare canon to refer to himself, alluding to his personal motto ("Nothing truer than truth") and to the pun on his name ("Vere" or "ver"). "Simplicity" is clearly foolishness, so the line likely refers to the low regard into which

Oxford has fallen during the preceding decade, when he withdrew from court. Finally, "captive-good" is again Southampton, and "Captain Ill" (again, capitalized) must refer to Cecil (with a pun on the second syllable of "Cecil"), who now controls his fate.

What a catalog! Everything has gone wrong. Good is defeated, truth is belied, Oxford's enemies have prevailed. What is there to live for? Only for Southampton who, somehow, still lives. This sonnet, written by Whittemore's reckoning on March 19, 1601, would have been composed one day after the other two condemned conspirators were beheaded. With executions taking place every few days, Oxford fully expected that the end would soon come for Southampton.

While recognizing, in Duncan-Jones' words, that this sonnet is "despairing," none of our commentators makes any coherent sense of the lines, finding *ad hoc* readings of each line. Duncan-Jones' summary is typical: "Weary of the corruption and hypocrisy of the age he lives in, the speaker longs for death, restrained only by the thought of abandoning his love." Why the poet would suddenly talk about "the corruption and hypocrisy of the age," or long for death on that account, is nowhere addressed.

Chapter 15
Turning Point –
Southampton Lives!

67   1   Ah! wherefore with infection should he live,

This first line of Sonnet 67, coming after the preceding seven sonnets with their dark forebodings of Southampton's execution, jumps out much as does Sonnet 27, indicating that something very important has just happened. It marks another major shift in tone, perhaps not as stark as that of Sonnet 27, but with a message even more momentous. In place of words that implied that Southampton is about to die, we now find the word "live."

All references to "time" vanish—the word is not used in any comparable context until Sonnet 77, and there it appears not as an executioner, but as limiting everyone's life. Line 2 notes "his" (Southampton's) "presence," Line 4 his "society." These are attributes of someone who is very much alive, not likely to die soon.

The remainder of this sonnet, and all that follow, confirm what Line 1 suggests. If Sonnet 27 records the beginning of his stay in the Tower on February 8, 1601, the conclusion is irresistible that Sonnet 67 records Oxford's reaction to the news that Southampton will not be executed. We infer that Oxford learned of this on or around March 20, 1601.

The sonnet is the only record of the point in time when at least a few people were informed that Southampton's life had been spared, documenting the latest date when that decision had been made.

Thus begins the next subset of the sonnets.

A further confirmation that Sonnet 67 marks a sharp shift in the narrative is provided by the symmetry such an interpretation reveals. Whittemore dates Sonnet 67 to March 20, the day after Sonnet 66. Sonnet 66 is the 40th sonnet since Sonnet 27, written on the date Southampton was arrested. Sonnet 67 thus begins a second set of forty "Prison Sonnets," culminating in Sonnet 106, the last one written while Southampton was in the Tower. The exact midpoint of the series of eighty prison sonnets lies between Sonnets 66 and 67. Such symmetry is not coincidental.

Such a *caesura* is not recognized by any traditional commentator because none of them recognizes this group *as* "prison sonnets." No commentator notices the dramatic change in tone, from discussions of death to presumptions of continued life for the beloved, between Sonnets 66 and 67.

The one-to-one correlation between the first forty prison sonnets and the number of days since Southampton's arrest is not maintained in the second group of forty. It appears likely that Oxford continued to write at the pace of one a day through Sonnet 87 (in which he reveals the legal basis by which Southampton was spared). But the final nineteen prison sonnets (88-106) span a period of twenty-four months, from April 1601 to April 1603. The urgency that drove Oxford to compose the first sixty prison sonnets had lessened dramatically. The pace became irregular, perhaps proceeding at the rate of one sonnet a month from April 1601 to February 1602, one every two months for the remainder of 1602, and then picking up in 1603 as news spread that Queen Elizabeth was approaching death; Sonnet 105 records her death on March 24. Sonnet 106 is a sendoff to the "Prison Sonnets," and was probably written between March 24 and April 10, 1603.

Such a reconstruction of probable dates is guesswork. The final arrangement was no doubt made after all were written; sonnets were lined up to correlate to various dates and to reflect the symmetrical structure of the series as a whole. But it appears all but certain, however, that certain sonnets were composed in "real time" to chronicle Oxford's day-to-day experience, especially within the first forty of the "Prison Sonnets." During the early days of Southampton's confinement, we can surmise that Oxford was under tremendous stress. Writing the sonnets would have been both therapeutic and functional. It is likely that Oxford was able to send sonnets to the imprisoned Southampton on some regular basis through messengers; it is also likely that Oxford himself was able to visit Southampton on occasion.

We now examine Sonnet 67 in detail.

Sonnet 67

67	1	Ah! wherefore with infection should he live,
67	2	And with his presence grace impiety,
67	3	That sin by him advantage should achieve
67	4	And lace itself with his society?

67	5	Why should false painting imitate his cheek
67	6	And steal dead seeing of his living hue?
67	7	Why should poor beauty indirectly seek
67	8	Roses of shadow, since his Rose is true?
67	9	Why should he live, now nature bankrupt is,
67	10	Beggar'd of blood to blush through lively veins?
67	11	For she hath no exchecker now but his,
67	12	And, proud of many, lives upon his gains.
67	13	O, him she stores, to show what wealth she had
67	14	In days long since, before these last so bad.

Though it announces that Southampton will not die, Line 1 asks "wherefore with infection should he live." The "infection" can only be that he is still a convicted traitor, and will remain in the Tower, stripped of all noble titles. Line 9 asks again "why should he live, now Nature bankrupt is." In the face of what we should think is welcome news—that Southampton will not be executed—we find equivocal statements, concerned with issues other than mortality, not celebrating his deliverance.

The third quatrain merits analysis first. Applying our knowledge that Elizabeth's bloodline will die out with her, we can conclude that it is she who is "Nature" and who is "bankrupt" (about to see her Tudor House die out), a reading confirmed in the next line, where she has been "beggared of blood"—denied any (acknowledged) descendants through whom her royal blood would flow ("to flow through lively veins"). In Line 1, Oxford asks why "should he [Southampton] live" which he repeats in 9: It is a valid question because the overarching purpose of his existence—at least in Oxford's mind—was to succeed Elizabeth and continue the Tudor lineage, a purpose which remains thwarted.

Line 11 is transparent—Elizabeth's only "exchequer" (bank) that can maintain her bloodline is "his" (Southampton's) exchequer (blood). In Line 12 the word "lives" is a subjunctive—the only chance to perpetuate her bloodline "lives" on the extant, if forlorn, possibility that Southampton might yet be acknowledged. I read "proud of many" as expressing how all England would rejoice, be proud of her and of their country, if she would ensure that the Tudor reign would continue through Southampton.

The couplet dashes that possibility. Elizabeth has decided to keep Southampton alive ("him she stores"), but she will not acknowledge him. She "stores" him because he has royal blood which represented her former "wealth" her heritable bloodline.

So we learn that although Southampton will live, he has not been pardoned, is still in the Tower, is still deemed a traitor, and consequently, all hope is dashed. One might ask, what did Oxford expect?

The tone and content of Sonnet 67 suggest that Oxford might have believed that if Southampton were spared at all, it would be by a royal pardon, which might mean he could still become king. It's possible that Oxford thought that if Southampton were spared, it would be because the Queen had finally decided to acknowledge him. That could explain Oxford's tempered reaction to the news that Southampton will not be executed. So understood, this sonnet is about the injustice that resulted from sparing Southampton's life: the true heir is permitted to live, while preparations proceed to crown another, as if no real heir existed.

The first line shows that Oxford is nonplussed by the situation. The "infection" is the continuing stain of Southampton's status as a convicted traitor. In effect, Oxford is asking "what's the point of not executing him if you're going to keep him in prison for the rest of his life as a nobody?" Where we might expect Oxford to be overjoyed that his son will not die, we find him lamenting that he will live, but still with the "infection" of being a convicted traitor.

The first quatrain continues in this vein, saying that by living, Southampton becomes a party to the "sin" of another (James) taking his place as the rightful successor. He "grace(s) impiety" by the "sin" of another's taking his place, which "achieve(s)...advantage" by means of his presence and bolsters ("lace[s]") itself by his existence ("society"). Since some insiders knew the truth about Southampton's royalty, Oxford is likely saying that keeping him alive reminds his putative supporters of their powerlessness. It also may reflect conditions that Southampton had to agree to, including not ever revealing who he really was or otherwise attempting to press a claim to be king.

Lines 5-6 are now transparent; they are a clear statement of Southampton's royalty and of the injustice of his being robbed of the succession. His "cheek" in Line 5 is his royal nature and the primacy of his claim to be king, which the "false painting" of the usurper James is merely imitating. Line 6 says that compared to Southampton's living existence as the true heir, the "false painting" is a "dead" thing, "steal(ing)" the succession from "his living hue" (with "hue" punning on Southampton's initials, HEW).

Lines 7-8 are the clearest in meaning: Why should Elizabeth ("poor beauty") "indirectly" seek "roses of shadow," that is, false roses, again a reference to James, when Southampton is the true Tudor Rose? "Indirectly" refers to the fact that James line of succession was indirect, as opposed to Southampton's.

The final couplet, following on the previous two lines' reference to Southampton as Elizabeth's only "exchequer," makes clear that Elizabeth did not spare Southampton in order to make him heir. The final half-line, "before these times so bad," gives the lie to every conventional analysis, which cannot explain why these recent days are so bad.

Sonnet 67 confounds traditional analysis for another reason, which should be recognized as further proof that our thesis is correct. None of our commentators notices that it is entirely in the third person, with "he" and "his" referring to the "beloved," to Southampton (instead of the common use of the second person or reference to my "love"), through Line 9, where "nature" is introduced as bankrupt, with no exchequer but "his." "She," in the traditional interpretations, is the rival lady. None of our commentators makes any effort to understand what "nature" means here, why she would be bankrupt, or why she would find her exchequer in "his."

Dynastic Disaster, or Tawdry Love Triangle?

Sonnet 67 follows hard on the despair of Sonnet 66 and on Oxford's railing against the "rage" of Elizabeth toward her own Tudor lineage in Sonnets 64 and 65. Sonnet 67 displays such an abrupt change in tone and content, so perfectly explained by our contention that this sonnet marks the moment that Southampton was definitively spared execution, that it confirms our reading that every sonnet between Sonnet 27 and 67 is about Southampton in prison, and that likewise every following sonnet through Sonnet 106 is likewise a "prison sonnet."

This eight-sonnet series (Sonnets 60-67) is thus revealed to contain Oxford's lamentations as he anticipates the execution of Southampton, capped by his mixed feelings upon learning that his life is suddenly spared. We have already sampled how the traditional commentators have especial difficulty with this series, resorting to discussions that abound in *non sequiturs* and unexplained discourses on Time, death, hypocrisy, etc., providing "explanations" of lines and quatrains that do not cohere with each other.

Here is Duncan-Jones' summary of Sonnet 67:

This follows on from the preceding sonnet's account of a hopelessly corrupt society, replacing the question of the speaker's death-wish with that of whether his friend should live. In existing in this environment, the fair youth lays himself open to exploitation and imitation; but he is kept alive by nature as an exemplar of what beauty was like in earlier, better days.

Why would the existence of a "hopelessly corrupt" society raise the question whether the friend should live? Why is whether he should live a question at all? What sort of "exploitation" might he be in danger of? What is meant by "imitation"? Who is "nature" to keep him alive? In the sonnet, "nature" is bankrupt, beggared of blood, and she lives through him (he is her only bank), so how does Duncan-Jones conclude that nature keeps the friend alive?

Burrow interprets the sonnet as follows:

> The opening question combines two distinct points of view: (a) a lament for the conduct of the friend: why should such a perfect creature spend time with worthless people? This requires the emphasis in reading the first line to be placed on infection, and carries a rebuke. As the poem progresses on to increasingly abstract concerns it is overwritten with (b) a lament for the times: why should such a perfect being exist in a corrupted world which is so unworthy of his perfection? This shifts the emphasis of Line 1 from infection to he ('who of all people deserves a better world'), and follows on from the satirical attack on present abuses in the previous poem.

"Infection" is interpreted not as something the friend has, but of what he is living in the midst of. Duncan-Jones agrees, though she notes a secondary meaning that the friend has some infection himself. By not showing how each line contributes to this explanation, Burrow fails to demonstrate how he arrives at this interpretation. His line glosses do not support this summary. Among other oddities, he reads "false painting" in Line 5 as facial makeup.

These examples of fruitless searches for intelligible meaning are again sufficient to prove that the paradigm within which they operate is bankrupt, and that their proffered readings could not possibly be what the poet intended.

The coherence of our reading of Sonnet 67, where every line contains allusions that make sense if interpreted as stated, is a very powerful confirmation that "we got it right," that the Whittemore paradigm, which posits 27-106 as relating to Southampton's time in the Tower for treason, has to be correct.

Chapter 16
But "Dost Common Grow"

S onnet 67 informed us that Southampton will live, but will remain in the Tower, without hope of becoming king. That reading is confirmed by the sonnets that immediately follow, just as our interpretation of Sonnet 27 was confirmed by the sonnets that followed it. The poet's concern for Southampton's expected death is now gone, replaced by a new concern for what lies ahead for him.

Sonnet 68

Sonnet 68 utilizes the metaphor of a map of history (with Southampton as the map), charting what was once possible for Tudor royalty, but is not possible now:

68	1	Thus is his cheek the map of days outworn,
68	2	When beauty lived and died as flowers do now,
68	3	Before the bastard signs of fair were born,
68	4	Or durst inhabit on a living brow;
68	5	Before the golden tresses of the dead,
68	6	The right of sepulchres, were shorn away,
68	7	To live a second life on second head;
68	8	Ere beauty's dead fleece made another gay:
68	9	In him those holy antique hours are seen,
68	10	Without all ornament, itself and true,
68	11	Making no summer of another's green,
68	12	Robbing no old to dress his beauty new;
68	13	And him as for a map doth Nature store,
68	14	To show false Art what beauty was of yore.

It immediately follows the sonnet that describes when Oxford learned that Southampton's life would be spared, but that he would not be pardoned or released. It reads like an open book when interpreted with our thesis, but is impossible to read coherently under any traditional interpretation. Here is a translation:

68	1	So, with Southampton now forever unable to be acknowledged as royal, the clock is turned back to earlier days

197

68	2	When the Queen's royal blood existed, but was destined to die with her, as in fact that Tudor Rose blood is now going to do,
68	3	To the days before the illegitimate, royal son of Elizabeth (Southampton) was born,
68	4	Or before those royal signs became manifest on his face;
68	5	Before Elizabeth's golden hair,
68	6	The inheritance of many ancestors, was shaved [before Elizabeth killed her lineage],
68	7	To pass the royal baton to a different lineage [James'];
68	8	Before Elizabeth's dead hair [royal blood] made another [James] royal:
68	9	In Southampton that royal lineage can be seen,
68	10	Without the outward trappings of royalty, just pure, true royal blood [with a pun on Oxford's motto],
68	11	Not taking his royal claim from someone else [like James is doing],
68	12	Not robbing a legitimate heir to stake his own royal claim [again, as James is doing]
68	13	And Elizabeth keeps him alive like a map [of what could have been]
68	14	Which shows the present counterfeit age what true royalty used to be.

Sonnet 68 looks backward—just what Oxford would be doing, as he contemplates the extinction of hope that Southampton would be acknowledged by Elizabeth. "Another" (lines 8 and 11) and "second life" on "second head" refer to James, who will displace Southampton as royal heir. "Bastard" is what Southampton was, but with "signs of fair," as "fair" means "royal." "Nature" is Elizabeth, who is "storing" Southampton in the Tower (recalling "him she stores" from Sonnet 67, Line 13), who is now a reminder (only to those few who know) of what true royalty once was (recalling "to show what wealth she had" from the same line).

Duncan-Jones interprets Sonnet 68 as ridiculing the practice of wearing wigs and "borrowed ornaments," and notes that since Elizabeth was one of the greatest offenders, it must be dated to after her death. But she also agrees that Sonnet 107 dates to 1603 or 1604, and further agrees that the sonnets are in proper order. Her two datings are mutually exclusive.

All four commentators agree that this sonnet is about the man's true beauty, as opposed to the false beauty of wigs and other adornments. None attempts to explain why such a disquisition on fashion would be interjected here.

Sonnet 69 contains a revelation that ties into history, providing yet another confirmation of our thesis.

Sonnet 69

69	1	Those parts of thee that the world's eye doth view
69	2	Want nothing that the thought of hearts can mend;
69	3	All tongues(the voice of souls) give thee that due,
69	4	Uttering bare truth, even so as foes Commend.
69	5	Thy outward thus with outward praise is crown'd;
69	6	But those same tongues that give thee so thine own
69	7	In other accents do this praise confound
69	8	By seeing farther than the eye hath shown.
69	9	They look into the beauty of thy mind,
69	10	And that, in guess, they measure by thy deeds;
69	11	Then, churls, their thoughts(although their eyes were) kind,
69	12	To thy fair flower add the rank smell of weeds:
69	13	But why thy odour matcheth not thy show,
69	14	The solye is this, that thou dost common grow.

Sonnet 69 is remarkable for several reasons. It illustrates how its real meaning is entirely foreign to any other reading of it. It also tells us something about Southampton in the immediate aftermath of his reprieve.

The sonnet is most productively analyzed by working backward from the end. The final five words are the key to its true meaning: "that thou dost common grow." The mandatory penalty for any nobleman convicted of a capital offense (in addition to execution) was forfeiture of his estates and his noble titles, which is to say to become a commoner. Once Sonnet 67 is properly read as announcing Southampton's reprieve from a death sentence, these final five words could hardly be more clear in stating that Southampton, though alive, remained a commoner.

To a contemporary Elizabethan audience, "common" would evoke precisely the meaning of "commoner," but that does not occur to any of our present-day commentators, who all gloss it as meaning "commonplace," "vulgar" or the like, or make no mention of it.

(Southampton would have been stripped of his titles and estates immediately upon his conviction a month before, but until his reprieve, that hardly mattered; it is only at this point, when he will now live, but with "infection," that Oxford rues the fact that he will live, but as a commoner. For Oxford, this fact would by itself have been a big deal. He was the first earl of the realm, and for his son, a former earl, to now be a commoner had to be a further cruel blow and sign of disgrace. Oxford may also be reflecting on his dashed hope that Southampton might have been pardoned, in which case he would not have remained a commoner.)

The first half of Line 14 contains a word that is generally understood to be a transposition. "Solye" is not a word. The word "solve" (with *y* erroneously substituted for *v*) was probably not intended; according to Booth, "solve" meaning "solution" was unknown at that time. But transposing the letters *l* and *y* would yield "soyle," one of the spellings for "soil." As a verb "soyle" was in use into the sixteenth century to mean "resolve, explain, answer (a question)." So "explanation" or "solution" is the likely meaning in Line 14, and makes perfect sense: That Southampton had been made a commoner is the solution to the question posed in Line 13, namely, why his "odour" did not match his "show." Given the word "grow" in the same line, the pun on "soil" as earth was likely intentional.

Line 12 helps us ascertain what is meant by "thy odour" and "thy show": "thy fair flower" is "thy show," and "the rank smell of weeds" is "thy odour." Clearly, "odour" is a negative, and therefore, must be the result of having become "common." We now have enough to start drawing conclusions: Southampton's being made a commoner was the outcome of his role in the Essex Rebellion, remaining in effect as the penalty now that his death sentence has been commuted. So, the "rank smell of weeds" corresponds to the "infection" of Sonnet 67.

This reading is confirmed by Line 10, where "thy deeds" are identified as the cause of "churls" (line 11) adding the smell of weeds to Southampton's "fair flower." "Thy deeds" refers to Southampton's role in the rebellion.

"Fair flower," utilizing what we already know, is a thinly disguised reference to Southampton's royal, Tudor blood, with "fair" meaning royal, and "flower" referring to the Tudor rose. Thus, Southampton, though he still carries royal Tudor blood, is now tainted by social demotion.

Line 11 tells us that this situation was the result of the actions perpetrated by "churls." Without doubt, the architect (the "churls") of Southampton's fate was Robert Cecil. While Queen Elizabeth would have had the final say, Cecil would have been able to convince Elizabeth of whatever course he pressed on her. In this sonnet, as in others, Oxford is using the plural to stand for the singular, no doubt to avoid making a too clear reference to Cecil.

Reading "churls" this way is cemented by the phrase "although their eyes were kind." Cecil was Oxford's brother-in-law, and they grew up together in the Burghley household as virtual brothers. "Kind" is used elsewhere by Shakespeare to mean kinship, and evidence exists that all but proves that this is the meaning here. In a letter from Oxford to Cecil dated by William Plumer Fowler, author of a collection of Oxford's letters,[xxxvi] to March of 1601, Oxford writes "I do assure you that you shall have no faster friend and well-wisher unto you than myself either in *kind*ness, which I find beyond mine expectation in you, or in *kindred*, whereby none is nearer than myself..." (emphases added). Clearly, both men saw each other as kindred to the other; no other reading of "kind" in this sonnet makes sense.

Lines 9 and 10 now read "They" (Cecil) "look into the beauty of thy mind" (knows full well that he is royal ["beauty"]), but Cecil evidently ("in guess") is choosing to act against him on the basis of his (mis)deeds.

This reading provides insight into lines 6-8. "Those same tongues" refers to "they" and "churls" and again represents Cecil. "That give thee so thine own" must refer to giving Southampton his life (commuting his death sentence). Cecil "confounds" (subverts) this gesture "in other accents" (in other ways), by "seeing farther than the eye hath shown." The "eye hath shown" refers to Southampton no longer facing death. "Seeing farther" than this fact would represent Cecil's knowing that he had royal blood (looking into the "beauty" of his mind), and making sure that it is burdened with the taint of his misdeeds.

Lines 1-2 would now represent Oxford's recognition that the commutation of Southampton's death sentence, without more (the "parts of thee that the world's eye doth view"), was all that could have been accomplished. "The thought of hearts" might even refer to Oxford's own heart, or perhaps to Oxford himself, saying that he could have done no better. Line 3's "All tongues" would again be Cecil, as it was Cecil who did "give thee that due," namely, his life; this reading is confirmed in Line 6, where we have established that "those same tongues" refers to Cecil. "Bare truth" likely means Cecil's decision to spare his life, which even Southampton's foes are forced to accept. Line 5 sets up the rest of the second quatrain by summarizing the import of the first quatrain: that Southampton lives, and that the people are grateful for this (or that Oxford himself is grateful for it), with Line 6 introducing "but" into the equation.

This interpretation fits perfectly with our reading of Sonnets 67 and 68 (and with 70 and beyond); it makes possible a coherent narrative that flows logically and transparently to the conclusion, that Southampton has been stripped of his noble titles and is now a commoner. Every alternate explanation must include *ad hoc* readings of words, phrases and lines that are highly speculative and that make no sense as a narrative.

In Sonnet 70, Oxford consoles Southampton, looking past his present humiliation, and seems to come to terms with Southampton's forfeiting all hope of being king:

Sonnet 70

70	1	That thou art blamed shall not be thy defect,
70	2	For slander's mark was ever yet the fair;
70	3	The ornament of beauty is suspect,
70	4	A crow that flies in heaven's sweetest air.
70	5	So thou be good, slander doth but approve
70	6	Thy worth the greater, being woo'd of time;
70	7	For Canker vice the sweetest buds doth love,
70	8	And thou present'st a pure unstained prime.
70	9	Thou hast pass'd by the ambush of young days,
70	10	Either not assail'd or victor being charged;
70	11	Yet this thy praise cannot be so thy praise,
70	12	To tie up envy evermore enlarged:
70	13	If some suspect of ill mask'd not thy show,
70	14	Then thou alone kingdoms of hearts shouldst owe.

The first two quatrains affirm that despite his misdeeds, Southampton's essence is still royal, as affirmed in Line 8, "And thou present'st a pure unstained prime." Line 9 refers to Southampton surviving the "ambush of young days" (his arrest and imprisonment for treason), Line 10 adding that he was neither executed nor pardoned ("victor being charged"). Lines 11-12 seem to say that though he may be praised, he will never receive the praise he deserves.

The final couplet attests to what the preceding twelve lines are about: "If your conviction for treason had not obliterated your ability to proclaim your royalty ("masked thy show"), then you would have been a reigning king."

Duncan-Jones typifies traditional interpretations of this sonnet by positing that the poet is "continuing the theme of the youth's bad reputation," which the poet sets out to defend "on the grounds that his surpassing beauty inevitably makes him the target of envious slander." Most of the sonnet could indeed support the notion that the young man is being slandered, perhaps because of his beauty. But the couplet obviates any such reading, making clear that the subject (young man) has some "suspect of ill" that is masking his "show," or beauty. Moreover, Duncan-Jones has just finished reading Sonnet 69 as the poet accusing the young man of being "degraded," which makes that reading incompatible with what she proposes for Sonnet 70.

Sonnet 71 begins a set of several sonnets where Oxford focuses on his own death, evidently expected soon. Sonnets 71 and 72 say that he, the poet, will disappear from history when he is dead, and warns Southampton to sever all ties to him, so as not to be tainted by association with him.

Sonnet 71

71	1	No longer mourn for me when I am dead
71	2	Then you shall hear the surly sullen bell
71	3	Give warning to the world that I am fled
71	4	From this vile world, with vilest worms to dwell:
71	5	Nay, if you read this line, remember not
71	6	The hand that writ it; for I love you so
71	7	That I in your sweet thoughts would be forgot
71	8	If thinking on me then should make you woe.
71	9	O if (I say) you look upon this verse
71	10	When I perhaps compounded am with clay,
71	11	Do not so much as my poor name rehearse.
71	12	But let your love even with my life decay,
71	13	Lest the wise world should look into your moan
71	14	And mock you with me after I am gone.

Sonnet 72

72	1	O, lest the world should task you to recite
72	2	What merit lived in me, that you should love
72	3	After my death(dear love) forget me quite,
72	4	For you in me can nothing worthy prove;
72	5	Unless you would devise some virtuous lie,
72	6	To do more for me than mine own desert,
72	7	And hang more praise upon deceased I

72	8	Than niggard truth would willingly impart:
72	9	O, lest your true love may seem false in this,
72	10	That you for love speak well of me untrue,
72	11	My name be buried where my body is,
72	12	And live no more to shame nor me nor you.
72	13	For I am shamed by that which I bring forth,
72	14	And so should you, to love things nothing worth.

In Sonnet 71 Oxford implores Southampton to forget him, if thinking about him will bring him trouble ("make you woe"). As to these sonnets, "do not mention my name in connection with them, or the world will mock you by associating you with me when I am gone."

The lament continues directly into the opening quatrain of Sonnet 72, that "if you are asked to say anything good about me, you won't be able to, so don't try. The only way you can praise me is to lie" (second quatrain). In the third quatrain, he says something extraordinary—"that even if (because you love me) you should speak well of me, what you would say would be untrue, and my name will be buried with my body and will not live on to shame either of us."

These deeply poignant lines are painfully prophetic. It took more than 300 years after Oxford's death for the truth of his life and identity to be discovered. His name was effectively buried with his body (ironically, we do not even know where he was buried), and he was nothing more than a footnote to history until well into the twentieth century. Even if he were not Shakespeare, Oxford played a vital role in creating the Elizabethan Renaissance. He was the leading patron of dozens of poets, playwrights and actors, a behind-the-scenes promoter of the high cultural level that was reached during Elizabeth's reign.

Line 11 of Sonnet 72 ("My name be buried where my body is") can only be rendered intelligibly if written by Oxford. If written by Shakspere, it makes no sense. If the poet were Shakspere, he is saying that the great Shakespeare, known throughout London for his acting, his poetry and his plays, will, when he dies, disappear from popular consciousness. That possibility is simply preposterous. *This line alone proves that Shakspere could not be the author of the* Sonnets (and if not of the *Sonnets*, then of nothing else of the Shakespeare corpus).

Tellingly, all four of our commentators are silent about this line. Given that they typically have something to say about most lines, the absence of commentary on this one bespeaks an inability by any of them to make sense of it.

Sonnets 73 and 74 continue the theme of Oxford forecasting his own imminent demise, reiterating that his death will free Southampton from the shame of his attachment to Oxford:

Sonnet 73

73	1	That time of year thou mayst in me behold
73	2	When yellow leaves, or none, or few, do hang
73	3	Upon those boughs which shake against the cold,
73	4	Bare ruin'd choirs, where late the sweet birds sang.
73	5	In me thou seest the twilight of such day
73	6	As after Sun-set fadeth in the West,
73	7	Which by and by black night doth take away,
73	8	Death's second self, that seals up all in rest.
73	9	In me thou see'st the glowing of such fire
73	10	That on the ashes of his youth doth lie,
73	11	As the death-bed whereon it must expire
73	12	Consumed with that which it was nourish'd by.
73	13	This thou perceivest, which makes thy love more strong,
73	14	To love that well which thou must leave ere long.

Sonnet 74

74	1	But be contented: when that fell arrest
74	2	Without all bail shall carry me away,
74	3	My life hath in this line some interest,
74	4	Which for memorial still with thee shall stay.
74	5	When thou reviewest this, thou dost review
74	6	The very part was consecrate to thee:
74	7	The earth can have but earth, which is his due;
74	8	My spirit is thine, the better part of me:
74	9	So then thou hast but lost the dregs of life,
74	10	The prey of worms, my body being dead,
74	11	The coward conquest of a wretch's knife,
74	12	Too base of thee to be remembered.
74	13	The worth of that is that which it contains,
74	14	And that is this, and this with thee remains.

In both sonnets Oxford expects to die soon, like a man at the end of his tether. The first quatrain of Sonnet 73 describes him as in the winter of his life, the second as in the twilight of the day, the third as the ashes after the fire of his life have burned themselves out, with the couplet telling Southampton to prepare himself to leave Oxford "ere long." Shakspere would still have been in his late thirties when these sonnets were written, creating a mystery as to why he would so fixate on his own apparently (to him) impending death.

Continuing in the same vein, Sonnet 74 adds a new element, namely, his instruction to Southampton on the importance of receiving these poems and making use of them after Oxford's death. The first quatrain says that when he (Oxford) dies, "my life hath in this line (the sonnets) some interest," and that the sonnets "with thee shall stay" "for memorial."

In the second quatrain he makes direct reference to transmitting them to Southampton, saying "when thou reviewest this" he will be examining something that is "consecrate(d) to thee;" Oxford adds that when he dies, the earth can have his body, but his spirit, "the better part of me," is Southampton's (in the form of the sonnets). The third quatrain continues, saying when Oxford is gone, Southampton will have lost only Oxford's "dregs," his body, "too base" to be worth remembering. The couplet is chilling in its assertion that Oxford's only value is what his spirit contains, "and that is this (the sonnets), and this with thee remains."

None of this is understood by the traditionalist critics. Kerrigan recognizes that the "this" of Line 14 is "this poetry," leaving undefined what he understands by that, while Duncan-Jones only sees it as "this poem." Nothing of interest is glossed by any of them about why the poet (Shakspere, for them, who was not yet forty in 1603) would be so fixated on his own demise, nor do they recognize that the poet is telling Southampton that the entire set of sonnets will be his "memorial." Above all, they are oblivious to what is most important about this sonnet, that the poet is telling his "friend" what will happen when he dies, when the sonnets will be his bequest to the friend, and will be much more important than his own physical existence. Nothing in the conventional understanding of *Shake-speares Sonnets* can provide a context in which the poet (if understood as Shakspere) would have told his friend that he expected to die soon, and that his life is far less important than his "spirit," as represented by the sonnets.

Chapter 17
Early Days in the Tower

I now discuss a few of the "Prison Sonnets" that I skipped over in my earlier discussion of this set, because we lacked the context and accumulated understanding to properly read them. I begin with one of the most famous and most frequently taught sonnets:

Sonnet 29

29	1	When, in disgrace with Fortune and men's eyes,
29	2	I all alone beweep my outcast state
29	3	And trouble deaf heaven with my bootless cries
29	4	And look upon myself and curse my fate,
29	5	Wishing me like to one more rich in hope,
29	6	Featured like him, like him with friends possess'd,
29	7	Desiring this man's art and that man's scope,
29	8	With what I most enjoy contented least;
29	9	Yet in these thoughts myself almost despising,
29	10	Haply I think on thee, and then my state,
29	11	(Like to the Lark at break of day arising)
29	12	From sullen earth, sings hymns at Heaven's gate;
29	13	For thy sweet love remember'd such wealth brings
29	14	That then I scorn to change my state with Kings.

Just two days after the arrest of Southampton on February 8, 1601, Oxford is lamenting the disgrace that has befallen his son, and is perhaps also sharing it, if his suspected role in helping the conspirators has come to light. "Deaf heaven" is certainly Elizabeth—"heaven" elsewhere refers to her—so perhaps he has already tried to intercede on Southampton's behalf.

In Line 8 the phrase "what I most enjoy" should mean Southampton's royalty, which now contents Oxford least (because Southampton is in the Tower). The remainder of the poem finds Oxford attempting to keep his spirits up, recording that his mood brightens every time he thinks of Southampton.

Sonnets 33 and 34 can now be understood as describing the new situation created by the failed rebellion and Southampton's imprisonment, and the dishonor and shame that pertain to both Southampton and Oxford.

Sonnet 33

33	1	Full many a glorious morning have I seen
33	2	Flatter the mountain-tops with sovereign eye,
33	3	Kissing with golden face the meadows green,
33	4	Gilding pale streams with heavenly alchemy;
33	5	Anon permit the basest clouds to ride
33	6	With ugly rack on his celestial face,
33	7	And from the forlorn world his visage hide,
33	8	Stealing unseen to west with this disgrace:
33	9	Even so my Sunne one early morn did shine
33	10	With all triumphant splendor on my brow;
33	11	But out, alack! he was but one hour mine;
33	12	The region cloud hath mask'd him from me now.
33	13	Yet him for this my love no whit disdaineth;
33	14	Suns of the world may stain when heaven's sun staineth.

The first two quatrains are an extended metaphor about the sun, which rises in its full glory, only to be suddenly masked by ugly clouds which hide it as it descends into the west "with this disgrace." While the sun is not explicitly mentioned, the poet says that he has seen many glorious mornings, only to then see "basest clouds" cover "his celestial face," unmistakably referring to the sun.

What the sun is a metaphor for is revealed in Line 9, whose opening words "even so" mean "just as in the case of the sun being masked by dark clouds, so...." Oxford virtually names the subject of the metaphor, with the locution "my Sunne one early morn did shine." The transparent pun on "Sunne," capitalized in the original, shows that the "Sunne" is not the literal sun, nor Oxford's male "friend," but his actual son. This meaning is also impelled by the use of "*my*" "Sunne," a peculiar phraseology under any other reading. As in many other locations, capitalization usually signifies a real person.

The silence of all four of our commentators on this line supports our interpretation. None of them makes any effort to explain Shakespeare's use of "my Sunne," demonstrating that they don't know what it, or the entire line, could mean. And, as usual, all four drop the capitalization in their transliterations.

The third quatrain continues, saying that his "Sunne" shone in "triumphant splendor," but only for one hour before being masked by "the region cloud." "One hour" clearly harks back to the sun metaphor, where a person's life is a day, and an hour would correspond to that person's youth. Where "basest clouds" hid the literal sun in Line 5, in Line 12 the "region cloud" masked his "Sunne" after the metaphorical hour. The reference to "the region cloud," doing to "my Sunne" what "basest clouds" did to the literal sun, is the clue that unlocks the entire sonnet.

While our commentators are compelled to speculate on Renaissance beliefs about "regions" in the sky where clouds could lurk, Whittemore, as others in the "PT" camp before him, realized that "region" is a near-anagram for "regina," a transparent reference to Queen Elizabeth. Coming as this sonnet does exactly a week after Southampton's arrest, the clear meaning is that by arresting Southampton, Elizabeth has hidden Southampton from Oxford and from the world ("forlorn world" in Line 7 is intended to have this connotation). The use of the singular ("the region cloud") cements the reading that this is a personification, not a reference to actual clouds. And the "region cloud" has masked "him" from the poet— again, "him" would hardly be the actual sun. The third quatrain recapitulates the sequence of the first two quatrains by moving from the metaphor to the actual narrative of Southampton's arrest by Elizabeth.

The reference to the sun having "sovereign eye" can now be seen as a metaphor for the royal Southampton—the connotation of "sovereign" as pertaining to the royal monarch is unavoidable. "Gilding" with "heavenly alchemy" also evokes royalty. "Disgrace" in Line 8 likely carries the primary meaning of "disfigure," as in the clouds disfiguring (by hiding) the sun, a meaning known from the 1550s, with a possible secondary meaning of "bring shame upon" (a meaning which first appeared in the 1590s).

The couplet, especially the second line, invites an unexpected interpretation. Examining Line 5, we note the word "permit," a verb without an obvious subject. Grammatically, the subject must be "glorious mornings," that is, the sun; thus, the second quatrain actually appears to blame the sun for allowing itself to become hidden by the clouds. This relates to Line 14 because of the likely actual meaning of "stain" and "staineth," to damage or blemish the appearance of, or to remove color from, meanings which were current from the 14th century. Those meanings would relate this line to the rest of the sonnet, where the issue is hiding (the color of) the sun, or the "color" (the person) of Southampton. Southampton's sin in Line 14 would be that he got himself arrested—"heaven" here being Elizabeth, he, "heaven's" (Elizabeth's) son (sun).

Sonnet 34

34	1	Why didst thou promise such a beauteous day,
34	2	And make me travel forth without my cloak,
34	3	To let base clouds o'ertake me in my way,
34	4	Hiding thy bravery in their rotten smoke?
34	5	'Tis not enough that through the cloud thou break,
34	6	To dry the rain on my storm-beaten face,
34	7	For no man well of such a salve can speak
34	8	That heals the wound and cures not the disgrace:
34	9	Nor can thy shame give physic to my grief;
34	10	Though thou repent, yet I have still the loss:
34	11	The offender's sorrow lends but weak relief
34	12	To him that bears the strong offence's cross.
34	13	Ah! but those tears are pearls which thy love sheds,
34	14	And they are rich and ransom all ill deeds.

The first quatrain continues directly from Sonnet 33, with lines 1-2 recapitulating the first quatrain and lines 9-11 of that sonnet, and lines 3-4 mirroring the second quatrain and Line 12. Here the onus is clearly on Southampton, who promised "such a beauteous day," only to "let base clouds," evoking the "basest clouds" and the "region cloud" of Sonnet 33, hide himself from Oxford.

The second quatrain seems to say that Southampton may now regret his involvement in the rebellion; but although regret may "heal the wound," it does not cure the disgrace of that involvement. Southampton's "shame" (line 9) does not help dispel "my grief"— his repentance (the word "repent" now makes clear what the "salve" is in Line 7) still leaves "me" with the loss of "you" and of the hope for him to become king. Southampton's sorrow is "weak relief" for Oxford, who is now bearing Southampton's cross. Then, as in several other sonnets, Oxford uses the couplet to contrast an upbeat comment against the previous twelve lines, to say that Southampton's tears are pearls, and do "ransom" his misdeeds.

These sonnets pose multiple challenges to the traditional perspective; none of our commentators attempts to discern a coherent narrative in either. Their efforts to explain "region cloud" as clouds in the upper atmosphere run aground first because they are clearly described as "basest clouds," which would be low-lying clouds, and second because the reference is to a single cloud. No explanation is attempted for Sonnet 33's reference in Line 9 to "my

Sunne," as already mentioned. Nor do any of them attempt an explanation of what Sonnet 34 as a whole is about, beyond claiming that it relates how the youth betrayed or dishonored the poet.

Sonnet 36

Sonnet 36 laments that Oxford and Southampton must henceforth have no connection to each other:

36	1	Let me confess that we two must be twain,
36	2	Although our undivided loves are one:
36	3	So shall those blots that do with me remain
36	4	Without thy help by me be borne alone.
36	5	In our two loves there is but one respect,
36	6	Though in our lives a separable spite,
36	7	Which though it alter not love's sole effect,
36	8	Yet doth it steal sweet hours from love's delight.
36	9	I may not evermore acknowledge thee,
36	10	Lest my bewailed guilt should do thee shame,
36	11	Nor thou with public kindness honour me,
36	12	Unless thou take that honour from thy name:
36	13	But do not so; I love thee in such sort
36	14	As, thou being mine, mine is thy good report.

This is another unusual sonnet when analyzed under the Stratford paradigm. All of our commentators disregard what it plainly says. It says that poet and friend must now be "twain" (separated), that "I [the poet] may not evermore acknowledge thee," and that "thou" can never honor "me" in public. This is no temporary state of affairs, as the poet understands the situation, nor did it come about as the choice of either party. Something has happened that is beyond the ability of either to alter.

But how can this separation be forever, without destroying the conventional interpretation of the succeeding sonnets? All conventional critics concur that poet and young man are depicted in many subsequent sonnets as being together. They ignore the clear import of these lines, not noticing the fatal contradiction their reading imposes on them.

Within the Stratford paradigm, the only explanation for this apparent contradiction is that the poet is lying or grossly exaggerating, that he says things in one sonnet that he forgets in the next. It is as if each sonnet stands alone. But we know that they do not.

Duncan-Jones illustrates this myopia, commenting on Sonnet

39 that "the poet proposes a separation which will enable him to praise his friend better while contemplating his merits in absence." But in Sonnet 36, the poet is saying that he and the friend are already separated, and will remain so forever—how can he be "proposing" a separation just three sonnets later? (Recall that in previous sonnets going back to Sonnet 27, the understanding was that the poet was suffering mightily from an enforced separation. Now, suddenly, are we to believe that he relishes it?)

The third quatrain stands out not only because the traditional view chokes on it, but because it explicitly discusses the core of our thesis: "acknowledgment." Here, Oxford states, "I can now never acknowledge you, Southampton. And you can never acknowledge me as your father without dishonoring yourself" ("tak[ing] that honor from thy name").

The beginning of the sonnet is also striking, with Oxford saying that as a result of Southampton's arrest, they are irremediably separated, even though they are of one blood, as father and son. Lines 3 and 4 appear to refer to Southampton's expected execution, which will leave Oxford as the sole bearer of Southampton's disgrace.

The second quatrain repeats the sense of Line 2, that they are linked by blood, but are forced to live separately by "spite," likely a reference to Elizabeth, since "spite" is the subject of lines 7-8, which say that while "spite" cannot change the fact of Southampton's royal blood ("love's sole effect"), it can prevent ("steal sweet hours from") the effect of Southampton's royalty ("love's delight").

Chapter 18
The Visit to the Tower
and the Deal with Cecil

W̶e turn now to Sonnets 43-53, a series of eleven sonnets that appears to document a visit by Oxford to Southampton in the Tower and a meeting between Oxford and Robert Cecil.

The first and last in this group use metaphors of shadows and substance. The nine in between are linked by their indication of continued separation of poet from friend. The traditional interpretation agrees with this view; this is because most of the nine involve extended metaphors for separation. The distinction between the conventional view and ours is one of context.

Sonnets 44 and 45 incorporate an extended metaphor about the four Aristotelian elements, in which, alone in all of the sonnets, the latter sonnet directly continues the metaphor.

Sonnet 44

44	1	If the dull substance of my flesh were thought,
44	2	Injurious distance should not stop my way;
44	3	For then despite of space I would be brought,
44	4	From limits far remote where thou dost stay.
44	5	No matter then although my foot did stand
44	6	Upon the farthest earth removed from thee;
44	7	For nimble thought can jump both sea and land
44	8	As soon as think the place where he would be.
44	9	But ah! thought kills me that I am not thought,
44	10	To leap large lengths of miles when thou art gone,
44	11	But that so much of earth and water wrought
44	12	I must attend time's leisure with my moan,
44	13	Receiving nought by elements so slow
44	14	But heavy tears, badges of either's woe.

Sonnet 45

| 45 | 1 | The other two, slight air and purging fire, |
| 45 | 2 | Are both with thee, wherever I abide; |

45	3	The first my thought, the other my desire,
45	4	These present-absent with swift motion slide.
45	5	For when these quicker Elements are gone
45	6	In tender Embassy of love to thee,
45	7	My life, being made of four, with two alone
45	8	Sinks down to death, oppress'd with melancholy;
45	9	Until life's composition be recured
45	10	By those swift messengers return'd from thee,
45	11	Who even but now come back again, assured
45	12	Of thy fair health, recounting it to me:
45	13	This told, I joy; but then no longer glad,
45	14	I send them back again and straight grow sad.

Sonnet 44 begins with the image of one's thoughts being able to bridge distances; the poet wishes his flesh were thoughts so that he could visit Southampton in person. The image is maintained until, in Line 11, having rued that this is not so, he must suffer "with my moan" the fact that "so much of earth and water" stands between the two of them. Earth and water are two of the four Aristotelian elements; that reference in Line 11 links directly to Sonnet 45, which opens with "the other two, slight air and purging fire," creating a seamless connection between the two poems. In the latter sonnet, air and fire are messengers to Southampton, flying, as thoughts did in Sonnet 44. Line 7 then refers to all four elements in combination ("my life, being made of four"); when the poet's substance is reduced to only two (earth and water) (while fire and air visit Southampton "in tender embassy of love to thee,") the poet is oppressed with "melancholy." When they return, with news of Southampton's good health, they "recure" his composition (making him whole once more) until the poet dispatches them again.

Sonnets 44 and 45 present two related conundrums for conventional analysis: why is a separation causing such melancholy on the part of the poet, and, assuming that Shakspere is either in London or Stratford (the two locations are about 100 miles apart, or a three-day journey at the time), what was the big deal? Do they record one particular trip back to Stratford, during which the poet felt melancholy about the separation?

When understood as referring to Southampton in the Tower, however, the two sonnets come alive as recording Oxford's anguish as the days passed. The separation is not one of physical distance, but of practicality.

The conventional critics all assume that it is the *poet* who has

214

traveled far from the friend. However, a number of references suggest it is the *friend* who has journeyed, or is in a place where he cannot be visited. The first occurs in Line 4 of Sonnet 44, "From limits far remote where thou dost stay." In Sonnet 45, as noted, the poet is sending air and fire to the friend, who bring back news of his health. The strong implication is that it is not the poet who is unable to travel, but Southampton.

Further confirmation that Southampton is in the Tower is provided in Line 8, with the reference to "the place" where he is. "The place" was a euphemism for the Tower: Essex used it with this meaning in a poem he composed just days before this sonnet would have been written. The term was used by the Lord High Steward speaking to Essex and Southampton at the end of their trial on February 19, 1601. It was later used by King James in his order releasing Southampton from the Tower in April of 1603.

Line 12 of Sonnet 44 poses an insuperable difficulty for our conventional critics, but yields a transparent meaning under our paradigm. The first ten lines are about how Oxford wishes he were an incorporeal thought, because as such he could visit Southampton instantaneously. He rues his not being so in Line 9, answering himself in Line 11 that he is "wrought" of "earth and water" (that is, matter), meaning that he cannot, of course, move as thought can. Then follows Line 12: "I must attend time's leisure with my moan." That is, he is restricted from visiting Southampton by "time." More precisely, he is waiting on ("I must attend") "time's leisure," which clearly means he is dependent on "time" to permit him to visit Southampton. In our context, "time" could only be Elizabeth or Cecil, and the use of the word "leisure" refers to nobility or royalty, so this says that Elizabeth is controlling access to Southampton in the Tower. Confirmation that "time" is an allusion to Elizabeth is provided by the several other sonnets in which time similarly refers to her.

Interestingly, all four critics understand "time's leisure" as definitely or possibly referring to waiting on the "leisure" of someone. Duncan-Jones quotes a 1963 edition of the sonnets edited by Ingram and Redpath, who render it as "a petitioner waiting on a great man, Time." Booth cites the same source slightly differently, as "the image appears to be that of a petitioner waiting on a great man." Burrow prefers his own variant, saying it means "wait on the whim of time, like a retainer awaiting the command of a lord," while Kerrigan prefers "(1) wait for time to pass; (2) wait until Time is ready to work in my favor (the poet is a humble petitioner waiting on the whim of a great man)."

I cite all four efforts to understand "time's leisure" because they again show the impossibility of making sense of crucial lines like this one under the erroneous standard paradigm. The "leisure" of Time, if time is not understood as an allusion to anyone, makes no sense. The alternate reading has the poet waiting on the whim of some nobleman (what nobleman), but for what? None has a suggestion. Why would a random nobleman be called "time?" Why would the poet suddenly say that the reason he can't visit his friend is that he must attend the whim of that nobleman?

Most tellingly, for all four critics, their reading of Line 12 following their discussion of the preceding lines, which are about the four elements and the separation of poet and youth, comes as a complete *non sequitur,* following from nothing before it, and relating in no way to what follows it. No stronger proof that the critics have no idea what is really going on here can readily be imagined. That this refers to Southampton in prison, where the Queen controls access, and that therefore access must "attend time's [the Queen's] leisure," makes sense of everything.

That several sonnets later a visit to Southampton is clearly described further confirms that the issue involves permission to visit Southampton in prison—if he were anywhere else, why would the poet need to get permission from anyone, much less the Queen, to visit him?

In Sonnet 45 fire and air now replace thought (actually, air is now likened to thought, fire to "my desire") as the elements that can make the trip to Southampton, saying that when they do, the poet "sinks down to death, oppressed with melancholy." Air and fire are "gone in tender embassy" which suggests an actual communication, with overtones of royalty ("embassy"). Oxford perhaps has been able to send Southampton a letter (maybe even enclosing some sonnets), and his anguish is in waiting for a reply. This makes Line 9 intelligible, that when the two elements return (with a response) Oxford is whole again; that interpretation is reinforced by Line 12, where the messengers have come back with assurance of Southampton's "fair health."

It is known from Privy Council records that Southampton was in poor health when first arrested, and received medical care for ague and swelling in several parts of his body. Sonnet 45 would have been written close to three weeks after his imprisonment, so Oxford would have been concerned for his health, so it seems highly probable that Oxford is referring to a real messenger who reported to Oxford that Southampton's health was improving.

Sonnets 46 and 47 are also linked by a common metaphor, the relationship between the poet's eye and his heart—in Sonnet 46 a rivalry, and in Sonnet 47 a partnership. Each organ provides a distinct way of knowing Southampton. Sonnet 46 features their competition to have exclusive access to "thy sight," ending in a mock trial where the split decision awards his eyes "thy outward part," and his "heart's right, their inward love of heart." This suggests a division between what the eye can see (the external appearance) and what the heart can know (the inward self, where love dwells).

Sonnet 48 finds Oxford directly lamenting that his beloved Southampton is in a place where he cannot help him, at the mercy of enemies who threaten to steal him away, even from within Oxford's own heart.

Sonnet 48

48	1	How careful was I, when I took my way,
48	2	Each trifle under truest bars to thrust,
48	3	That to my use it might unused stay
48	4	From hands of falsehood, in sure wards of trust!
48	5	But thou, to whom my jewels trifles are,
48	6	Most worthy of comfort, now my greatest grief,
48	7	Thou, best of dearest and mine only care,
48	8	Art left the prey of every vulgar thief.
48	9	Thee have I not lock'd up in any chest,
48	10	Save where thou art not though I feel thou art,
48	11	Within the gentle closure of my breast,
48	12	From whence at pleasure thou mayst come and part;
48	13	And even thence thou wilt be stol'n, I fear,
48	14	For truth proves thievish for a prize so dear.

In the third quatrain, Oxford visualizes Southampton confined only in his own breast (heart and mind), where he (Southampton) can come and go as he pleases, in clear contrast to where he actually is. The final couplet expresses Oxford's fear that Southampton's execution is imminent, where his royalty ("a prize so dear") is a truth that will be extinguished, and that when it happens, will steal Southampton even from Oxford's breast.

The opening quatrain seems to refer to the sonnets themselves, the "trifles" of Line 2, hidden "under truest bars" and "in sure wards of trust" (perhaps a reference to Southampton) where he (the poet) could use them, but where they would be "unused" by the "hands of falsehood" (the authorities). The second quatrain commences (line 5) by saying that compared to Southampton ("thou"), the sonnets ("jewels") are, again, "trifles," and that Southampton, Oxford's greatest comfort in life, has now become the source of his greatest grief. Line 8 bemoans that Southampton is left to be the prey of thieves (those who will shortly execute him).

Sonnet 48 is built upon a recurring theme of thievery, which fittingly describes someone who has been taken and whose life will soon be stolen. The first quatrain is about protecting the sonnets from being stolen by "hands of falsehood"; the second quatrain is about how Southampton is prey for "every vulgar thief" (who wants to steal his life); the third quatrain sets up the couplet by saying that Southampton is safe at least in Oxford's own breast, only to have the couplet say that thieves may steal him even from there (by executing him).

Sonnet 49 stands out for its use of the phrase "Against that time" to begin all three quatrains, followed by the couplet which refers to Southampton leaving "poor me." "That time" is almost surely the prospect that Southampton may be permitted to live, on pain of being forever separated from Oxford (and of agreeing never to claim to be of royal blood). If so, this sonnet most likely documents Oxford's effort to broker a deal with Robert Cecil to spare Southampton's life, albeit with strict conditions involving distasteful sacrifices. A number of documents exist attesting that Cecil desired to save Southampton, if it could be done; while he may have been disingenuous in some of them, he clearly desired to be seen as wanting to help him. More likely, it was always in his power to save Southampton, and he played up its difficulty to exact a high price from those lobbying on Southampton's behalf (we do not know if anyone besides Oxford was lobbying, and there are no historical documents that show his involvement). This sonnet would appear to reflect Oxford's proffer to Cecil, if not also at least a provisional agreement with him. (I say "provisional" because subsequent sonnets, especially 61-66, appear to reflect continuing despair that Southampton will still be executed, which suggests that Oxford later believed there was no deal.)

Sonnet 49

49   1   Against that time (if ever that time come)
49   2   When I shall see thee frown on my defects,

49	3	When as thy love hath cast his utmost sum,
49	4	Call'd to that audit by advised respects;
49	5	Against that time when thou shalt strangely pass
49	6	And scarcely greet me with that sunne thine eye,
49	7	When love, converted from the thing it was,
49	8	Shall reasons find of settled gravity,--
49	9	Against that time do I ensconce me here
49	10	Within the knowledge of mine own desert,
49	11	And this my hand against myself uprear,
49	12	To guard the lawful reasons on thy part:
49	13	To leave poor me thou hast the strength of laws,
49	14	Since why to love I can allege no cause.

Assuming, as seems all but certain, that "that time" is Southampton's release, or at least a commutation of his death sentence, we can see that each quatrain presents a similar structure: a second line that refers to Oxford, and concluding lines that document the sacrifices involved in making the deal to save his life.

The first quatrain begins by qualifying "if ever that time come," making clear this is not yet a done deal. Line 2 suggests that when Southampton is released (or reprieved), he will not be happy with the terms (giving up his royal claim) that Oxford had to agree to (Southampton will "frown on my defects"). Line 3 spells this out: "thy love" is Southampton's royalty, which will "cast his utmost sum," or die, in the sense that it will never be acknowledged. Line 4 says that his royal claim will be "called to that audit" based on advice ("advised respects"), surely, Oxford's advice (and perhaps Cecil's too). "Audit" is a legal term; other legal terms appear in the next two quatrains, strongly implying that the deal itself is a legal matter.

The second quatrain refers to "that time when thou shalt strangely pass," where "strangely" surely means "as a stranger," as they are required to be to each other as part of the deal. Line 6 recalls Line 2 in suggesting that Southampton will hardly relish greeting Oxford. Line 6 also all but identifies him as Oxford's son, with the use of "that sunne thine eye," an obvious play on the pun of "sunne/son." This line could also be referring to part of the deal, that Southampton must publicly ignore Oxford. Line 7 echoes line 3, saying that his royal blood "love" is "converted from the thing it was" to something less. Similarly, Line 8 strongly suggests a legal issue, like Line 4, where the decision to abjure his royal claim is based on "reasons" "of settled gravity."

*Figure 8 - 3rd Earl of Southampton in
the Tower in 1603, in a painting
attributed to John de Critz.*

The third quatrain states that Oxford is steeling himself against the moment of Southampton's release or reprieve, including his own role ("mine own desert") in brokering the deal. Line 11 is telling: Oxford is taking his own hand against himself, as Line 12 makes clear, to preserve the deal that obscures Southampton's royalty ("guard the lawful reasons on thy part"). Oxford will deny Southampton's royalty and his paternity.

Casting a "sum" and being "called to audit" suggest legal proceedings. Line 12 makes this explicit, mentioning the "lawful reasons" that must be adhered to as part of the deal. The import is that for Southampton to live, the fact of his royal blood must be forever concealed, along with any knowledge of Oxford as his father.

Sonnet 50 has Oxford riding a horse away from what was undeniably a meeting with the "friend" (Southampton). This confirms that he would have been in London in Sonnet 49, so it is virtually assured that he negotiated the deal with Cecil that we inferred from that sonnet. Sonnet 50 therefore strongly supports our reading of Sonnet 49, suggesting that while the deal wasn't yet final, its terms had been formulated and presented to Southampton. The knowledge revealed in Sonnet 50 of their meeting now permits reading back into Sonnet 49 that Southampton was probably not happy about the terms, explaining why Oxford anticipates that Southampton will "frown on [Oxford's] defects," and "scarcely greet [him] when" he will pass him in future.

Sonnet 51 continues the theme of Oxford's horse, here expressing Oxford's desire to speedily return to Southampton.

Sonnet 52 likewise suggests that Oxford is able to visit Southampton, but only occasionally. The first two quatrains appear to be justifications for doing pleasurable things only infrequently, so as to heighten the pleasure when doing them. The third quatrain applies this principle to Southampton:

52	9	So is the time that keeps you as my chest,
52	10	Or as the wardrobe which the robe doth hide,
52	11	To make some special instant special blest,
52	12	By new unfolding his imprison'd pride.

Lines 9 and 10 say that "time" (Elizabeth) keeps Southampton hidden as Oxford's "chest" keeps its riches hidden (referring back to the first quatrain's metaphor) or as a "wardrobe" (closet) hides a "robe," permitting only "some special instant special blest" when Oxford can visit him ("unfolding his imprisoned pride"). "Imprisoned" all but broadcasts that Southampton is in the Tower.

Sonnets 43 and 53, bracketing the nine sonnets we have just surveyed, trade heavily in the metaphor of shadows and shades.

Sonnet 43

43	1	When most I wink, then do mine eyes best see,
43	2	For all the day they view things unrespected;
43	3	But when I sleep, in dreams they look on thee,
43	4	And darkly bright are bright in dark directed.
43	5	Then thou, whose shadow shadows doth make bright,
43	6	How would thy shadow's form form happy show
43	7	To the clear day with thy much clearer light,
43	8	When to unseeing eyes thy shade shines so!
43	9	How would(I say) mine eyes be blessed made
43	10	By looking on thee in the living day,

43	11	When in dead night thy fair imperfect shade
43	12	Through heavy sleep on sightless eyes doth stay!
43	13	All days are nights to see till I see thee,
43	14	And nights bright days when dreams do show thee me.

This sonnet recalls Sonnet 27, where Oxford most clearly visualizes Southampton in the Tower at night, but by day has a murkier image of him. The first quatrain repeats that perception, confirming that there has been no change in Southampton's situation (which sets up Sonnet 49's new information that there now exists hope for Southampton's survival and possible release). Line 5 describes Southampton as having a shadow that radiates and makes others' shadows bright, prompting Oxford to wonder how bright it would be in the full light of day. The third quatrain reiterates the thought as the poet remarks that, if he could look on Southampton by day, how "blessed" he would be, given how bright he already seems at night. The couplet conveys a more specific message, that Oxford so far (this is day 17 in the Tower for Southampton) has not been able to visit Southampton. "All days are nights to see till I see thee." This suggests that the visit recorded in Sonnet 50, one week later, was the first.

Sonnet 53 picks up the "shadow" metaphor, but varies its treatment.

Sonnet 53

53	1	What is your substance, whereof are you made,
53	2	That millions of strange shadows on you tend?
53	3	Since every one hath, every one, one shade,
53	4	And you, but one, can every shadow lend.
53	5	Describe *Adonis* and the counterfeit
53	6	Is poorly imitated after you;
53	7	On *Helen's* cheek all art of beauty set,
53	8	And you in *Grecian* tires are painted new:
53	9	Speak of the spring and foison of the year;
53	10	The one doth shadow of your beauty show,
53	11	The other as your bounty doth appear;
53	12	And you in every blessed shape we know.
53	13	In all external grace you have some part,
53	14	But you like none, none you, for constant heart.

Here we find an encomium to Southampton. It opens with "What is your substance," and ends with there is none like you "for constant heart." In between we learn that "millions" of shadows focus on him, and that Southampton, as just one shadow himself, can "lend" to every one of these millions. I read this as referring to Southampton's essence as the heir apparent, to whom all England should owe allegiance and obedience. *That* is his substance. The second quatrain directly invokes Adonis as a poor counterfeit for Southampton, a reference to Oxford's 1593 poem *Venus and Adonis*, which was dedicated to Southampton. Lines 7-8 refer to Elizabeth ("Helen" is an unmistakable allusion to her) as the creator of Southampton, endowing him with royal blood (she created him ["set...all art of beauty...(and) painted (him) new"]).

The third quatrain then reads like an open book. Line 9 refers to the spring and the fall harvest ("foisin"), "the one" (spring) in Line 10 showing only a shadow of Southampton's royal blood (when he was young), "the other" (the abundant fall harvest) in Line 11 showing his full royal self; this is reinforced by Line 12's saying that he is royal ("blessed") in every way. The couplet concludes this paean to Southampton, saying that externally, he is part of everything (and everyone—the "millions" of Line 2), and is peerless for what lies within him, his true essence

.

Chapter 19
"Rival Poet"...or a Mirror?

Moving to the post-reprieve sonnets (those that begin with Sonnet 67), we come to the third of the four major "mysteries" of the sonnets that every commentator attempts to explain, the identity of the so-called "rival poet" apparently alluded to in Sonnets 78-86

We have already resolved our first mystery, the nature of the relationship between the poet and the younger man in Sonnets 1-126, as father and royal son (burying for good any notion of it being homosexual), and the second, the identity of the young man, who is Southampton. We have implicitly resolved the fourth mystery, the identity of the so-called "Dark Lady" of Sonnets 127-152, by having identified the woman who is referenced in a number of places in the first 126 sonnets as Elizabeth, such that Sonnets 127-152 have to relate to the same woman.

In their attempts to identify the "rival poet," conventional analysts have argued for Spenser, Marlowe, Chapman, Daniel, Nashe, Essex and many other writers, the respective proponents of each trying to find correspondences between lines in Sonnets 78-86 and lines penned by their preferred candidate. This approach is not intrinsically flawed, but the test of its utility lies in what it yields. Rollins in his *Variorum* catalogs the attempts of several dozen scholars from 1840 to 1940 to find such correspondences for more than a dozen candidates; he concludes that the results are disappointing. While a few resonances can be discerned, no definitive identification of any of the proposed candidates as the likely "rival poet" has emerged, and the situation has not changed in the succeeding seventy-five years.

All four of our conventional commentators list the leading candidates, and conclude that any one of them might be the rival, but add that it is just as likely that Shakespeare chose to create a composite figure. They sagely make no attempt to seek internal evidence in the sonnets for who might have been intended, implicitly admitting that they have no idea who this set of sonnets is referring to. Their failure is analogous to the way that the police in Poe's *Murders in the Rue Morgue* failed to solve their case. Here, our commentators (and all other scholars) are trapped in the assumption that a distinct "other" poet—another human being who is also a poet—is referred to. It cannot occur to them that the "other" is "Shakespeare" (understood as a pseudonym) because they believe the *poet* to be Shakespeare.

In fact, the sonnets themselves conclusively *prove* that no one else could have been the "rival poet.". To recognize the proof, however, it is necessary to actually read the poems and make sense of each line and quatrain. When this is done, a striking conclusion appears: the primary characteristic of the "rival" is that "he" is *praising Southampton*, and several sonnets appear to be asking the question: *who can best represent Southampton's qualities in poetry?* This gives us a litmus test to apply to any candidate to be the rival. Under this test, no poet who wasn't known to be praising Southampton in verse need be considered as a candidate. As none of the traditional scholars can point to any poet who fills the bill as publicly praising Southampton, at least after 1595 (and certainly not after his 1601 arrest), this test excludes every candidate ever proposed as the "rival poet."

The implication of this fact is enormous. The context mandates that the "other poet" must also have done, or be doing, what the author/poet (Oxford) is doing, capturing Southampton's essence for posterity; otherwise, there is no rivalry. In that context, the "rival" can be neither a single poet nor a composite. An alternate explanation is required.

To start sorting out this seeming paradox, we bear in mind that the poet is Oxford; the young man is Southampton, Oxford's son by Elizabeth; the date is 1601, when Southampton is in the Tower; his life has just been spared, but at the cost of never revealing his royal lineage or otherwise seeking the kingship of England.

With that knowledge, let us now examine the nine so-called "rival poet" sonnets, Sonnets 78-86. This series demands being analyzed as a single unit.

Most crucial to unlocking the true meaning of this sequence are the repeated references to the poet/author (i.e., Oxford) being unable to continue writing his praises of Southampton, and unable to make his writing public. Sonnet 80's statement that the other poet "make[s] me tongue-tied speaking of your fame" recalls Sonnet 66's reference to "art made tongue-tied by authority"; Sonnet 85 repeats this claim in its opening line, with "My tongue-tied Muse" holding her silence. Sonnet 79 states that his sonnets "are decayed" and his Muse has given another poet "place." Sonnet 82 states that the praise that the author/poet had been giving to Southampton is no longer sufficient, and that Southampton has to look elsewhere for it. Sonnet 83 refers to the author/poet's "silence" and his "being dumb" and "mute." Sonnet 85 contrasts the other poet's ability to "write good words," while the author/poet can only "think good thoughts," later characterized as "dumb (unspoken) thoughts." And in Sonnet 86, the final sonnet of this sequence, he says that his brain, the womb of his "ripe thoughts," has become their tomb, and that the writings of the other poet have "struck me dead." The couplet says that the other poet's writing has drained and "enfeebled mine."

Our conventional interpreters further misread these sonnets to declare that the rival was a *superior* poet. But these sonnets say no such thing. They *do* say that the rival has *supplanted* the author, a very different point. The standard reading is well represented by Duncan-Jones' comment on Line 2 of Sonnet 80, that "a better spirit" "suggests both a superior being and a more inspired writer."

To the contrary, in reality, these sonnets frequently mention *limitations* in the rival's praise of Southampton, and several times comment that the author/poet's own writings are still excellent. Sonnet 78 tells Southampton to "be most proud of that which I compile," while "others' works" merely "mend the style." Sonnet 79 deprecates the other poet's writing as being merely imitative, depending entirely on its subject, "robbing" Southampton only to give him back what is his. Sonnet 81 makes no mention of the other poet, but harks back to previous sonnets in stating that only through these sonnets will Southampton live on in the hearts and minds of men, "such virtue hath my Pen" (belying any suggestion that the author/poet doubts his own poetic excellence). Sonnet 82 characterizes the other poet's writing as "Rhetoric" which devises "strained touches" and as "gross painting," while the author/poet's "plain words" "truly" capture Southampton's essence. Sonnet 84 says that the other poet can "but copy" what he sees in Southampton, and will be famous only for his "style." Not one commentator grasps that the poet is affirming his own *superiority* to the "rival"—precisely the opposite of the standard interpretation.

In fact, the real "rival" to Oxford, the actual author of the sonnets, is "Shakespeare," the public face that must now, according to the deal with Cecil, masquerade as a person distinct from Oxford. In a stroke, every unanswered question about the identity of the "rival poet" is solved. We shall see how each of the nine sonnets explores a facet of what Oxford is relating about the relationship between him and his alter ego, "Shakespeare." The rivalry only concerns the circumstance that the author/poet (Oxford) cannot freely praise Southampton in his poetry, whereas the "other poet" ("Shakespeare") can do so (*via* the dedications to Southampton of the narrative poems, under the "Shakespeare" pseudonym).

Far from being a self-deprecating lament that the poet is overmatched by an unidentified rival, these sonnets are strong confirmation that Oxford has had to forever bury knowledge that *he* is Shakespeare as a part of the deal with Cecil to spare Southampton's life; merely agreeing never to reveal Southampton's royalty was not enough. This must have been sweet revenge for Cecil against Oxford, a payback for Oxford's parodying and mocking Cecil and his father Burghley in plays such as *Hamlet*.

Sonnet 81

I begin with Sonnet 81; like a few others, it contains references that do not make sense if Shakspere is the poet, and which unlock some aspect of the hidden story of what the sonnets are really about. In Sonnet 81, this second element is very strong confirmation that Oxford has had to agree to bury forever the fact of his being "Shakespeare."

81	1	Or I shall live your Epitaph to make,
81	2	Or you survive when I in earth am rotten;
81	3	From hence your memory death cannot take,
81	4	Although in me each part will be forgotten.
81	5	Your name from hence immortal life shall have,
81	6	Though I (once gone) to all the world must die:
81	7	The earth can yield me but a common grave,
81	8	When you entombed in men's eyes shall lie.
81	9	Your monument shall be my gentle verse,
81	10	Which eyes not yet created shall o'er-read,
81	11	And tongues to be your being shall rehearse
81	12	When all the breathers of this world are dead;
81	13	You still shall live (such virtue hath my Pen-)
81	14	Where breath most breathes, even in the mouths of men.

The key lines are lines 4 and 6-7, which convey the same message: "my name," that is, the name of the poet/author, "will be forgotten"; "I, once gone, to all the world must die: The earth can yield me but a common grave." (We noted Line 6 previously in discussing a cognate line from Sonnet 72, but the primary point bears repeating.) The message is astounding, or should be for any proponent of the Stratfordian paradigm, because under it William Shakespeare, the highly esteemed playwright, is saying that he will die unheralded and unremembered. This is impossible. Were William Shakespeare the true name of the poet, and were he Shakspere of Stratford, he simply could not have written those lines.

Figure 9 - The only rival that a proud Oxford (pictured here in the famous Welbeck portrait, circa 1576) could really have in his Elizabethan world would be his alter-ego, "Shake-speare" (himself).

Our four critics fail to recognize that they even have a problem. Duncan-Jones comes closest to sensing that something is amiss, observing that "The paradoxical claim that *Sonnets* will be remembered for its subject-matter (the fair youth), not for its author, is here taken to its farthest extremes." She doesn't seem to realize that the author is saying that his *name* will be forgotten, which applies to all of his known works, including the *Sonnets*. She clearly is thinking of the "fair youth" being remembered, but somehow not the sonnets (bearing the author's name, Shakespeare) that tell his story (and his name). She fails to address how if the sonnets are remembered, can their author be forgotten, given that his name (if it's Shakespeare) will be permanently attached to them?

Burrow restates Line 6 to say "I must lose at once my existence and my reputation in the eyes of the world." Burrow has accurately paraphrased the line, but, like Duncan-Jones, fails to ask why the author, were he Shakespeare, would say such a thing. Booth and Kerrigan say nothing about these lines.

The first two lines of the sonnet say that either Oxford will outlive Southampton and make his epitaph, or Southampton will outlive Oxford. The quatrain goes on to say that in either event, death cannot take away Southampton's fame ("from hence your memory death cannot take"), but that Oxford will be utterly forgotten.

The second quatrain restates this duality even more starkly: "Your name (Southampton) from hence immortal life shall have," "though I (Oxford)," once dead, "to all the world must die," to lie in a "common grave," while Southampton will be "entombed in men's eyes." Shakespeare's fame was already great and still rising; such statements would be absurd. The author of this sonnet could not possibly have been Shakespeare if that was his real name.

But if "Shakespeare" were Oxford's pseudonym, and if he had been forced to permanently conceal his authorship of the "Shakespeare" corpus as part of the deal for Southampton's life, such a statement would be an accurate prophecy—so accurate that it holds true to this day, though Whittemore's books, and hopefully this one, may one day help to finally falsify it.

It should be noted that with Southampton in disgrace and in the Tower, the assertions in lines 3 and 5 about how death cannot take away Southampton's memory and how his name will have "immortal life" are both absurd under the conventional interpretation.

In the context of this nine-sonnet sequence, Sonnet 81 offers the clearest statement that the author (Oxford) will achieve no fame or recognition under his own name, and will be unknown, despite the praise that his sonnets will provide to Southampton. While the other poet is not referred to in Sonnet 81, he is implicitly referenced; for the sonnets to make Southampton famous, they would have to be published under the name Shakespeare.

"Your monument shall be my gentle verse" (line 8) is the

clearest statement so far that Oxford intends the sonnets to be Southampton's monument—"monument" understood as a structure that marks where famous people are buried. It was from this line that Whittemore took the title for his *The Monument*. Lest there be any confusion about whether the poet feels inferior to any "rival," he affirms that the sonnets will have the power to keep Southampton's name famous even when all persons then living are dead, "such virtue hath my pen."

Let us now examine in sequence the other sonnets of this series.

Sonnet 78

78	1	So oft have I invoked thee for my Muse
78	2	And found such fair assistance in my verse
78	3	As every *Alien* pen hath got my use
78	4	And under thee their poesy disperse.
78	5	Thine eyes that taught the dumb on high to sing
78	6	And heavy ignorance aloft to fly
78	7	Have added feathers to the learned's wing
78	8	And given grace a double Majesty.
78	9	Yet be most proud of that which I compile,
78	10	Whose influence is thine and born of thee:
78	11	In others' works thou dost but mend the style,
78	12	And Arts with thy sweet graces graced be;
78	13	But thou art all my art and dost advance
78	14	As high as learning my rude ignorance.

The first quatrain begins the series with its mention of "every Alien pen" as having gotten the use of the author's verse, and under the name of Southampton, "dispersed" it. This already lessens the likelihood that another real person could be the "other" poet, because no other poet appropriated poems from Oxford (or "Shakespeare"). Only Oxford's pseudonym might be said to have so "got[ten] my use." Even more telling, of whom but "Shakespeare" could it be said that they "disperse[d]" "their poesy" "under thee"? While it is true that other poets dedicated poems to Southampton in the early 1590s, only *Venus and Adonis* and *The Rape of Lucrece*, first published in 1593 and 1594 and frequently reprinted, with their effusive dedications to Southampton under the name "William Shakespeare," could be said to have been distributed "under thee."

The phrase "every Alien pen" cements this reading, if we recall Oxford's propensity to use "ever" and "every" to allude to himself, playing on "E. Ver" for Edward Vere. "Alien" is capitalized. If "every" were to be read as "E. Ver's," then the "Alien pen" would be E. Vere's "alien" pen, or his pen name. Thus, "every Alien pen" refers to the publicly identified author of *Venus and Adonis* and *Lucrece*: "Shakespeare."

The first quatrain refers to one (or more) poets who have praised Southampton in poetry and enlisted Oxford's help in being able to do so. If our context is correct, it is 1601 and Southampton is still in the Tower and still in disgrace. At that time, what poet would choose to praise Southampton? None did. Traditional scholars avoid dealing with this glaring anomaly because they don't recognize the time frame as connected to Southampton's incarceration—once that is understood, the notion that any other poet would then be praising Southampton becomes untenable.

Any difficulty evaporates if it is a desperate Oxford praising his royal but disgraced son. If he's made the deal we posit he has, one effect is to sever the connection between Oxford and "Shakespeare," permanently orphaning the pseudonym and preventing Oxford from ever claiming authorship of the "Shakespeare" works. The effect, and likely the intent, of such a separation is to make "Shakespeare" now appear to be a real person. This may be the genesis of what became, a decade and a half later, the effort to pin the identity of "Shakespeare" on the recently deceased Shakspere of Stratford.

It might be asked why this was an issue, since Oxford was already unknown to the public as the author of "Shakespeare's" works. Putting ourselves in Oxford's shoes, we can assume that before the failed Rebellion, he remained hopeful that Elizabeth would acknowledge Southampton and make him heir apparent. The Rebellion dashed that hope. We can also imagine that, prior to the Rebellion, Oxford wanted to abandon the pseudonym at some point, and publicly take credit for the works of "Shakespeare." The reference in 1598 in *Palladis Tamia* to Oxford as the greatest playwright for comedy (almost certainly engineered by Oxford himself), and the appearance in print of many of his plays with "William Shakespeare" indicated as the playwright for the first time, even if they were pirated, lend weight to this presumption.

It makes sense not only that Southampton had to agree never to proclaim his royal status, but also that Oxford had to agree never to reveal it (hence the need for the "deep cover" of an Aesopian revelation of it in the sonnets); otherwise the author of the fawning dedications to Southampton in *Venus and Adonis* and *The Rape of*

Lucrece would be revealed to be Oxford, and it wouldn't be hard to connect the dots from there.

Some people at that time suspected that the name "William Shakespeare" was a pseudonym. As Katherine Chiljan ably demonstrates in her book, *Shakespeare Suppressed*, suggestions to that effect began to appear in print very shortly after *Venus and Adonis* appeared in 1593. It is impossible to determine how many persons knew that the identity behind the Shakespeare mask was Oxford, but it must have been an open secret among many at court and among other writers.

For that reason alone, until the aftermath of the Essex Rebellion, Oxford must have assumed it was only a matter of time before either the "secret" became so well known that his identity as Shakespeare would become common knowledge, or he would be permitted to openly announce it. Thus, it must have devastated him to have to strike a bargain barring him from claiming the authorship. I, with Whittemore, read these nine sonnets as Oxford ruefully reporting that his *alter ego*, Shakespeare, would now become a separate entity that would never be linked to him, and would forever be linked to his plays and poems.

Returning to Sonnet 78, we see that the second quatrain recites how Oxford has received his entire inspiration from Southampton, amplifying the message of the first two lines—Oxford was "dumb" (without the power to speak the truth) until Southampton's eyes taught him to write ("sing"), and was ignorant (unknowing) until those eyes taught him to fly aloft—to write the sonnets. Those eyes taught Oxford to write poetry.

Lines 9-10 say that the sonnets should make Southampton most proud, as they are entirely born of him, and reaffirm that they are of the highest poetic quality ("be most proud of that which I compile"). It should also be noted that the use of the word "compile," which meant "to bundle together" suggests that the sonnets were parts of a broader whole, not just a sequence of unrelated poems.

The assertion that the sonnets are born of Southampton is also conveyed in the dedication to *Shake-speares Sonnets*, which states that the dedicatee [Southampton] is "the onlie begetter of these ensuing sonnets." And of course, as Sonnet 76 states, *all* the sonnets are of Southampton: "I always write of you."

Lines 11-12 characterize the "others' works" (by our reading, the two narrative poems by Shakespeare dedicated to Southampton) as inferior to the sonnets, wherein the author merely "mend[s] the style" and "grace[s]" the other's work "with thy sweet graces" ("with your royalty," if "sweet" retains its former meaning). The final couplet reaffirms that Southampton is Oxford's entire inspiration, saying that, in contrast to the "others," for him, "thou art all my art," and that without Southampton to inspire him, he would have been ignorant.

Although the dedications of the two long poems were to Southampton, it is doubtful that many readers would have understood the poems themselves also to be about him. Indeed, they were mainly about Oxford and Elizabeth, with a few slight hints of a connection to Southampton; the allegorical references of Venus and Lucrece to Elizabeth may have been transparent, but those of Adonis and Tarquin to Oxford would have been understood by only a few. Thus, as vehicles to preserve the knowledge of Southampton's royalty by the union of Elizabeth and Oxford, the poems are indeed inferior to the sonnets. Only in the dedications is there language to suggest that Southampton was being addressed as a king or as royal.

In contrast, Oxford intends the sonnets as comprising a monument specifically for Southampton. While Sonnet 79 appears to justify the notion that a rival, superior, poet has come on the scene, it returns to the deficiencies of this "other."

Sonnet 79

79	1	Whilst I alone did call upon thy aid,
79	2	My verse alone had all thy gentle grace,
79	3	But now my gracious numbers are decay'd
79	4	And my sick Muse doth give an other place.
79	5	I grant (sweet love) thy lovely argument
79	6	Deserves the travail of a worthier pen,
79	7	Yet what of thee thy Poet doth invent
79	8	He robs thee of and pays it thee again.
79	9	He lends thee virtue and he stole that word
79	10	From thy behavior; beauty doth he give
79	11	And found it in thy cheek; he can afford
79	12	No praise to thee but what in thee doth live.
79	13	Then thank him not for that which he doth say,
79	14	Since what he owes thee thou thyself dost pay.

The first six lines imply that something has impeded Oxford's ability to produce his verse. Lines 1-2 say that until recently, he alone was deriving his inspiration from Southampton, and was capturing his "gentle grace" well. But suddenly (lines 3-4), his sonnets ("my gracious numbers") are "decayed" and someone else has supplanted Oxford as the poet of Southampton. This appears to reflect the consequence of the deal with Cecil, where Oxford is to be muzzled, leaving "Shakespeare" as the only poet who can praise Southampton. The sonnet concedes that Southampton does indeed merit a "worthier pen," but he immediately says that "thy poet" (line 7) simply reflects Southampton back to himself. He is "robbing Southampton and paying it back to him," stealing his virtue and lending it back again, describing the beauty that he found in Southampton's face, providing only that praise that already lives in Southampton. This seems to anticipate subsequent references to the other poet's writing as like a painting, reflecting only what can be seen by the eye. He is contrasting what the other poet is doing with what Southampton merits and deserves. This rival poet is *not* the "worthier pen" that Southampton deserves, but one who, like the "others" in Sonnet 78, reflects only the surface of Southampton, not the deeper essence which Oxford and his Muse have been supplying.

One possible reading of Line 3 is that Oxford fears that the sonnets may not see the light of day. If so, it would appear to be a momentary fear, as by Sonnet 81 he is confident that his sonnets will live forever.

The next sonnet can be seen to take these ideas further, with the poet contrasting himself to the "other" not as "decayed," but simply as weaker.

Sonnet 80

80	1	O, how I faint when I of you do write,
80	2	Knowing a better spirit doth use your name,
80	3	And in the praise thereof spends all his might,
80	4	To make me tongue-tied, speaking of your fame!
80	5	But since your worth (wide as the Ocean is)
80	6	The humble as the proudest sail doth bear,
80	7	My saucy bark (inferior far to his)
80	8	On your broad main doth wilfully appear.
80	9	Your shallowest help will hold me up afloat,
80	10	Whilst he upon your soundless deep doth ride;
80	11	Or (being wreck'd) I am a worthless boat,
80	12	He of tall building and of goodly pride:
80	13	Then if he thrive and I be cast away,
80	14	The worst was this; my love was my decay.

In the first quatrain, Oxford writes that he is "faint" because he can never use his own name in connection with Southampton, whereas a "better spirit," Shakespeare, can, with the repeated imputation that the praise heaped on Southampton by Shakespeare (presumably in the dedications) makes Oxford tongue-tied—a restriction brought about by Oxford's deal with Cecil.

The second quatrain would read "since your worth (your royal self) is so great, that both the humble and the proud can tell of it, so my (humble) boat, though overshadowed by Shakespeare's, will still be there next to you." The third quatrain appears to say that Oxford will be content with just a little attention from Southampton. Line 11 foreshadows the couplet, anticipating his demise, which Line 13 returns to, saying that if Shakespeare thrives, and Oxford "is cast away," at least he will have sacrificed himself for Southampton, "my love."

Then follows Sonnet 81, which drops all mention of another poet, and reaffirms the importance and excellence of Oxford's sonnets. When several coded words are correctly deciphered, Sonnet 82 emerges as the clearest proof so far that the other poet is indeed Shakespeare:

Sonnet 82

82	1	I grant thou wert not married to my Muse
82	2	And therefore mayst without attaint o'erlook
82	3	The dedicated words which writers use
82	4	Of their fair subject, blessing every book
82	5	Thou art as fair in knowledge as in hew,
82	6	Finding thy worth a limit past my praise,
82	7	And therefore art enforced to seek anew
82	8	Some fresher stamp of the time-bettering days
82	9	And do so, love; yet when they have devised
82	10	What strained touches Rhetoric can lend,
82	11	Thou truly fair wert truly sympathized
82	12	In true plain words by thy true-telling friend;
82	13	And their gross painting might be better used
82	14	Where cheeks need blood; in thee it is abused.

This sonnet returns to the theme identified in Sonnet 78, after making the most explicit reference yet to the "Shakespeare" dedications to Southampton in 1593 and 1594. The first line says that Southampton is not tied to Oxford, and that he therefore may, without blame ("attaint") cherish ("o'erlook," as in "read again") the dedications ("the dedicated words") which "writers"

("Shakespeare") use. The entire phrase, "The dedicated words which writers use of their fair subject," is a clear allusion to the two dedications to "their fair (royal) subject (Southampton)." The final phrase, "blessing every book," that is, each dedication "blesses" a long poem ("book"), reinforces this reading. The appearance of "every" is also a reference to Oxford, as if to say "E. Ver's" book.

The second quatrain says that thou art so fair (royal) in knowledge (inner essence) as in hue (outward appearance, with a likely pun on Henry Wriothesley's initials ("hew," the actual spelling of "hue" in this sonnet), that "thy worth" is beyond what Oxford can praise. Lines 7-8 add that he needs to find "some fresher stamp" to praise him in the "time-bettering days" (the present, with Southampton now reprieved). This likely refers to Oxford's inability to openly reveal the royalty of ("praise") Southampton. The poet immediately tells him to find some "fresher stamp" (an alternate way to "praise his worth"), but then indicates that the best that he will find represents only "what strained touches rhetoric" can offer up; he is again implying that this will *not* represent or replace the true inspiration that has been demonstrated in Oxford's sonnets. Lines 11-12 then refer to Oxford himself, with four references to "true"/"truly" as the only one who can capture Southampton in poetry. The final couplet describes the best that "others" can do as "gross painting" better reserved for lesser personages than Southampton.

Sonnet 83

In Sonnet 83 the other poet is not mentioned until the last line. It describes how Oxford has been silent about Southampton, and perhaps how that silence saved his life.

83	1	I never saw that you did painting need
83	2	And therefore to your fair no painting set;
83	3	I found (or thought I found) you did exceed
83	4	The barren tender of a Poet's debt;
83	5	And therefore have I slept in your report,
83	6	That you yourself being extant well might show
83	7	How far a modern quill doth come too short,
83	8	Speaking of worth, what worth in you doth grow.
83	9	This silence for my sin you did impute,
83	10	Which shall be most my glory, being dumb;
83	11	For I impair not beauty being mute,
83	12	When others would give life and bring a tomb.

| 83 | 13 | There lives more life in one of your fair eyes |
| 83 | 14 | Than both your Poets can in praise devise. |

The first quatrain says that the "painting" (recall the "gross painting" of Sonnet 82) made by others was unnecessary, and that the poet thought Southampton far exceeded what a poet could capture. The second quatrain says that Oxford therefore remained silent about him ("I slept in your report") because you yourself (Southampton) would show the inadequacy of any poet's description of you, trying to speak of your royalty ("your worth").

The third quatrain contains the curious suggestion that Southampton took Oxford's silence for a sin, when remaining silent was actually the most glorious thing Oxford could have done, because it meant that Oxford did not "impair" Southampton's beauty. As "beauty" refers to Southampton's royalty, this says that Oxford's silence about Southampton was necessary, i.e., that not revealing his royal descent helped prevent his execution. Line 12 supports this reading, implying that others had advised Southampton to reveal his true royal self ("give life"), which would have brought "a tomb."

The couplet returns to the theme of Southampton's excellence, saying it exceeds both Oxford's and Shakespeare's abilities to properly praise it. The use of the phrase "both your poets" suggests a softening of the contrast between them, a sense reinforced in the next two sonnets. Again, as no other poet was celebrating Southampton in writing, this phrase alone refutes all standard understandings of the "rival poet" sequence.

Sonnet 84:

84	1	Who is it that says most? which can say more
84	2	Than this rich praise, that you alone are you?
84	3	In whose confine immured is the store
84	4	Which should example where your equal grew.
84	5	Lean penury within that Pen doth dwell
84	6	That to his subject lends not some small glory;
84	7	But he that writes of you, if he can tell
84	8	That you are you, so dignifies his story,
84	9	Let him but copy what in you is writ,
84	10	Not making worse what nature made so clear,
84	11	And such a counterpart shall fame his wit,
84	12	Making his style admired every where.
84	13	You to your beauteous blessings add a curse,

84 14 Being fond on praise, which makes your praises worse.

Sonnet 84 is closely paired with Sonnet 83, as its opening line, "Who is it that says most, which can say more" follows seamlessly from Sonnet 83's "both your poets." It asks, which of us (Oxford or Shakespeare) can say more about Southampton's true nature. "Praise" in Line 2 is defined as the reality that "you alone are you," with "alone" ("all one") evoking Southampton's motto, a "you" in whom is "immured" "the store," surely, his royal blood.

At first glance, the second quatrain might appear to be referring to Shakespeare as "he that writes of you." I believe that a more consistent reading of the quatrain follows logically from Line 1, that he is describing either and both of them. Lines 5-6 say that "it is a miserly writer who does not lend to his subject some glory," which I interpret to mean that the writer who does not chronicle Southampton's royalty is withholding something (displaying "lean penury"). Lines 7 and 8 would then mean that "any poet who writes of you and *can* tell who you really are (that you are royal), will bring dignity to his subject."

The third quatrain advises both poets that all they need to do to be famous is to copy what is already within Southampton, not covering up his royalty ("what nature [Elizabeth] made so clear [created by having Southampton]").

The couplet cautions that Southampton's "beauteous (royal) blessings" also carry a curse (presumably his treason, and probably also that his royalty cannot be revealed), such that openly praising his royalty will make trouble for him.

This reading leads directly into the next sonnet:

Sonnet 85:

85 1 My tongue-tied Muse in manners holds her still,
85 2 While comments of your praise, richly compiled,
85 3 Reserve their Character with golden quill
85 4 And precious phrase by all the Muses filed.
85 5 I think good thoughts whilst other write good words,
85 6 And like unletter'd clerk still cry 'Amen'
85 7 To every Hymn that able spirit affords
85 8 In polish'd form of well-refined pen.
85 9 Hearing you praised, I say "Tis so, 'tis true,'
85 10 And to the most of praise add something more;
85 11 But that is in my thought, whose love to you,
85 12 (Though words come hindmost) holds his rank before.

| 85 | 13 | Then others for the breath of words respect, |
| 85 | 14 | Me for my dumb thoughts, speaking in effect. |

The opening line appears to say that after all, you, Shakespeare, must carry the torch, since I, Oxford, am "tongue-tied" (presumably still "by authority"), while you can proclaim Southampton's praise and "Character." "I (can only) think good thoughts" while "other[s] write good words," which I applaud.

Sonnet 85 seems to represent Oxford's acceptance that only Shakespeare can be known publicly as an author. Perhaps it represents his decision to publish the sonnets in the future under the "Shakespeare" name. This much is clear: Without disparagement, Oxford ("I") says he will praise the "good words" of others, cry "Amen" to their efforts, will say "'Tis so, 'tis true" about their praises of Southampton, while he himself will only think "good thoughts," and even "add something more," but only in thought. The couplet asks Southampton to respect Shakespeare for his public words and Oxford for his silent thoughts.

Sonnet 86

We come finally to Sonnet 86, the last of the series, the one most often cited in defense of the traditional "rival poet" thesis. Ironically, by any interpretation, it is an affirmation that the poet deems himself superior to the rival:

86	1	Was it the proud full sail of his great verse,
86	2	Bound for the prize of (all too precious) you,
86	3	That did my ripe thoughts in my brain inhearse,
86	4	Making their tomb the womb wherein they grew?
86	5	Was it his spirit, by spirits taught to write
86	6	Above a mortal pitch, that struck me dead?
86	7	No, neither he, nor his compeers by night
86	8	Giving him aid, my verse astonished.
86	9	He, nor that affable familiar ghost
86	10	Which nightly gulls him with intelligence
86	11	As victors of my silence cannot boast;
86	12	I was not sick of any fear from thence:
86	13	But when your countenance fill'd up his line,
86	14	Then lack'd I matter; that enfeebled mine.

Sonnet 86 asks in several ways if the other poet's verse was superior to Oxford's; the conclusion is that it was not. What "enfeebled" Oxford's poetry was when Southampton's "countenance filled up his line." In light of everything we have discussed, this is another way of describing how the public association of Southampton with Shakespeare has eclipsed Oxford, rendering it impossible for Oxford to reveal his own authorship—thus creating an "authorship mystery."

Oxford is now saying that "Shakespeare" is no longer Oxford's creation and is no longer under his control. The name now comes under the effective control of Robert Cecil. Oxford's two long poems are in print under the pseudonym "Shakespeare," as are an increasing number of his plays (and a few "Shakespeare" sonnets are circulating privately, as Meres reported in 1598); there is no longer any possibility of suppressing the Shakespeare name. So, to preserve the secrets that Cecil must suppress about Southampton's royal blood, and Oxford's relationship to Southampton, "Shakespeare" has become Cecil's tool against Oxford. Although "Shakespeare's" works are all created by Oxford, the Shakespeare name is no longer Oxford's property, but Cecil's. The placement of these sonnets in the sequence is no accident. With Southampton now spared, Cecil is pressing the *quid pro quo* that Oxford must fulfill, which is here chronicled. The fact that in the very next sonnet (87) Oxford reveals the legal basis for Southampton's reprieve from execution further supports the view that in the "rival poet" sequence Oxford is detailing the terms of the deal, and that it has nothing to do with the traditional view that some flesh-and-blood poet has emerged as a "rival" for Southampton's affections.

Chapter 20
Final Prison Sonnets

W e now revisit Sonnet 87, which richly rewards a detailed
review:

Sonnet 87:

87	1	Farewell! thou art too dear for my possessing,
87	2	And like enough thou know'st thy estimate:
87	3	The Charter of thy worth gives thee releasing;
87	4	My bonds in thee are all determinate.
87	5	For how do I hold thee but by thy granting?
87	6	And for that riches where is my deserving?
87	7	The cause of this fair gift in me is wanting,
87	8	And so my patent back again is swerving.
87	9	Thyself thou gavest, thy own worth then not knowing,
87	10	Or me, to whom thou gavest it, else mistaking;
87	11	So thy great gift, upon misprision growing,
87	12	Comes home again, on better judgment making.
87	13	Thus have I had thee, as a dream doth flatter,
87	14	In sleep a King, but waking no such matter.

Following on the previous nine sonnets (especially Sonnet 81,
which says "to all the world I die") the opening line is poignant:
"Farewell, thou are too dear for my possessing," followed by Line
4's "My bonds in thee are all determinate" (ended). Line 3 says that
Southampton's own worth allows him to be released from any
bonds tying him to Oxford. In the second quatrain Oxford says that
he doesn't deserve to have continuing ties to Southampton; there is
no longer any reason for them to have a relationship. The third
quatrain adds that when Southampton first gave Oxford the gift of
a relationship, he did so because he did not know his own worth, or
he mistook Oxford's worth; but now his "gift," having grown
because his death sentence has been commuted (he has life and the
potential to still make something of it), is returned to Southampton,
who should now use better judgment by severing himself from
Oxford.

Why, we might ask, would Oxford so denigrate himself and say that he is unworthy to "hold thee" any longer? One possibility is that he is saying that, although he succeeded in getting Southampton's life spared, he failed to secure a full pardon which would have (in Oxford's view) increased the possibility that he could have been named heir to the throne.

He also may be reflecting another provision of the deal he struck with Cecil, which likely included a severing of ties between Oxford and Southampton. One would assume that the two continued to maintain some connection, shown by Southampton's presumed possession of the sonnets after Oxford died, but that may have been illicit; or perhaps the deal was that there would be no further public tie between them.

It could also be a statement that Oxford has done everything he can for Southampton, and Southampton is now on his own. Since Oxford has always treated Southampton as his noble superior or royal sovereign, he would put the onus on himself for not being worthy enough to deserve Southampton.

The final couplet, already cited, is astounding. Seen in context, it confirms Southampton's royalty. The dream metaphor is just that, a metaphor for the reality that Southampton could have been king.

We now turn to several of the sonnets that closely precede 107.

Sonnet 97:

97	1	How like a Winter hath my absence been
97	2	From thee, the pleasure of the fleeting year!
97	3	What freezings have I felt, what dark days seen!
97	4	What old December's bareness every where!
97	5	And yet this time removed was summer's time,
97	6	The teeming Autumn, big with rich increase,
97	7	Bearing the wanton burden of the prime,
97	8	Like widow'd wombs after their Lords' decease:
97	9	Yet this abundant issue seem'd to me
97	10	But hope of Orphans and un-fathered fruit;
97	11	For Summer and his pleasures wait on thee,
97	12	And, thou away, the very birds are mute;
97	13	Or, if they sing, 'tis with so dull a cheer
97	14	That leaves look pale, dreading the Winter's near.

The reference in line 2 to "the fleeting year" strongly suggests that this sonnet was written on the first anniversary of the Rebellion, which would put it in February 1602. ("Fleeting" was also used as slang for "being imprisoned in the Fleet Street prison," so its use here likely was also intended as a pun evoking Southampton's imprisonment.) This suggests that Oxford wrote (or assigned) one sonnet a month after writing Sonnet 87 in April of 1601.

It also says that the period of absence between them has been "a fleeting year." Nothing in the standard interpretation suggests that poet and young man ever had a separation of a year, and nothing in that reading can explain how such a long, clearly enforced, such separation would be possible.

The sonnet describes how painful this year has been for Oxford during his enforced "absence...from thee," which made summer and fall feel like winter. Summer, which ordinarily would have produced a bounty to be harvested in the fall, yielded to Oxford but a "hope of Orphans" and "unfathered fruit." This is a clear reference to Oxford and Southampton's father-son relationship, after it was severed by the deal that Oxford had to strike. And "thou away" (line 12) confirms that it is Southampton who is away, not Oxford, and that the separation has lasted for an entire year. Such a long separation cannot be explained under the Standard Interpretation.

Sonnet 104 appears to refer to the second anniversary of the Rebellion, placing it in February 1603. If so, that means that six sonnets (98-103) span an eleven-month period. Whittemore assigns two-month intervals to Sonnets 98-102, taking us through December 1602, and assigns Sonnet 103 to January 1603. If Sonnet 105 were assigned to March, and Sonnet 106 to late March (perhaps when Elizabeth died on March 24) or early April, it would bring us to April 10, 1603, for Sonnet 107.

Precise dating can only be guesswork. But the dates proposed are likely close to what Oxford intended. Also, it seems unlikely that all sonnets were actually written in real time. Oxford could easily have assigned specific sonnets to particular dates after the fact. It is the symmetry and balance that matter.

Sonnet 98 indicates that it was written in April of 1602, judging from the first quatrain:

98	1	From you have I been absent in the spring,
98	2	When proud-pied April (dress'd in all his trim)
98	3	Hath put a spirit of youth in every thing,
98	4	That heavy *Saturn* laugh'd and leap'd with him.

The explicit reference to April, and to the spring, following immediately after Sonnet 97 about winter, makes this dating highly likely. Furthermore, an astrological event involving Saturn occurred that month.

Sonnet 100:

Sonnet 100, which we would date to August 1602, suggests that Oxford has not written any sonnets for a while, and is chiding himself:

100	1	Where art thou, Muse, that thou forget'st so long
100	2	To speak of that which gives thee all thy might?
100	3	Spend'st thou thy fury on some worthless song,
100	4	Darkening thy power to lend base subjects light?
100	5	Return, forgetful Muse, and straight redeem
100	6	In gentle numbers time so idly spent;
100	7	Sing to the ear that doth thy lays esteem
100	8	And gives thy pen both skill and argument.
100	9	Rise, resty Muse, my love's sweet face survey,
100	10	If Time have any wrinkle graven there;
100	11	If any, be a *Satire* to decay,
100	12	And make time's spoils despised every where.
100	13	Give my love fame faster than time wastes life;
100	14	So thou prevent'st his scythe and crooked knife.

The opening lines recall the previous references to Southampton as the topic that inspires his "Muse," "gives thee all thy might." The second quatrain beckons her to return, and "redeem in gentle numbers" "time so idly spent." "Numbers" refers to sonnets; he wants to continue writing them. The third quatrain becomes more serious, referring to "time's spoils." "Time" is almost certainly Elizabeth, and the muse's task is to use the sonnets to restore Southampton's reputation ("my love's sweet [royal] face"), by erasing any "wrinkle[s] graven there," making these ravages against Southampton's royal being "despised everywhere."

The couplet completes the thought, ordering the muse to hurry to make Southampton so well known that his ruin by Elizabeth (time's "scythe"—Elizabeth's death) and by Cecil (time's "crooked knife"—alluding yet again to the hunchback Cecil)—can be forestalled.

Sonnet 101

Sonnet 101, no doubt written a year or more after *The Phoenix and Turtle,* resumes the discussion of truth and beauty, in the fading embers of Elizabeth's reign. It is a marvel of construction, where Oxford engages in a dialogue between himself and his "Muse," which is his poetic inspiration. It also demonstrates the importance of grasping the significance of everything in the sonnet, not resting until grammar, syntax and metaphor all make sense.

101	1	O truant Muse, what shall be thy amends
101	2	For thy neglect of truth in beauty dyed?
101	3	Both truth and beauty on my love depends;
101	4	So dost thou too, and therein dignified.
101	5	Make answer, Muse: wilt thou not haply say
101	6	'Truth needs no colour, with his colour fix'd;
101	7	Beauty no pencil, beauty's truth to lay;
101	8	But best is best, if never intermix'd?'
101	9	Because he needs no praise, wilt thou be dumb?
101	10	Excuse not silence so; for't lies in thee
101	11	To make him much outlive a gilded tomb,
101	12	And to be praised of ages yet to be.
101	13	Then do thy office, Muse; I teach thee how
101	14	To make him seem long hence as he shows now.

Oxford's "Muse" is set up as the foil, accused of slacking off and neglecting her responsibility, which, Oxford reiterates, is to report Southampton and his royalty to future generations. "Truth and beauty" again figures prominently in this sonnet.

Line 1's describing his Muse as "truant" suggests that Oxford may have stopped writing sonnets for a time, his creative juices temporarily not flowing, leading the subject matter "truth in beauty dyed" to have been neglected. The poet then says that "truth and beauty" depends on his "love," a clear reference to Southampton, which completes his reference to the three persons whom every sonnet is about. He then asks if the Muse justifies her delinquency by saying that "truth needs no color" and "beauty (needs) no pencil," i.e., that truth and beauty are self-sufficient and have no need of the Muse, and furthermore (in Line 8) that it would be better if truth and beauty were not involved with each other.

Then the poet asks, does the fact that Southampton "needs no praise" (meaning "because Southampton, being royal, cannot be improved upon") excuse the Muse's silence? "No," the poet makes clear, because only the Muse (via the sonnets) can make Southampton "outlive a gilded tomb," "be praised of ages yet to be" and appear to the world "long hence" as he is now (royal).

The first line's meaning is self-evident, but Line 2's "thy neglect of truth in beauty dyed" is not. If the Muse is "neglecting" something, it must be the same "argument" and "invention" we have already discussed. By that reading, "truth in beauty dyed" must mean Southampton. With "truth" again standing for Oxford, and "beauty" for Elizabeth, this line would then be an allusion to Southampton by reference to his parentage (truth "in" beauty could perhaps even be a reference to their sexual union that produced Southampton).

The third line confirms that Southampton ("my love") is again the centerpiece of the poem, on which "truth and beauty" depend ("depends" may be required for the rhyme, or it may be in the singular in order to render "truth and beauty" as singular). Line 4 establishes that the Muse likewise depends on Southampton, and is dignified by him. Again, this reading is consistent with our understanding of what the constant "argument/invention" is throughout the sonnets.

Lines 5-8 appear to represent Oxford musing (pun intended) on whether things would have been better if Southampton had never been born: Oxford (Truth) could have managed fine on his own ("needs no color") and Elizabeth (Beauty) likewise (needing "no pencil" to enhance her royalty). He then asks his Muse whether it would have been best (the "best is best") if they (Oxford and Elizabeth) had "ever been intermix'd." It is hard to read "intermix'd" in this context without seeing it as their sexual liaison that produced Southampton. This quatrain begins by asking whether Oxford's Muse would rather ("haply") argue this excuse for going truant. It ends without an answer.

As discussed, *The Phoenix and Turtle*, published in 1601 just after the Essex Rebellion, featured "Truth and Beauty," to be understood as Oxford and Elizabeth, which Sonnet 101 is clearly echoing.

Line 9 picks up with Southampton ("he"), who needs no praise because he is royal, but who does need the sonnets (which the Muse has composed) to ensure that knowledge of his royalty is preserved. The answer to the question posed to the Muse in the second quatrain is implicitly answered in the negative. However, the last six lines inform us that Oxford has now given up hope that Elizabeth will acknowledge Southampton; the only thing that can be done is to preserve the knowledge of his royal blood.

Once again, our commentators provide no enlightenment. On the meaning of "intermixed," those who gloss it concur that the point is that it is better not to "adulterate" truth with beauty or vice versa. For Duncan-Jones, this reading of Line 8 contradicts her reading of Line 2, where she describes "truth in beauty dyed" as "truth which is an integral part of the beauty it inhabits." If truth inhabits beauty, and is an integral part of it, how can Line 8 imply that truth can adulterate it? The artistic domains of sketching and painting might be considered distinct disciplines that should not adulterate each other (even though sketches are often the basis of paintings), but the truth and beauty for which they are metaphors share no such mutually exclusive distinctions. Another challenge to the traditionalist attempt to understand Sonnet 101 comes from the premise that the poet's Muse has neglected her duty, and needs to be reactivated. If the poet is Shakspere, there is no good explanation, no context that could explain why the poet would claim that his Muse wants to quit.

Our reading—that Oxford is tired, discouraged and disheartened but has decided to soldier on with his sonnet project— not only makes sense of this sonnet, but is also consistent with Sonnet 100. It has a similar theme, with Oxford chiding his Muse, "Where art thou, Muse, that thou forget'st so long to speak of that which gives thee all thy might?"—namely, Southampton. This sonnet, too, suggests that Oxford, worn out from stress and in ill health, forced to abandon hope that Southampton would ever be king, has seen his poetic powers dry up. He cannot concentrate; he cannot produce sonnets the way he did a year or so earlier. Oxford is trying to will himself to hold out, to not stop writing, to not give up on creating the monument to his son that offers the only hope of preserving the memory of who he really was.

Sonnet 103 (by Whittemore's hypothesis written roughly four months later than Sonnet 101) also begins by strongly chiding his muse that, despite having the great "scope" of Southampton to write about, she is guilty of "poverty" of expression, with "argument all bare," anticipating Sonnet 105's expansion on this theme.

Sonnet 104 switches gears, and is reminiscent of Sonnet 97 in reviewing the two years that have now passed since Southampton was last a free man.

Sonnet 105, also discussed previously, almost certainly corresponds to the death of Elizabeth on March 24, 1603. Her death was the trigger for discussing what "might have been" had she acknowledged Southampton (and Oxford as the father) and brought them into the royal residence to live as a family.

Sonnet 106

Sonnet 106, surely written just after Elizabeth's death, is Oxford's summing up of the wreckage of Southampton's royal hopes, and a statement of what might have been:

106	1	When in the Chronicle of wasted time
106	2	I see descriptions of the fairest wights,
106	3	And beauty making beautiful old rhyme
106	4	In praise of Ladies dead and lovely Knights,
106	5	Then, in the blazon of sweet beauty's best,
106	6	Of hand, of foot, of lip, of eye, of brow,
106	7	I see their antique Pen would have express'd
106	8	Even such a beauty as you master now.
106	9	So all their praises are but prophecies
106	10	Of this our time, all you prefiguring;
106	11	And, for they look'd but with divining eyes,
106	12	They had not skill enough your worth to sing:
106	13	For we, which now behold these present days,
106	14	Had eyes to wonder, but lack tongues to praise.

Line 1's haunting phrase, "When in the chronicle of wasted time," is Oxford's characterization of Southampton's life, especially of the last few years when his royal aspirations had to be buried. The rest of the sonnet explores what Oxford sees in that chronicle. It is also possible that he sees "chronicle" in a broader sense, as the chronicle of the kings of England, as in his history plays, or at least of the Tudor monarchs—the time would truly be "wasted" for the Tudor lineage, now at the point of its cessation. This broader reading fits well with my reading of the meaning of "wights."

In Line 2 the poet sees "descriptions of the fairest wights." "Wight" was an archaism even then for living beings, persons, often referring to those strong and courageous in warfare. The use of the word, and the characterization of "wights" as "fairest" (royal, perhaps), suggest he may be referring to previous Tudor monarchs, which would make Line 3 a reference to royalty propagating itself ("beauty making beautiful old rhyme," the "old rhyme" possibly referring to the fact that Henry VII and Henry VIII produced heirs, something that Elizabeth did not do). "In praise of ladies dead" could refer solely to Elizabeth (using a plural for a singular, as employed elsewhere), or to both Elizabeth and Queen Mary, and "lovely knights" a likely reference to the male Tudor rulers.

In that context the second quatrain states that in the present adulation of Elizabeth ("blazon" means praising of admirable qualities, and also was often used to refer to royalty, "sweet beauty's best" would be Elizabeth), praising her every feature, Oxford sees "their" (the referent is the "wights" of Line 2) "antique Pen" "express[ing] even such a beauty as you master now." If the "wights" are the earlier Tudor monarchs, their "antique Pen" would be their spirits looking down on the current time; their "expressing a beauty" would mean their expectation that Elizabeth would have produced an heir. "As you master now" is surely a reference to the sufficiency of the royal blood that Southampton "mastered" which could have been used to make him the heir they expected, a reading reinforced by the connotation of "master" as "king."

This reading makes sense of lines 9-10, wherein their "praises" (best rendered here as their royal blood, for which they would have been "praised") would have prophesied the continuation of the House of Tudor, in effect "prefiguring" Southampton ("all you prefiguring"). The next two lines fit perfectly with this reading, saying that "they" (these spirits of earlier time) "looked (down)," but with "divining (divine) eyes," which confirms our reading of "wights" as the spirits of the Tudor monarchs. Line 12 records their inability to intervene and help Southampton to succeed Elizabeth (they "had not skill enough your worth [royal blood] to sing [make known])." This could also mean that the argument for continuing the Tudor lineage was not strong enough to persuade Elizabeth to proclaim Southampton her heir.

The couplet follows from all this. "We," that is, "we contemporaries" (as distinguished from the "wights" of days gone by), who *now* behold the situation, know the truth, that Elizabeth had indeed produced a suitable heir, but we lack the ability to make that knowledge public.

I offer this analysis as a striking example of the power of the new paradigm to extract a consistent meaning from every line of a sonnet, to produce a reading that is also consistent with the entire thesis of all the sonnets.

Chapter 21
Final Reckoning

Everyone recognizes that Sonnet 126 definitively ends the series of sonnets addressed to the young man, and that Sonnet 127 begins a new sequence of twenty-six sonnets, all concerned with a woman whom most commentators read (or misread) as dark-skinned, hence the moniker "the dark lady." But what of the twenty sonnets from 107 to 126, written after Southampton's release from the Tower?

Southampton was released and restored to favor (and would soon be restored to his earldom), but only because he had promised never to reveal his royal status. Contemplating his part in all this, Oxford viewed himself as having told a monumental lie, one that sinned against truth, religion (succession was sanctioned by God, through the Church) and all England.

The poet's ambivalence is evident in a number of the later prison sonnets we have already examined. It is more pronounced in these final twenty sonnets directly addressed to Southampton. In some, Oxford appears to beg forgiveness for the role he has played, and in others to justify it. He describes how he is at war with himself, and emphasizes that he does indeed stand for truth.

Dating the Sequence

Virtually all commentators miss the reference to one of the most clearly datable events in the entire series, which appears in the first line of Sonnet 125: "Wer't ought to me I bore the canopy," followed in Line 2 by "With my extern the outward honoring." Our four commentators define "canopy" as something that would have been carried for a visiting foreign dignitary. Only Duncan-Jones suggests that it could also be a canopy for a monarch. Assigning the sonnet to 1604, she surmises that the canopy was the one used in James' procession through London in 1604, which would fit her Pembroke thesis.

The problem faced by the commentators is obvious: If Stratford Shakspere, a commoner, is Shakespeare, the canopy could not be one carried only by members of the nobility at major occasions of State.

The line indicates that the poet himself—Oxford—had the opportunity to carry a canopy. Whether he actually did so is not clear. He may have been physically unable to perform the task; he died in June 1604, and is believed to have been in failing health during his later years. What matters is the indisputable conclusion that the poet *must* be a nobleman. This is another of the several references that, by themselves, prove that Shakspere *couldn't* have been Shakespeare.

The second line establishes that the canopy was not used for a visiting dignitary, but for a more important occasion. Elizabeth died on March 24, 1603. James did not arrive in London until after Elizabeth's procession and funeral; the public procession that would normally have accompanied his coronation on July 25 was postponed until 1604 because the plague was raging at that time. The only major event of State during this time that would have involved a procession with a canopy was the funeral procession and burial of Elizabeth on April 28, 1603.

The span from April 10 to April 28 is nineteen days, which, surely not coincidentally, matches the number of sonnets from 107 to 125. Counting Sonnet 126, the universally recognized *envoi* sonnet concluding the first 126 sonnets, this makes a final set of twenty sonnets, which, when added to the eighty from 27-106, yields a total of 100 sonnets from Southampton's arrest to the final disposition of the only person who could have made him king, Queen Elizabeth. Oxford intended exactly this structure for his sonnets. Such a structure made them a true "monument" for Southampton. The existence of exactly 100 sonnets—a century— linked by a common theme and thread located in the exact center of the entire series, is dispositive of any question that this structure was not intentional.

With nineteen sonnets to cover the nineteen days from April 10 to April 28, we have the same correspondence that we saw in the first forty "Prison Sonnets," where each sonnet is intended to represent one day. The likelihood is, as Whittemore proposes, that with the release of Southampton, Oxford resumed writing a sonnet to correspond with each day, culminating with Sonnet 125 on April 28, 1603.

Whittemore's assumption proves productive. Under it, the sonnet series comes to a chronological end at Sonnet 125, with the funeral and burial of Queen Elizabeth. Even though all possibility of Southampton's being acknowledged as king died much earlier, her interment marks the unfortunate end of the Tudor lineage, which, Oxford knows, didn't have to end this way.

There was nothing left for Oxford to say. With that "same...thing" (Sonnet 108, lines 6-7) now finished, what would have been the purpose of more sonnets? Sonnet 125 is chronologically the last sonnet; it chronicled the latest event in the series. Sonnet 126 has a different structure (technically, it is not in sonnet form). It was probably written later than Sonnet 125, intended as an *envoi*, or sendoff, with no temporal anchor.

What's New to Speak?

When Southampton was released on April 10, 1603, as announced in Sonnet 107, what more could Oxford say to or about him? Would it be the last sonnet, now that the issue of Southampton's royal blood is a dead letter? It was not, and the next one seems to explain why.

There we find that Oxford asked himself the same question:

Sonnet 108

108	1	What's in the brain that Ink may character
108	2	Which hath not figured to thee my true spirit?
108	3	What's new to speak, what new to register,
108	4	That may express my love or thy dear merit?
108	5	Nothing, sweet boy; but yet, like prayers divine,
108	6	I must, each day say o'er the very same,
108	7	Counting no old thing old, thou mine, I thine,
108	8	Even as when first I hallow'd thy fair name.
108	9	So that eternal love in love's fresh case
108	10	Weighs not the dust and injury of age,
108	11	Nor gives to necessary wrinkles place,
108	12	But makes antiquity for aye his page,
108	13	Finding the first conceit of love there bred
108	14	Where time and outward form would show it dead.

Sonnet 108 asks, "What's in the brain" to say that hasn't been said already, "what's new to speak?" Line 4 once again identifies the purpose of every sonnet: "That may express my love or thy dear merit?" The poet is asking "What is new to say that expresses my relationship as your father ('my love') or your royal blood ('thy dear merit')."

The second quatrain returns to the theme of Sonnets 76 and 105, answering that there is "nothing" new. "I must each day say o'er the very same, counting no old thing old," just as one says the same prayers every day. Line 7 again refers to his relationship to Southampton, "counting no old thing old," meaning "I never tire of talking about it," and "thou mine, I thine" meaning "you as my son, me as your father." Line 8 reads: "Even as when first I hallow'd thy fair name," that is, "just as this relationship has existed since the first day I saw you, and I (or we) named you." The choice of "hallow'd" also suggests a christening ceremony and a consecration, the conceptions of royal and sacred being virtually synonymous given the divinity of kings.

The final six lines could then be rendered as:

So, your eternal royal blood in your newly freed body
Is not subject to getting old or wearing out,
Nor will it show itself old in outward appearance,
But will rather be eternal (subjugate history and make it its servant),
It (your royal blood) knows it was bred in your person
Despite the fact that to all the world at this point, it is hidden and unknown ("dead")

In other words, Southampton's royalty, which now exists in the person of a freed prisoner ("love's fresh case"), is no longer a prisoner of the past and is not subject to aging. It has risen above history, even though no one knows about it.

Note the use of the appellation "boy" in Line 5, a reference to Southampton as Oxford's son, not to a child or young adult, which, when coupled with "sweet," yields "my royal son."

Rift with Southampton?

The tone abruptly changes with Sonnet 109, which appears to belie that the remaining sonnets will be "more of the same." Oxford appears to be on the defensive, responding to unspecified charges or accusations, presumably from Southampton. If Sonnet 108 strongly echoes Sonnets 76 and 105, again affirming that "(I) write still all one, ever the same," Sonnets 109-125 appear to be anything but such a continuation. The shift in tone between the end of Sonnet 108 and the opening line of Sonnet 109 is dramatic: "O, never say that I was false of heart."

Sonnet 110 opens with "Alas 'tis true, I have gone here and there." Sonnet 111 opens with "O for my sake do you wish fortune chide." Line 1 of Sonnet 112 is "Your love and pity doth th' impression fill," and of Sonnet 113, "Since I left you, mine eye is in my mind." All five of these sonnets seem to describe a dialogue with Southampton or a response to something Southampton has communicated to Oxford. Southampton appears to have been critical of him, presumably for some aspect of the deal with Cecil. Sonnet 113 confirms that Oxford and Southampton met, possibly on the day after his release. The opening line in Sonnet 109 is Oxford's first response to an accusation that Southampton presumably leveled at him during that meeting, to the effect that Oxford had been "false of heart."

Sonnet 109

Sonnet 109 begins with an apparent appeal to Southampton not to consider the deal that Oxford struck with Cecil as having sold him out. It continues with an appeal to Southampton never to believe that Oxford was anything but loyal to him:

109	1	O, never say that I was false of heart,
109	2	Though absence seem'd my flame to qualify.
109	3	As easy might I from myself depart
109	4	As from my soul, which in thy breast doth lie:
109	5	That is my home of love: if I have ranged,
109	6	Like him that travels I return again,
109	7	Just to the time, not with the time exchanged,
109	8	So that myself bring water for my stain.
109	9	Never believe, though in my nature reign'd
109	10	All frailties that besiege all kinds of blood,
109	11	That it could so preposterously be stain'd,
109	12	To leave for nothing all thy sum of good;
109	13	For nothing this wide Universe I call,
109	14	Save thou, my Rose; in it thou art my all.

Line 2 says that though it might appear that during Southampton's imprisonment Oxford was "false of heart," in reality (lines 3-4) Oxford could no more separate from himself than from his soul, which lies within Southampton's breast ("in thy breast doth lie"). Line 5 says that in Southampton's breast is "my home of love," to which "I return again," and bring water to erase any stain "I" may have committed. The reference to "bringing water" may also likely be intended to reference Oxford's ceremonial role in the coronation of James, to be held on July 25, as "water-bearer to the monarch."

In the third quatrain, Oxford says that no matter what frailties he might have had, none would have induced him "to leave for nothing all thy sum of good" (line 12), which he reiterates in the couplet, saying "For nothing this wide Universe I call, Save thou, my Rose, in it thou are my all." To Oxford the "wide Universe" is nothing except for Southampton, "my (Tudor) Rose," who is the only thing of importance.

Sonnet 110

Sonnet 110 opens by stating that he agrees with something Southampton said about him (something negative). "Alas, 'tis true," Oxford admits, followed by an admission of what Oxford has done to himself by having struck this deal:

110	1	Alas, 'tis true I have gone here and there
110	2	And made myself a motley to the view,
110	3	Gored mine own thoughts, sold cheap what is most dear,
110	4	Made old offences of affections new;
110	5	Most true it is that I have look'd on truth
110	6	Askance and strangely: But, by all above,
110	7	These blenches gave my heart another youth,
110	8	And worse essays proved thee my best of love.
110	9	Now all is done, have what shall have no end:
110	10	Mine appetite I never more will grind
110	11	On newer proof, to try an older friend,
110	12	A God in love, to whom I am confined.
110	13	Then give me welcome, next my heaven the best,
110	14	Even to thy pure and most loving breast.

Oxford says he has "gor'd mine own thoughts, sold cheap what is most dear," (line 3), and has "looked on truth askance and strangely" (lines 5-6). He explains in lines 7-8, that these "blenches" (deviations from truth) "gave my heart (Southampton) another youth (new life, being spared execution)," that his terrible actions ("worse essays") nonetheless proved how much he loved Southampton. He comments in Line 9 that "Now all is done, have what shall have no end," meaning, it's all over. He states that he will never again attempt to prove Southampton's royalty, but will remain "confined" to Southampton, described as a "God in love," meaning, a royal King, ordained by God. The couplet asks Southampton to give him welcome to his "pure and most loving breast," a plea to heal any rift that may have developed between them.

Sonnet 111

Sonnet 111 invokes images of the sacrifice that Oxford had to make in his efforts to help Southampton, listing some of the penances that Oxford is prepared to do to wipe away his stain:

111	1	O, for my sake do you with Fortune chide,
111	2	The guilty goddess of my harmful deeds,
111	3	That did not better for my life provide
111	4	Than public means which public manners breeds.
111	5	Thence comes it that my name receives a brand,
111	6	And almost thence my nature is subdued
111	7	To what it works in, like the Dyer's hand:
111	8	Pity me then and wish I were renew'd;
111	9	Whilst, like a willing patient, I will drink
111	10	Potions of Eisel 'gainst my strong infection
111	11	No bitterness that I will bitter think,
111	12	Nor double penance, to correct correction.
111	13	Pity me then, dear friend, and I assure ye
111	14	Even that your pity is enough to cure me.

The sonnet opens with what appears to be a reproach from Southampton, that "you (Southampton) wish to chide fortune (or Oxford himself) on account of me (for my misdeeds)," supported by Line 2, saying that fortune ("the guilty goddess") was the cause of those "harmful deeds." In the rest of the sonnet Oxford seeks to do penance, and to beg for Southampton's pity. Lines 3-4 can be read as "(my harmful deeds) for my life did no better than secure your rehabilitation ('public manners') and the restoration of your earldom ('public means')."

Line 5 says that "my name receives a brand" (branding was a form of punishment for criminals), meaning that Oxford has suffered some disgrace. Line 6 continues with "my nature is (almost) subdued" to become like the ink that dyers use ("dye" also often meant a marker of a crime, as a stain). The third quatrain turns to the subject of Oxford's willingness to do penance. In lines 9-10, he says that he would willingly drink "potions of Eisel" to heal his "infection." "Potions of Eisel" signifies the vinegar that Christ was given while on the cross. The stain can only be the deal he made never to support Southampton's claim to the throne, which to Oxford constituted a crime and an act of dishonesty. The couplet returns to the direct entreaty with which the sonnet began, asking Southampton at the very least to pity him, which alone would cure him.

Sonnet 112

Sonnet 112 picks up where Sonnet 111 leaves off, referring in the first line to Southampton's "pity," pairing it with his "love," and saying that Southampton's "love and pity" are the only things of importance to Oxford.

112	1	Your love and pity doth the impression fill
112	2	Which vulgar scandal stamp'd upon my brow;
112	3	For what care I who calls me well or ill,
112	4	So you o'er-green my bad, my good allow?
112	5	You are my All the world, and I must strive
112	6	To know my shames and praises from your tongue:
112	7	None else to me, nor I to none alive,
112	8	That my steel'd sense or changes right or wrong.
112	9	In so profound Abysm I throw all care
112	10	Of others' voices, that my Adder's sense
112	11	To critic and to flatterer stopped are.
112	12	Mark how with my neglect I do dispense:
112	13	You are so strongly in my purpose bred
112	14	That all the world besides methinks are dead.

The first quatrain says that Oxford doesn't care what the public thinks of him, as long as Southampton will excuse or overlook his faults ("o'er-green my bad") and acknowledge his good ("my good allow"). The second quatrain states that only Southampton can inform Oxford of his "shames and praises," that no one else can tell Oxford about right and wrong. In the third quatrain, Oxford says that he throws the opinions of others into the abyss, that he is deaf ("my adder's sense") to the words of critics and flatterers alike (those who in Line 3 call him "well or ill"). The couplet concludes by saying that "you are everything to me," and that no one else matters (aside from "you," "methinks" "all the world aside from [you] are dead" [of no interest] [to me]).

Sonnet 113 begins by making clear that Oxford recently "left" Southampton, which almost surely occurred shortly after Southampton was released.

Sonnet 116

Moving to Sonnet 116, we have a special treat—a sonnet which on its surface level is quintessentially eloquent about what true love is, but which conveys an Aesopian message that has nothing to do with the surface meaning. It is among the handful that are most widely read and recited. Its popularity stems in part from the fact that there is no internal reference to the gender of the object of love, permitting the presumption that it refers to ordinary (heterosexual) romantic love.

However, as with all of the first 126 sonnets, it *is* to Southampton. Its true message is not about the quality of permanence of love between two persons, but about the permanence of the love between Oxford and his royal son, and the permanence of Southampton's royalty, which not even Time can alter. Possibly no other sonnet presents simultaneously such a seemingly coherent surface message together with an underlying, true message that is opposite from that surface reading. (We shall see on closer examination below that the seeming coherence of the surface reading is actually largely an illusion.)

116	1	Let me not to the marriage of true minds
116	2	Admit impediments. Love is not love
116	3	Which alters when it alteration finds,
116	4	Or bends with the remover to remove:
116	5	O no! it is an ever-fixed mark
116	6	That looks on tempests and is never shaken;
116	7	It is the star to every wandering bark,
116	8	Whose worth's unknown, although his height be taken.
116	9	Love's not Time's fool, though rosy lips and cheeks
116	10	Within his bending sickle's compass come:
116	11	Love alters not with his brief hours and weeks,
116	12	But bears it out even to the edge of doom.
116	13	If this be error and upon me proved,
116	14	I never writ, nor no man ever loved.

The surface meaning, that "true love" is a transcendent, constant quality, proves unsustainable on closer analysis. First, we have already established the correct context, which is Oxford speaking of Southampton after his release. Second (unnoted by all but one conventional scholar) is that this is not an abstract discourse on love, but is Oxford responding to something that Southampton has stated, perhaps that either the father-son bond between them or his royal blood had been altered by changed circumstances. Oxford is arguing back, saying that neither our love (our relationship) nor your royalty have been altered just because some externalities have changed ("it alteration finds"). "O no, it is an ever-fixed mark," Oxford continues, that isn't shaken even by tempests, and is a star to every ship on the sea—perhaps a reference to how the world should regard Southampton as a king.

Alone among traditionalist commentators, Helen Vendler has astutely recognized that Sonnet 116 is the poet's reply to something that the young man has said, presumably something to the effect that their love has impediments, and must come to terms with changes ("alterations"). In *The Art of Shakespeares Sonnets*, she writes that this sonnet is usually read as "a definition of true love," to which she contrasts her view that it "springs from the fiction of an anterior utterance by another which the sonnet is concerned to repudiate."[xxxvii] She finds that the prevalence of negative words and the overall syntax strongly suggest that the poem is a rebuttal to arguments made by the young man that maintain the opposite of every quality of love extolled in this sonnet.

Expressing amazement that her insight has gone unnoticed, Vendler writes:

> No reader, to my knowledge, has seen "Let me not to the marriage of true minds" as a coherent refutation of the extended implied argument of an opponent, and this represents an astonishing history of critical oversight, a paradigmatic case of how reading a poem as though it were an essay, governed by an initial topic sentence, can miss its entire aesthetic dynamic. Because many readers still seek, in the anxiety of reading, a reassuring similarity of patterning among quatrains rather than a perplexing difference, and prefer to think of the Sonnets as discursive propositional statements rather than as situationally motivated speech-acts, we remain condemned to a static view of any given sonnet.[xxxviii]

This is truly an insightful observation. It accurately describes how Whittemore and I approach each sonnet, seeking to determine what is happening, what is the dynamic between quatrains, what "off-scene" issue or fact is being responded to, if any, and how each sonnet is constructed. Her phrase "discursive propositional statements" aptly characterizes the conventional readings of many passages throughout the sonnets, which turn those sonnets into abstract commentaries on random topics, rather than the focused "situationally motivated speech-acts" that Vendler, and Whittemore and I, concur they really are.

Vendler's observation that so many readers fail to see the "perplexing difference" that sometimes appears between quatrains in a sonnet also accords with the approach Whittemore and I employ. The way that Shakespeare frequently uses quatrains within a sonnet to make contrasting points, or to build up a single point by going from the particular to the general, demands that close attention be paid to sonnet construction. The pity here is that

Vendler, as a Stratfordian, cannot begin to apply the gift of her insights to actually solve the *Sonnets*, a handicap compounded by her core belief that the "young man" was a fictive poetic device, not a real person.

The opening reference to "true" minds recalls Oxford himself; Southampton, as Oxford's son, might also be said to share the appellation "true" by inheritance from Oxford. "Love is not love which alters when it alteration finds" says that the quality of true royalty will not alter when it encounters changed circumstances (such as those Oxford and Southampton now face), nor "bend" with "the remover." "Alteration" most likely also refers to the accession of James ("the alteration of succession" was a contemporary phrase denoting royal succession), as it plays with the related word "alters" earlier in the line. Line 4 must remain cryptic to a traditionalist reading; in the correct context, there is no mystery as to what has been "removed"—Southampton's claim to the throne—nor by whose agency—Cecil is "the remover." "Bends" likely also is intended to evoke Cecil's hunchback. This line is cautioning Southampton not to permit Cecil to come between them.

The second quatrain again recalls Oxford with "ever-fixed mark," saying that Southampton's royalty ("love") is a constant star; though his "worth's unknown" (literally—his royalty is unknown), his value ("height") is perceived.

Lines 9-10 present Time (capitalized in the original) as Death: "rosy lips and cheeks" evoke the Tudor rose and Elizabeth, both of which have just been cut down by Time's "bending sickle's compass." "Love's not Time's fool" means that Death can cut down Elizabeth, even eradicate the Tudor line, but it cannot conquer "Love"—the fact of Southampton's royalty. This royalty ("Love") is not affected by the vicissitudes of Time (aka Death) (it does not change with Time's "brief hours and weeks"), but will radiate even to eternity ("doom") (evoking previous statements that knowledge of Southampton and his royalty will outlast marble monuments and last till the Last Judgment).

The couplet emphatically asserts Oxford's confidence in the truth of what he has written in the previous twelve lines.

We can now see that even the seeming coherence of the popular understanding of this sonnet is much less than first meets the eye. The sonnet seems to say that the only kind of love that is "true" is a constant love that remains even when the beloved no longer loves back, nor "bends with the remover to remove," which begs for an explanation for what "remover" is. Not even tempests can shake it, we are told in Line 6, and it is like the North Star, guidepost to every ship at sea, though its "worth's unknown," an odd phrase under this reading. The third quatrain says that love transcends the flesh and lasts until eternity. While "Love's not Time's fool" might be glossed as "Love transcends mortality" (line 10 makes clear that "Time" is the grim reaper), the rest of lines 9 and 10 appear to say just the opposite—that "rosy lips and cheeks" will be cut down by Time. Line 12 appears anomalous, suggesting that love is eternal—but how could mortal love transcend the lifetime of the lover, much less last forever? The couplet is then absurd—it appears to say that if this interpretation of love is not true, then love has never existed in the world, and he, Shakespeare, has never written anything.

Booth concurs that Sonnet 116 is problematic, noting that its "virtues...are more than usually susceptible to dehydration in critical comment. The more one thinks about this grand, noble, absolute, convincing, and moving gesture, the less there seems to be to it." Our other commentators are also at pains to explain some of its passages, indicating that even conventional scholars recognize defects in the surface reading.

Sonnets 117 and 118

In Sonnet 117, Oxford returns to the theme that while Southampton may have many justified accusations to make against him, including neglect, in his own defense, he (Oxford) "did strive to prove the constancy and virtue of your love" (Southampton's royal claim to the throne).

The first two quatrains of Sonnet 118 state that to save Southampton, Oxford had to make himself sick. The third quatrain strongly alludes to how the evil or "ill" of the deal that Oxford made, and that Southampton went along with, led to the greater good of a peaceful transition of power:

118	9	Thus policy in love to anticipate
118	10	The ills that were, not grew to faults assured
118	11	And brought to medicine a healthful state
118	12	Which, rank of goodness, would by ill be cured:

The sonnet is anchored on imagery from medicine, that it is often necessary to induce an illness to reach eventual health. The first quatrain describes taking medicines that lead to sickness and "purg[ing]" to expel the illness. The second quatrain builds on this, to say that Oxford fed on "bitter sauces," becoming "diseased" in preparation for doing good. The third quatrain is difficult to decode, but the general meaning appears to be that the issue of Southampton's royalty ("policy in love") had to be resolved (that is, buried) to forestall "faults assured" and bring "medicine" (England) to a "healthful state" (a peaceful state with the transition to James). The resulting goodness was thereby "cured" by "ill," the ill of the deal that had to be made, which was bitter medicine for Oxford. "Ill" also evokes "Captain Ill" of Sonnet 66, Cecil (the second syllable of whose name is a homonym for "ill"), as does "the ills" of Line 10.

The couplet then tells us:

| 118 | 13 | But thence I learn, and find the lesson true, |
| 118 | 14 | Drugs poison him that so fell sick of you. |

That is, having sacrificed his "health" by taking the "drugs" of the deal, Oxford learned that those drugs "poison[ed] him [Oxford]" that "so fell sick [on account] of you."

This sonnet restates ideas that Oxford put forth in many other sonnets; here the message is as clear as it is poignant. Oxford is tormented by the awfulness of what he has had to do, and can't help second-guessing himself. There was no good course of action, only a choice between bad and worse.

Sonnet 119

Sonnet 119 continues the medical metaphor, repeats that "ill" has gained more than it has lost, and suggests that Oxford is finally moving to a resolution of the tension he feels:

119	1	What potions have I drunk of *Siren* tears,
119	2	Distill'd from Limbecks foul as hell within,
119	3	Applying fears to hopes and hopes to fears,
119	4	Still losing when I saw myself to win!
119	5	What wretched errors hath my heart committed,
119	6	Whilst it hath thought itself so blessed never!
119	7	How have mine eyes out of their spheres been fitted
119	8	In the distraction of this madding fever!
119	9	O benefit of ill! now I find true
119	10	That better is by evil still made better;
119	11	And ruin'd love, when it is built anew,
119	12	Grows fairer than at first, more strong, far greater.
119	13	So I return rebuked to my content
119	14	And gain by ill thrice more than I have spent.

The first quatrain continues from Sonnet 118 the notion of

taking a terrible potion. The second laments the "wretched errors" his heart committed thinking itself "blessed," and describes how his eyes ache from "madding fever." The third suddenly changes the evaluation, stating that "I find true" the "benefit of ill" (the ill he did was worth it), that "evil" made "better" even "better," and that "ruined love" became more royal than ever ("grows fairer than at first") when he was given his life again ("built anew"). Summing up in the couplet, Oxford announces that though he has been rebuked, he gained three times more than he lost ("spent") by the "ills" he committed.

Sonnet 120

In Sonnet 120 Oxford begins to transition from what could be called the *mea culpa* attitude of many of the preceding sonnets to the affirmation of his own truth in Sonnet 125, a process of seeking inner peace. Sonnet 120 begins with statements of mutual injury, develops to the point in the third quatrain where "you" *versus* "I" becomes "our," and proceeds to the couplet, where each party has a mutual obligation toward the other.

120	1	That you were once unkind befriends me now,
120	2	And for that sorrow which I then did feel
120	3	Needs must I under my transgression bow,
120	4	Unless my Nerves were brass or hammer'd steel.
120	5	For if you were by my unkindness shaken
120	6	As I by yours, y'have pass'd a hell of Time,
120	7	And I, a tyrant, have no leisure taken
120	8	To weigh how once I suffered in your crime.
120	9	O, that our night of woe might have remember'd
120	10	My deepest sense, how hard true sorrow hits,
120	11	And soon to you, as you to me, then tender'd
120	12	The humble salve which wounded bosoms fits!
120	13	But that your trespass now becomes a fee;
120	14	Mine ransoms yours, and yours must ransom me.

The first quatrain states that the "sorrow" Oxford had experienced (during the prison years) when Southampton "was once unkind" must be tempered by the fact of his own transgression at that time. "Unkind" may also refer to "kind" as Southampton as Oxford's son, a tie that had to be officially severed (making him "un-kind"), or even to a period when perhaps they were not allowed to contact each other.

In the second quatrain, where Oxford asks if Southampton was as "shaken" by Oxford's unkindness as he was of Southampton's, he says "y'have passed a hell of Time," suggesting that he, as Oxford, suffered mightily, also evoking that the suffering was by Elizabeth's ("Time['s]") hand. Lines 7-8 add that he (Oxford) has not spent time thinking about how he has suffered for Southampton's crime (his treasonous role in the Rebellion). The third quatrain starts by referring to "our night of woe" (Southampton's prison term) and ends by mentioning how Southampton tendered Oxford "the humble salve," possibly a reference to the "salve" of Sonnet 33, which was Southampton's repentance for what he had done.

The couplet states that Oxford has ransomed Southampton for his trespass, for which Oxford paid the "fee" (which we know to be his anonymity, and silence on Southampton's parentage and royalty), in exchange for which Oxford tells Southampton he must now ransom Oxford (which we know means being sure to publish the sonnets so that Oxford will not be lost to history).

Whittemore sums up the meaning of this last line:

> Southampton's fee (to ransom Oxford from his obliteration) is to see that this monument of verse gets into print; though the sonnets are preserving "the living record" of Southampton, they also contain Oxford's life and truth: "And death to me subscribes,/ Since spite of him I'll live in this poor rhyme"—Sonnet 107, lines 10-11; therefore, with Southampton having been liberated, it's Oxford who is now "supposed as forfeit to a confined doom" (Sonnet 107, Line 4) and his life (in the eyes of posterity) is in his son's hands, i.e., Southampton is "A god in love, to whom I am confined" –Sonnet 110, line 12.[xxxix]

Sonnets 121-122

Sonnet 121 returns to the theme of how popular opinion is to be ignored in evaluating Oxford. The "false adulterate(d)" views others hold of him should have no weight. In the third quatrain, he quotes Yahweh from the Old Testament, saying "No, I am that I am," adds that those who cite his faults only reveal their own, and concludes the quatrain saying that their "rank thoughts" cannot be relied on to recount his deeds:

121 12 By their rank thoughts my deeds must not be shown
121 13 Unless this general evil they maintain,
121 14 All men are bad, and in their badness reign.

Grammatically, Line 12 must be connected to the couplet, as

there is no punctuation at the end; that compels the reading that "my deeds must not be reported by those 'others' who will report them falsely, unless they inhabit a world in which all men are bad, and therefore badness reigns." I interpret this as saying that if it turns out that evil has triumphed in the world, then these evil "others" will provide the only report (a false one) of Oxford's deeds.

This couplet leads directly into Sonnet 122, which records Oxford entrusting the sonnets to Southampton's care.

122	1	Thy gift, thy tables, are within my brain
122	2	Full character'd with lasting memory,
122	3	Which shall above that idle rank remain
122	4	Beyond all date, even to eternity;
122	5	Or at the least, so long as brain and heart
122	6	Have faculty by nature to subsist;
122	7	Till each to razed oblivion yield his part
122	8	Of thee, thy record never can be miss'd.
122	9	That poor retention could not so much hold,
122	10	Nor need I tallies thy dear love to score;
122	11	Therefore to give them from me was I bold,
122	12	To trust those tables that receive thee more:
122	13	To keep an adjunct to remember thee
122	14	Were to import forgetfulness in me.

Surprisingly, none of our commentators recognizes that "tables" refers to the sonnets themselves; they read "tables" as "notebook" and speculate about whether the "gift" is a blank book or one containing writings (whether of the friend or the poet our commentators are not clear on). All of them read the poem as an apology by the poet to the friend for having given away this notebook. To whom it might have been given, why he would do such a thing if it meant so much to the friend, or why it would matter to the friend if in fact the notebook were blank are not addressed.

All the commentators recognize that Sonnet 126 is the final sonnet to or about the friend, and correctly see Sonnets 123-126 as therefore wrapping up the series. But they do not see Sonnet 122 in any broader context, and, as so often before, they attempt to read it as *sui generis*, seeking to tease a meaning with only local relevance. They thereby miss several clear markers that belie their interpretations.

First, a gift once given becomes the property of the recipient. The expression "thy gift" could just as well be the gift *from* the poet, after it has been given, as it could be a gift from the friend. In context, the former is the required interpretation, a possibility none of our commentators considers. The clear meaning of lines 11-12, that the poet was the giver ("to give them from me"), and the friend the receiver (properly parsed as "that thee receive"), is likewise missed.

More importantly, none recognizes the resonance of lines 3-8 with the passages in several earlier sonnets stating that the sonnets will ensure that knowledge of the true nature of the "friend" will endure until the end of time. These lines clearly state that the "tables" "shall...remain beyond all date, even to eternity," or, at least until Judgment Day, the likely meaning of "so long as brain and heart" (that is, people) continue to "subsist." Lines 7-8 say that "thy record" (the story recorded in the sonnets) will exist until "oblivion" erases that memory ("his part of thee") from "each" person then alive. This final reference to writings lasting until the end of time refers to the same writings—the sonnets themselves— that all previous such references clearly allude to, proving that "tables" *are* the sonnets.

Line 1 informs us that the sonnets are Oxford's gift to Southampton ("Thy gift, thy tables"), and that Oxford has no need to retain a written copy as he has them all in his brain ("are within my brain"). He concludes the sonnet by returning to this point, saying that if it were otherwise, he would be guilty of forgetfulness of Southampton ("were to impart forgetfulness in me."). Lines 11-12, best paraphrased as saying "therefore I am making bold to give these sonnets ('tables') to you, to (en)trust them that you may receive them" all but cry out that Oxford, sensing his own impending death, is entrusting the sonnets to Southampton to publish, which is the only way for them to endure.

Sonnets 123-125 are the final sonnets in the "real time" sequence that began with Sonnet 1, ending in Sonnet 125, which references the day that Elizabeth was formally laid to rest, a fitting date to end the saga of Elizabeth, Oxford and Southampton. (Sonnet 126, while technically the last of the "fair youth" series, is a "sendoff," *envoi* sonnet and has a different role from 123-125 in wrapping up the sequence). For the last time, Oxford assesses the wreckage of the hope that his royal son might become king, thereby ensuring the survival of the Tudor Dynasty, and he revisits the roles that the two of them played in saving Southampton's life.

Sonnet 123

In Sonnet 123, Oxford figuratively gives the finger to fate, "Time" and the world. He states his insistence that against the appearance of change in history, he, Oxford, is not fooled, and is constant. Oxford is boldly announcing that he knows what really happened with the succession of James, and who Southampton really is, and that he will not cease telling that story, even though everyone else may think they are seeing a new chapter in history.

123	1	No! Time, thou shalt not boast that I do change:
123	2	Thy pyramids built up with newer might
123	3	To me are nothing novel, nothing strange;
123	4	They are but dressings of a former sight.
123	5	Our dates are brief, and therefore we admire
123	6	What thou dost foist upon us that is old,
123	7	And rather make them born to our desire
123	8	Than think that we before have heard them told.
123	9	Thy registers and thee I both defy,
123	10	Not wondering at the present nor the past,
123	11	For thy records and what we see doth lie,
123	12	Made more or less by thy continual haste.
123	13	This I do vow and this shall ever be;
123	14	I will be true, despite thy scythe and thee.

Line 1's statement that "I" do not change contrasts with the following lines, all addressed to "Time," here understood not as Elizabeth, but as history or fate. First, Oxford mentions "pyramids" built up recently, most likely the accession of James (pyramidal obelisks were constructed on triumphal arches built to greet James in March of 1603), which, to Oxford, are "nothing novel," and merely repeat previous history ("dressings of a former sight"). The second quatrain says that people prefer to go with the flow of the present rather than recognize the truth of what is really happening, making what Time is "foisting" on them cleave "to our desire," in effect, that people prefer to forget the past and see what they want to see.

We know that Oxford wasn't concerned with any matters of general interest. The denial of the right of the true king of England is still the subject of every sonnet. I think that "dressings" in Line 4 is key, and foreshadows the claim that history "doth lie" in Line 11, as dressings are things that cover something up—in this case, the truth about Southampton. The "former sight" would then be

Southampton's royalty, and the prospect of his being acknowledged by Elizabeth that existed before the Essex Rebellion.

The third quatrain bolsters this interpretation, starting with the statement that Oxford defies both Time's "registers" (historical records) and Time itself (via the agency of the sonnets); Oxford is not "wondering" about the past or the present, because he knows the truth, against which Time's "records, and what we see doth lie." The only lie documented in the sonnets is the denial of the truth of Southampton's royalty, so surely this is what "Time" and Time's "registers" are lying about.

The couplet is defiant, recalling Line 1, "I vow, for ever and ever, that I will be 'true'" (I will stand for and will tell the truth) such that even death ("thy scythe and thee") cannot make me change. The "ever" of Line 13, and "true" of Line 14 both evoke Oxford's emblematic wordplay with his name.

Sonnet 124

Even more defiantly, Sonnet 124 throws down the gauntlet to history, and to those who have denied Southampton his due, while making a startling admission that confirms the underlying premise of our thesis.

124	1	If my dear love were but the child of state,
124	2	It might for Fortune's bastard be unfather'd'
124	3	As subject to Time's love or to Time's hate,
124	4	Weeds among weeds, or flowers with flowers gather'd.
124	5	No, it was builded far from accident;
124	6	It suffers not in smiling pomp, nor falls
124	7	Under the blow of thralled discontent,
124	8	Whereto the inviting time our fashion calls:
124	9	It fears not policy, that *Heretic*,
124	10	Which works on leases of short-number'd hours,
124	11	But all alone stands hugely politic,
124	12	That it nor grows with heat nor drowns with showers.
124	13	To this I witness call the fools of time,
124	14	Which die for goodness, who have lived for crime.

The first two quatrains contrast what Southampton would have been had he been merely the subject of circumstance ("but the child of state") to what he really was, a unique individual not swayed by popular vicissitudes (not falling "under the blow of thrilled discontent"), instead meant to soar above the fray. The first quatrain states that Southampton was not subject to "Time's love" (where he would be a flower among other flowers) or "Time's hate" (where he would be a weed among other weeds), in both cases dependent on external circumstance. The second quatrain states that he was neither a sycophant ("suffer[s](ing) not in smiling pomp") to power, nor a rebel. Line 5 also informs us that Southampton was a planned child ("builded far from accident"), in contrast with any other child ("child of state")—planned, of course, by Oxford and Elizabeth for a higher purpose.

The third quatrain contrasts "policy" with being "politic," using a delightful play on the similarity of the sound of these words whose meanings couldn't be more opposite. "Policy" is to be understood (and in this instance our commentators agree) as expediency, scheming, the betrayal of truth (most likely for short-term temporal advantage), whereas to be "politic" is to be prudent, sagacious, provident, wise, guided by principle not expediency. Line 12 reaffirms that it is steady, unaffected by changes around it ("heat," "showers").

The couplet requires a paraphrase to make the meaning of the syntax clear. It might be stated as "To the truth of the above I call as witnesses the population (the fools of time), who die in a state of grace despite living lives of sin." The meaning of "fools of time" almost certainly has to mean the population, as those who in Sonnet 123 have no historical memory and just see the present as if it is new, not understanding it. This line also echoes "Love's not time's fool" in Sonnet 116, where Love is *not* fooled by time. "Fools of time" most likely also refers to those who believe the false history that does not recognize Southampton's royalty. This line would then be calling them to witness the truth of Southampton.

The meaning of the last line of this sonnet is subject to much speculation on the part our commentators, who wonder whether it might refer to religious martyrs, plotters (like the Gunpowder Plotters) or deathbed converters. Most likely, since the fools of time are those who are subject to the circumstances of life, who curry favor, who go in for pomp and show, they live their lives largely in sin ("have lived for crime"), and only at the end of their lives seek forgiveness and absolution for their sins ("which die for goodness"). Or the "crimes" could be living their lives currying favor, blowing this way and that, without grounding principle, the same people he has been talking about at points throughout the sonnets. (It is also possible, as suggested by Vendler, that there was a popular adage at the time about people who live for crime who die for goodness, to symbolize those whose "values change with the weather."[xl])

Sonnet 125

Sonnets 125 and 126 are the final sonnets in which Oxford sums up the entire set of sonnets. In them, he comes to terms with his life, and where things have ended up at the moment that Elizabeth, the royal mother of his royal son Southampton, is finally interred, the thirty-year effort to see him acknowledged as her heir has come to an end, and Oxford has had to content himself with producing the sonnets to report to all succeeding ages the truth of who Southampton was. Sonnets 127-152 do not follow the first 126 in time, but rather double back and retrace the 26 months of Southampton's imprisonment, and Sonnets 153-154 are a set by themselves. So we find that Sonnets 125 and 126 carry Oxford's final accounting of where things stand between him, Southampton, Elizabeth, and Time, here a metaphor for history and mortality.

125	1	Were 't ought to me I bore the canopy,
125	2	With my extern the outward honouring,
125	3	Or laid great bases for eternity,
125	4	Which proves more short than waste or ruining?
125	5	Have I not seen dwellers on form and favour
125	6	Lose all, and more, by paying too much rent,
125	7	For compound sweet; Forgoing simple savour,
125	8	Pitiful thrivers, in their gazing spent?
125	9	No, let me be obsequious in thy heart,
125	10	And take thou my oblation, poor but free,
125	11	Which is not mix'd with seconds, knows no art,
125	12	But mutual render, only me for thee.
125	13	Hence, thou suborn'd *Informer*! a true soul
125	14	When most impeach'd stands least in thy control.

The first quatrain clearly refers to the day of Elizabeth's funeral, April 28, 1603, at which Oxford would have had the right, which he likely did not exercise, to bear the canopy that a team of top nobles would have borne. He says that he could have honored her by so doing, thereby honoring her in public, or he could have honored her by building a monument that in time would waste away or be ruined. The implication is that he did neither, because neither had any meaning, confirmed by the fact that Oxford in his own name made no public statement honoring Elizabeth at her death, unlike virtually every other literary figure and important noble of the realm. This striking omission fits well with the Whittemore view that bitterness against Elizabeth had consumed Oxford—with good reason. This bitterness, tending toward hate, is what Whittemore sees as underlying the "dark lady" sonnet series (127-152), and would explain why Oxford saw no reason to honor her publicly.

Conversely, the fact that the great "Shakespeare," universally recognized for both his plays and poetry, took no notice of the passing and funeral of Elizabeth, his sovereign and patron, is impossible to explain under the presumption that he was Shakspere. This shocking omission represents one more anomaly to be swept under the rug by traditional scholars; Shakspere, were he "Shakespeare," would have had every motive to be lavish in his public praise for Elizabeth [before whom his plays had been performed in the palace for several years], while also currying James' favor. The silence from "Shakespeare" was deafening.

The second quatrain echoes the message that appears in several other sonnets immediately preceding this one, that the vast majority of all people are "dwellers on form and favor," that is, they value and strive to achieve recognition and favor with the powerful, preferring form to substance, favor to principle. They lead complicated lives, forgoing simplicity ("simple savor"), in their thriving, spending themselves with "gazing" at external things. This quatrain is likely also to be a specific commentary on England's accepting James, transferring allegiance from the dead Elizabeth to the interloper who has been accepted to replace her, when a true heir was denied the ability to receive his rightful inheritance and be a legitimate king.

The third quatrain and couplet begins with an emphatic "No" signaling Oxford's break from all that precedes in this sonnet. Not until line 9 is the grammatical second person introduced in the form of an unnamed "thou" who is clearly Time, explicitly called out in previous sonnets but left implicit here. "Time" has represented Elizabeth in some earlier sonnets, and in Sonnet 106 Oxford speaks of the "Chronicle of Wasted Time," where Time represents the duration of Elizabeth's reign, which has just come to an end. Time is also clearly death, in that all people die at a certain point in time, and their life is measured in terms of time, and that only something which is immortal can be said to conquer death. These six lines are Oxford having his final reckoning with Time, his ultimate adversary.

He begins by saying that he wishes to be "obsequious in thy heart," which I read as an offer to serve Time (the meaning of obsequious at that time was "prompt to serve," from Latin words meaning dutiful (the alternate meaning, that had just become current in the 1590s, of fawning or sycophantic is almost certainly not intended). Line 10 asks Time to receive his "oblation," which means gift or "pious donation," though I doubt that the sense of pious is intended here. This oblation is "poor but free," not adulterated ("mixed with seconds") nor containing any artifice ("knows no art")—by strong implication, in contrast with the ordinary gifts of others such as those characterized in the second quatrain, which are presumably not free, but intended to curry favor.

Line 12 begins "But mutual render..." "Render" would continue the thought begun by "take thou my oblation...", being a request to Time to do an exchange with Oxford, "only me for thee." What an extraordinary statement! Here is Oxford, dealing with Time. It brings to mind later literary figures such as Faustus making deals with Satan. I believe that Oxford is comparing his own mortality, which we know he was feeling as his health was already in decline, with the immortality that he has poured into his sonnets. We know that he saw the sonnets as lasting until eternity, with a message worthy of being read by untold future generations. What could the "oblation" (gift) be but the sonnets. In Sonnet 123 Oxford directly told Time that the history it records is lies, and that Oxford will be true despite Time. Here, I believe he is saying that Time can have Oxford's mortal body, but Oxford (and by implication Southampton) will have immortality through the sonnets—Oxford and Time rendering each other—each "yielding" (the likely meaning of render) to the other—in effect, a tit-for-tat with Time.

Then comes the shocking couplet. Seemingly out of nowhere, Time is called a "suborned Informer!" I believe this can only refer to what is made explicit in Sonnet 123, where Time is clearly telling the story of the victors, of Cecil in particular, who get away with lying about history (and above all about who Southampton really was). Then, in contrast to this, Oxford says that he (and likely Southampton), a "true soul" ("true" invokes Oxford, and by extension his son Southampton), is least in the control of Time when he is most put upon, most overwhelmed by adversity ("impeached" carries meanings of "hindered," "captured," "impeded," "trapped," etc.). That is, having suffered everything he (and Southampton) have suffered, by the very travails they have experienced, they are most free of Time. The sonnets will live for eternity, despite the thwarting of Southampton's proper destiny, and the besmirching of Oxford's reputation.

What a conclusion to this entire series of sonnets! Oxford has finally made peace with all that has happened. He and Southampton are free, by virtue of their steadfast upholding of the truth of Southampton's royal blood and inheritance, even if the vicissitudes of time have prevented them from expressing it in public.

Sonnet 126

The series formally concludes with Sonnet 126, noteworthy for its unusual construction. It consists of only twelve lines of poetry; lines 13 and 14 are two pairs of parentheses bracketing line-length empty spaces. The rhyme scheme of the twelve lines of verse (aabb ccdd eeff) is also different from all the rest.

Oxford opens with an explicit address to Southampton as his son:

126	1	O thou, my lovely Boy, who in thy power
126	2	Dost hold time's fickle glass, his sickle, hour;
126	3	Who hast by waning grown, and therein show'st
126	4	Thy lovers withering as thy sweet self grow'st;
126	5	If Nature (sovereign mistress over wrack)
126	6	As thou goest onwards, still will pluck thee back,
126	7	She keeps thee to this purpose, that her skill
126	8	May time disgrace and wretched minutes kill.
126	9	Yet fear her, O thou minion of her pleasure!
126	10	She may detain, but not still keep, her treasure:
126	11	Her *Audit* (though delay'd) answer'd must be,
126	12	And her *Quietus* is to render thee.
126	13	( )
126	14	( )

"O thou, my lovely Boy." In April of 1603 Southampton would have been twenty-nine. Men of that age were not addressed as "boys." Also, "Boy" is capitalized.

Under our thesis, there is no mystery at all—Southampton *was* Oxford's boy. And what is Oxford's parting message to him?

First, he states that he has mastered Time—he holds Time's "fickle glass" and his sickle, or "scythe" (the two items Time is traditionally depicted carrying). He describes Southampton as "by waning grown" (by abandoning his claim to the throne he has regained his freedom and noble status), and thereby, in contrast to Oxford ("thy lovers withering"), he continues to grow ("thy sweet self grow'st").

The third couplet introduces Nature, clearly in contrast to time.

If "wrack" is read as Time (bringing everyone to "wrack and ruin"), it says that Nature holds some power over Time. "As thou goest onwards" almost surely means "as you proceed onwards toward death, at the hands of Time." Saying then that Nature "will pluck thee back" means that she will pull you back from Time. The following couplet reinforces this interpretation, that Nature will keep you out of Time's clutches because she has the skill to disgrace Time and to kill minutes (units of time).

The fifth couplet (lines 9-10) warns that Nature, too, must be feared, identifying her as having dominion over Southampton ("thou minion of her pleasure"). Though "she may detain" Southampton (keep him away from death for a while), she can't do so indefinitely ("but not still keep her treasure"). Lines 11-12 say that Nature may delay "her Audit" (her reckoning of Southampton's life; the word is capitalized and italicized in the original text), but the audit must eventually be completed, and the "Quietus" (the document certifying that Nature is released from a debt, also capitalized and italicized in the original) is to surrender "thee" to death.

In previous sonnets we have seen time associated with the fickleness of popular opinion and changing policy and with Elizabeth herself. Nature in some previous sonnets was also Elizabeth herself, but with Elizabeth now dead, she is not the referent here. Nature would appear to be the personification of some higher purpose, perhaps the manifestation of constancy against the inconstancy of Time. It is in conflict with Time, and can delay, but not prevent, death. Oxford's parting advice to Southampton is to trust in Nature and stay true to himself and his unacknowledged royal blood.

As to the two final blank lines, set off by parentheses, Whittemore speculates that this is intended to signify that as Southampton's life is unfinished, so are the sonnets. The insertion of the parentheses was made by the poet himself, to show that he was not composing a poem of just twelve lines. The two empty lines also suggest that the poet cannot know how Southampton's life will turn out because he will die soon, presumably well before Southampton.

Although the series of sonnets to Southampton is finished, the entire set is not. We now turn to Sonnets 127-152, about the mysterious woman whom conventional analysis cannot correctly identify.

Chapter 22
"My Mistress," Queen Elizabeth

We now come to the sequence of sonnets that relates to the final major "mystery" of the sonnets—the identity of the "dark lady," as she is conventionally called, the subject of Sonnets 127-152. After writing 126 sonnets to the young man, why does the poet suddenly begin to write to and about a woman? The principal emotions expressed in many of these sonnets are hatred and disparagement, rather than love. The switch in focus should be especially troubling to proponents of the homosexual hypothesis, but it doesn't make a lot of sense even to those who find some sort of "manly friendship" in the relationship between the poet and the young man.

However, if Sonnets 1-126 are understood according to our thesis, with the recurring *dramatis personae* of Oxford, Southampton and Queen Elizabeth, Sonnets 127-152 must be about Elizabeth. That another woman would be introduced at this point makes no sense. Moreover, several of these sonnets refer back to the "friend," who must be the same "friend" of 1-126, thus ensuring that the woman in the first 126 sonnets must be the same woman.

Even a quick scan of Sonnets 127-152 reveals that they are not about a love-struck poet writing to his paramour. Too many lines are hostile, negative, conflicted, or otherwise impossible to interpret as describing a romantic or sexual attachment.

Under the traditional paradigm, if the author is Shakspere, and the sonnets are about a love triangle involving poet, young man and an unidentified woman, then every sonnet in this group must be seen to fit that pattern. But a sonnet-by-sonnet examination reveals enormous problems with this interpretation. Indeed, in the explanations offered by our four commentators we see the same incoherent, inconsistent and contradictory readings as we found in their analyses of the first 126 sonnets.

The very designation of "dark lady" is a tortured and unsustainable reading of these sonnets, even under the Stratfordian hypothesis. While lines in a few of the later sonnets ostensibly support this characterization, it is Sonnet 127, the first in the series, that provides the bulk of the fodder for this misapprehension. Interestingly, Burrow questions the designation of "dark lady," noting that "Sonnet 127 begins a group of sonnets which are chiefly about a mistress with dark hair and dark eyes whom Shakespeare never calls a 'lady,' let alone the 'dark lady' favored by his biographical critics." He notes that "scores" of candidates have been proposed over the years.

He is correct that the sonnets never refer to a "dark lady," but that is the extent of what he gets right. He follows convention in describing her as having "dark hair" and "dark eyes," despite the fact that neither her hair nor her eyes are ever actually described by the poet as "dark." Sonnet 127 calls her eyes "Raven black" and Sonnet 130 compares her hair to "black wires"; these are the only references to their color anywhere in the sonnets. Her hair is nowhere else even referred to, and while literally speaking, black hair can be considered "dark," the two words are not synonyms, each bearing distinct symbolic meanings; "dark" hair is generally thought of as brunette, not black—when hair is truly black, it is so labeled. Most commentators, in fact, describe her as brunette.

As for her eyes, they are mentioned ten times in this group of sonnets, yet in none of the other nine instances is there any hint of their color. The actual color of her eyes was of no significance to Shakespeare. Furthermore, humans do not have truly black colored eyes (unless they suffer from a rare genetic defect). Again, a figurative meaning is almost certainly the correct one, bolstered in Sonnet 127 and elsewhere by the discussion of her eyes as "mourning" or "mourners"—black being the color of mourning.

In sum, the entire designation of the lady as "dark" based on physical traits is unsupportable. Only one of our commentators has even an inkling of this fact.

Duncan-Jones exemplifies the sloppy analysis that leads to the "dark lady" moniker: "Initiating the 'dark lady' sequence, the speaker claims that 'fairness' of complexion is no longer esteemed, since it can be falsely appropriated by means of cosmetics; fashionably, therefore...he (the poet) rejoices in a mistress with dark eyes (by implication, dark complexion)...whose eyes seem to mourn in mocking regret for the false reputation for beauty enjoyed by other women, while asserting their own aesthetic superiority."

To borrow a legal phrase, Duncan-Jones has "assumed facts not in evidence." Complexion is neither explicitly mentioned nor reasonably inferable from any lines in this sonnet. Her claim that "cosmetics" are being referred to is likewise unwarranted. From cosmetics, Duncan-Jones continues with assertions that Sonnet 127 is saying that "fairness" is no longer esteemed, that her eyes are "mourning in mocking regret" for "false reputation(s) enjoyed by other women." There is no support for any of her conclusions.

Booth imputes the same references to hair, saying that "black" means brunette and "ugly," i.e., the opposite of "beautiful." That claim is not justifiable. The word is not intended to refer to physical beauty (or the absence of it)—here, as everywhere, "beauty" refers to royalty, or royal blood.

Only Kerrigan avoids the assumption that the "dark" aspect is either hair or complexion, noting that by Sonnet 131, "black" applies to the woman's actions; he is on the right track, though he identifies the wrong actions, writing that she is "decidedly dark in her love-life."[xli]

"Black" is used nine times in this section of sonnets to describe the lady's character, nature or actions, which accords perfectly with Whittemore's contention that in these sonnets Oxford is railing against Queen Elizabeth for not acknowledging Southampton. "Dark" is used only once in the entire section, in Line 14 of Sonnet 147, again in reference to her character. The replacement of a textual "black" by "dark," as a matter of common agreement among traditional critics, is yet another instance of failing to read what the sonnets actually say, and imputing a meaning foreign to the true one.

Whittemore contends that Sonnets 127-152 were written in parallel with the eighty prison sonnets (27-106) previously discussed. They are, however, directed at Elizabeth, rather than Southampton. In Sonnets 27-126, the "thou" or "you" is Southampton, and the third party, when she appears, is Elizabeth; here (with one exception), the "thou" or "you" is Elizabeth, and the third party is Southampton.

This shift permits Oxford to say something very different in these sonnets. The overriding emotions are conflicted, with Oxford confronting Elizabeth in three different roles: as his sovereign, to whom he owes liege loyalty; as his partner in creating Southampton, who he believes then betrayed him and Southampton; and as his opponent, even his enemy, for her refusal to acknowledge Southampton and for her intention to execute him. This emotional conflict provides an explanation for the "love-hate" message in many of these sonnets.

Sonnet 127

Under Whittemore's construction, Sonnet 127 corresponds to the moment of Southampton's arrest on February 8, 1601, and would therefore line up next to Sonnet 27, exactly 100 sonnets prior. The repeated use of the words "black" and "mourn," and of other negative words ("slandered," "shame," "disgrace," "woe") suggest a context similar to that described in Sonnet 27. Its language strongly suggests that it refers to the first days after the arrest, and all that is implied by that development which is strongly suggested by the opening quatrain, which appears to describe Southampton's sudden disgrace:

127	1	In the old age black was not counted fair,
127	2	Or if it were, it bore not beauty's name;
127	3	But now is black beauty's successive heir,
127	4	And Beauty slander'd with a bastard shame:

The first quatrain defies intelligible interpretation under the conventional reading. The inability of our four chosen commentators to make any sense of it at all is striking. Duncan-Jones suggests that "what used to be called beauty—a 'fair complexion'—has acquired a bad reputation." Booth is convinced the lines are about brunettes versus blondes, with beauty "being itself thought bastard (because genuine, natural beauty may be taken to be cosmetically achieved)." Burrow reads Line 1 as saying that "coloring (dark hair and dark eyes) was not considered beautiful," and reads Line 4 as saying that "beauty is publicly shamed with having borne a bastard...beauty is both the source of due succession and its own illegitimate offspring." Kerrigan fares no better, starting with "in the olden days darkness was not considered beautiful, or if it were, it was not called so," and ending with "darkness, considered the legitimate heir of Beauty, is granted beauty's name, while beauty (what is fair), regarded as Beauty's illegitimate offspring, loses...the name of its parent." None of these comments make any sense.

When the poem is read as discussing the suddenly changed political situation for Southampton, Oxford and Queen Elizabeth after the Essex Rebellion, the opening quatrain becomes intelligible. "In the old age" means "before the rebellion," and "black" almost surely means Southampton in Line 3, and therefore also in Line 1—there using the term that will characterize him after he has committed treason in the Rebellion. "Not counted fair" likely means that Southampton wasn't recognized as royal, or (line 2), if he was so recognized by a few, he did not bear Elizabeth's Tudor name in public. In Line 3, Southampton, the "successive heir" to Elizabeth, is now truly "black" because of his crime, which slanders Elizabeth with his shame, as he is her bastard son.

The rest of the sonnet follows:

127	5	For since each hand hath put on Nature's power,
127	6	Fairing the foul with Art's false borrow'd face,
127	7	Sweet beauty hath no name, no holy bower,
127	8	But is profaned, if not lives in disgrace.
127	9	Therefore my Mistress' eyes are Raven black,
127	10	Her eyes so suited, and they mourners seem
127	11	At such who, not born fair, no beauty lack,
127	12	Slandering Creation with a false esteem:
127	13	Yet so they mourn, becoming of their woe,
127	14	That every tongue says beauty should look so.

The second quatrain appears to refer to Southampton's having been denied his rightful place by the machinations of those around Elizabeth (chief among them Robert Cecil), saying that many people tried to influence Elizabeth ("Nature's power"), using artifice and deceit ("fairing the foul with Art's false borrowed face"), such that "sweet beauty" (almost certainly Southampton) was not seen as heir apparent ("hath no name," no lineage), and had no "holy bow'r" (sacred, royal seat).

The third quatrain refers to Elizabeth, the "Mistress" of this entire set of sonnets. It says that her eyes are "black" because they are in mourning for someone not lacking beauty (that is, having royal blood, i.e., Southampton), but who was "not born fair" (he was not acknowledged). "Slandering Creation" suggests that "Creation" (which is capitalized in the original text) is Southampton (created by Elizabeth and Oxford), who is now slandered by a false understanding of who he really is. The couplet states that their (her eyes') woe is sufficient cause for mourning, and that the whole world is mourning with her.

The commentators, who all endorse a reading that this sonnet is about cosmetics and physical appearance (based mainly on the first six lines), struggle to maintain that reading in the remainder of the sonnet, only to abandon it entirely in the next sonnet. They never ask why Shakespeare would interject such an odd discussion here, in the initial sonnet of a new section. Read as the new paradigm understands it, it is a most fitting introduction to the series.

Sonnet 128

Sonnet 128 clearly is to Elizabeth, shown by the reference to the virginals, the harpsichord-like instrument which she loved to play, and to the terms "blessed" (a synonym for sacred, as in "sacred majesty") and "sweet fingers" (sweet meaning royal):

128	1	How oft, when thou, my music, music play'st,
128	2	Upon that blessed wood whose motion sounds
128	3	With thy sweet fingers, when thou gently sway'st
128	4	The wiry concord that mine ear confounds,
128	5	Do I envy those Jacks that nimble leap
128	6	To kiss the tender inward of thy hand,

The metaphor of the virginal is used to say that Oxford wishes he had access to her hands, to kiss them, in place of "Jacks that nimble leap" to kiss them. Booth notes that "jack" was "a standard term of abuse for any worthless fellow and for impudent upstarts in particular." Since the time of composition of this sonnet was likely just after the trial—Whittemore believes it was the actual day on which Essex was executed—Oxford was likely referring to his own outcast situation with respect to the Queen, compared with that enjoyed by sycophants rallying to her against the Essex faction (perhaps reflecting the same sentiment shown in Sonnet 30, "When in Disgrace with Fortune and mens eyes").

Sonnet 130

Sonnet 130 can be understood as Oxford attacking Elizabeth in the days immediately after Southampton's arrest. We have a unique window on this sonnet because it appears to be a mirror image of a poem almost nineteen years earlier. Whittemore cited it from a book published in 1582 (*Hekatompathia or The Passionate Century of Love,* by Thomas Watson, which was dedicated to Oxford) that is clearly about Queen Elizabeth, and that Whittemore attributes to Oxford. This poem, which praises the Queen, contains eight lines (out of eighteen) that appear to be virtual mirror images of lines in Sonnet 130, including using the same words describing the same bodily features. While the 1582 poem uses these terms to glorify Elizabeth, Sonnet 130 gives the same terms a negative connotation. Here are some of the corresponding lines:

1582 poem: Her lips more red than any Coral stone
Sonnet 130: Coral is far more red than her lips' red

> *1582 poem:* Her neck more white, than aged Swans that moan,
> Her breast transparent is, like Crystal rock
> *Sonnet 130:* If snow be white, why then her breasts are dun [dull grey brown]

> *1582 poem:* On either cheek a Rose and Lily lies
> *Sonnet 130:* I have seen Roses damasked, red and white
> But no such roses see I in her cheeks

> *1582 poem:* Her sparkling eyes in heav'n a place deserve
> *Sonnet 130:* My Mistress' eyes are nothing like the Sunne

> *1582 poem:* Her words are music all of silver sound
> *Sonnet 130:* That Music hath a far more pleasing sound [than her words]

> *1582 poem:* Her breath is sweet perfume, or holy flame
> *Sonnet 130:* And in some perfumes is there more delight
> Than in the breath that from my Mistress reeks

Such a correspondence can hardly be a coincidence. The conclusion is inescapable that the author of Sonnet 130 was also the author of the 1582 poem. Since the earlier poem is almost certainly describing Queen Elizabeth, Sonnet 130 must also be about her. If so, this sonnet alone strongly confirms the new reading of Sonnets 127-152 as being about Elizabeth, and by extension, confirms Whittemore's reading of the preceding sonnets.

This reading, of course, negates all traditionalist interpretations of this sonnet, not merely Duncan-Jones', again showing the implications of viewing the sonnet from the perspective of a different paradigm.

Sonnets 131-133

In Sonnet 131, Oxford calls Elizabeth "tyrannous" and "black" because she intends to execute Southampton. The couplet reads: "In nothing art thou black save in thy deeds, And thence this slander as I think proceeds." Using a contemporary meaning for "slander" ("bad situation, evil action; a person causing such a state of affairs," from the Online Etymological Dictionary), a new meaning emerges: "this slander (evil action)…proceeds" from "thy (black) deeds," referring to the impending execution. The couplet also makes clear that the "dark lady" is *not* black (or dark) in physical properties— only in deeds—definitively disposing of the basis for the standard "dark lady" appellation for her.

Sonnet 132 returns to the sub-theme of Sonnet 127 and

Elizabeth's mourning eyes, which he likens to the sun and moon for becoming her face as sun and moon become the morning and the evening, but which he now describes as mourning for him (Oxford), in what seems like a state of self-pity.

Sonnet 133 uses the word "friend" to refer to Southampton, and plays with the word "heart." It starts by cursing Elizabeth's heart that is bringing suffering to both Oxford and Southampton and later offering his own heart ("Prison my heart in thy steel bosom's ward") if it will get Southampton out of prison ("then…let my poor heart bail…my friend's heart…").

Sonnet 134

Sonnet 134 seems to be devoted entirely to the fact that Elizabeth has Southampton, their son, in the Tower facing death:

134	1	So now I have confess'd that he is thine,
134	2	And I myself am mortgaged to thy will,
134	3	Myself I'll forfeit, so that other mine
134	4	Thou wilt restore, to be my comfort still:
134	5	But thou wilt not, nor he will not be free,
134	6	For thou art covetous and he is kind;
134	7	He learn'd but surety-like to write for me
134	8	Under that bond that him as fast doth bind.
134	9	The statute of thy beauty thou wilt take,
134	10	Thou usurer, that put'st forth all to use,
134	11	And sue a friend came debtor for my sake;
134	12	So him I lose through my unkind abuse.
134	13	Him have I lost; thou hast both him and me:
134	14	He pays the whole, and yet am I not free.

"(H)e is thine" imparts the information that "he" (Southampton) is in her prison, and "I," Oxford, am subject to "thy" (Elizabeth's) power to decide his fate. Oxford would gladly forfeit himself to save Southampton (by "forfeit," Oxford may be referring to his offering to conceal his own role as "Shakespeare," or possibly any claim to be Southampton's father). Lines 5-6 affirm that Elizabeth will not budge. "(H)e is kind" harkens back to Sonnet 105, where he refers to Southampton as "kind," a synonym for "kindred," in this context, meaning "son."

The meaning of the third quatrain is not entirely clear, but the couplet seems to sum up the situation, where Oxford has lost Southampton, and Elizabeth has lost both of them. Southampton will have paid the full penalty (death), but Oxford is still heavily affected, and suffers with Southampton. This sonnet corresponds to the situation in the last days before Southampton's reprieve (described in Sonnet 67), when Oxford was at his lowest point.

Interestingly, over a hundred years ago, one Shakespeare scholar correctly divined the truth of this sonnet, confirming the reading presented here. Edward J. White, in his 1911 *Commentaries on the Law in Shakespeare,* wrote of Sonnet 134: "This verse clearly refers to the confinement of Southampton in the Tower and the former verse [133] expresses the Poet's desire to be permitted to go his bail by substituting his own person for that of his friend, in jail." Since White believed the poet was Shakspere, he leaves unexplained how he thought the man from Stratford could have made such an offer on Southampton's part, much less to the Queen of England, but his insight is still noteworthy.[xlii]

Sonnets 135-136 are typically cited as weighing against the case for Oxford as Shakespeare because they play with the word "will" (the word is frequently, though not consistently, capitalized and italicized in the two poems) in myriad ways, ending, in Line 14 of Sonnet 136, with the statement "for my name is Will." These two sonnets do not appear to relate to Southampton, but rather to Oxford's relationship with Elizabeth. They do not support the case against Oxford as Shakespeare, since Oxford's pseudonym "William Shakespeare" can just as well be the referent for this line and others that seem to refer to the poet's name.

Sonnet 137

In Sonnet 137, Oxford appears to be observing, and ruing, the fact that the deal he has secured for Southampton, or is attempting to secure, is based on a lie that he is forced to live and propagate:

137	1	Thou blind fool, love, what dost thou to mine eyes,
137	2	That they behold, and see not what they see?
137	3	They know what beauty is, see where it lies,
137	4	Yet what the best is take the worst to be.
137	5	If eyes corrupt by over-partial looks
137	6	Be anchor'd in the bay where all men ride,
137	7	Why of eyes' falsehood hast thou forged hooks,
137	8	Whereto the judgment of my heart is tied?
137	9	Why should my heart think that a several plot
137	10	Which my heart knows the wide world's common place?
137	11	Or mine eyes seeing this, say this is not,
137	12	To put fair truth upon so foul a face?

| 137 | 13 | In things right true my heart and eyes have erred, |
| 137 | 14 | And to this false plague are they now transferr'd. |

"Love" here would appear to be Oxford's love for Southampton, and lines 3-4 seem to say that his eyes know what "beauty" (royalty) is and where it is (in Southampton), but are forced to live with the reality that Southampton is in the "worst" condition. In lines 7-8 he accuses "Love" of forging hooks tying his heart to the falsehood induced in his eyes. The third quatrain appears to ask why his heart, which knows Southampton is in the Tower, is forced to go along with his eyes in pretending that this awful situation is "fair" ("to put fair truth upon so foul a face"). This is not the first sonnet in which Oxford contrasts eyes and heart. The couplet sums up the state of affairs, where Oxford says that both his eyes and his heart "have erred" and are "now transferred...to this false plague."

Sonnet 140

In Sonnet 140 we find a remarkable statement. Oxford appears to threaten the Queen that he will reveal all if she doesn't act wisely ("Be wise as thou art cruel" or else):

140	1	Be wise as thou art cruel; do not press
140	2	My tongue-tied patience with too much disdain;
140	3	Lest sorrow lend me words and words express
140	4	The manner of my pity-wanting pain.
140	5	If I might teach thee wit, better it were,
140	6	Though not to love, yet, love, to tell me so;
140	7	As testy sick men, when their deaths be near,
140	8	No news but health from their Physicians know;
140	9	For if I should despair, I should grow mad,
140	10	And in my madness might speak ill of thee:
140	11	Now this ill-wresting world is grown so bad,
140	12	Mad slanderers by mad ears believed be,
140	13	That I may not be so, nor thou belied,
140	14	Bear thine eyes straight, though thy proud heart go wide.

Harking back to his phrase "art made tongue-tied by authority" from Sonnet 66, Oxford suggests that "sorrow" will give him tongue to reveal why he is in such pain, if he is pressed. In the second quatrain, he says he should be treated the way a sick man is treated by his doctor, who tells him good news. In the third quatrain, he virtually evokes Hamlet's madness, which is the cover Hamlet uses to say things he couldn't if not thought mad—here, he says that if he (Oxford) despairs, he may go mad and "in my madness might speak ill of thee" (tell the truth about Elizabeth and Southampton), which would be believed by an "ill-wresting world grown so bad." The couplet says that, so that Oxford won't appear to go mad, and Elizabeth therefore not be exposed ("belied"), her eyes must be honest (her outward, public self—what she actually does), even if her heart is not in agreement.

Sonnets 141-144 again reflect Oxford's conflicted relationship with Elizabeth, tied to her as her subject, by love, and by Southampton, yet he is striving to get her to spare him (and hopefully to pardon and restore him).

Sonnet 145 is unique in the entire collection of sonnets, for being in iambic tetrameter rather than pentameter. This variance corresponds with an equally unique alteration in voice—this sonnet is written as if by Southampton. The "I" and "me" point to Southampton in the Tower, the sonnet describing his reaction to being spared execution. This would strongly suggest that this sonnet can be matched with Sonnet 67 and dated to about March 20, 1601.

Sonnet 145

145	1	Those lips that Love's own hand did make
145	2	Breathed forth the sound that said 'I hate'
145	3	To me that languish'd for her sake;
145	4	But when she saw my woeful state,
145	5	Straight in her heart did mercy come,
145	6	Chiding that tongue that ever sweet
145	7	Was used in giving gentle doom,
145	8	And taught it thus anew to greet:
145	9	'I hate' she alter'd with an end,
145	10	That follow'd it as gentle day
145	11	Doth follow night, who like a fiend
145	12	From heaven to hell is flown away;
145	13	'I hate' from hate away she threw,
145	14	And saved my life, saying 'not you.'

Referring to Elizabeth, Southampton describes (line 3) how he "languished for her sake" in prison, where her command ("those lips") (line 3) expressed hatred (his death sentence). Lines 4-7 say that when Elizabeth saw Southampton's "woeful state," "Straight in her heart did mercy come," leading her to "chide" her tongue that had previously doled out "doom," and (line 8) taught her tongue to greet Southampton "anew."

Lines 9-12 express how she altered her "hate," like day following night. The couplet couldn't be more explicit: Having relented, no longer "hat(ing)" Southampton, she (literally) "saved my life, saying, 'Not you.'"

Following directly, Sonnet 146 can be understood as an appeal to Queen Elizabeth even at this late date to consider the consequences of not acknowledging Southampton as her son. There is even a suggestion that she abdicate in favor of Southampton.

Sonnet 146

146	1	Poor soul, the centre of my sinful earth,
146	2	My sinful earth these rebel powers that thee array;
146	3	Why dost thou pine within and suffer dearth,
146	4	Painting thy outward walls so costly gay?
146	5	Why so large cost, having so short a lease,
146	6	Dost thou upon thy fading mansion spend?
146	7	Shall worms, inheritors of this excess,
146	8	Eat up thy charge? is this thy body's end?
146	9	Then soul, live thou upon thy servant's loss,
146	10	And let that pine to aggravate thy store;
146	11	Buy terms divine in selling hours of dross;
146	12	Within be fed, without be rich no more:
146	13	So shalt thou feed on death, that feeds on men,
146	14	And death once dead, there's no more dying then.

Oxford is describing Elizabeth as she nears death, and the end of her dynasty. "Pour soul" (Elizabeth), the center of all England ("my sinful earth") on whose terrain Elizabeth is "array(ing)" "rebel powers" (a reference to James, or to the danger of civil war on her death), he entreats, "why are you permitting your inner essence (your royal legacy) to fade while you maintain outward show?" We see here, as in Sonnet 69 and others, the contrast between "outward show" and "inward essence." Here the "outward show" ("Painting thy outward walls so costly gay") is her court and courtiers—the maintenance of all the pomp and ceremony of the Elizabethan court, which belies its inner rot and its disastrous future ("pine within and suffer dearth").

The second quatrain expands on the theme, referring to the "large cost" of something that will last only a very short time ("having so short a lease"), the expenditure on a "fading mansion," which will soon become fodder for worms. That he is referring as much to her physical body, which contains the royal blood that will soon die with her, is made clear when he asks "is this thy body's end?"

The third quatrain offers her an alternative, to "aggravate [increase] thy store" (her essence) by "Buy[ing] terms divine" (recognizing Southampton and permitting the dynasty to continue, which is doing the "divine" work of God), in exchange for relinquishing the last few inconsequential years of her rule ("selling hours of dross"). She is urged to propagate her Tudor blood ("Within be fed") by giving up the trappings of Queen ("without be rich no more") in favor of Southampton.

The couplet promises that if she does, she will defeat death ("feed on death"). Having done so, her future (and the dynasty's) will be secure.

In the next sonnet, Oxford describes how the situation has driven him mad:

Sonnet 147

147	1	My love is as a fever, longing still
147	2	For that which longer nurseth the disease,
147	3	Feeding on that which doth preserve the ill,
147	4	The uncertain sickly appetite to please.
147	5	My reason, the Physician to my love,
147	6	Angry that his prescriptions are not kept,
147	7	Hath left me, and I desperate now approve
147	8	Desire is death, which Physic did except.
147	9	Past cure I am, now Reason is past care,
147	10	And frantic-mad with evermore unrest;
147	11	My thoughts and my discourse as madmen's are,
147	12	At random from the truth vainly express'd;
147	13	For I have sworn thee fair and thought thee bright,
147	14	Who art as black as hell, as dark as night.

The first eight lines are an extended metaphor on how he is made sick by his "love" (his emotions toward Southampton and the Queen's refusal to acknowledge him); his "reason," which would normally act as his physician, has left him because he has not followed its advice. He says his "love" is like a fever that promotes its own illness. The third quatrain says that with reason having fled, Oxford is made "frantic mad," his "thoughts" and his words "as madman's are," wildly lying ("at random from the truth").

The "truth" is that "thee" (Elizabeth) are "black as hell, as dark as night," while "I have sworn thee fair, and thought thee bright."

287

The deal he has made is eating away at him; the dishonesty, the sin against truth, that Oxford had to commit, is driving him mad.

The next four sonnets (Sonnets 148-151) continue in this mode of hatred and disparagement of Elizabeth, a tone broken only in Sonnet 152, the final sonnet in the sequence, which clearly corresponds to the death of Elizabeth. It is a final reckoning of the lies and dishonesty that Elizabeth has forced Oxford into, which is her sad legacy to him:

Sonnet 152

152	1	In loving thee thou know'st I am forsworn,
152	2	But thou art twice forsworn, to me love swearing,
152	3	In act thy bed-vow broke and new faith torn,
152	4	In vowing new hate after new love bearing.
152	5	But why of two oaths' breach do I accuse thee,
152	6	When I break twenty? I am perjured most;
152	7	For all my vows are oaths but to misuse thee
152	8	And all my honest faith in thee is lost,
152	9	For I have sworn deep oaths of thy deep kindness,
152	10	Oaths of thy love, thy truth, thy constancy,
152	11	And, to enlighten thee, gave eyes to blindness,
152	12	Or made them swear against the thing they see;
152	13	For I have sworn thee fair; more perjured eye,
152	14	To swear against the truth so foul a lie!

This sonnet is entirely about lying, as shown in terms such as "forsworn," "bed-vow broke," "new faith torn," "two oaths' breach," "perjured," "swear against the thing they see," "perjured eye," and "swear against the truth so foul a lie." Oxford begins by saying that he has had to utter one major lie ("I am forsworn"), but that Elizabeth has lied twice. First, she broke her "bed-vow," and second, she turned on Oxford and Southampton after Southampton was born ("after new love bearing"). "Bed-vow" is construed by our traditionalist commentators as a promise made when the poet and the woman made love, but such a conjecture connects to nothing else. Understood as referring to Elizabeth's vow to Oxford when they decided to conceive Southampton, it becomes a startling reference to that very act. "New love bearing" refers to Southampton, using "bear" in the sense of "bear a child," the natural outcome of having sexual relations. A bed vow can't exist unless the two partners are bedding together.

Lines 3 and 4 so strongly support our thesis that it is worth a detour to see how our commentators deal with them. Trying to make sense of "new love bearing," some of them offer readings that are mutually exclusive. For Booth, it means either "(1) feeling love for someone new (i.e., for me); (2) feeling love for someone new (i.e., for someone who has replaced me); (3) bearing the physical weight of a new lover, allowing a new lover to lie with you." This is unintelligible.

Duncan-Jones posits similar contradictory options, saying that the phrase may be read "as suggesting that the woman…is recently married, and already expressing *new hate* for her husband, in favor of love for the speaker; or that she has betrayed both her husband and the speaker in favor of some third party." Kerrigan maintains that the "new love" is definitely not the poet, that it means "entertaining new affection (affection for someone new). With a further quibble released by the sexual suggestions of 'bearing': the mistress bears the burden of a new lover in her bed."

Getting back to the sonnet itself, we see how the theme of "forswearing" is amplified in the second quatrain, where Oxford says he hasn't just lied once, but twenty times: "I am perjured most." What has he lied about? About Elizabeth, praising her when he should have been condemning her. "My vows are oaths but to misuse thee" (oaths to lie about you), he writes, while he had actually lost all faith in her. Line 9 continues the theme, saying that his lying oaths spoke of her "kindness" (her goodness, her virtue), oaths of her truth and constancy. Lines 11-12 say that Oxford helped shine a favorable light on her ("gave eyes to blindness" to "enlighten" her), or made people believe a lie about Elizabeth.

The couplet completes the sonnet and the entire series of bitter poems to Elizabeth: Oxford has sworn all good things about Elizabeth, perjuring his eye, swearing "so foul a lie" against the truth.

Truth is revealed as the paramount goal of Oxford's life. Upholding it is his family's motto, but he has been forced to heinously violate that duty, depriving Southampton of his rightful place as king, and England of its rightful Tudor heir. Oxford's parting sonnet documents this colossal sin against truth.

Sonnets 153-154: Epilogue as Prologue

Sonnets 153 and 154 are universally described as outliers, two poems that seem not to fit well with the rest. They are not clearly about Southampton, or the Queen, or even the poet. They are based on a six-line epigram by Marianus Scholasticus (a fifth-century Byzantine poet) about Cupid and his torch. Cupid entrusts the torch to his nymphs while he takes a nap; the nymphs decide to extinguish it in the water in order to quench man's passions, but instead, the torch burns the water, and makes it warm.

I read both sonnets as allegories for Elizabeth's attempt to extinguish the knowledge of Southampton's royal blood, represented by the plunging of the torch (Southampton's royal blood) into cold water. That the torch prevailed and heated the water is intended to represent that, at least for Oxford, the issue of Southampton's royalty is something that could not have been, and was not, extinguished.

Sonnet 153 was probably written years earlier than the rest of the sonnets, perhaps just after Oxford had slept with the Queen in 1573, or more likely after a visit he made to the city of Bath while the Queen was also there (for the first and only time) in the summer of 1574. The reference in Sonnet 153 to "bath" (lines 11-12: "I, sick withal, the help of bath desired, and thither hied") all but confirms that Oxford did indeed go there to see Elizabeth. Perhaps the metaphor of Elizabeth trying to quench Cupid's torch was intended to represent her decision not to openly raise the child (which would have required marrying Oxford, as she may have led him to believe she would do) but to place it in the Southampton household. Admittedly, we are in the realm of speculation, but it is not impossible that Elizabeth attempted to hide from Oxford what became of the child, and that Oxford found out, which would represent the victory of Cupid's torch ("Love's fire") over Elizabeth's cold water. With that knowledge Oxford could begin to urge that their child be acknowledged, which is what the *Sonnets* is really about.

By this reading Sonnet 153 tells us that Oxford found no satisfaction in Bath. The only cure lay in "my mistress' eye," that is, in the domain of her power to decide if and when to acknowledge Southampton.

Sonnet 154 relates the same story of Cupid and his "maidens," one of whom is a "Virgin" (Elizabeth) who disarms him (steals his torch). The couplet confirms again that "Love's fire heats water, water cools not love," meaning that Elizabeth's effort to bury the knowledge of Southampton's royalty will fail. Sonnet 154 was written later; perhaps it was the last sonnet that Oxford wrote, as a second bookend to match the first represented by Sonnet 153.

Chapter 23
Symmetry and the Monument

The Monument

As noted, the method of analysis that Whittemore and I have employed is to take *Shake-speares Sonnets* to mean what they actually say. Our job as critics and analysts is to make coherent sense out of every sonnet; when something is clearly stated, it cannot be ignored or glossed in a mechanical or irrelevant fashion. I have provided many instances where important statements *are* so glossed or ignored by our four chosen traditional commentators.

A dramatic illustration of this is also the basis for the title of Whittemore's magnum opus, *The Monument*. His choice was not arbitrary, but dictated by the poet himself. In two of the most revealing and important sonnets, 81 and 107, the poet states unambiguously that "Your monument shall be my gentle verse," and "And thou in this ['this poor rhyme,' i.e., the sonnets] shalt find thy monument," respectively. The implications of these two lines are vast and powerful. First, the poet is saying that the sonnets *collectively* constitute a monument to his subject—they are not a collection of diverse, unconnected or unrelated poems loosely associated by virtue of describing a supposed relationship between two men and a woman, but a unified, coherent paean to their subject, Southampton—the poems being "barren of new pride," "ever the same," "to constancy confined," "one thing expressing," etc., in the words of Sonnets 76 and 105, as we have seen.

More important, they *are* a monument. In Shakespeare's day, all kings were honored after death by monuments made of stone. The sonnets refer to these ostensibly permanent structures several times in order to claim that the sonnets will outlive them. The entire set of sonnets must be understood as representing *what will remain after Southampton dies* as his memorial, something which is equivalent to (and in a sense greater than) a physical, stone monument. Understood thusly, can anyone continue to maintain that the sonnets chronicle the vicissitudes of a love triangle involving two men and a woman? Could anyone believe that such a narrative could constitute a fitting monument to someone whose memory is intended to be preserved until the end of time? The poet's clear statement that the sonnets are a monument to their subject (whom we know to be Southampton) is further proof that the traditional interpretation of the sonnets is untenable.

Despite the clarity of the poet's assertion that the sonnets constitute a monument to their subject, not one of our commentators (nor any other scholars, to my knowledge) show the slightest awareness that the poet has said what he so plainly states. All four of them fail to comment on the use of the word "monument" or that the poet has stated that the sonnets *are* a monument, in Sonnet 107, and, of the three who do refer to the word in Sonnet 81, none draws any useful inferences from it.

Structure and Symmetry

In Shakespeare's time, structure and symmetry were important in art to a degree that is difficult for our modern mind to comprehend. Symmetry was at the heart of Greek art, which only recently had been rediscovered and which provided models for the Italian Renaissance, the spirit of which Oxford played a major role in bringing to England. It was also an age when people were fascinated with numbers, numerology, astrology, ciphers and codes. The choice of the number of poems to be included in a collection or sonnet cycle, especially the number 100, was never accidental. In the 14th century, Boccaccio included exactly 100 stories in his *Decameron*. Thomas Watson published 100 poems in his 1582 *Hekatompathia, or The Passionate Century of Love*. Several other well-known sonnet cycles also consisted of 100 poems.

To my knowledge, Edgar Fripp is the only traditional scholar to notice that Sonnets 27-126 formed a century in the exact middle of the cycle. Fripp wrote in his 1938 *Shakespeare, Man and Artist* that "Centuries or 'hundreds' of literary pieces were in fashion...of Songs, Sonnets, Prayers, Sermons, Hymns, Sentences, Flowers, Points of Husbandry, Emblems, Medical Observations, or what not....*The Hekatompathia or Passionate Century of Love* by Thomas Watson...may have served as a model for Shakespeare's Century of Sonnets....Shakespeare's Sonnets 27-126 are a century."[xliii]

Other traditional scholars do not discern the "century" in the middle of the sonnets because they don't see a division between Sonnets 26 and 27; instead, they see one between Sonnets 17 and

18 (at the end of the "Procreate Sonnets," which they misconstrue as the "Marriage Sonnets"). Since the *caesura* between Sonnets 26 and 27 is universally overlooked, the traditional camp sees the first 17 urging marriage, followed by a group of 109 to the same young man, and 26 to the "dark lady" (plus the final set of two). The resulting "pattern," 17/109/26/2, does not reveal the true structure.

The Whittemore interpretation, that Sonnet 27 relates to the day on which Southampton was arrested for treason after the failure of the ill-fated "Essex Rebellion," explains this dramatic change in tone. The case becomes airtight that indeed, the structure of 26/100/26 was intentional, and that the middle 100 sonnets are unified.

We have already seen how the "middle century" itself is composed of eighty prison sonnets (Sonnets 27-106, written between February 8, 1601, and April 9, 1603), followed by twenty written shortly after Southampton's release from the Tower. It appears that Oxford decided to add the latter group to the eighty prison sonnets so as to bring the core to exactly 100. There were nineteen days from the date Southampton was released (April 10, 1603) to the date of Elizabeth's funeral on April 28. Dating Sonnet 125 to the latter date, based on the reference to the "canopy," Oxford needed only to add one final sonnet, a sendoff or *envoi*, to complete the series that became the central group of 100.

Thus, the "century" is itself divided 80/20. It can hardly be a coincidence that *The Hekatompathia* of 1582 (which was dedicated to Oxford and to which he almost certainly contributed, perhaps in large part) was also divided into a series of eighty and a series of twenty.

Preceding the middle century, the first twenty-six sonnets were all written before Southampton was twenty-seven years old, strongly suggesting that each sonnet was intended to represent a year of his life. The fact that Southampton turned twenty-seven in 1600 would suggest that the nine sonnets (18-26) following the seventeen "Procreate Sonnets" were written one a year from 1592 through 1600 (with Sonnet 27 intended to be written before his twenty-eighth birthday in 1601), yielding a total of twenty-six sonnets that had been completed by the time tragedy struck on February 8, 1601. It is highly probable that the first seventeen were written on or around Southampton's seventeenth birthday, specifically intended to correspond to his age. This much is conceded even by many traditional scholars. It is easy to further conclude that, once having matched the number of sonnets to

Southampton's age, the poet continued the practice for the next nine years—until Southampton's arrest changed everything.

Southampton's arrest at age 27, when Oxford had written twenty-six sonnets created a "yardstick" which would resonate throughout the structure of the sonnets. Before 1601, there is no good reason to believe that Oxford had plans to publish the sonnets (Francis Meres wrote in 1598 of Shakespeare's "sugar'd sonnets" circulating among his "private friends"), that he thought of them as having any particular structure, or that they represented a monument to Southampton.

But if Oxford decided in 1601 to create a series of 100 sonnets related to Southampton's arrest, and to dedicate them to him as a monument, as Sonnets 81 and 107 tell us he did, the existence of the preceding twenty-six and the need for symmetry dictated the creation of a back-end set of another twenty-six. But as it was now pointless to continue the narrative of Southampton's life past the interment of his mother, Elizabeth, which buried forever any hope that Southampton would be recognized as her rightful heir, the final set could not continue the narrative of the first 126. Yet, this final twenty-six needed to be connected to his purpose. We are compelled to assume that during the 1601-1603 period Oxford had been composing sonnets in addition to those he included in his 100-sonnet Southampton narrative, which he now used to make this second twenty-six-sonnet series. That Sonnets 127-152 turn out to be bitter poems directed against Elizabeth confirms the truth of the new paradigm.

Two final sonnets complete the series, making a total of 154. Although the last two sonnets are important for other reasons, they can safely be ignored in terms of the symmetry of the remainder of the sonnets, as they are clearly tacked on, as if (as Whittemore suggests) to invite the reader to start over with Sonnet 1 and read them again. I therefore discuss the structure of the sonnets, or the monument, as consisting of 152 sonnets.

Examining the eighty Prison Sonnets more closely, we note further details of structure. Southampton's reprieve from a death sentence is documented at Sonnet 67, the exact midpoint of this group. Sonnet 67 initiates a new sequence that no longer anticipates Southampton's imminent death, but turns to other matters. Once again, a precise division that subdivides a set of eighty sonnets into two groups of forty further confirms the correctness of the interpretation. Because we can date the execution of the last of the conspirators to the thirty-ninth day of Southampton's incarceration

(March 18, 1601), with his own execution expected to follow two days later, we can safely conclude that Sonnet 66, the fortieth sonnet since his imprisonment, was written on March 19, which was the fortieth day since his arrest. That Oxford would learn of Southampton's reprieve from execution on the forty-first day is likely a coincidence, which permitted him to implement the symmetry of forty pre-reprieve sonnets, and forty post-reprieve ones. So, with Sonnet 67 Oxford laid down another marker.

Yet another marker appears exactly twenty sonnets later, in Sonnet 87, with the description of the legal device by which Southampton was spared execution, namely, misprision of treason; that divides the second group of forty into two subgroups of twenty sonnets each. There are good reasons to assign the twenty sonnets from Sonnet 67 through Sonnet 86 to the twenty days following Southampton's reprieve from his death sentence, as it is unlikely that Oxford would have had to wait longer than that to learn of the reduction of the treason charge.

If that is accepted, then the second twenty sonnets from Sonnet 87 to 106 must cover the period from April 1601 to April 9, 1603. Sonnet 97 then stands as yet another marker, further subdividing these twenty into two groups of ten. Sonnet 97 begins "How like a winter hath my absence been from thee, the pleasure of the fleeting year!" If the preceding ten sonnets, Sonnets 87-96, are assigned one to a month, starting with April 1601 (where the previous twenty sonnets left off), Sonnet 96 would correspond to January 1602, and Sonnet 97 to February 1602, exactly one year ("the fleeting year") since Oxford would have seen Southampton as a free man ("my absence...from thee").

It is not necessary to assume that Oxford actually wrote each sonnet during the month or day we are assigning, but rather that when he came to assemble the entire series, he deliberately arranged them as we describe. Once he was well embarked on the project and had begun to conceive of the series as his monument for Southampton (by no later than Sonnet 81), he most likely planned that there would be eighty sonnets as of the date of Southampton's release (which he likely knew would happen on James' accession), and that another twenty sonnets would complete the century.

In February of 1602, he could not know how much longer Southampton would be in the Tower; thus, he could not have planned how to correlate sonnets 98-106 with specific months. However, when Elizabeth died in March of 1603, ensuring Southampton's imminent release, Oxford could assign Sonnets 98-

102 to the ten months from March 1602 through December, each sonnet assigned to a two-month period. Then Sonnet 103 would correspond to January 1603, Sonnet 104 to February, Sonnet 105 to March (most likely to March 24, the date of Elizabeth's death), and Sonnet 106 to April (almost certainly to April 9, the day before Southampton's release). Sonnet 104 (which we assign to February of 1603) may also be intended to mark the second anniversary of Southampton's incarceration, with its reference to "three winters cold" which would be the winters of 1601, 1602 and 1603. However, the sonnet also refers to three springs, summers and autumns, so this identification is not certain. What matters is that Oxford did allocate these ten sonnets to the time between the first anniversary of Southampton's arrest (Sonnet 97 in February of 1602) and his release on April 10, 1603.

One final "coincidence" is that Southampton, who was twenty-six at the time of his arrest, was imprisoned for almost exactly twenty-six months.

With Whittemore, I contend that these arguments in support of his paradigm based on structure and symmetry are not secondary or minor, and certainly not coincidental, but constitute strong supporting evidence of its validity. Those who continue to dispute the new paradigm are obliged to account for these structural features and relate them to the content of the sonnets as they understand it.

We can safely assume that Oxford did not originally intend to create a cycle of the sort he eventually produced. The structure suggested itself only after Southampton's arrest, when Oxford's purpose would have changed dramatically, from just writing sonnets to his slightly wayward son to writing sonnets chronicling what seemed certain to be a tragedy of monumental proportions—that a son of the monarch, whose true identity was unacknowledged, faced execution. Even while doing everything he could behind the scenes to spare Southampton's life (and, if possible, get him exonerated), Oxford had to prepare for the worst case scenario, that Southampton would be executed, in which case only these sonnets would exist to tell his story to posterity. It does not matter exactly when Oxford decided on the exact structure we see today; what matters is that it was intentionally created, which fact is one more strong confirmation of the correctness of the Whittemore paradigm.

Chapter 24
Summary and Conclusion

Summary

The case laid out in the preceding pages, that Shakespeare's sonnets were about Shakespeare's own son, Henry Wriothesley, the 3rd Earl of Southampton, that Shakespeare himself was actually Edward deVere, the 17th Earl of Oxford, and that Southampton's mother was Queen Elizabeth herself, *uniquely makes sense of Shakespeare's sonnets.* The evidence has provided multiple proofs that the author could not have been the orthodox candidate, William Shakspere of Stratford, and could only have been Oxford. (See Appendix III for a recapitulation of many of these proofs from within the *Sonnets.*)

Shake-speares Sonnets thus, by themselves, proves the dual case—who Shakespeare wasn't, namely, Shakspere of Stratford, and who he was, namely, Oxford. Once their true meaning is laid bare, under the paradigm that Whittemore developed, the *Sonnets* proves to be the most powerful evidence in existence for the truth of the hypothesis first put forward by Thomas Looney in 1920 that Oxford was Shakespeare. Ironically, very few defenders of the Oxfordian thesis have shown themselves prepared to embrace the truths that can be teased from these poems, and they have thereby overlooked the most powerful argument they could use on behalf of the case for Oxford.

Prior to Whittemore's discoveries, a courageous few Oxfordians had recognized enough evidence within the *Sonnets* to draw the correct conclusion that Southampton was Oxford's and Elizabeth's son. This conclusion *per se* is not Whittemore's achievement. His unique contribution is the realization that the *Sonnets* was a project driven by Oxford's torment in the aftermath of the failed Essex Rebellion on February 8, 1601, that left his son Southampton in the Tower of London, condemned to death. Whittemore alone recognized that Sonnets 27-106 chronicle Southampton's twenty-six month period of confinement in the Tower for treason, and that Sonnets 107-126 chronicle the nineteen days following his release on April 10, 1603, culminating with

Sonnet 125, written on the day of the funeral of Queen Elizabeth, followed by Sonnet 126, an *envoi* or postscript to the entire Southampton saga. This recognition in turn revealed a set of exactly 100 sonnets, bookended by two sets of twenty-six sonnets (1-26 and 127-152), creating a symmetrical structure that cannot have been accidental.

When viewed in light of references within a number of sonnets to the sonnets themselves as constituting a monument to Southampton, such a structure confirms that a monument is precisely what Oxford created to honor and preserve the memory of his royal son for future generations. The sonnets also contain striking evidence that the price Oxford paid for having Southampton's life spared was his forced agreement never to reveal that he was the flesh and blood author behind the "Shakespeare" pseudonym. Whittemore's unique contribution was seeing all of the sonnets as a monument to Southampton, and discovering that each one can thereby be understood in totally new ways, ways that resolve all of the anomalies that cannot be explained within the old paradigm, while confirming the conclusion

that Southampton was the royal son of Elizabeth and Oxford.

Whittemore's discoveries also include solving for the first time the mystery of who the supposed "rival poet" was in Sonnets 78-86, namely, the Shakespeare name versus Oxford the actual author, and the mystery of who the "dark lady" of Sonnets 127-152 was, namely, Queen Elizabeth, toward whom Oxford maintained a very conflicted "love-hate" relationship.

The case made in these pages against Shakspere's authorship of *Shake-speares Sonnets* is compelling. The helplessness of all of our orthodox critics shown by the manifest failure of their attempted explications of so many passages from so many sonnets, as laid out in this book, is proof that the orthodox reading cannot be correct. With that recognition, the alternate paradigm laid out in these pages deserves a thorough, fair, open-minded and comprehensive review. It is high time the true author whom we have known as the incomparable "Shakespeare" be recognized for who he really was; this volume seeks to advance that recognition.

Conclusion

We have shown that *Shake-speares Sonnets* is the chronicle of the demise of the Tudor dynasty, which was directly caused by Elizabeth's refusal to acknowledge her illegitimate son by Edward de Vere, the 17th Earl of Oxford, the actual flesh-and-blood author behind the "Shakespeare" pseudonym. It is the painfully personal saga of Oxford, the father of the young man who could have become king, who had to watch as his son was arrested and condemned to death by a jury led by himself, even as he lobbied behind the scenes for his life. The tragedies are multiple, for Oxford, for Southampton, and for England, deprived as it was of a direct successor to Elizabeth and forced to accept the alien, Scottish, Catholic King James. The reigns of James and his son, Charles I, were disastrous; the monarchy itself was toppled in 1648.

Numerous excellent books demonstrate that most of Shakespeare's works are just as much about high matters of state as the *Sonnets*. Once the full extent of the political nature of plays such as *Hamlet, Othello, Romeo and Juliet* and others is understood—which can happen only when Oxford is accepted as Shakespeare—it can be seen that the corpus we know as "Shakespeare's" was written by a nobleman, a leading insider in Elizabeth's court, as part of an ambitious political agenda to help inspire England to come together to fight the foreign enemies it faced, to deal with the corruption of the state, and to ensure harmony rather than civil war. In that light it should be no surprise that the *Sonnets* is also political. Given the highly sensitive nature of their true meaning, they had to be written in disguise, one which has escaped detection for 400 years. Now that their true meaning has been discovered, many opportunities exist for scholars to refine the precise readings of each sonnet, and to properly read those that remain difficult to understand. That will bring an even deeper level of understanding of the *Sonnets*. Such a reexamination will hopefully create well-deserved interest in *all* the sonnets, not just in the handful of favorites we all recognize. Many poetic gems come alive under the correct interpretation of what they are about, just waiting to be discovered by a wider audience.

This Book's Challenge to Stratfordian Orthodoxy

To reiterate the point, this book challenges Shakespearean orthodoxy, possibly to a greater degree than any other book in recent memory. While doubts about Shakspere's authorship began in the 19th century, the correct author was only first identified in print in 1920. Orthodoxy, ensconced in academia, has attempted since that time to man the bilge pumps to keep the Good Ship Shakspere afloat, employing every approach from silence to ridicule to debate. All the while the credibility of their case continues to erode, as more and more people become skeptics of Shakspere or advocates of Oxford as the true author.

Nonetheless, the tipping point that would bury the orthodox paradigm has not yet arrived. It took the academic profession of geology nearly fifty years to recognize that Alfred Wegener had been right about continental drift, but eventually the notion that continents move became the new doctrine. In just under a hundred years, the academic profession of Shakespeareana has yet to furl its flag and accept that they "got the wrong guy," and move on to explore the exciting new world of Shakespeare studies that will open up once they finally accept the inevitable.

While the evidence that Shakspere was not, and could not, have been Shakespeare is, in my opinion, virtually conclusive, the case for Oxford, which I believe is just as strong, has so far lacked the kind of evidence from within the works that would make it impossible to resist.

Ironically, it is in the *Sonnets* that Oxford's authorship is most clear—in fact, recognizing Oxford as Shakespeare is the only alternative that can explain the *Sonnets* at all. One purpose of this book is to identify numerous passages that orthodox criticism cannot make sense of, but that yield a consistent, coherent and efficient reading under the new paradigm. This book represents a unique challenge to orthodoxy because it employs four well-respected modern scholars on the *Sonnets* as foils to expose the bankruptcy of their readings. I know of no other book that has attempted to do this. This creates a compelling case that no matter who the author of the *Sonnets* may have been, it cannot possibly have been Shakspere. It had to be someone who was a nobleman, and one who cared for Southampton very deeply yet without a hint of the relationship being romantic, homoerotic, or any brand of ordinary friendship.

Even without the touchstone of the new paradigm—that the author was Oxford and that Southampton was his son by Elizabeth—the analysis in this book demolishes the credibility of all orthodox scholarship on the *Sonnets*. While orthodoxy has been occupied fending off Oxfordian challenges concerning the authorship of the plays, I doubt that orthodoxy would have thought that their point of greatest vulnerability, their true Achilles heel, is actually these pesky sonnets.

Once it is recognized, as it must be, that Sonnets 27-106 are about Southampton during his incarceration in the Tower of London from 1601 to 1603, the game is up. Correctly read, these eighty sonnets can be seen to contain multiple instances of Oxford's signature, such as his self-portrayal as simultaneously Southampton's "advocate" and "adverse party."

All that remains is to follow the evidence where it leads, as I have done throughout this book. *Only* if Southampton is Oxford's illegitimate son by Elizabeth can the sonnets be understood. Once this is accepted, a fascinating narrative unfolds that resolves scores of anomalies that orthodox scholarship gags on (if it attempts to explain them at all) into a coherent interpretation of the entire 154-sonnet sequence.

I anticipate this book will begin to draw negative attention from orthodox scholars, and that the first salvos will ridicule as preposterous the core premise of Oxford's "trinity," in the hope that such ridicule will suffice to deter serious consideration of all that I have presented. However, ignoring powerful arguments will only work for so long before the orthodox camp will need to actually try to refute this book's repeated demonstrations of the futility of the orthodox reading.

This Book's Challenge to Oxfordian "Orthodoxy"

Also as noted, it also challenges Oxfordian "orthodoxy." For three-quarters of a century, those affirming their belief that Southampton was a "Prince Tudor" have been generally marginalized and ridiculed even within the Oxford movement. The publication of *The Monument,* and Whittemore's subsequent persistent advocacy of his theory of the *Sonnets,* has led to a gradually widening circle of Oxfordians who concur with his thesis.

The resistance to it is doubly ironic in that it mirrors the resistance of Stratfordians against the Oxfordian hypothesis. In both cases, those opposed cry out that "there is no evidence" for key parts of the new theory—that Oxford was Shakespeare in the one case, that Oxford, Southampton and Elizabeth formed a "royal family" in the other. The case for Oxford, and the case for Whittemore's thesis, both depend on literary evidence, and each represents the only solution that accords with that literary evidence.

That Oxfordian attacks on Whittemore's thesis are bankrupt is shown by the inability of those who reject it to explain the sonnets in any other way. In fact, I believe it the case that most Oxfordians who reject Whittemore's view fall back on some version of the

Stratfordian Standard Interpretation that the sonnets are about the poet (replacing Shakspere with Oxford), Southampton and an unknown lady who have a weird three-way up-and-down relationship. Some Oxfordians openly support the view that Oxford was homosexual or bisexual, and those that don't have no explanation for why the sonnets appear to support that conclusion.

I challenge Oxfordians who maintain that Whittemore has it all wrong. My challenge is to take my arguments in the order I present them, chapter by chapter, theorem by theorem, and identify where they disagree, and why. Do they accept my reading (following Whittemore) of Sonnet 107, which is close to what even many Stratfordians believe? If so, then what about Whittemore's take on Sonnet 27? And so on. That is, this book presents a solution to the clues—the anomalies—in a logical order; there is nothing illogical about someone who sees and concurs with the logic up to a point, and then says, "hmm, I don't agree with this next step," provided they have a *reason* for doing so. I welcome feedback and critical comment from anyone who would follow along and tell me at exactly where they draw the line.

It's Time for Justice to Finally Be Served

Shakespeare is unique in modern history in the degree to which he has become timeless and universal, delighting audiences today just as much as he delighted them in his own time, his plays the most performed of any playwright in history, selected sonnets among the most read and recited of any poems ever written. For that reason, if no other, it should matter a great deal to us today that we honor the correct author of the plays and poems. Borrowing my subject matter and most of my analysis from Hank Whittemore, to whom the world owes its gratitude for finally unraveling what the sonnets were really about, I have sought to present it here in a fashion all my own, making the case for the new paradigm in the most logical order possible. I am confident that this presentation will unlock these unsurpassed poetic gems to a new generation of readers, and facilitate a new world of appreciation and analysis, while accelerating the acceptance of Oxford as Shakespeare, and the Whittemore "Monument" paradigm as the solution to the 400-year-old riddle of *Shake-speares Sonnets*.

May Edward de Vere, the 17th Earl of Oxford, finally take his rightful place in the public eye as the supreme and subline "William Shakespeare."

Appendices

Appendix I
The Great Shakespeare Fraud

Two Centuries of Skepticism

For two centuries, many people have doubted that William Shakspere of Stratford could have produced the towering literary achievements that constitute the output associated with the name of "William Shakespeare."

The essence of the case can be simply stated: there is no contemporary documentary evidence that Shakspere had anything to do with writing the plays and poems of Shakespeare, and what is known about his life is so inconsistent with the life that the real author had to have had, that his being the author is impossible. The known life of William Shakspere is that of a semiliterate man who hoarded grain in a famine, frequently went to court to hound debtors for paltry sums and aspired to join the "gentle" class in England's highly stratified society. It is primarily the incongruity between the soaring accomplishments in a dozen fields of endeavor, including being the greatest wordsmith in the English language, that the author Shakespeare possessed, and the few known achievements of William Shakspere, that has convinced the following people, among many others, that Shakspere wasn't Shakespeare:

Writers: Walt Whitman, Nathaniel Hawthorne, Samuel Taylor Coleridge, Ralph Waldo Emerson, John Greenleaf Whittier, Henry James, Thomas Hardy, Mark Twain, James Joyce, John Galsworthy and Daphne DuMaurier.

Political figures: Benjamin Disraeli, Lord Palmerston, Otto von Bismarck, Charles de Gaulle and Senator Paul Douglas.

Public figures: Charlie Chaplin, Sigmund Freud, Orson Welles, Helen Keller, Malcolm X, Paul Nitze and Claire Booth Luce.

Historians: Crane Brinton and David McCullough.

Shakespearean actors: Sir John Gielgud, Derek Jacobi and Mark Rylance.

Supreme Court Justices: Oliver Wendell Holmes, Harry Blackmun, Lewis Powell, Sandra Day O'Connor and John Paul

Stevens.

An honor roll of doubters by itself does not prove the case, of course. But it illustrates that the belief that Shakspere of Stratford couldn't have been Shakespeare is very far from a crackpot, wild, "conspiracy" theory that can be airily dismissed as the view of a lunatic fringe.

The Case Against Shakspere

The case against William Shakspere of Stratford-upon-Avon as the author of the literary works we attribute to "Shakespeare" is, in my opinion, conclusive. Dozens of irrefutable arguments exist, any one of which is sufficient to prove this impossibility. The only reasons the myth persists are the existence of a "united front" of academic scholars whose reputations would be ruined if they were to admit that Shakspere wasn't Shakespeare, and the credulity that most uninformed people naturally give to these self-proclaimed "experts." In the introduction to her book, *Shakespeare Suppressed*, Katherine Chiljan offers a concise explanation of why the myth persists. After characterizing Shakespeare as "the epitome of high art and culture, the fount of knowledge, the biggest contributor to modern English language, [and] the master dramatist whose 400-year-old plays are performed, read and appreciated today, every day, in many languages," she writes:

> The Shakespeare professor or expert, however, would have you believe that a man with scant education, no evidence he could write (other than a crude signature), and no evidence during his lifetime that he was in fact a professional writer, was the same erudite, witty and super-brilliant wordsmith, Shakespeare. Left with so few facts about his personal life and literary career, the very best that the expert can do for the great author, the creator of so many gorgeous verses, and fascinating, lovable and psychologically complex characters, is to make guesses. Nothing but endless speculations and fantasies are offered to explain how England's greatest author reached the pinnacle of literary achievement. But does the professor look at the historical record? Apparently, he does not. If he did, he would see how obvious it is that his man, the Stratford Man, was not the great author, Shakespeare. And with only a little extra effort he would also see that the

concept of the Stratford Man as Shakespeare is a very old and well-orchestrated fabrication. He would see that the maker of this fabrication or myth was Ben Jonson, directed and sponsored by William Herbert, 3rd Earl of Pembroke, and that their instrument was Shakespeare's First Folio, published in 1623. This book of collected plays suggested for the very first time that "William Shakespeare" and an undistinguished businessman with a similar name who hailed from Stratford-upon-Avon were one and the same. The Stratford Man had been dead for seven years when the book was launched. Jonson and Pembroke's deception remained for the most part undetected for over two centuries. But by the time that unbiased observers were starting to catch on, the Shakespeare professor or expert had evidently become enamored with the idea that a boy with humble origins, little schooling and no connections had transformed himself into a polyglot, a polymath, a master of rhetoric, and a sophisticated, traveler, a man of the world who could create timeless literary masterpieces. Any evidence that contradicted this picture was ignored, and that is the situation as it stands to this day.[xliv]

The result is that virtually all students, when they are introduced to Shakespeare in school, are not even informed that there is a "controversy" over authorship, much less that the case for Shakspere lacks a shred of contemporary evidence and depends on absurd assumptions about what a minimally educated country boy could magically accomplish. This chapter presents a brief review of the strongest evidence against Shakspere. In the bibliography I cite many other works which provide a full account of the case against him.

Multiple Categories of Proofs

I have chosen to highlight eight types or categories of proof, each of which contains multiple specific items of evidence, many of which could stand alone as sufficient to prove the case:

1) The complete disconnect between the personality and commoner status of Shakspere and the personality and clearly noble status of Shakespeare.
2) Issues posed by "Shakespeare's" authorship of not just the plays, but also the two narrative poems, and the *Sonnets*, and other anomalies involving the appearance of the name

"Shakespeare."

3) Shakspere's "positives": known characteristics of Shakspere that are incompatible with his being Shakespeare.

4) Shakspere's "negatives": missing characteristics of Shakspere that he would had to have possessed if he were the author.

5) Fields of knowledge that Shakespeare demonstrates mastery of, but that Shakspere could not have mastered.

6) Specific items of knowledge displayed in the plays that Shakspere couldn't have known.

7) "Dogs that didn't bark" (people who knew Shakspere, or knew of Stratford when Shakspere lived there but who never mentioned knowing, or knowing of, the great dramatist).

8) Other proofs and indications that Shakspere couldn't have been Shakespeare.

To support the traditional case for Shakspere as Shakespeare, orthodoxy relies on three main pillars: (1) the close similarity of the two names (in an era when spelling was admittedly haphazard); (2) the fact that Shakspere was a shareholder in several London theater companies and may have had some other peripheral connection to the London acting scene; and (3) the prefatory materials in the First Folio of 1623. Some other items are also typically introduced into evidence, but they are inferential at best and Chiljan (among others) does a masterful job of demonstrating how they count against his authorship, not for it.

Tellingly, the known documentary evidence of the life of the historical Shakspere of Stratford is thin—ironically, too thin to show that he could have been Shakespeare, but not thin enough to hide why he could not have been. It is sufficient to paint a portrait of a real person but, unfortunately for the Stratfordian camp, someone without a single characteristic that one would associate with the author of the plays and poems, someone with personality traits inconsistent with being the author, and someone who was never recognized during his own lifetime as the writer we know as "Shakespeare." No more than a few dozen documents exist that pertain to the activities of Shakspere. Most of them refer to mundane money matters, or to Shakspere's efforts to secure his father the right to bear a coat of arms. None points to Shakspere as a playwright or an actor or, with one possible exception, to someone with any connection to the theater at all. There is no contemporaneous evidence that Shakspere was ever an actor, much less a playwright or poet. The earliest cited evidence for Shakspere as an actor comes from Ben Jonson, who in 1616, just weeks after Shakspere died, listed "William Shake-speare" as an actor in several of his plays performed fifteen years earlier, conveniently and hardly coincidentally timed so that the living Shakspere couldn't protest the reference.

The most powerful pieces of evidence adduced by Stratfordian defenders are the dedications and poems in the sixteen pages of front matter to the 1623 First Folio. While many have pointed out anomalies and contradictions within those pages, Chiljan provides a well-researched and powerful demonstration of how that section was a carefully constructed fraud, intended to point toward Shakspere without being too explicit (as many people were still alive who knew the truth), and which also explains *why* Jonson and Pembroke, who also played a major role in producing the First Folio, perpetrated it.

The Personality and Class of Shakspere and Shakespeare

Great artists draw on their life experiences in their art; one of the factors that makes their art great is its "truth." Shakespeare was one of the most prolific dramatists in history, author of some three dozen known (and some possibly unknown) full-length plays, two long narrative poems, a collection of 154 sonnets, and a few shorter poems. The wealth of imagery, the range of plots and material, the psychological insights into people, the implicit view of humanity (and the difference that class makes), the understanding of so many domains of knowledge, the immense vocabulary used (including the invention of nearly 2,000 new words), all are universally acknowledged as the output of "Shakespeare."

None of that is consistent with the known biography of Shakspere. The meager documentary evidence of Shakspere's activities starts and finishes with activities involving making money, mainly by lending small sums or by investing in several theater companies or theaters (as well as hoarding grain during a famine). Shakspere clearly sought to acquire the title "gentleman" by obtaining a coat of arms, which he managed to do for his father, who was granted one in 1596 (it was later found to have been improperly granted). Several records show him seeking legal redress for small debts. The conclusion that he was a money-conscious commoner who was focused on becoming rich in an outlying town is inescapable.

How could such a one produce an enormous corpus of work in which are found innumerable instances of extreme generosity, acts based on devoted friendship and love, while the same corpus bespeaks no interest in earning money whatsoever? Shakespeare's lead characters, and the plots of his plays, have no relationship with a single thing known about Shakspere. Such a huge chasm between life and art does not exist for any other writer.

The evidence that the author Shakespeare was an aristocrat, a member of the high nobility, is equally overwhelming:

1) The plays reflect knowledge of many domains that only a high nobleman could know about.

2) The plays' heroes and heroines are all members of the nobility; the common people are all either foils or fools, generally introduced for comic relief.

3) Many specific references in the plays can only be understood as proof that the author was a nobleman.

4) Numerous writings of the period by contemporaries contain clear references to Shakespeare as a nobleman (see Chiljan for an excellent review of this evidence).

5) From no later than 1595, and possibly earlier, plays now identified as by "Shakespeare" were being performed at court for Queen Elizabeth, something unthinkable were the author an itinerant playwright from the boondocks.

6) There are multiple indications that Shakespeare not only knew, but was on intimate terms with, Queen Elizabeth; such a relationship would only have been possible for a member of the high nobility.

7) Several prominent members of the court, above all Lord Burghley, are clearly lampooned in several plays, something that no commoner could have gotten away with, but a high lord could have.

8) Many references in the plays are to events that only a member of the court would have known about.

"Shakspere" the Playwright, as a Poet First?

The very first public appearance of the name "Shakespeare" is toxic for the Shakspere hypothesis, because it appears in print not as the writer of popular plays, but as the author of two popular (and very high quality) narrative poems published in 1593 and 1594. It is problematic because the entirely circumstantial case for Shakspere relies on hypothesizing a story that an itinerant from Stratford joins a London acting company, finds he has a talent for playwriting, and begins to write plays for the acting companies. For Shakspere to have been a highly polished poet *before* he was recognized as a playwright, but was still quite young, strains credulity and upends the only plausible narrative in defense of the traditional account. Since the first plays under the name "Shakespeare" were not published until 1598, why there was such a gap before his plays started being published, and then with so little fanfare, considering the continuing popularity of the two narrative poems which were frequently reprinted? It is a mystery the Shakspere camp is hard-pressed to explain.

Why, if Shakspere had experienced success in the poetic realm, and created a fan base for his works, did he not capitalize on it by bringing out his plays in print or by writing any more long poems? The traditional belief is that he had begun writing plays around 1590-91, but had to stop for over a year when London theaters were closed because of the plague, and so turned to poetry. All of this— that he was even in London by 1590, that he was involved with acting companies in any capacity, that he was an actor, that he was a playwright, and that he was an accomplished poet—is pure speculation, without an iota of documentary evidence, other than the differently-spelled name "William Shakespeare" on the two poems. The traditional belief is hardly credible even on its own terms. If Shakspere were as accomplished a poet as Shakespeare's poems demonstrate, and had suddenly become well known among the literati of London, he surely would not have junked his new-found fame (and fortune) to return to the anonymous world of the theater where he was still a nobody.

Given the immediate popularity of both poems in 1593 and 1594—reprintings began very shortly after each first print run—it is unexplainable under the Stratfordian premise that nothing more was heard of the Shakespeare name until 1598.

How Shakspere could have been able to write such highly polished poems at all, with no prior evolution as a poet—works which showed great familiarity with classical mythology, and which could only have been the culmination of years of experience as a poet —is beyond rational explanation by the Stratfordian camp. That camp is already hard-pressed to explain how Shakspere could have acquired the erudition in several dozen major domains of knowledge demonstrated in the plays—all acquired while browsing in bookstalls (Shakspere owned no books), as traditionalists are compelled to assert.

Poetry and playwriting are distinct skills. I cannot think of another well-known poet who also wrote plays, or a famous playwright who wrote great poetry. But the oddity of Shakspere being able to dash off these two lengthy poems doesn't end here. How could a complete unknown get published at all? Had the poems capped his playwriting career, one might imagine that he would have had no trouble finding a publisher, based on his reputation. But *Venus and Adonis* preceded the first play published under the Shakespeare name by five years. That a commoner with no record of any literary achievement could get such a poem published and to have it instantly so well received is extremely unlikely.

It gets worse for the Stratfordian advocates. Conventional analysis considers the presumed relationship between Shakspere and Henry Wriothesley, 3rd Earl of Southampton, to have been that of client and patron, with Shakspere having secured the young nobleman's patronage around 1593-94. The "evidence" for this supposition are the laudatory dedications to Southampton in *Venus and Adonis* and *Lucrece,* each effusive in its praise of him. Some conventional scholars posit that the 1593 dedication was written to solicit Southampton as a patron by flattering him, and that by the time of the second poem, Southampton had become his patron. But there is no documentary evidence that Shakspere of Stratford ever had Southampton as a patron, met him or even knew him at all. Neither supposition is anything more than that. They are both artifacts of accepting that Shakspere was Shakespeare—the dedications exist, authored by "Shakespeare," so how else could Shakspere have been their author?

The "premature" appearance of the two poems creates an additional complication for the patronage conjecture: if Southampton became Shakspere's patron by 1594, what became of that relationship? According to the theory, Shakspere was already writing plays that were being performed. Why didn't Southampton arrange to have some of them published? Why didn't Southampton have a relationship to Shakspere's putative acting company? Why is there no documentary record of any relationship, from this date forward, of Southampton to Shakspere?

These questions are unanswerable, for the simple reason that *there was no such relationship*. The conundrums posed by the publication of these two poems all but prove that Shakspere could *not* have been their author.

Since no one has ever proposed that the "Shakespeare" of the plays was a *different* Shakespeare from that of the two poems, Shakspere could therefore have been the author of neither.

The *Sonnets* poses even greater problems for the Shakspere hypothesis. It is useful to mention here just one telling circumstances in the context of the Stratfordian patronage claim. Those traditionalists who concur that the young man addressed in the *Sonnets* is Southampton explain this by reference to the patronage relationship they believe is proven by the 1593 and 1594 dedications. Having become patron and client by 1594, the two men started having the relationship that many traditionalists believe the first 126 sonnets describe. Even apart from the issue of whether that relationship was homosexual, the tone of these sonnets, if presumed to be between a commoner and one of the leading noblemen of the day, is impossible to imagine.

The required interpretations of many sonnets from the traditionalist perspective put Southampton in a compromised, pejorative light. He is shown at times fickle, moody, inconstant, and easily tempted by the mysterious lady. How could Shakspere the commoner address an earl in such intimately familiar and unflattering terms? If he had he done so in a sonnet, would he have dared to show it to Southampton? Especially after he had ceased to be his patron? Wouldn't both of them have strenuously objected to these revelatory poems being published? Despite the internal evidence mentioned above, that the author clearly wanted them published, any view that they are about Shakspere and Southampton requires that neither party would have wanted them published, even if the relationship was not homosexual. But published they were.

Was Shakspere arrested for his libelous portrayal of a top earl of the realm? If the *Sonnets* was published without Shakspere's permission, did he do anything about it? Was any notice taken when these salacious poems suddenly turned up? No. Their appearance was a non-event.

None of this makes sense within the Shakspere paradigm. This reality calls for a different paradigm, one capable of yielding compelling explanations for *why* Southampton would want them published. Only Whittemore's "Monument" paradigm supplies those explanations.

Shakspere's "Positives"

By "positives," I refer to aspects or features of Shakspere's known life that argue against his being Shakespeare. This litany is well known, and only requires a quick listing here:

1) Only six signatures of Shakspere exist; all are ill-formed, appearing to be the handwriting of someone who was illiterate or semiliterate. How could a person who can barely write his name be Shakespeare?

2) Shakspere's gravestone carries an engraving of doggerel, apparently written by him. How could, and why would, Shakespeare have so disgraced himself with such an epitaph?

3) Shakspere's daughters, Susanna and Judith, were illiterate. Would the real Shakespeare not have educated his own daughters—a point made stranger by the myriad depictions in Shakespeare's plays of highly educated women?

4) Shakspere's detailed will mentions not a single book or manuscript, nor did it contain a bequest to the town grammar school or a provision for the education of his granddaughter. How could this be for the real Shakespeare, especially as the wills of other educated people did mention books (expensive items in those days), made provision for the education of female relatives, and made bequests to schools?

5) Shakspere's only recorded activities in London involve receipt of money, an extremely odd fact if he was really the playwright Shakespeare—that he would be known in that town only for pecuniary matters, but not for playwriting.

6) Shakspere's will bequeaths the sum of 26 shillings to "buy …rings" for three members of the King's Men acting company. Were he the real Shakespeare, well-known and universally praised, and assuredly well-off due to his success, why would he make such a provision in his will to only three of his acting fellows and for such paltry sums, given the value of his overall estate)? Why was even this limited bequest interlineated, meaning he omitted it in the first draft of his will, as if someone needed to remind him later?

Collectively, these and the few other known facts about Shakspere represent anomalies for which no credible explanation has ever been adduced by Stratfordian defenders. Each of them strongly disproves the possibility of Shakspere being Shakespeare.

Shakspere's "Negatives"

By "negatives," I mean things that would have to be true if Shakspere had been Shakespeare, but are not.

1) Shakspere had become relatively rich, for a commoner, by 1603. As an actor or playwright, he could not have earned so much money, so he had to have devoted a major portion of his life to earning it in other ways. This would have precluded his having time to act, to do the necessary research reflected in his plays, and to actually write the plays and poems.

2) At best, Shakspere had a grammar school education (and there is no documentary evidence of even that). He would have to have given himself the equivalent of a university education, including mastery of several foreign languages, to have written the plays. It strains credulity that a minimally educated commoner was somehow able to master the vast array of domains that Shakespeare clearly did, including specialized ones such as law, without leaving any evidence of it. There is no evidence that he ever purchased or owned a single book (traditionalists try to explain away this lack by claiming he browsed in bookstalls and borrowed books from printers; there is, of course, no evidence that he did either).

3) Shakspere, the documented money-grubbing miser, left not one scrap of evidence that he made money from selling plays, or had any interest in making money from them. His known biography would suggest that, had he written the plays, he would have left documentary evidence of making money from them. The irony here is extreme: most of the documentary evidence that exists about Shakspere is how he sued people for small sums and hoarded grain in a famine. That such a person would invest no effort to make a shilling from selling and publishing plays that were highly popular, and could have brought him even greater wealth, is beyond improbable.

4) As discussed, Shakespeare's two long, narrative poems appeared in 1593 and 1594, when Shakspere was age twenty-nine and thirty, five years before the first play

appeared with his name on it. The dedications in the two poems to the 3rd Earl of Southampton are written in a manner that makes them inconceivable as coming from a commoner. No attempt to explain them as "Shakespeare's" bid to cultivate Southampton as a patron makes sense. There is no evidence that Shakspere and Southampton met or even knew each other.

5) In a 1598 publication, *Palladis Tamia,* Francis Meres lists twelve Shakespeare play titles. Four more Shakespeare plays are known to have been performed by then. Since few traditionalists believe that Shakspere wrote any plays before 1590, we are required to believe that this actor (acting itself was a full-time job) wrote seventeen plays in eight years in his spare time (during which he would also have had to spend much time haunting bookstalls and pubs to garner the vicarious knowledge he lacked). The unlikelihood of all this is great. Chiljan has also found, in the writings of others before 1598, allusions to lines in sixteen additional Shakespeare plays, bringing the total to thirty-three that Shakspere would have had to have written in an eight-year span —about a play every three months.

As with the "positives," each of these points independently suggests that Shakspere couldn't have been Shakespeare.

Shakespeare's Fields of Knowledge

Much has been written on the enormous erudition displayed in Shakespeare's works. It is not merely that Shakespeare showed familiarity with many disciplines, but rather that he demonstrated consummate *mastery* of them. One example is his knowledge of the law, which scholars have shown to have been so sophisticated, and so accurate, that only one who had received legal training (which Shakspere did not receive, but Oxford did) could possibly have written the legal references in the plays. Another example is quotations from French sources for which English translations existed, but where Shakespeare made his own retranslation— something that Shakspere (for whom there is no evidence he knew French) could not have done.

1) Shakespeare's works display a deep knowledge of the following disciplines: law, botany (Shakespeare had a detailed knowledge of dozens of flowers that grew only in the gardens of aristocrats), zoology (Shakespeare

demonstrated a precise understanding of the behavior of many animals, especially birds), astronomy, French and Italian (Shakespeare clearly was fluent in both languages), Latin (while grammar schools taught Latin, Shakespeare's depth of knowledge bespeaks one who has gone far beyond grammar school knowledge—Shakespeare was so steeped in it that he invented hundreds of new English words based on Latin roots), and classical mythology (hundreds of references permeate Shakespeare's works—something that a grammar school graduate would have been hard-pressed to correctly inject into his work).

2) Shakespeare's works also show knowledge that only one raised in the world of the nobility would know, or only one who had had certain experiences could know: falconry (Shakespeare makes numerous, accurate references to this sport, which was reserved to the nobility), military affairs, seamanship, medicine and music.

3) Shakespeare's word use, by various counts at between 17,000 and 21,000 words, triple the number used in the King James Bible, 250% greater than the number used by Milton, bespeaks someone steeped from earliest childhood in readings of the greatest literature. He also invented nearly 2,000 new words.

Ben Jonson, who came from humble beginnings like Shakspere and lacked a university education, is known to have worked hard as an adult to rectify his lack of education as a child, but he never came close to rivaling Shakespeare's erudition and knowledge. Shakspere's known biography ensures that he would have had vastly less time than Jonson to try to remedy his lack of formal education. No amount of self-study could have filled in the gaps in his background, which would have been necessary for him to do if he were the real Shakespeare.

Specifics in the Plays That Shakspere Couldn't Have Known

One of the strongest proofs that Shakspere could not have written the works of Shakespeare comes from the mountain of detail in the plays that reflects specific knowledge about foreign geography, art, culture, places and people, things that no one who hadn't visited these places could possibly have known. The

Stratfordian response is that it is not impossible, because "Shakespeare" did it—a tautology that exposes the weakness of the intended argument. They are compelled to claim that Shakespeare simply picked up every such detail from tavern conversations with travelers or seamen. Here are just a few examples:

1) That Shakespeare had knowledge of the street layouts of several Italian cities is proved in *The Shakespeare Guide to Italy,* by Richard Paul Roe. The playwright's knowledge of Venice, Verona, Padua and other Italian locations is specific, detailed and, most of all, accurate (these are cities that Oxford spent time in during his 1575-76 trip to Europe; Shakspere never left England).

2) Shakespeare describes Milan as a seaport. Generations of scholars have laughed about that, but Roe has established that in the 1570s (when Oxford would have visited the city), it had a canal linking it to the sea, and seagoing ships docked there.

3) Shakespeare's description of Roussillon Castle as being five days travel north of Lyon was also scoffed at by scholars (because the city of Roussillon is in the Pyrenees, nowhere near Lyon), but it turns out that a castle of that name lay precisely five days travel north of Lyon—and was clearly the setting for *All's Well That Ends Well.*

4) Knowledge of obscure facts about foreign artistic figures, such as that Giulio Romano, generally known as a painter, was also a sculptor, a fact that only a visitor to Italy would have known.

The inability of anyone who hadn't traveled abroad (and to these specific locations) to make such references is, by itself, conclusive proof that the Stratford man could not have been Shakespeare.

The Dogs that Didn't Bark

In the famous Arthur Conan Doyle mystery "Silver Blaze," Sherlock Holmes solves the case by recognizing that the murderer fled past the victim's dog, but that since no bark came from the animal, the murderer must have been someone known to and trusted by the dog. The inverse of this well describes the case against Shakspere. The failure of any of many "dogs" to "bark" demonstrates that Shakspere *could not* have been Shakespeare.

Were the author of the plays and poems the man from Stratford, people in Stratford would have known him, and been proud of him, some of whom would have recorded mention or discussion of him in writings that would have come down to us. Also, several travelogue-type books were published in the early 1600s which included chapters on Stratford-upon-Avon, and in none of these is Shakespeare mentioned, even when lesser men from the town were. Some of the other instances where "dogs didn't bark" are:

1) Shakspere's death was a non-event in England, inconceivable for one so publicly acclaimed during his lifetime. There was no funeral, no eulogy, no recorded notice by anyone, only silence.

2) Both his life and death were non-events in Stratford, an impossibility if he had been recognized locally as the famous Shakespeare.

3) Dr. John Hall, a physician who married Shakspere's daughter Susanna, lived in Stratford, and who wrote a lot, never once mentioned his father-in-law. Similarly, Shakspere's two adult daughters and his granddaughter (who lived until 1670) are not known to have mentioned his name. Had he been the great Shakespeare, is it conceivable that they would never have made mention of it?

4) Thomas Greene, town clerk of Stratford for over ten years, knew Shakspere, but made no mention of him as being Shakespeare. Greene did record a conversation he had with Shakspere, but it was about a real estate matter.

5) William Camden, writing a history of England in 1607, describes a number of famous Stratfordians, but makes no mention of Shakespeare.

6) The playwright and poet Michael Drayton, who lived twenty-five miles from Stratford, published a series of poems mentioning famous men from every county in England, but did not mention Shakespeare.

7) Dr. James Cooke, an army doctor, visited Shakspere's daughter Susanna Hall in 1649, purchased her late husband's medical casebooks and had them printed. In the introduction to them he recounted his conversation with Susanna, during which Cooke never asked her about her supposed famous father, nor did Susanna mention him, nor was there any reference made to any books or manuscripts he might have left her. Cooke's only interest was in Dr.

Hall's writing, inconceivable had Susanna's father been Shakespeare.

8) Fulke Greville, born near Stratford, was appointed recorder for the town from 1606 to 1628, charged with recording court proceedings, and was also a poet and playwright who was personally acquainted with Ben Jonson and George Chapman, but never indicated knowledge that Shakspere was Shakespeare.

9) Richard Burbage and William Kemp, named with Shakspere in a 1595 document for receiving payment for a theatrical performance in that year (who therefore clearly knew Shakspere) never left any indication that they knew Shakespeare.

Other Disproofs of Shakspere's Authorship

A great many other items of evidence also prove the impossibility that Shakspere wrote Shakespeare. I summarize here five of the most powerful.

1) The dedication to the 1609 edition of *Shake-speares Sonnets* refers to the author as "our ever-living poet," a clear reference to a person who has already died. Oxford died in 1604; Shakspere lived until 1616, and was very much alive in 1609.

2) With a single exception in 1598, there are no contemporary commentaries that refer to Shakespeare as a playwright, despite a plethora of publications that discussed, or mentioned, other playwrights, and despite the appearance of Shakespeare name's on the two narrative poems, and, starting in 1598, on sixteen plays. This vacuum cannot be explained if Shakspere were a well-known commoner playwright like Ben Jonson, but is readily explained if Shakespeare were a high-ranking nobleman who for many reasons would not be permitted to publish works in his own name, and for the same reason could not be referred to, even under a pseudonym, for fear of revealing his identity.

The one exception in 1598, in a publication by one Francis Meres, *Palladis Tamia,* praising "Shakespeare" as one of England's favorite and best dramatists, may be the proverbial "exception that proves the rule." *Palladis* was published during what amounts to an interregnum following the death of William Cecil, Lord Burghley,

Queen Elizabeth's top counselor, and before his successor and son, Robert Cecil, had established himself in his father's former position. Since the Cecils were the political opponents of Oxford, it would be likely that Oxford might have attempted to use this brief period following William Cecil's death to try to come out of the shadows, preparing the way to reveal himself as Shakespeare. With Robert Cecil's rapid accession to power, this window would have closed quickly, as Robert could be expected to force Oxford back into the shadows. No one can explain why, were Shakspere the author, a contemporary reference to him as the playwright would have been so long delayed and so briefly acknowledged, only to be dropped again for the duration of his career. (To be sure, following the publication of this book, the name "Shakespeare" started to be attached to individual copies of the plays that began to be published, in all cases seemingly not by the author or with authorial permission—the relevance of the reference in *Palladis Tamia* was that it was the only published non-fiction work of the time that mentioned Shakespeare as a playwright among other playwrights.)

3) In *Shakespeare Suppressed*, Katherine Chiljan has identified some ninety-three instances where other authors have referenced lines from Shakespeare plays in publications that are "too early" to be referring a play that Shakspere could have written. Traditional scholars have constructed a set of dates for when they believe each play was likely first acted, none before 1590. If Shakspere were Shakespeare, these examples could only be explained by saying that Shakspere cribbed all of these lines that appear in thirty of his plays, from fifty-three different sources written by thirty different people, some of whom were neither writers nor playwrights. Such dependence on plagiarism makes no sense. Why an author so otherwise supremely talented (as shown by his work as a whole) would bother to, or need to, crib a tiny percentage of his lines from other sources, defies explanation. The necessary—and obviously correct—explanation is that all of these instances were quotes *from* Shakespeare plays that existed, perhaps in earlier versions, before 1590, which means the works they came from couldn't have been written by Shakspere.

4) There are also at least eight plays with titles or subjects so similar to those of known Shakespeare plays that the inference is inescapable that they were either earlier drafts by Shakespeare of the plays we now know as his, or plays by others that Shakespeare plagiarized to a significant degree. The traditional view needs to turn Shakespeare into a wholesale plagiarist for some of his plays, leaving open the question why a playwright so capable of creating many plays on his own would choose to plagiarize about a quarter of them. The explanation that he was revising his own earlier versions of them is not only far more plausible, but also explains why none of these earlier plays have survived (some of them surely would have, if they had written by other authors). But because the references to these earlier plays date from before 1590, traditional scholars must reject this preferable interpretation.

Case Closed: No Contest

Entire, excellent books expound and expand on most of the points summarized here, but even this short summary of the evidence that Shakspere of Stratford-on-Avon could not possibly have authored the works of Shakespeare redundantly proves the point beyond a shadow of a doubt. Nonetheless, I wish to present a final argument that draws from several points made above, adds some additional information, and combines all the information into a slightly different argument than we've yet examined, which by itself I believe is utterly unanswerable from the Stratfordian perspective. Whether or not one finds that the case that Oxford was Shakespeare persuasive, the view that Shakspere was is simply untenable.

The argument starts from the premise that we are dealing with a human being who, no matter how talented, still has only 24 hours in a day, which time must be allocated among many tasks, from sleeping, traveling and eating, to earning money, practicing a profession (or more than one), reading, learning, and, for the author of Shakespeare, of course, writing. The issue I want to focus on is to catalog the activities that Shakspere (assuming for the sake of argument that he *was* Shakespeare) would have had to have devoted time to, assuming, again for the sake of argument, that we accept the reconstruction of his life from about 1585 to 1600 or so that the standard story relates. That is, I propose taking the traditional version of his biography *on its own terms*, and looking at some implications that I have seen no one, whether Stratfordian or Oxfordian, draw.

The traditional view posits that Shakspere, having married Anne Hathaway in November of 1582 at the age of 19 (she was 26), and having had 3 children by 1585, stayed in Stratford earning a living (how is not known) until the late 1580s, with 1589 often given as the year he went to London. There is zero documentary evidence that he left Stratford for London at any time before the first documented reference to him appeared in 1595, but let's accept that in 1588 or 1589 he went to London to be an actor, as the standard story assumes. (The strongest purported reason for believing that he was in London by 1589 is that the first of Shakespeare's Henry VI plays began being acted by no later than 1590—this of course is not evidence that Shakspere was in London then—to assert so is simply circular reasoning.)

If he became an actor in 1589, there are several overlooked implications. First, acting was an extremely arduous occupation, requiring huge amounts of time each day to memorize new lines, rehearse, and then perform. Second, actors were considered vagabonds, and the pay was very low. These facts are inconvenient, because they beg two obvious questions. First, if the pay was so low, how could Shakspere have made enough to support himself in London *and also support his wife and three children* in Stratford, which he clearly did, since they would otherwise have gone to the poor house. Not one source I have consulted notes this problem. Second, if he was a full-time actor (and how else could he have become relatively famous in a short period, as the standard story posits), how and when did he find time to write anything, much less polished plays that he apparently started turning out with regularity almost as soon as he landed in London?

The effective impossibility of the above is merely the beginning of the matter. We have the issue of how did/could Shakspere have acquired all of the enormous range and quantity of knowledge and understanding in all the areas catalogued above, that no one disputes are displayed in the plays and poems, plus master fluent French and Italian, and master the English language to become the greatest wielder of it in history? In effectively no time at all. Let's grant the most generous view of Shakspere's schooling at the Stratford Grammar School, that he emerged with a solid grounding in Latin and acquaintance with some of the Latin classics (very strong evidence suggests this is not the case, but let's grant it for the sake of argument). A point I have seen noted nowhere else is that, since the only requirement to enter the grammar school was basic literacy of a sort that a seven-year-old could have acquired, and since it was *Latin,* not *English,* that was taught there, as a grammar school graduate, Shakspere would have had no significant contact with *English,* certainly no English literature, no significant reading of any sort. To the contrary, Shakespeare utilized the largest vocabulary by a factor of two or more compared with the next-most literate writers of his era—something utterly unimaginable for someone not educated from an early age in English, several foreign languages and literature in both English and several foreign languages, as only the upper nobility and royalty were typically educated. How, and where, could Shakspere possibly have developed the ability to deploy English as Shakespeare did, "out of the box" within months of arriving in London with at best a Stratford Grammar School education, which, in Stratford, consisted almost entirely of "blab school" rote memorization of Latin grammar?

That is, on just the score of his competence in *English,* how could Shakspere conceivably have begun writing Shakespeare plays within a few months of arriving in London, with nothing more than a second-grade (at best) knowledge of the language, much less all the other fields of knowledge that Shakespeare's works display (law, botany, falconry, military matters, seamanship, medicine, geography, astronomy, Scripture, classical literature, heraldry, etc.)? Where did his enormous vocabulary come from? When did he/could he, have acquired it?

And of course, he needed no period of years to hone and develop his craft—his masterpieces just emerged full-blown and mature from his pen in his first literary effort. Not to mention, how and where did he acquire the deep knowledge and understanding of English history and politics, just a few months into his first stay in London, that are displayed so masterfully in the Henry VI plays, recording a hugely unsettled and complicated period in England's political history.

The standard reply of Stratfordians to the charge that Shakspere couldn't possibly have had the educational and experiential background that Shakespeare had, is to say that Shakspere picked up all the knowledge displayed in the plays by browsing books in bookstalls, perhaps having access to private libraries, and by conversations with travelers and seamen in taverns. To believe that anyone could master fluent French or Italian in this way is to be gullible in the extreme. And many of the fields are ones where no books likely existed for one to peruse. And try to picture someone spending hours every day in a bookstall reading books that he never buys—how long would the bookseller let that go on? And a point I've not seen noted elsewhere, at any given time, wouldn't bookstalls have displayed only a tiny fraction of all the books Shakespeare clearly would have read—merely the few titles in print at that time? How could Shakspere have found titles not currently being sold? Booksellers weren't tantamount to modern libraries— the only collections of books that existed that we de facto libraries were the collections owned by members of the nobility, like the excellent library maintained by Lord Burghley, that the actual Shakespeare (Edward de Vere Lord Oxford) and a generation later the 3rd Earl of Southampton, had access to during their formative years.

And think of how people learn. They sit down to read, they do some writing, and above all, it takes time, lots of it, for even the most gifted intellectuals to master huge amounts of knowledge in many disparate fields. How much time could Shakspere realistically spend each day, or each week, playing catch-up on his woefully inadequate education, standing and reading books on the street without buying them—all in order to pour this knowledge into his plays? It strains credulity well beyond the breaking point!

But since we have already accounted for all, or almost all, of Shakspere's day, just in his acting capacity, where did he find the time for all this browsing? Worse, and this point is likewise one I've seen nowhere else, *even if,* let us say, Shakspere could have mastered all this knowledge by browsing books in bookstalls over the course of his adult life, surely at the very least it would have taken him years to get to the point where he could *start* writing what Shakespeare wrote in his plays. It takes people years in school to master far less, going full-time. That is, his education, at least most of it, would have to have occurred *before* he began writing the plays in which that knowledge is on display. And we are talking about someone who started in 1589 with very limited schooling in *English*, no less. How long does it take someone to read a 300-page book? 5 hours? 8 hours? More? Multiply that by the number of books one would need to read. Spread it out over, say, fifteen years, or even just ten. It's still a lot of time.

But by the standard story, Shakspere was popping out plays within months of hitting London. There is simply no conceivable way, even if it might have been possible over a decade or more, to acquire such encyclopedic knowledge in a matter of months—while acting full-time—and while writing the plays at a more prolific rate than any other playwright in history. The fairy tale of browsing bookstalls and talking to travelers is simply absurd, and collapses of its own weight when its implications are examined.

But the conundrums of the Shakspere biography don't stop even here. Because, to review, Shakspere had to be earning enough to both support himself in London *and* send enough back home to support his family. It is simply impossible that he could have been doing that on an actor's salary. *If he was in London at all,* he *had* to have had a second source of income. Which, given the fact that the only records that pertain unmistakably to Shakspere during his adult life relate to being a businessman, would strongly suggest that he began some sort of business in London. Really, *if* he was there, he simply had to have done so.

But wait, this would have taken time, probably a lot of time, and time Shakspere couldn't possibly have had. How could he have worked as some sort of businessman *and* still found time to act (not to mention learn, browse bookstalls, and write plays at a feverish pace)? Adding in the requirement that he put in, say, 50% of his time in his other business, the already impossible calculation just becomes even more fanciful.

There is a simpler explanation. Another fact of Shakspere's life, accepted by all, is that he paid £60 for the second largest house in Stratford, in 1597. This was a goodly sum of money. There is no way he had earned it acting, or even play writing, which wasn't even a profession at all at that time. And there is no evidence he received any money from the two poems in 1593 and 1594. So by 1597, he was clearly a successful businessman. He soon also bought extensive land holdings, including some that were agricultural. He also bought lands that paid him tithes. And he lent money. So, by all extant records, Shakspere was a successful businessman.

Another generally overlooked point is that almost all of his business dealings, especially in the earlier years, were in Stratford. No credible evidence exists that Shakspere made his money as a businessman in London. It was in Stratford that he owned property. It was only much later that he acquired part-ownership in a couple of theaters in London. The Stratfordian camp cannot afford to admit this, but it was clearly the case that Shakspere would have had to spend whatever time he allocated to his business(es) *in Stratford,* not in London, since that is where the businesses were located. So how could he have been an actor, and written plays for London acting companies, while domiciled much, if not most, of the time in Stratford? Clearly, he couldn't. The simplest explanation is that what you see is what you get: Shakspere *was* a businessman, *not* an actor or playwright. All the evidence points to that, none of it points to acting or playwriting. That's where his money came from. That's where his time went. As the saying goes, "follow the money."

So, given the known date of 1597, by when he was wealthy enough to afford £60 for a house, he clearly had to have been working as a businessman for a number of years before 1597. His father's business had collapsed in the 1580s, so he had no help from that quarter. The 1597 purchase of New Place, and the subsequent further real estate purchases over the next decade, confirm that whatever his business was, he was relatively successful at it. But, *this is bad news for the standard Shakspere story*, because it means that it is *absolutely necessary* to assume that a significant portion of Shakspere's time was devoted to his business, week in, week out. Maybe it could go in spurts, with a few months intensively, then some months off, let's say, to act in London, but year-in, year-out, it would seem necessary to assume that he must have spent at least 25-50% of his time on his business.

Such an assumption is fatal to whatever shreds of belief in the Shakspere myth someone might have held onto to this point. I posit, which I have not seen anyone else lay out, that to Shakspere's already impossible daily, weekly and yearly schedule that already had to accommodate being a full-time actor, the equivalent of a fulltime student browsing bookstalls or private libraries, and a prolific writer of plays, that he was at least a part-time businessman. This is a further factor that simply makes utterly absurd the notion that this man could have been the author who wrote 37 plays, two long narrative poems, and the *Sonnets,* displayed encyclopedic knowledge on so many topics, and demonstrated the greatest command of the English language in history, and did it only as a part-time activity, while he split the remainder of his time between acting and tending to his business. Truly, when the facts are laid out thusly, based on nothing but the Stratfordian side's *own reconstruction* of Shakspere's life, how can *anyone* hold on to the fairy tale told by the academic community. **Case closed.**

Appendix II
The Sonnets v. Shakspere

While this book's purpose is to explain the real meaning of the sonnets, we early on had to specify that the poet had to be Oxford, not Shakspere of Stratford-upon-Avon. And we showed, starting with our analysis of Sonnet 35, that the sonnets themselves pointed to Oxford in lines in a number of sonnets, providing confirmation of this assumption. And at the end, understanding the poet to be Oxford was one key to unlocking the meaning of every sonnet we analyzed. The overwhelming productivity of this assumption in making sense out of virtually every sonnet, where all alternative attempts premised on Shakspere being the poet fail so miserably to make sense even of individual sonnets, much less the collection taken as a coherent narrative, effectively proves that Oxford had to have been the poet. And since we know the poet was known by the name "Shakespeare," the sonnets, somewhat ironically, represent the strongest evidence in existence that Oxford was the flesh and blood author behind the "Shakespeare" pseudonym.

The case for Oxford that derives from all the evidence amassed by nearly a century of research by scores of Oxfordian researchers, totally apart from the evidence we have shown from within the sonnets, is, in my opinion, already extremely strong, to the point of being conclusive, based on a very large array of evidence and arguments of various types. All of the evidence is ultimately literary, in that the works we know as "Shakespeare's" contain innumerable passages that require the characteristics in their author that Oxford, and only Oxford, is known to have had (and that Shakspere did not, and could not, have had).

Apart from bolstering the case for Oxford as Shakespeare, the sonnets also conclusively prove that even if Shakespeare were not Oxford, he could not possibly have been Shakspere. This is because the sonnets are unique among all of the other works in being written in the first person, which carries the consequence that the author, whoever he was, frequently says things about himself. And some of these things simply cannot be true of the author had he been Shakspere. That is, *the sonnets, uniquely among all of Shakespeare's works, contain evidence, of a different type than that found elsewhere, that the author couldn't have been Shakspere.*

The significance of this is that, for a reader initially skeptical about the assumption that the poet was Oxford, these passages that disqualify Shakspere do not require accepting any of the premises of the Whittemore paradigm. That is, they are independent proofs that Shakspere could not have written these sonnets, because were Shakspere the author, he would have been alive and highly acclaimed as the author of the published poems and plays by "Shakespeare," while the cited lines bespeak someone who is unknown, who will die unheralded, and who is relying on posthumous circulation of the sonnets to make Southampton famous, and to preserve memory of himself.

All of the lines I have culled in the list below have been noted in the preceding pages where the relevant passages are discussed. As a convenience to the reader, I have compiled them below as a handy reference guide to how the sonnets definitively, without recourse to any other information or evidence, prove that whoever Shakespeare really was, he wasn't Shakspere of Stratford.

Sonnet Proofs that Shakspere Wasn't Shakespeare

1. Sonnet 107 documents Southampton's release from prison, confirming that Shakespeare continued to write sonnets to Southampton even after his utter disgrace and conviction for treason. That Shakspere, who supposedly sought and obtained Southampton as a patron in 1593 or 1594, stayed loyal to him ten years later, despite his imprisonment, when Southampton could do nothing to help Shakspere, is improbable in the extreme. (pp. 30-38)

2. Sonnet 87's use of "misprision" demands the meaning of "misprision of treason" (understandably, as Southampton was convicted of treason), but the conventional narrative makes no mention of Southampton's treason, and misreads "misprision" accordingly. It is not conceivable that Shakspere as Shakespeare would have continued to support Southampton under these circumstances, much less continue as his client (with Southampton his patron). (p. 55)

3. Shakspere could not have been both Southampton's "adverse party" and his "advocate," nor an accessory to some process that was pulling Southampton away from him, as related in Sonnet 35. (p. 58)

4. A majority of Stratfordian critics hold that Southampton was the young man of the sonnets, and most further concur

that Sonnets 1-17 had to relate to the period when Burghley and likely even the Queen, were urging Southampton to marry Elizabeth Vere, which would date this initial sequence to 1590. But that date is impossibly early for Shakspere, who would have just arrived in London, a goof four years before convention believes he began seeking Southampton's patronage. (p. 66)

5. The tone, often scolding and disparaging, taken in many passages in the first set of sonnets (Sonnets 1-17), would have been totally impossible from a commoner to an earl— they would have been seen as impertinent even if from another nobleman under most circumstances. Shakspere could not have addressed Southampton this way and not suffered the consequences. (p. 69)

6. It also strains credulity that Shakspere could have produced such polished sonnets so early in his career, just months after leaving Stratford. (p. 70)

7. Sonnet 1's description of Southampton as "the world's fresh ornament," discussed in several locations, cannot be reconciled with the standard interpretation, nor can any other references to the interest the "world" has, will have, or should have, in the "young man" (Southampton). (p. 75)

8. Sonnet 18 says that the sonnets will live as long as men are alive, and will tell of Southampton. Under the conventional reading, there is nothing in the narrative involving Shakspere that would possibly warrant preserving for future generations. (p. 91)

9. Sonnet 55 says that Southampton will "pace forth" and be praised "even in the eyes of all posterity that wear this world out to the ending doom," a claim that would be preposterous if the poet were Shakspere and the content of the sonnets the standard narrative of a 3-way love triangle. (p. 95)

10. Queen Elizabeth's motto, *Semper Eadem,* ("Ever the Same") is quoted in Line 5 of Sonnet 76 and Line 4 of Sonnet 104. The context of both is not praise of Elizabeth (the allowed context for such allusions), but a statement of what is constant in the sonnets—that is, that Elizabeth is one of the three persons of the sonnets. It is impossible that Elizabeth could be the woman in the sonnets if Shakspere were the poet. (p. 108)

11. Sonnet 10 says that Southampton is "beloved of many." Why would Shakspere say this about seventeen-year-old Southampton, just appearing at Court for the first time? (p. 126)

12. Sonnet 10 has the poet asking Southampton to "make thee an other self, for love of me." Why would Shakspere say his request was "for love of me?" No possible reason exists for Skaspere to make such a request of his supposed patron. (p. 126)

13. In Sonnets 81 and 107, the poet says that the sonnets will be a monument to Southampton that will outlast bronze monuments and be spoken of by unnumbered generations to come. Nothing in the biography of Shakspere, nor in the conventional interpretation of the sonnets, provides any basis for seeing the sonnets as such a monument. (p. 156)

14. Sonnet 76 says that every sonnet is fundamentally saying the same thing as every other sonnet, which is manifestly not the case with the standard interpretation involving Shakspere, so that interpretation can't be correct, nor can the poet be Shakspere. (p. 168)

15. Sonnet 76 also says that in every sonnet "I always write of you," which is emphatically *not* the case with the standard interpretation, which posits all sorts of betrayals, separations and reconciliations, and which reads some sonnets as abstract discourses on random topics that are emphatically *not* about Southampton. (p. 168)

16. Sonnet 76 also says that the sonnets represent an "invention" that is disguised (kept "in a noted weed"), such that "every word doth almost tell my name." Such an assertion is meaningless if Shakspere/Shakespeare were the author, as his name was no mystery, but rather almost universally known. (p. 172)

17. In Sonnets 71-4, the poet makes clear he believes he is near death, and is preparing for it ("in me thou seest the twilight" of his life, "no longer mourn for me when I am dead," "after my death...forget me quite", etc.) Nothing can explain why Shakspere, in his late '30s or early '40s when this have been written, and in good health, as far as anyone knows, would be fixated in this way on his impending death, hence Shakspere would never have penned these lines. (p. 203-5)

18. In Sonnet 72, the poet says that his name will be "buried where my body is," something utterly impossible if

Shakspere were Shakespeare, as his name was already far too famous to conceivably not continue to be famous for generations. (p. 205)

19. Sonnet 73 also states that when he dies, the loss of his wretched life is of no consequence, and that all that matters is the survival of the sonnets that he is bequeathing to Southampton. None of this could possibly apply to Shakspere, then at the height of his powers and famous for his plays, if the conventional view were correct. (p. 205)

20. In Sonnet 74, the poet informs the young man that he is entrusting the sonnets to him, and that the only value of the poet's life is what the sonnets contain, "and this with thee remains." Such a dedication of the sonnets to the young man, under the standard interpretation, makes no sense. It is impossible that Shakespeare (if he were Shakspere), at the height of his popularity, would say that his physical being will be "too base to be remembered" and that only the sonnets will contain the poet's value. (p. 206)

21. Sonnet 81 says that when he (the poet) dies, "each part will be forgotten." Shakspere, at the height of his popularity, were he Shakespeare, could not conceivably have written this. (p. 227)

22. Sonnet 81 continues with more assertions to the same effect, that would be equally impossible coming from Shakspere: "I, once gone, to all the world must die," and "the earth can yield me but a common grave." (p. 227)

23. The opening two lines of Sonnet 97 strongly imply that the poet and friend have been separated for a year, something the standard interpretation cannot explain and does not try to. (p. 242)

24. Sonnet 125 carries the famous line "Were 't ought to me I bore the canopy," which effectively says that the poet either did bear a canopy, or had the right to. Only members of the nobility would have born a canopy for important state events, such as Elizabeth's funeral which is surely the context here. Shakspere could not possibly have borne a canopy. (p. 270)

Appendix IV
Oxford

The case for Oxford as Shakespeare differs from the case against Shakspere in being circumstantial (at least until publication of *The Monument* in 2005), if still very strong. No item of "hard" evidence, such as a signed play or a third party confirmation, has come to light that proves beyond a doubt that Oxford wrote Shakespeare. A mountain of evidence strongly suggests that Oxford was Shakespeare, and it continues to grow as Oxfordian scholars continue their research. (The reader is referred to the bibliography for a list of excellent books for further reading.)

I shall not attempt to summarize all the evidence that exists for Oxford as Shakespeare. Suffice it to say that Oxford had every qualification to be Shakespeare that Shakspere lacked: the education, the training as a nobleman, the travel on the continent, and the life experiences that whoever wrote Shakespeare clearly had. Oxford was also known to be passionately interested in poetry and the stage. He was known to have written poetry starting at a young age, to have translated several works into English, to have written an early version of a "Shakespearean" sonnet, and to have patronized two acting companies. Hundreds, if not thousands, of specific references in the plays have been found that connect to Oxford's life, and virtually none to Shakspere's. Practically all of the anomalies for the Shakspere case disappear when Oxford is understood as the true author.

Oxford as Poet as Well as Playwright

One topic warrants brief coverage because of its signal importance both for the case against Shakspere, and the case for Oxford, namely, the ability of Oxford to have been the author of *Venus and Adonis* and *The Rape of Lucrece*, the two narrative poems that were published in 1593 and 1594 with the name "William Shakespeare" on them.

If the author was Oxford, and it was he who wrote the two dedications to Southampton, there is no difficulty in understanding how an older earl might write such effusive tributes to a younger earl. Oxford and Southampton surely knew each other well as members of a tiny aristocracy. Both grew up in the household of William Cecil, later Lord Burghley, as wards of the crown when their fathers died during their respective minorities. Having married Cecil's daughter Anne, Oxford's ties to Burghley continued long after he had left the household. Also, as a leading lord Oxford had frequent official contact with Burghley, evidence of which is preserved in the documentary record, including numerous letters.

It is safe to conclude that Oxford knew Southampton from the early 1580s, when the latter was still growing up in the Burghley household. They certainly had to know each other quite well by the early 1590s, by which time Burghley was strongly pushing Southampton to marry Oxford's daughter Elizabeth, a union that the Queen herself must have favored, as Southampton was her royal ward and Burghley would not have proceeded without her consent.

We also know that Oxford and Southampton shared a passionate interest in the theater and performance of plays. It is hard to imagine them not working together to further that cause.

Unlike Shakspere, Oxford was accomplished enough both as a poet to produce two long poems by 1594, and as a playwright to produce plays. Oxford had already written a number of poems that had appeared under his own name, some as early as the 1570s. His skill at poetry was such that the seminal book on poetry, George Puttenham's *The Arte of English Poesie*, published in 1589 by Richard Field (who went on to publish "Shakespeare's" two long poems in 1593 and 1594), included *high praise for Oxford as a poet* and included a sample of his verse. Other praises of Oxford as a poet were published during the 1590s. Oxford even wrote an early sonnet around 1573, using the same meter and rhyme scheme as that employed in *Shake-speares Sonnets*. Thus, we have a timeline of the poet's maturation, and evidence that the 1593-94 narrative poems were the product of creative efforts that had begun at least two decades earlier—a far more believable scenario than that of the two long narrative poems being Shakspere's very first attempts at poetry.

Oxford Brings the Italian Renaissance to England

An extremely strong proof that Oxford wrote the Shakespeare canon is provided by a myriad of references, introduced almost incidentally in many plays, that reflect intimate and first-hand knowledge of many cities in Italy and significant portions of France—exactly the terrain that Oxford traversed during his sixteen-month tour of Europe in 1575-76. Some of these references are cited in Appendix I as specifics that Shakspere could *not* have known. Oxford, perhaps more than anyone else in England, had the opportunity to travel, and stay, often for weeks at a time, in a city, which enabled him to become intimately familiar with it. Oxford's travels on the Continent are well documented.

William J. Ray usefully summarizes resonances of Oxford's trip to Italy in a number of the plays:

> To throw out more biographical facts connecting his Italian journey to what he later wrote: On the Rialto is a statue of a hunchback, El Gobbo, revered by Venice's people. De Vere made hunchbacked Gobbo Shylock's faithful servant. At Messina, De Vere met Don John, a Spanish hero-commander. Don John appears in 'Much Ado About Nothing'. During the Genovese civil war Prospero Fattinanti became the new duke. De Vere made Prospero the old duke in 'The Tempest'. On Twelfth Night in Siena, the venerated Piccolomini, playwright and friend to De Vere, directed his own play, 'The Deceived'. The play featured two sets of siblings marrying their opposites after a shipwreck. 'Twelfth Night' adapted the plotline and the occasion De Vere first saw it. Siena's cathedral had a circular mosaic depicting "The Seven Ages of Man". Jacques in 'As You Like It' tells the same story as the mosaic. At Venice's Carnival, high and low acted and danced together in the revels, setting aside identity for the night. This cathartic celebration is echoed in 'Henry V' and 'Antony and Cleopatra'.[xlv]

Returning home in mid-1576, Oxford proceeded to literally father the Elizabethan Renaissance. He was criticized for his "Italianate" ways, even as he sought to bring England up to the cultural level he had partaken of in Italy. Several excellent biographies document his activities to patronize promising playwrights and poets in order to promote the cause of drama in England, including sponsoring several play companies. While these activities do not constitute proof that he was "Shakespeare," the fact that so many Shakespeare plays were first performed in Elizabeth's court, before being shown at the public theaters, and that "Shakespeare" was such a favorite of Elizabeth's, cries out for rational explanation under the Shakspere hypothesis. With Shakespeare understood as Oxford, the close connection of "Shakespeare" to the inner court is easily explainable.

Shakespeare and the Law

One of the most noted characteristics of Shakespeare's corpus is its extensive use of legal terminology, references, and reasoning. Because the "Shakespeare" from Stratford had no known legal training, the legal competence exhibited by Shakespeare presents a serious conundrum to the traditionalist defender of the faith.

It is no surprise that many traditionalists have long maintained that, despite their quantity and seeming quality, the legal usages in Shakespeare's works do not indicate that the author must have had legal training. A detailed account of the history of the debate over the quality of Shakespeare's legal knowledge by Oxfordian scholar Mark Alexander convincingly demonstrates that the Stratfordian effort is in vain. The author of Shakespeare's plays and poems was, beyond any reasonable doubt, one who had studied the law, mastered it, conversed with other lawyers to hone his knowledge, and had so imbibed the spirit and letter of the law that correct usages (or deliberately mangled usages uttered by ignorant characters) appear abundantly not only where one would expect them, but elsewhere, in metaphors or other casual contexts where only one steeped in law would ever reach into its vocabulary for literary purposes.

In "Shakespeare's Knowledge of Law, A Journey Through the History of the Argument,"[xlvi] Alexander meticulously analyzes every book or important article that has attempted to debunk Shakespeare's knowledge of law. The article is a fascinating study that can be only briefly summarized here. Essentially, those seeking to debunk Shakespeare's legal knowledge use three arguments: 1) that Shakespeare's use of legal terminology in the plays, while extensive, was not unusual, and that a number of other contemporary authors used as many or more legal terms; 2) that Shakespeare's usage of legal terms did not imply that he had to have had formal legal training, because the specific usages he employs were of the type that informed people of that era could have possessed without legal training; and 3) that Shakespeare made a number of egregious errors in his use of legal terms that no one trained in the law would have made.

Refuting those arguments, Anderson presents specific examples and presents a compelling case for the following:

1) Shakespeare uses legal terms more frequently than any other contemporary; this alone is no claim to have had legal training, but refutes a common claim to the contrary.

2) The quality of Shakespeare's legal usages is extraordinary, and that some of them reflect a deep connection to the law unlikely to be accessible to anyone not formally trained in it.

3) Shakespeare not only uses legal terms correctly even for more arcane concepts, but that he also mangles certain legal terms uttered by characters who would not be expected to know the law—i.e., characters who ought to know the law use legal terms correctly, and those who do not know the law use them incorrectly, often to comic effect.

4) Shakespeare not only uses legal terms correctly when a legal matter was at issue, but also uses legal metaphors and puns in other instances, unerringly. In Anderson's words, "[the argument that Shakespeare had had legal training] would best be shown by the fact that he used legal metaphors and similes and puns that arise in places where one does not expect forensic terminology. In other words, Shakespeare's mind exhibits the kind of training in law that comes with deep, long-term study—a mind that naturally views the world in legal metaphors. This distinction is lost on many later writers."[xlvii]

5) Shakespeare makes no errors of legal usage except when it is clearly intentional.

The conclusion is inescapable that Shakespeare had to have had extensive, formal legal training, of the sort available only at one of the Inns of Court, involving years of study and the interaction with lawyers and other students that would have honed a sharp legal mind. Since Shakspere had no known legal training, this point alone proves he could not have written Shakespeare's plays. Oxford, by contrast, attended Gray's Inn after graduating from Oxford, fully qualifying him to have displayed the level of legal knowledge manifested in the plays.

The Compleat Aristocrat

One of the most telling criteria that John Thomas Looney listed as among those that the author behind "Shakespeare" surely possessed was that he was an aristocrat, and a leading noble at that. The fields of knowledge that Shakespeare mastered (listed as negatives in Appendix I that Shakspere could have known little or nothing about), are of a nature that only a member of the high nobility would have acquired. These include Shakespeare's detailed and accurate knowledge of falconry, a sport reserved for the upper nobility, as well as of botany; only the highest nobles could afford to maintain botanical gardens of the sort that "Shakespeare" clearly was familiar with.

In addition, Oxford was fluent in Latin, French and Italian; Shakespeare's works contain instances where he made his own translation of passages from French or Italian sources, in cases where no translation existed (ruling out Shakspere's ability to have done so), and in cases where they did exist but Shakespeare chose not to use them.

One of the most important clues that Shakespeare was an aristocrat is that all of his leading characters are from the nobility, and that his non-noble characters are inserted for comic relief or other purposes, and almost uniformly are presented in a pejorative light. One of the few things of Shakspere's biography that can be asserted with certitude is that he was a social climber who helped his father obtain a questionable coat of arms, and that he clearly aspired to join the gentry class as a prosperous middle-class businessman. He would have to have had a profound self-hatred to have portrayed his class so negatively, and to have been obsequious in the extreme to have portrayed members of the nobility so favorably. Authors write from their own experience. The experience manifested in Shakespeare's plays is that of one born and bred to the upper nobility.

The Evidence from the Plays

Further compelling evidence comes from the plays themselves, but it is not feasible to present it here: the reader is referred to the bibliography. One illustration, from *Hamlet*, will be noted to represent the quality of this evidence. It has often been remarked that Polonius appears to be a representation of Lord Burghley, and the case is effectively proven when it is noted that the list of precepts that Polonius reads to his son before he leaves Elsinore is so close to an actual list that Burghley wrote for his son Robert Cecil, that Shakespeare, whoever he was, had to have had knowledge of it. The list wasn't published until the 1620s, long after *Hamlet* had been published and several years after Shakspere's death. Shakspere could not possibly have had access to it (nor, even if he had, could he have referred to it in a play and escaped without punishment). Oxford, almost uniquely, could, because he grew up in the Cecil household. Moreover, Burghley was the most powerful person in the realm after Elizabeth. His portrayal in *Hamlet* is far from flattering, and it can hardly be doubted that everyone in the Court recognized him in the bumbling figure of Polonius, and laughed at him for it. Who in all of England could have dared to mock him in this way and have gotten away with it? Only someone very high up in the nobility and the Court, and who had the protection of the Queen against the possibility of retribution from Burghley. It is known that Elizabeth enjoyed tweaking her closest advisors; she probably relished Oxford's sense of humor in this instance. Oxford was the first earl of the realm, by hereditary right, and if anyone could take such license and get away with it, it was he.

Oxford and Ovid

A final item that points to Oxford as Shakespeare should be noted. All Shakespeare scholars agree that Shakespeare's references to classical mythology are legion, and that he drew heavily from Ovid's *Metamorphoses* for them. It can hardly be a coincidence that when Oxford was still living in the Burghley household in the 1560s, one of his tutors was Arthur Golding, who was also his uncle. Golding was a Puritan, but in 1567 he published a translation of the fifteen books of the *Metamorphoses*, a poem hardly calculated to instill Puritan values. *Metamorphoses* is a rollicking romp through a large swath of Greek and Roman mythology, sometimes considered to be a "mock epic" poem, celebrating the triumphs of humans and human passions (especially love) over the gods. Many scholars have noted that it is odd that Golding would have chosen to translate such a bawdy, non-Christian work, notwithstanding his disclaimers in the printed edition that the reader should ignore the heretical content of the poem and draw morals consistent with Christian virtue. Golding went on to translate many works of Calvin and never again translated anything like *Metamorphoses*.

A likely explanation for this anomaly is that it was Golding's nephew and tutee who actually created the translation, just at the age, 15-17, when Oxford, highly accomplished in Latin, would have been capable of it. It could have begun as an exercise, and metamorphosed (pun intended) into a full translation. It would not be surprising if Golding, seeing its high quality, recognized that it was worthy of being published, in the spirit of making the great classics available in English. Part of the translation appeared in print in 1565, lending support to the notion that Oxford had been given a single chapter to translate, and that Golding then encouraged him to complete the entire book, a feat he accomplished within two more years.

Shakespeare critics all agree that this particular translation of *Metamorphoses* reverberates mightily throughout Shakespeare's works. "The phraseology of Golding's translation so frequently reappears in Shakespeare's page," wrote Sir Sidney Lee, "especially by way of subsidiary illustration, as almost to compel the conviction that Shakespeare knew much of Golding's book by heart."[xlviii] Or, more likely, Shakespeare/Oxford is quoting his own translation. No tortured explanation for why Ovid's work so permeates "Shakespeare's" works need be provided once Oxford is recognized as Shakespeare and as the author of the Ovid translation.

I have presented more than enough evidence to show that it is at least highly plausible that Oxford could have been Shakespeare. Of course, as I have shown, the *Sonnets,* correctly understood, clinches the case for Oxford the way no other evidence does. Nonetheless, I hope that the reader will be inspired to explore these topics in more detail by seeking out some of the sources cited in the bibliography to get a comprehensive understanding of the wealth of other evidence that also shows that Shakespeare had to be Oxford.

Appendix IV
Oxford/Shakespeare's
Other Poems

[Hank Whittemore contributed the following brief review of the four other poems credited to Shakespeare, which, when read from the perspective of the Whittemore Monument paradigm, are of the same cloth, telling about the same people—himself (Oxford), Queen Elizabeth, and, in three of them, Southampton.]

Shakespeare's Four Other Poems Unlocked

by Hank Whittemore

In addition to the *Sonnets*, the other four published poems attributed to Shakespeare all lend support to the theme of an intimate Oxford-Elizabeth relationship: *Venus and Adonis*; *Lucrece*, or *The Rape of Lucrece*; *The Phoenix and Turtle*; and *A Lover's Complaint*. All four can be viewed as allegorically representing their love affair and/or sexual union, with at least two (*Venus and Adonis* and *The Phoenix and Turtle*) clearly indicating an offspring and royal heir.

Venus and Adonis of 1593 carried the first appearance of the name William Shakespeare, used as the printed signature for the dedication to Southampton. The story of the poem features Venus, goddess of Love and Beauty, attempting to seduce the young god Adonis, who runs away only to be attacked and killed by a wild boar; then, however, comes a birth:

And in his blood that on the ground lay spilled,
A purple flower sprung up...

Venus was one of the goddesses associated with Queen Elizabeth; for example, she was called Venus in *Euphues his England* (1580) by Oxford's secretary John Lyly, who dedicated that prose work to the earl. The Shakespeare poem appears to be an allegorical representation of the Queen's own seductive behavior toward Oxford—at least by 1571, after he had arrived at court at twenty-one, but possibly beginning back in his teenage years when he was her first royal ward. The purple flower clearly symbolizes a royal heir; Venus speaks to it as a mother to her son with blood rights to succeed her:

'Poor flower,' quoth she, 'this was thy father's guise...
Sweet issue of a more sweet-smelling sire...
Thou art next of blood, and 'tis thy right...

The poem concludes with a vision of Elizabeth retaining her public image as the Virgin Queen who had never married or given birth, thereby refusing to acknowledge the child. Venus flies off in her chariot drawn by silver doves –

Holding their course to Paphos, where their Queen
Means to immure herself and not be seen.

One striking feature of *Venus and Adonis* is the presence of thirty-six lines of dialogue, spoken by Venus to Adonis, urging him to procreate in much the same language used in the first seventeen sonnets to Southampton and for the same reasons: "Beauty within itself should not be wasted....Seeds spring from seeds, and beauty breedeth beauty;/ Thou wast begot, to get it is thy duty....Upon the earth's increase why shouldst thou feed,/ Unless the earth with by increase be fed?/ By law of nature thou art bound to breed,/ That thine may live when thou thyself art dead;/ What is thy body but a swallowing grave,/ Seeming to bury that posterity/ Which by rights of time thou needs must have,/ If thou destroy them not in dark obscurity?/ If so, the world will hold thee in disdain,/ Sith in thy pride so fair a hope is slain...."

Lucrece followed a year later, in 1594, also dedicated to Southampton. [The dedications of these two narrative poems are the only such epistles the poet-dramatist would ever make to anyone, thereby uniquely linking Henry Wriothesley to "Shakespeare" for all time.] Once again the queen in the title appears to represent Elizabeth, this time not as the sexual aggressor, but as Lucrece, renowned for her chastity; and now Oxford is allegorically no longer the victim, but Tarquin, the rapist.

In effect, *Venus and Adonis* and *Lucrece* present two sides of the same story, both leading to sexual union and an unacknowledged offspring. In each case, the aggressive party indirectly brings about the death of the desired party. In this case Queen Lucrece takes her own life, by implication also killing the unborn child conceived as a result of the rape.

[Also in 1594 Thomas Nashe dedicated some bawdy verse to Southampton entitled *Choice of Valentines*, discovered in manuscript only in the twentieth century, with lines such as: "Pardon, sweet flower of matchless Poetry/ And fairest bud the red rose ever bore....Ne blame my verse of loose unchastity/ For painting forth the things that hidden are." The red rose symbolizes the House of Lancaster, identifying Elizabeth as mother of Southampton, a scion of the Tudors.]

The Phoenix and Turtle was published in 1601, soon after the failed Essex Rebellion and when Southampton was imprisoned in the Tower. The poem is part of a collection called *Love's Martyr* and includes the printed (and hyphenated) signature of William Shake-speare. Elizabeth is now the Phoenix, one of her most cherished names, signifying the mythical bird consumed by fire every 500 years but rising again from its own ashes; and Oxford is the Turtledove, her mate.

The poem is a funeral dirge for both birds ("this Turtle and his Queen"), along with their hopes for posterity, which have died because of Southampton's crime. "Love and Constancy is dead,/ Phoenix and the Turtle fled/ In a mutual flame from hence...."

"Beauty, truth and rarity"—Elizabeth, Oxford and Southampton—"Grace in all simplicity,/ Here enclosed in cinders lie/....Leaving no posterity:/ 'Twas not their infirmity,/ It was married chastity"—indicating Oxford and Elizabeth were betrothed, or virtually married, but that she chose to maintain her image as the chaste Virgin Queen—"Truth and Beauty buried be...."

[The last line recalls Sonnet 14 to Southampton, telling him that "truth and beauty shall together thrive/ If from thy self to store thou wouldst convert,/ Or else of thee this I prognosticate:/ Thy end is Truth's and Beauty's doom and date."]

A Lover's Complaint was printed in the 1609 quarto of the *Sonnets*, following the full sequence of 154 numbered verses; it appears to represent an early stage of the Oxford-Elizabeth love affair. The woman is clearly Elizabeth, with her "monarch's hands" and "folded schedules" which she peruses and tears to shreds. In the poem she tells the love story to an old man, from her point of view, and proceeds to describe her young lover as a nobleman who fits a description of Oxford.

"So on the tip of his subduing tongue/ All kinds of arguments and questions deep," she says of the young man, who "had the dialect and different skill,/ Catching all passions in his craft of will:/ That he did in the general bosom reign" and "What with his art in youth and youth in art," she finally "threw my affections in his charmed power,/ Reserved the stalk and gave him all my flower/.... For, lo, his passion, but an art of craft,/ Even there resolved my reason into tears;/ There my white stole of chastity I doffed,/ Shook off my sober guards and civil fears...."

The evidence that Shakespeare's other poetry reinforces the royal contents of the Sonnets would explain the failure to include those poems in the First Folio of Shakespeare works published in 1623. [Ben Jonson's folio of 1616 included both plays and poetry.] None of the published poems, nor any of the sonnets, was printed in the Folio, which also made no mention of Southampton, despite his importance to Shakespeare. Powerful interests were apparently intent upon obscuring any notion that "Shakespeare" was a nobleman, much less that Oxford and Elizabeth had produced a son and royal heir in the person of Southampton, who was alive in 1623 and whose Tudor blood would have posed an unthinkable threat to King James and the Stuart dynasty.

Appendix V
Southampton Poem to
Elizabeth from the Tower

[Below is an article by Hank Whittemore discussing the poem that Southampton wrote to Queen Elizabeth most likely some time during March 1601, pleading for mercy to spare his life, and which may indeed have played a part in securing his ultimate reprieve from a death sentence. It is based upon a presentation made at the 2013 Shakespeare Authorship Studies Conference at Concordia University in Portland, Oregon, and subsequently published in *A Poet's Rage* (2013).[xlix]]

Southampton's Tower Poem

by Hank Whittemore

Henry Wriothesley, third Earl of Southampton, wrote a 74-line poem from his prison room in the Tower of London to Queen Elizabeth in February or March of 1601, begging for the royal mercy. I would like to present strong evidence that during this same period in the Tower he received some of the private Shakespearean sonnets from Edward de Vere, seventeenth Earl of Oxford that helped to guide him in the composition of his poem to the Queen.

The Tower

He had been imprisoned on the night of February 8, 1601, after the so-called rebellion of that day had failed; he and Robert Devereux, second Earl of Essex, stood trial eleven days later; both were found guilty of high treason and sentenced to be executed. Essex was beheaded six days later, on the morning of February 25; and then Southampton began to languish in his prison room waiting to be executed. The earl wrote his poem to Elizabeth during the next three or four weeks, no later than the twentieth of March, the approximate time when he was unexpectedly spared the death penalty. His sentence was quietly commuted to perpetual imprisonment—not only quietly, but secretly, because no official record of the reprieve has ever been found.

His poem written in the Tower was discovered by Lara

Crowley, assistant professor of English at Texas Tech University, and printed in the winter 2011 issue of *English Literary Renaissance*. Professor Crowley found it in the British Library, in a collection of miscellaneous folios prepared in the 1620s or 1630s. It was preserved as a scribal copy entitled "The Earl of Southampton prisoner, and condemned, to Queen Elizabeth." The 74 lines consist of 37 rhymed couplets in iambic pentameter—as in the lines of the Shakespeare sonnets (five feet or ten beats per line) and more specifically as in the rhymed couplets of Sonnet 126, the envoy or postscript to the fair youth series written to and about Southampton. The newly recovered scribal copy represents the only poem Southampton is known to have written.

Professor Crowley calls it a "verse letter" to the Queen—although a literary work, it is nonetheless nonfictional and functional—intended as a means of communication and persuasion. Crowley also refers to it as a "heartfelt plea" by Henry Wriothesley for his life. She focuses on several key issues.

One is the authenticity of the poem. In this regard she cites certain details within the poem that would be known only to Southampton himself and just a few others—the prison doctor, the Lieutenant of the Tower and Secretary Robert Cecil. Also favoring authenticity is that Southampton wrote several letters to the Privy Council, as well as one to Cecil—and many of the key words in the poem are also employed in these letters.

A second issue is the question whether Southampton wrote the poem all by himself or with someone's help. Is it even possible, Crowley wonders, that some more "practiced" poet wrote it for him? Could such help have come from Mr. Shakespeare? Highly improbable, given the restricted access to Southampton, but she puts forth the question and lets it float out there.

A third matter to which she gives attention is the literary quality of the poem. Crowley notes the work is "unpolished," adding however that we might predict such lack of polish from a man expecting to face the executioner's axe at any moment. However imperfect it may be, she writes, "the poem proves lyrical, powerful and persuasive."

Robert Cecil

Most important to Crowley is that the poem triggers a historical question that has never been satisfactorily answered: Why was Southampton spared? There must have been a concrete reason; but there is nothing in the record, from the government or from anywhere else, with an explanation of what happened. The professor dismisses any idea that Cecil was moved to save Southampton out of sympathy. At this point he had the power— apparently even over Elizabeth—to make, or not make, this decision; and if he did make sure that a convicted traitor was spared, he would have demanded something that he dearly wanted in return.

Of course, what he dearly wanted now was to bring James of Scotland to the throne. At stake was Cecil's own position behind the throne, not to mention his life; and now he faced a long, uncertain time of waiting for the Queen to die, during which time he had to conduct a secret and even treasonous correspondence with James that her Majesty might discover at any moment. It would take more than two years—a period of almost unbearable tension for Robert Cecil; and the question, given these high stakes, is what he might have demanded and gotten in return for sparing Southampton's life.

The Southampton Tower Poem was of interest to me right away, because I realized it could have some bearing upon the theory of the Shakespeare sonnets as expressed in my book *The Monument*. A central aspect of the theory is that on the night of the failed rebellion, Edward de Vere began to write a string of sonnets—a sequence that he ultimately arranged in correspondence with each day (or night, if you will) until Southampton was either executed or given a reprieve. Oxford knew that Southampton's fate would be determined sooner rather than later; in fact it took approximately forty days and forty nights until the reprieve; in my view, no matter what the precise number of days, Oxford deliberately lined up exactly forty sonnets from number 27 to number 66.

I believe he arranged this sequence to equal forty sonnets in order to have it correspond with the forty days and forty nights that Jesus spent fasting in the wilderness, as in the Gospel of Matthew; and part of the evidence for this conjecture is in Sonnet 76, where he points to that very section of the Gospel:

"And when he had fasted forty days and forty nights.... And when the tempter came to him...he answered and said, 'It is written, Man shall not live by bread alone, but by every word that proceedeth from the mouth of God'"—Matthew, 4.4

In rather blatant correspondence, Oxford writes:

"That every word doth almost tell my name, showing their

birth, and where they did proceed"—Sonnet 76

Now if those forty sonnets correspond with the forty days from February 8, 1601, to March 19, 1601, we then have Southampton in the Tower during the very same time, waiting to learn his fate—and we know that in those days and nights he wrote his letters to the Council and to Cecil and additionally his poem to Elizabeth, pleading for mercy. So if the theory of forty sonnets (27 to 66) during that time is correct, we should be able to find some relationship between Oxford's sonnets to Southampton and Southampton's poem to the Queen.

First, a few markers:

"When to the Sessions of sweet silent thought
I summon up remembrance of things past"—Sonnet 30

Given the premise that the sonnet is written just when Oxford is summoned to the sessions or treason trial, it would seem to be extraordinary corroboration.

Thy adverse party is thy Advocate—Sonnet 35

["Your (legal) opponent is also your (legal) defender."—Katherine Duncan-Jones, editor, the Arden edition]

"Thy adverse party is thy Advocate" would describe Oxford's role on the tribunal at the trial, having to be Southampton's adverse party by voting to find him guilty and sentence him to death, but also promising to work behind the scenes as his advocate or legal defender.

To my knowledge, this is the only explanation of that line that links it to a specific historical and biographical event—that is, the trial, and Oxford's role on the tribunal—and also in terms of its accuracy and precision as a recognized legal reference. Moreover, the line serves to suggest that Oxford had some way of helping Southampton—helping him write those letters to the Council, not only with words but with guidance about what to say to the queen—and that he may have urged Southampton to plead with Elizabeth through poetry in the first place. It would be logical to infer that in playing his role as "advocate" or defense counsel, Oxford either helped him write the poem, or at least suggested its themes.

Essex wrote a much longer poem to Elizabeth from the Tower, during the few days between the trial and his execution. In that case, however, it was absolutely necessary for Cecil to destroy Essex by sending him to his death; therefore I would think it fairly certain that he made sure Elizabeth never did see the Essex poem. In Oxford's case, however, the proposition here is that he made a deal with Cecil, which included supporting the succession of King James of Scotland on the English throne and severing his relationship to "Shakespeare" and any connection to Southampton. In return, Cecil would make it possible for Oxford to help Southampton gain a reprieve. Given the likelihood that Oxford advised Southampton to write a poem to her Majesty, the question is how he might have helped him—which brings us to another marker, this one in Sonnet 45, when Oxford refers to:

> Those swift messengers returned from thee,
> Who even but now come back again assured
> Of thy fair health, recounting it to me.

There are two topics here—one, he appears to be referring to messengers on horseback riding back and forth between Oxford's home in Hackney and the Tower—and this may well indicate that he's been able to get copies of sonnets delivered to Southampton. This, in my view, is possible and even probable— first, because of Oxford's high rank and seeming ability to get away with so much, apparently because the Queen protected him; second, because John Peyton, Lieutenant of the Tower, had been appointed by Cecil back in 1598, and owed his allegiance to him; and third because if Oxford made a deal with Cecil, it was in the Secretary's best interest to enable such communication between Oxford and Southampton, so that Oxford could play his part by helping him. That would include the proposition here—my hypothesis—that as part of such communication, copies of the sonnets got into Southampton's hands in the Tower.

The other aspect of these two lines of Sonnet 45 is the clear reference to Southampton's health. It is on the record that he had fevers and swellings in his legs and other parts of his body; but he was being treated and apparently his health was steadily improving. In his poem to the Queen, Southampton refers specifically to his leg problem.

> I've left my going since my legs' strength decayed…

It turns out that within Southampton's Tower poem, as predicted, there's a strong correspondence with Oxford's Shakespearean sonnets.

Southampton's Poem

At least forty-seven key words in the Shakespearean sonnets also appear in Southampton's poem, of which the following twenty-three words might be emphasized:

Blood, Buried, Cancel, Condemned, Crimes, Dead, Die, Faults, Grave, Grief, Ill, Liberty, Loss, Mercy, Offenses, Pardon, Power, Princes, Prison, Sorrow, Stain, Tears, Tombs...

There are at least four distinct themes shared by both the Sonnets and the Southampton poem.

1. Crime—Fault—Offence—Ill Deed

2. Grief—Loss—Sorrow—Tears

3. Prison—Death—Tomb—Buried

4. Plead—Mercy—Pardon—Liberty

(1) The Crime - Fault - Offence

"The *offender's* sorrow lends but weak relief
To him that bears the strong *offence's* cross."
(Sonnet 34)

"I beg liberty to cancel old *offences...*
Better go ten such voyages than once *offend*
The majesty of a Prince, where all things end" (Southampton)

"All men make *faults,* and even I in this"
(Sonnet 35)

"Where *faults* weigh down the scale"
(Southampton)

"To you it doth belong
Yourself to pardon of self-doing *crime*"
(Sonnet 58)

"Let grace so...
Swim above all my *crimes*"
(Southampton)

(2) The Grief - Loss - Sorrow

"But day doth daily draw my *sorrows* longer,
And night doth nightly make *grief's* length seem stronger"
(Sonnet 28)

"Sorrow, such ruins, as where a flood hath been
On all my parts afflicted, hath been seen:
My face which *grief* plowed..."
(Southampton)

"Though thou repent, yet I have still the loss"
(Sonnet 34)

"And I with eating do no more engross
Than one that plays small game after great *loss*"
(Southampton)

And also in this category, a comparison:
"To *dry* the *rain* on *my storm-beaten face*"
(Sonnet 34)

"And in the wrinkles of my cheeks, tears lie
Like furrows *filled with rain*, and no more *dry*" (Southampton)

(3) The Prisoner - Condemned - Awaiting Execution—Feeling Buried Alive.

Here I think is an amazing comparison—first, Oxford pictures Southampton and his friends in prison, who are not yet executed, but existing unseen in the darkness of coming death—and he weeps while picturing Southampton himself as a living grave.

"Then can I drown an eye (un-used to flow)
For precious friends *hid in death's dateless night*...
How many a holy and obsequious tear
Hath dear *religious* love stolen from mine eye...
Thou art the *grave where buried love doth live*..."
(Sonnets 30 & 31)

Second, Southampton in turn pictures the prison itself as a grave or tomb, in which he is buried alive, and legally dead, that is, found guilty of treason and condemned to death.

"While I yet breathe, and sense and motion have
(For this a *prison* differs from a *grave*),
Prisons are living men's tombs, who there go
As one may, sith say *the dead* walk so.
There *I am buried quick*: hence one may draw
I am *religious* because *dead in law*."
(Southampton)

(4) The Monarch's Unique Power to Pardon

Given that unique power of the monarch to grant a pardon, we find Oxford writing to the Earl of Southampton as if the prisoner himself was a royal prince or a king who is somehow able to help himself:

"The imprisoned absence of your liberty...
To you it doth belong
Yourself to *pardon* of self-doing *crime*"
(Sonnet 58)

"Not to live more at ease (Dear Prince) of thee
But with new merits, *I beg liberty*...
If faults were not, how could great Princes then
Approach so near God in *pardoning* men?"
(Southampton)

We know Oxford's concept of the monarch being able to substitute mercy for justice—as he would write to Cecil later, on May 7, 1603, just ten days after Elizabeth's funeral, when the Earl of Southampton had already been liberated by such mercy from James, whom Oxford appears to be thanking indirectly through the Secretary:

"Nothing adorns a king more than justice, nor in anything doth a King more resemble God than in justice, which is the head of all virtue..."

Two years earlier, in the Tower prison, Southampton expresses the same idea by writing that "mercy" is an "antidote to justice"— mercy as a remedy to ensure the right kind of justice:

Wisdom and valor common men have known,
But only mercy is the Prince's own.
Mercy's an antidote to justice...
(Southampton)

He associates the Queen with the miracle worker who cured Naaman's condition, and mentions the River Jordan, thereby linking Elizabeth with Christ, the ultimate exemplar of mercy.

Had I the leprosy of Naaman,
Your mercy hath the same effects as Jordan. (Southampton)

The vast majority of these key words fall not only between Sonnet 27 and Sonnet 66, but, moreover, virtually all of the key words come from the first twenty of these. Most of those words are actually located within the first ten sonnets—within the sequence of Sonnet 27 to Sonnet 36—and the key words from these ten sonnets are also used by Southampton in his poem to the Queen:

Sonnets 27 to 36:

Sonnet 28—Sorrows, Grief

Sonnet 30 –Death, Grieve, Moan, Losses, Sorrows

Sonnet 31—Dead, Buried, Tear, Religious, The Dead, Grave, Buried

Sonnet 32—Death, Died

Sonnet 33—Stain, Staineth

Sonnet 34—Rain, Grief, Loss, Offender, Sorrow,

Offence, Tears, Ill

Sonnet 35—Grieved, Stain, Faults, Fault, Plea

Sonnet 36—Blots [stains]

The proposition suggested here is that upon the night of the failed rebellion, Edward de Vere began to write and compile sonnets that would ultimately correspond with the days and nights of waiting to see if Southampton would live or be executed. The further proposition is that Oxford, while trying to work a deal with Cecil to save Southampton's life, was able to send messages— including some of these sonnets—to Southampton in the Tower.

Now, with the discovery of a poem that Southampton himself wrote to the Queen, the added proposition is that he drew upon Oxford's sonnets for words, concepts or themes as well as inspiration. Given the preponderance of such words and themes within the forty sonnets between 27 and 66, covering those forty days, the further proposition is *that Southampton drew mainly from these particular sonnets, which, as a practical matter, would have been delivered to him in the Tower before any of the others.*

I suggest that the foregoing evidence amounts to very near certainty, if not absolute proof, that the real-life context of these particular Shakespearean sonnets is in fact the plight of Southampton in prison after the failed Essex Rebellion and his desperate need for a reprieve from the Queen; and that—in this context of time and circumstance—Elizabeth becomes the so-called Dark Lady of Sonnets 127 to 152, wherein we find:

"Straight in her heart did *mercy* come"—Sonnet 145

Below is a modern-English version of the Southampton Tower
Poem (February-March 1601), with the couplets separated.
Emphasized are key words that also appear (in one form or
another) within the Shakespearean "century" of Sonnets 27—126.

The Earl of Southampton Prisoner, and Condemned, to Queen Elizabeth:

Not to live more at ease (Dear Prince) of thee
But with new merits, I beg **liberty**

To **cancel** old **offences**; let grace so
(As oil all liquor else will overflow)

Swim above all my **crimes**. In lawn, a **stain**
Well taken forth may be made serve again.

Perseverance in **ill** is all the **ill**. The horses may,
That stumbled in the morn, go well all day.

If **faults** were not, how could great Princes then
Approach so near God, in **pardoning** men?

Wisdom and valor, common men have known,
But only mercy is the Prince's own.

Mercy's an antidote to justice, and will,
Like a true **blood**-stone, keep their bleeding still.

Where **faults** weigh down the scale, one grain of this
Will make it wise, until the beam it kiss.

Had I the leprosy of Naaman,
Your mercy hath the same effects as Jordan.

As surgeons cut and take from the sound part
That which is **rotten**, and beyond all art

Of healing, see (which time hath since revealed),
Limbs have been cut which might else have been healed.

While I yet breath and sense and motion have
(For this a **prison** differs from a **grave**),

Prisons are living men's **tombs**, who there go
As one may, sith say the **dead** walk so.

There I am **buried** quick: hence one may draw
I am **religious** because **dead** in **law**.

One of the old Anchorites, by me may be expressed:
A vial hath more room laid in a **chest**:

Prisoners condemned, like fish within shells lie
Cleaving to walls, which when they're opened, **die**:

So they, when taken forth, unless a **pardon**
(As a worm takes a bullet from a gun)

Take them from thence, and so deceive the sprights
Of people, **curious** after rueful sights.

Sorrow, such **ruins**, as where a flood hath been
On all my parts afflicted, hath been seen:

My face which **grief** plowed, and mine eyes when they
Stand full like two nine-holes, where at boys play

And so their fires went out like Iron hot
And put into the forge, and then is not

And in the **wrinkles** of my **cheeks**, **tears** lie
Like **furrows** filled with **rain**, and no more **dry**:

Mine arms like hammers to an anvil go
Upon my breast: now **lamed** with beating so

Stand as clock-hammers, which strike once an hour
Without such intermission they want power.

I've left my going since my legs' **strength decayed**
Like one, whose stock being spent give over trade.

And I with eating do no more engross
Than one that plays small game after great **loss**

Is like to get his own: or then a pit
With shovels emptied, and hath spoons to fill it.

And so sleep visits me, when **night's** half spent
As one, that means nothing but complement.

Horror and fear, like cold in ice, dwell here;
And hope (like lightning) gone ere it appear:

With less than half these miseries, a man
Might have twice shot the Straits of Magellan;

Better go ten such voyages than once *offend*
The Majesty of a Prince, where all things end

And begin: why whose sacred prerogative
He as he list, we as we ought live.

All mankind lives to serve a few: the throne
(To which all bow) is sewed to by each one.

Life, which I now beg, wer't to proceed
From else whoso'er, I'd first choose to bleed

But now, the cause, why life I do implore
Is that I think you worthy to give more.

The light of your countenance, and that same
Morning of the Court favor, where at all aim,

Vouchsafe unto me, and be moved by my **groans**,
For my **tears** have already worn these stones.

Appendix VI
Sonnet Theorems 1-19

The nineteen Sonnet Theorems we derived in Part I are reprinted here in order, as a help in seeing how they logically build on one another to construct the evidentiary case for the hypothesis that the *Sonnets* are about Elizabeth, Oxford and their royal son Southampton. They should be thought of as equivalent to theorems in mathematics, where a theorem is a statement proved to be true based on previous theorems and/or new conceptions that are shown to be true. Once proven, each theorem can be used to justify other theorems that will be true if those earlier theorems are true.

Sonnet Theorem 1: The author of the sonnets intended that they be published, which is the only conclusion that can be drawn from the statements in at least eight sonnets that the author wants the sonnets to be read by the world and last until the end of time. [p.34]

Sonnet Theorem 2: The relationship of young man to poet in Sonnets 1-126 cannot be homosexual because they were intended for publication (see Theorem 1), and the consequences for both poet and young man would be dire if the poems described such a relationship; nor can it have been some species of "friendship" or "manly love," because that would not justify the claims made that the sonnets, and Southampton's name, would be made famous until the end of time. Therefore, the relationship must be of a different type, such as between blood relatives. [p. 34]

Sonnet Theorem 3: The sonnets are in the order the author intended, demonstrated by the author's description of them as constituting a "monument" and as being an eternal historical record, which bespeaks their being a unitary document in a structured order rather than a mere collection of poems. [p. 35]

Sonnet Theorem 4: Lines 5-8 of Sonnet 107 reference the death of Elizabeth, the accession of James, and the palpable public relief and joy at the peace and calm with marked James' accession. [p. 35]

Sonnet Theorem 5: Sonnet 107 celebrates the release of Southampton from the Tower on April 10, 1603, by order of James I, and was quite likely written on that date. [p. 36]

Sonnet Theorem 6: Because Sonnet 107 describes the release of Southampton from prison, Southampton must be the addressee and subject of all preceding sonnets, as the "friend," "love," "young man," "fair youth," etc. Sonnets 1-106 are therefore to and about Southampton. [p. 36]

Sonnet Theorem 7: Since all sonnets through Sonnet 126 are about the same man, the remainder of the sonnets in this series (Sonnets 108-126) are also to and about Southampton. [p. 37]

Sonnet Theorem 8: Sonnet 27 was written on, and chronicles the night of, the failed Essex Rebellion, February 8, 1601, when Southampton and others were arrested for high treason and put in the Tower of London. [p. 49]

Sonnet Theorem 9: The series of eighty sonnets from Sonnet 27 to 106 chronicles Southampton's period of confinement in the Tower of London from the day of his arrest on February 8, 1601, until the day of his release on April 10, 1603, and should therefore be identified as the "Prison Sonnets." [p. 49]

Sonnet Theorem 10: Sonnet 87 chronicles the legal device that must have been used in Southampton's case, namely, that his sentence was commuted from the capital offense of high treason to the non-capital offense of misprision of treason. [p. 55]

Sonnet Theorem 11: The early Prison Sonnets, especially Sonnet 35, establish that Southampton has committed a serious crime or "trespass," i.e., treason, arising from his role in the Essex Rebellion. [p. 61]

Sonnet Theorem 12: Sonnet 30 chronicles how Edward de Vere, the Earl of Oxford, was "summoned" to the "sessions" of the House of Lords to be part of a jury to condemn the Essex Rebellion conspirators. [p. 61]

Sonnet Theorem 13: Sonnet 35's reference to the poet being simultaneously the "Advocate" and the "adverse party" of Southampton bears only one possible interpretation: that Oxford, as a member of the jury that must condemn Southampton to death is his "adverse party," but that he is simultaneously doing what he can behind the scenes to save his life, as his "advocate." [p. 62]

Sonnet Theorem 14: Based on Theorems 12 and 13, it is now conclusively established that the poet is Edward de Vere, 17th Earl of Oxford, who sat in the sessions of Parliament that condemned Southampton and others to death. As the commoner Shakspere could not have had anything to do with the trial, he could have been neither Southampton's advocate nor adverse party, and hence could not have been "Shakespeare." [p. 62]

Sonnet Theorem 15: Shakspere was not Shakespeare, because, as the subject of the sonnets is Southampton (Theorems 6 and 7), it is impossible that twenty-six-year-old Shakspere could have written these sonnets in 1590, when Southampton was sixteen; Shakspere had yet to produce anything that would commend him as competent to write poetry, or plays, nor is it credible that a commoner could write poetry that so scolds and patronizes one of the highest earls in the land. [p. 70]

Sonnet Theorem 16 "Beauty" as used in the "Procreate Sonnets" refers not to physical beauty, but to the bloodline that the poet desires Southampton to pass on. [p. 84]

Sonnet Theorem 17: Southampton had to have been Oxford's son. Having ruled out that the relationship between Shakespeare and Southampton could be either homosexual or some species of "manly friendship," we must conclude that it had to have been one based on blood (parental or close relative). The relative ages of Oxford and Southampton, and the concern expressed in Sonnets 1-17 that Southampton pass on his bloodline (his "beauty") practically rule out that the relationship was anything but father and son. [p. 85]

Sonnet Theorem 18: There is something transcendent about Southampton and his bloodline (his "beauty" as presented in the "procreate sonnets"), the subject of the sonnet series, which leads Oxford to state that the truth about him will be of interest and import to future ages, as evidenced by his increasingly grandiose claims for the importance of the sonnets and what they reveal about the subject, as most strongly demonstrated in Sonnets 54 and 55. [p. 95]

Sonnet Theorem 19: Southampton was the royal son of Queen Elizabeth and Oxford, and his royal blood is the subject of Sonnets 1-126. The word "beauty" in Sonnets 1-18 is a coded reference to this royal blood, which must be passed on so that the Tudor dynasty will not die out. The fact of his having royal Tudor blood in direct succession from Elizabeth, making him perhaps the only living person other than Elizabeth to have such blood, and hence that he carried within himself possibly the only means to continue the House of Tudor, explains the poet's far-reaching statement of the importance of Southampton that will make him live on, in the sonnets at least, for ages to come. [p. 131]

Appendix VII
Index of Sonnets Analyzed

The sonnets listed in this index are ones that are discussed in some detail, with at least 2-4 lines being presented in the discussion, or, in many cases, the whole sonnet being reproduced for detailed analysis.

Sonnet	Chapter	Page	Sonnet	Chapter	Page
64	14	182-3	107	2	31
65	14	186	108	21	252
66	14	188	109	21	254
67	15	192-3	110	21	255
68	16	197-8	111	21	256
69	16	199	112	21	257
70	16	202	116	21	257-8
71	16	203	118	21	261-2
72	16	204	119	21	262
73	16	205	120	21	263
74	16	206	121	21	264
76	13	168-9	122	21	265
78	19	230	123	21	266-7
79	19	232	124	21	268
80	19	233	125	21	270
81	19	227	126	21	273
82	19	234	127	22	278-9
83	19	235	128	22	279
84	19	237	130	22	280-1
85	19	238	134	22	282
86	19	239	137	22	283-4
87	4	53	140	22	284
87	20	241	145	22	285
97	20	242	146	22	286
98	20	243	147	22	287
100	20	243-4	152	22	288
101	20	244-5	153	22	290
105	13	173	154	22	290
106	20	248			

Appendix VIII
Contacting the Author and Informing the Public

I certainly hope that the conscientious reader who has taken the time to read the sonnets quoted in this book in conjunction with the text critiquing the traditional readings and offering the alternative reading discovered by Hank Whittemore and honed by myself has been convinced at the very least that the conventional reading of the *Sonnets* is hopelessly flawed and essentially useless as a guide to what the sonnets are about, and is at least intrigued if not fully convinced of the correctness of the new paradigm put forward in these pages.

I fully understand that it takes more than the ordinary level of concentration and time to fully appreciate the arguments made here. And the reader who was unaware of the Authorship Controversy before beginning has had to make a double paradigm shift, first away from believing that Shakspere of Stratford wrote Shakespeare, and that the Earl of Oxford *was* Shakespeare, and second that the *Sonnets* are about what Whittemore discovered, that they are centered on Southampton's tenure in prison, and the implications for him, and for England, of his being the possible but never-to-be acknowledged next Tudor king of England.

I hope it is self-evident that our reading here makes every sonnet interesting and worthy of being read and studied, and by replacing the insipid and so often illogical or absurd readings from traditional critics, totally and positively transforms the experience of reading the sonnets—all of them, not just a pre-selected few that are all most students are ever exposed to.

It may not be obvious to the reader new to the Controversy how important replacing Shakspere with Oxford is for understanding and appreciating the plays as well. I can assure you that comparable transformations of paradigm will occur when it is realized that most of the plays are also highly political, and that Oxford's motivation for most of them was to further a political agenda. He sought to instruct the rulers of England on how statecraft should be conducted, either by positive or negative example, and also held up a mirror on human nature to help those in power govern more wisely. And he also recognized the need to instill patriotism in the general population, most importantly in the years leading up to the

Spanish Armada in 1588. It is not accidental that his plays were written to be great popular entertainment as well as lessons in statecraft and personal integrity, and that they were very popular when performed in public theaters and equally popular when performed in private performances for Elizabeth and her inner circle.

I therefore commend the reader to begin sampling some of the books in the bibliography on the Controversy, toward which end I hope that my annotations will be of service.

As noted in the Appendix I, doubters that Shakspere could have been Shakespeare became numerous in the 19th century, including such figures as Lord Palmerston, Benjamin Disraeli, Walt Whitman, Henry James, Mark Twain, Thomas Hardy, and in the 20th century, Oliver Wendell Holmes, Sandra Day O'Connor, Sir John Gielgud, Sigmund Freud, and David McCullough, to name just a few. The discovery of the only entirely convincing candidate to have been the person behind the pseudonym, Edward de Vere, 17th Earl of Oxford, by Thomas Looney 99 years ago opened a window at last that finally enabled an understanding of the entire corpus in its true light and context. For those readers who see the relevance of "getting the right man," I can assure you the reward of reading a few of the books in the bibliography listed under the heading "The Case for Oxford" will be very great. The real-life Shakespeare/ Oxford was the prime mover of the Elizabethan Renaissance, who literally single-handedly imported from Italy conceptions and inspirations that he then imparted to dozens of poets and playwrights in the next 20 years, many of whom he also personally sponsored for parts of their careers.

In short, finally correcting a 400-year-old injustice of misat-tribution of the author of the incomparable Shakespeare corpus to a mediocre businessman from Statford who was likely semi-literate at best is a travesty that it behooves us to finally correct. There is a movement in the United States working to do just that, spearheaded by the Shakespeare Oxford Fellowship, an organization which meets annually, and whose members conduct research, write books and articles, and do outreach, including speaking engagements, to educate the public on Oxford as the real Shakespeare. Their website is https://ShakespeareOxfordFellowship.org, and they publish a quarterly newsletter which covers their activities, reviews new books on the topic, and presents original research. They also respond to requests for speakers for public events which tend to draw nice attendance, and readers of this book are encouraged to

361

reach out to them and request a speaker.

I also have set up a website focused on the *Sonnets* with a similar outreach mission, www.hiddeninplainsight.org. I shall be posting various articles here, and also maintaining a blog that readers of the website may access and comment on. I would love to have feedback, and to respond to questions that readers may have. Readers may also reach me directly by email, at ShakespearesSonnets@hiddeninplainsight.org. Feedback, debates, comments, and questions are all welcome, and I will endeavor to reply to all questions asked. And I also am available for speaking opportunities to present the essence of the Whittemore paradigm on the sonnets to audiences any place I am able to get to. Please email me with any requests for me (or Hank Whittemore) to speak on the topic of this book, and we will see if a lecture from one of us is feasible.

Peter Rush
Leesburg, VA
May 22, 2019

Annotated Bibliography

Elizabethan England

Chambers, E.K., *The Elizabethan Stage*, 1923
> Massive research in four volumes.

Campbell, Oscar James, *Reader's Encyclopedia of Shakespeare*, 1966
> A treasure of information about Shakespeare's work and contemporaries.

Complete Pelican Shakespeare, 2002
> One of several invaluable editions of the Shakespeare works.

Stratfordian Biography

Lee, Sidney, *A Life of William Shakespeare*, 1898
> Lee wrote the original long entry for Shakespeare in the Dictionary of Biography in the nineteenth century. [He also wrote the biography of Edward de Vere, Earl of Oxford for the Dictionary of National Biography (DNB).] Lee writes that Sonnet 107 "makes references that cannot be mistaken to three events that took place in 1603 – to Queen Elizabeth's death, to the accession of James I, and to the release of the Earl of Southampton [from the Tower]." On the other hand, he also believed that Sonnet 107 was written "almost a decade" after the other sonnets – a view that has become entrenched, preventing recognition that the prior eighty sonnets correspond with the earl's prison years during 1601-1603.

Honan, Park, *Shakespeare: A Life*, 1999
> This book was billed as "the most complex, accurate, and up-to-date narrative of Shakespeare's life ever written," and many of the leading Shakespeare scholars concur even today. Honan agrees that Sonnet 107 refers to the succession of 1603; otherwise, he shuns any serious attempt to link the sonnets to a documentary narrative of specific persons and events.

Prior to the Oxfordian Movement

Greenwood, Sir George, *The Shakespeare Problem Restated*, 1908
> Probably the most forceful and articulate anti-Stratfordian work until Looney in 1920, he boldly speculates that the true author will be found "among cultured Elizabethan courtiers of high position." On the final pair of sonnets, 153-154, he perceives (correctly, I believe) an allusion to "the poet's

'Mistress,' the Virgin queen, and to the City of Bath," asking, "Was Shakspere at Bath with the Queen? I think it probable that 'Shakespeare' was."

The Case for Oxford

Looney, J. Thomas, *"Shakespeare" Identified*, 1920
> The breakthrough book that launched the Oxfordian theory of authorship.

Miller, Ruth Loyd, *"Shakespeare" Identified and Oxfordian Vistas*, 1975
> The full set in four volumes includes a wealth of Oxfordian research.

Ogburn, Charlton Jr., *The Mysterious William Shakespeare*, 1984, 1992
> The massive work that gave new life to the Oxfordian movement.

Fowler, William Plumer, *Shakespeare Revealed in Oxford's Letters,* 1986
> Fifty letters of Edward de Vere and hundreds of links to the Shakespeare works.

Ogburn, Charlton Jr., *The Man Who Was Shakespeare*, 1995
> Updating his previous work and now agreeing with Prince Tudor theory.

Whittemore, Hank, *100 Reasons Shake-spear was the Earl of Oxford,* 2016
> A treasure trove of material, much of it not covered, or not covered in anywhere near the detail as it here, in other sources, including dozens of fascinating correspondences between specimens of Shakespeare's known writings and writings, or other specifics of the biography, of Oxford, plus many other biographical facts of Oxford which all enhance the items of evidence that very strongly, if still circumstantially, support the attribution of authorship to Oxford.

Chiljan, Katherine, *Shakespeare Suppressed*, 2011
> In addition to impressive work on the Shakespeare authorship question in relation to contemporary Elizabethan history, she develops further evidence on Southampton's life as a Prince Tudor until his death, possibly by murder, in 1624. Chiljan provides possibly the best coverage and explanation available of all of the specific items of putative evidence adduced by the Stratfordian side, showing persuasively why they are not convincing. In addition to several new avenues of proof that

Shakspere couldn't have been Shakespeare, she presents a unique and powerful explanation of how the actual publication of the *Sonnets* likely triggered the publication of the *First Folio* fourteen years later as the basis for creating the myth that William Shakspere of Stratford was the great author. Her book suffers at a few points from not openly identifying Oxford as the real Shakespeare (though she confirms in her introduction that she believes it), and more importantly from not adopting Whittemore's thesis on the *Sonnets,* but it is still an outstanding work.

Steinburg, Steven, *I Come to Bury Shakspere,* 2013

This is a most remarkable and excellent addition to the literature proving that Shakspere couldn't have been Shakespeare, which covers the case that dismisses the Stratfordian camp's putative evidence for Shakspere with more completeness and finality than any other work I am aware of. Steinburg exhaustively delves into key issues such as whether the Stratford grammar school could possibly have prepared anyone to be well educated (it couldn't have), and all of the other pillars of the Stratfordian case, and demolishes them with a finality from which they cannot recover. It also covers elements of the evidence that Oxford had to be Shakespeare, some of which I've seen nowhere else, such as his treatment of an otherwise odd work in the collection, *Timon of Athens.* He does for the Shakspere case what I do with the Stratfordian case on the *Sonnets,* that is, he cites and quotes copiously from the leading defenders of the Stratfordian case, voices such as Kathman's, pointing out the flaws of their attempted defense of the indefensible case for Shakspere. A very well-written, thoroughly delightful and highly original work all interested in Shakespeare should read.

The Case for the Sonnets as About Southampton as Oxford's and Elizabeth's Son

Whittemore, Hank, *The Monument,* 2005

The monumental (no pun intended) represents the fruits of over a decade of work on the sonnets, and presents the fruits of Whittemore's finally "cracking the code" that unlocked the true meaning of the *Sonnets,* as that meaning is also unfolded in this current book. It includes a long introductory section, and then presents every sonnet, followed by a "translation" of each line of every sonnet into what the underlying actual story appears to be be—the story of Oxford, his son by Elizabeth, and Elizabeth herself. Following this is a line-by-line discussion where key words are explained, and resonances, and other uses of the same words and phrases, from the plays are presented. The 918 page tome is now also available in a less expensive Kindle edition.

Whittemore, Hank, *Shakespeare's Son and His Sonnets,* 2010
A much shorter, more summary presentation of the author's breakthrough understanding of the *Sonnets* as about Southampton, Oxford's son by Elizabeth, and the despair of Oxford after the failed Essex Rebellion put Southampton in the Tower, narrowly escaping execution.

Biographies of Oxford
Ward, B. M., *The Seventeenth Earl of Oxford,* 1928
The first full biography, based on the original documents.
Nelson, Alan H., *Monstrous Adversary,* 2003
The most complete documentary record, but tainted by anti-Oxford bias.
Anderson, Mark, *Shakespeare by Another Name,* 2005
This is the most popular Oxfordian biography of Edward de Vere to date and is particularly strong in its coverage of the earl's travels in Italy. Whittemore shared his manuscript of *The Monument* with Anderson prior to publication; as a result, Anderson cited many sonnets as corresponding with events from the failed Essex Rebellion of February 8, 1601, onward: for example, Sonnets 30, 35, 46, 68, 69, 70, 71, 72, 73, 74 and 76, adding, "As the scholar and author Hank Whittemore recently pointed out, the nineteen sonnets beginning with Sonnet 107 appear to present daily meditations that culminate with the interment of the house of Tudor."

Biographies of Southampton
Stopes, Charlotte, *The Life of Henry, Third Earl of Southampton,* 1922
The first and still most complete biography.
Rowse, A. L., *Shakespeare's Southampton,* 1965
Includes Rowse's acceptance of Southampton as Fair Youth of the Sonnets.
Akrigg, G.P.V., *Shakespeare and the Earl of Southampton,* 1968
He agrees with Sonnets 1-17 as urging Southampton to marry Elizabeth Vere in the early 1590s and, too, with Sonnet 107 as

celebrating Southampton's release from the Tower in April 1603 as a result of Elizabeth's death and the accession of King James, who ordered his liberation.

"Prince Tudor" Theory

Allen, Percy, *The Life Story of Edward de Vere as "William Shakespeare,"* 1932

> In the appendix he gives evidence that Oxford and Queen Elizabeth were lovers and that she may have borne his son.

Ogburn, Dorothy and Charlton, *This Star of England*, 1952

> This massive volume explores Oxford's life in relation to the Shakespeare works and offers the first detailed scenario of evidence that Oxford and the Queen were the natural parents of a male heir, born in 1574 and placed as a changeling in the Southampton household.

Sears, Elisabeth, *Shakespeare and the Tudor Rose*, 1990, 2003

> Picking up from the Ogburns' work, she offers a detailed description of the maneuverings of Robert Cecil in the latter part of Elizabeth's reign, preventing Southampton from inheriting the crown and forcing Oxford to bury his identity as author of the Shakespeare works.

Beauclerk, Charles, *Shakespeare's Lost Kingdom*, 2010

> This is the most articulate and profound portrait of Oxford-Shakespeare's relationship to the Queen and the "identity" crisis that he endured. Beauclerk views Oxford as the son of Elizabeth and Thomas Seymour, born in 1548 when she was fifteen; and he also views Oxford and the Queen as the natural parents of Southampton. These highly controversial views provide Beauclerk with enormous explanatory power when dealing with the Shakespeare works including the Sonnets, in regard to which he agrees with *The Monument*.

Chiljan, Katherine, *Shakespeare Suppressed*, 2011

> See listing under "The Case for Oxford," above. Listed here because it presents the most fully documented case for the Elizabeth-Oxford-Southampton parent-child relationship of any book I am aware of other than *The Monument,* some of which evidence is included in this book.

The Sonnets – Stratfordian Commentary

Drake, Nathan, *Shakespeare and His Times*, 1817

> In two volumes; Drake is first to identify Southampton as the young man of the Sonnets.

Massey, Gerald, *The Secret Drama of Shakespeare's Sonnets Unfolded*, 1866-72
>   He explores Southampton's relationship to the Sonnets in the greatest depth so far.

Rollins, Hyder Edward, *A New Variorum Edition of Shakespeare: The Sonnets, Vol. 2,* 1944
>   An invaluable compilation of commentary about the Sonnets up to this date.

Rowse, A.L., *Shakespeare's Sonnets: The Problems Solved*, 1964, 1973
>   He attempts to briefly explain and/or paraphrase each sonnet, emphasizing Southampton as the Fair Youth, but with little if any new evidence of linkage to Shakespeare or historical evidence.

Hotson, Leslie, *Mr. W.H.,* 1965
>   He is the first (and only) Stratfordian to declare that the younger man of the Sonnets must be a royal prince; therefore, he disqualifies Southampton, who is but an earl.

Wait, J.C., *The Background to Shakespeare's Sonnets*, 1972
>   He includes much biographical and historical information, with Southampton as Fair Youth.

Vendler, Helen, *The Art of Shakespeare's Sonnets,* 1997
>   She provides commentary and insights on the rhetorical structure of each sonnet.

The Sonnets - Editions

Booth, Stephen, *Shakespeare's Sonnets*, 1977-2000

Kerrigan, John, *William Shakespeare: The Sonnets and A Lover's Complaint,* 1986

Duncan-Jones, Katherine, *Shakespeare's Sonnets* (Arden), 1997

Mowat, Barbara & Werstine, Paul, *Shakespeare's Sonnets and Poems* (Folger), 2004

Burrow, Colin: *Oxford Shakespeare: The Complete Sonnets and Poems*, 2008

Endnotes

[1] Hyder Edward Rollins, *A Variorum Edition of Shakespeare's Sonnets* (New York, NY : ??; 1944).

[2] John Hollander, contributing editor, *The Complete Pelican Shakespeare* (New York, NY : Penguin Books, Inc.; 2002) p. 59.

[3] Barbara A. Mowat and Paul Werstine, eds. *Shakespeare's Sonnets and Poems* (Folger Library edition) (New York, NY : Simon& Schuster Paperbacks; 2006) pp. 13-14

[4] Ibid, pp.

[5] Neil L. Rudenstine, *Ideas of Order, A Close Reading of Shakespeare's Sonnets* (New York : whatever press, 2014), *passim.*

[6] Stephen Booth, ed. *Shakespeare's Sonnets* (New Haven : Yale University Press, 1977).

[7] Colin Burrow, ed. *The Complete Sonnets and Poems* (Oxford : Oxford University Press, 2002).

[8] Katherine Duncan-Jones, ed. *Shakespeare's Sonnets* (rev. ed., Arden Shakespeare; Methuen Drama, 1997; 2010).

[9] John Kerrigan, ed. *The Sonnets and A Lover's Complaint* (Penguin Books, 1986, 1999).

[10] T. W. Baldwin, *William Shakespeare's Small Latine and Less Greeke* (Illinois : Illinois University Press, 1944), Vol. 2, p. 663, as cited in Steven Steinberg's *I Come to Bury Shakspere* (Middletown, Deleware : Café Padre Printing, 2013) p. 84.

[11] Mark Andre Alexander, "Shakespeare's Knowledge of Law: a Journey Through the History of the Argument," 2000. <http://shakespeareoxfordfellowship.org/shakespeares-knowledge-of-law/>

[xii] Booth, *op. cit.,* p. 342.

[xiii] Kerrigan, *op. cit.,* pp. 313-318.

[xiv] William E. Boyle, "Unveiling the *Sonnets.*" *Discovering Shakespeare : A* Festschrift *in Honour of Isabel Holden,* Daniel Wright, Ed. (Portland, OR : Shakespeare Authorship Research Centre, 2009), pp. 63-85.

[xv] Roberts, Clayton, and Owen Duncan. "The Parliamentary Undertaking of 1614." *English Historical Review* (93:368 [1978]), p. 494 (cited in Boyle, *op. cit.*, p. 70).

[xvi] John Rastell. *Exposicions of the Termes of the Lawes of England.* (London : Richard Tottell, 1567), p. 153 (cited in Boyle, *op. cit.*, p. 74).

[xvii] Boyle, *op. cit.,* p. 74.

[xviii] Hank Whittemore, "1601: Authorize thy trespass with compare…" *Shakespeare Matters*, (3:4, Summer 2004), pp 19-20.

[xix] Boyle, *op. cit.,* p. 70.

[xx] See Appendix IV for the text of Whittemore article, very slightly edited from its published version.

xxi Booth, *op. cit.,* p. 149.

xxii Katherine Chiljan. *Shakespeare Suppressed* (San Francisco : Faire Editions, 2011),. p. 280.

xxiii Chiljan, *op cit,* pp. 83-89.

xxiv Burrow, *op. cit.* p. 15

xxv *The Monument,* op. cit. p. 136.

xxvi Hank Whittemore. *The Monument* (Marshfield, MA : Meadow Geese Press, 2005), p. xxxv.

xxvii *Ibid.,* pp. 18-19.

xxviii *Ibid.,* pp. 18-28.

xxix *The Monument,* pp. 141-160.

xxx G.P.V. Akrigg. *Shakespeare and the Earl of Southampton,* (Cambridge : Harvard University Press, 1968) pp. 47-48.

xxxi Paul E. J. Hammer. "Shakespeare's *Richard II*, the play of February 7, 1601, and the Essex Rising." *Shakespeare Quarterly* (59:1, Spring 2008), pp. 1-35

xxxii *Ibid.,* pp. 305-333.

xxxiii *Ibid.,* pp. 305-310.

xxxiv Akrigg, *op. cit.,* pp. 140-142.

xxxv *Ibid.,* pp. 311-326.

xxxvi William Plumer Fowler. *Shakespeare Revealed in Oxford's Letters* (Portsmouth, NH : Peter Randall, 1986), p. 577.

xxxvii Helen Vendler. *The Art of Shake-speares Sonnets,* (Cambridge : Harvard University Press, 1997), pp. 488-491.

xxxviii *Ibid.,* pp. 491-492.

xxxix Whittemore, *op. cit.,* p. 629.

xl Vendler, *op. cit.,* p. 528.

xli Kerrigan, *op. cit.,* p. 58.

xlii Edward J. White. *Commentaries on the Law in Shakespeare* (St. Louis : F.H. Thomas Law Book Co, 1911). I am indebted to Hank Whittemore for providing this reference.

xliii Edgar Fripp. *Shakespeare : Man and Artist,* (London : H. Milford, Oxford University Press, 1938), pp. 322-325. I am indebted to Hank Whittemore for providing this reference.

xliv Chiljan, *op. cit.,* p. 1

xlv William J. Ray. "The Life and Work of Edward De Vere," <http://www.wjray.net/shakespeare_papers/shakespeare-sonnets.htm>

xlvi Alexander, *op. cit.*

xlvii Alexander, *ibid.*

xlviii Mark Anderson. *Shakespeare By Another Name* (New York : Gotham, 2005), pp. 26- 27

xlix "Southampton's Tower Power," in *A Poet's Rage* (Somerville, MA : Forever Press, 2013), pp. 73-88.

Made in the USA
Las Vegas, NV
25 April 2021